Australasian Language Technology Association Workshop

(ALTA 2014)

Melbourne, Australia
26-28 November 2014

Editors:

Gabriela Ferraro
Stephen Wan

ISBN: 978-1-63439-636-3

Printed from e-media with permission by:

Curran Associates, Inc.
57 Morehouse Lane
Red Hook, NY 12571

Some format issues inherent in the e-media version may also appear in this print version.

Printed by Curran Associates, Inc. (2015)

Association for Computational Linguistics
209 N. Eighth Street
Stroudsburg, Pennsylvania 18360

Phone: 1-570-476-8006
Fax: 1-570-476-0860

acl@aclweb.org

Additional copies of this publication are available from:

Curran Associates, Inc.
57 Morehouse Lane
Red Hook, NY 12571 USA
Phone: 845-758-0400
Fax: 845-758-2634
Email: curran@proceedings.com
Web: www.proceedings.com

Gold Sponsors:

As Australia's national science agency, CSIRO shapes the future using science to solve real issues. Our research makes a difference to industry, people and the planet. We're doing cutting-edge research in collaboration technologies, social media analysis tools and trust in online communities. Our people work closely with industry and communities to leave a lasting legacy.

SEEK is a diverse group of companies, comprised of a strong portfolio of online employment, educational, commercial and volunteer businesses. SEEK is listed on the Australian Securities Exchange, where it is a top 50 company with a market capitalization close to A$6 billion. With exposure to 2.5 billion people and over 20 per cent of global GDP, SEEK makes a positive contribution to peoples lives on a global scale. SEEK Australia currently receives over 26.6 million visits per month. The SEEK experience is seamless across desktop, mobile and iPad and currently over 54 per cent of all visits to seek.com.au are via mobile devices.

Silver Sponsors:

Research happens across all of Google, and affects everything we do. Research at Google is unique. Because so much of what we do hasn't been done before, the lines between research and development are often very blurred. This hybrid approach allows our discoveries to affect the world, both through improving Google products and services, and through the broader advancement of scientific knowledge.

Other Sponsors:

We would like to thank IBM Research for sponsoring the prize for this year's ALTA 2014 Shared Task.

ALTA 2014 Workshop Committees

Workshop Co-Chairs

- Gabriela Ferraro (National ICT Australia)
- Stephen Wan (CSIRO)

Workshop Local Organiser

- Lawrence Cavedon (RMIT)

Programme Committee

- Timothy Baldwin (University of Melbourne)
- Wray Buntine (Monash University)
- Alicia Burga (Universitat Pompeu Fabra)
- Lawrence Cavedon (RMIT University)
- Nathalie Colineau (DSTO)
- Trevor Cohn (University of Melbourne)
- Lan Du (Macquarie University)
- Dominique Estival (University of Western Sydney)
- Ben Hachey (University of Sydney)
- Gholamreza Haffari (Monash University)
- Graeme Hirst (University of Toronto)
- Nitin Indurkhya (University of New South Wales)
- Sarvnaz Karimi (CSIRO)
- Su Nam Kim (Monash University)
- Alistair Knott (University of Otago)
- François Lareau (Université de Montréal)
- David Martinez (University of Melbourne)
- Tara McIntosh (Google)
- Meladel Mistica (Intel Corporation)
- Diego Mollá (Macquarie University)
- Anthony Nguyen (Australian e-Health Research Centre, CSIRO)
- Joel Nothman (University of Sydney)
- Scott Nowson (Xerox Research Centre Europe)
- Cécile Paris (CSIRO)
- David Powers (Flinders University)
- Lizhen Qu (NICTA)
- Will Radford (Xerox Research Centre Europe)
- Horacio Saggion (Universitat Pompeu Fabra)
- Andrea Schalley (Griffith University)
- Rolf Schwitter (Macquarie University)
- Karin Verspoor (University of Melbourne)
- Ingrid Zukerman (Monash University)

Preface

This volume contains the papers accepted for presentation at the Australasian Language Technology Association Workshop (ALTA) 2014, held at the RMIT University in Melbourne, Australia on 26–28th of November, 2014.

The goals of the workshop are to:

- bring together the Language Technology (LT) community in the Australasian region and encourage interactions and collaboration;
- foster interaction between academic and industrial researchers, to encourage dissemination of research results;
- provide a forum for students and young researchers to present their research;
- facilitate the discussion of new and ongoing research and projects;
- increase visibility of LT research in Australasia and overseas and encourage interactions with the wider international LT community.

This year, we are pleased to present 20 peer-reviewed papers selected for the ALTA Workshop, including 10 full papers, 6 short papers, and 4 papers that will be presented as posters. We received a total of 30 submissions. Each paper was reviewed by three members of the program committee. The reviewing for the workshop was double blind, and done in accordance with the DIISRTE requirements for E1 conference publications. Furthermore, great care was taken to avoid all conflicts of interest.

This volume covers a diverse of set topics as represented by the selected papers. This year, a number of papers describe applications of language technology, with domains ranging from biomedicine to emergency management. As in previous years, we aim to provide to foster the career development for research students by providing opportunities to receive feedback. Our hope is that both students and staff alike will enjoy the papers presented and that the workshop will continue to be a forum for our community to build new research relationships and collaborations.

The proceedings include the abstract of the invited talk by Dr. Jennifer Lai, from IBM Research. This volume also contains an overview of the 2014 ALTA Shared task and descriptions of the systems developed by three of the participating teams. These contributions were not peer-reviewed.

We would like to thank, in no particular order: all of the authors who submitted papers to ALTA; the program committee for the time and effort they put into maintaining the high standards of our reviewing process; the local organiser Lawrence Cavedon for taking care of all the physical logistics and lining up some great social events; our invited speakers Jennifer Lai and Maarten de Rijke for agreeing to share their extensive experience and insights with us; Trevor Cohn for agreeing to host a great tutorial, and Sarvnaz Karimi and Karin Verspoor, the program co-chairs of ALTA 2013, for their valuable help and guidance in preparing this volume. We would also like to acknowledge the constant support and advice of the ALTA Executive Committee for providing input critical to the success of the workshop.

Finally, we gratefully recognise our sponsors: CSIRO, SEEK, Google, and IBM Research. Their generous support enabled us to fund student paper awards, travel subsidies to attend and present at ALTA, catering for the event, and to fund the prize for the ALTA 2014 Shared Task.

Gabriela Ferraro and Stephen Wan
ALTA Workshop Co-Chairs

ALTA 2014 Programme

Wednesday 26th of November 2014 Pre-workshop tutorials

13:30–17:00 (Break 15:00-15:30)	*Gaussian Processes for NLP* Trevor Cohn (University of Melbourne)

Thursday 27th of November, 2014

08:50–09:00	Opening remarks
09:00–10:00	Joint ALTA-ADCS Keynote Maarten de Rijke *Diversity, Intent, and Aggregated Search*
10:00–10:30	Coffee break
Session 1	
10:30–11:00	Sunghwan Kim, John Pate and Mark Johnson *The Effect of Dependency Representation Scheme on Syntactic Language Modelling*
11:00–11:30	Haoxing Wang and Laurianne Sitbon *Multilingual lexical resources to detect cognates in non-aligned texts*
11:30–12:00	Tudor Groza and Karin Verspoor *Automated Generation of Test Suites for Error Analysis of Concept Recognition Systems*
12:00–13:30	Lunch break
Session 2: Joint ALTA-ADCS Session	
13:30–14:00	Jie Yin, Sarvnaz Karimi and John Lingad (ADCS Paper) *Pinpointing Locational Focus in Tweets*
14:00–14:30	Johannes Schanda, Mark Sanderson and Paul Clough (ADCS Paper) *Examining New Event Detection*
14:30–15:00	Kristy Hughes, Joel Nothman and James R. Curran (ALTA Paper) *Trading accuracy for faster named entity linking*
15:00–15:30	Alexander Hogue, Joel Nothman and James R. Curran (ALTA Paper) *Unsupervised Biographical Event Extraction Using Wikipedia Traffic*
15:30–16:00	Coffee break
Session 3	
16:00–16:30	Su Nam Kim, Ingrid Zukerman, Thomas Kleinbauer and Masud Moshtaghi *A Comparative Study of Weighting Schemes for the Interpretation of Spoken Referring Expressions*
16:30–16:45	Mohammad Aliannejadi, Masoud Kiaeeha, Shahram Khadivi and Saeed Shiry Ghidary *Graph-Based Semi-Supervised Conditional Random Fields For Spoken Language Understanding Using Unaligned Data*
16:45–17:00	Dominique Estival and Steve Cassidy *Alveo, a Human Communication Science Virtual Laboratory*
17:00–17:30	Awards and ALTA business meeting
19:00–	Conference dinner

Friday 28th of November, 2014

09:00–10:00	ALTA Keynote Jennifer Lai *Deep QA: Moving beyond the hype to examine the challenges in creating a cognitive assistant for humans*
10:00–10:30	Coffee break
Session 4	
10:30–10:45	Jennifer Biggs and Michael Broughton *OCR and Automated Translation for the Navigation of non-English Handsets: A Feasibility Study with Arabic*
10:45–11:00	Simon Kocbek, Karin Verspoor and Wray Buntine *Exploring Temporal Patterns in Emergency Department Triage Notes with Topic Models*
11:00–11:30	Bella Robinson, Hua Bai, Robert Power and Xunguo Lin *Developing a Sina Weibo Incident Monitor for Disasters*
11:30–12:00	Michael Niemann *Finding expertise using online community dialogue and the Duality of Expertise*
Session 5: ALTA Shared Task	
12:00–12:450	Diego Mollá *ALTA 2014 Shared Task overview*
12:00–12:450	Shared Task Winner (TBA) *Presentation Title TBA*
12:30–13:30	Lunch break
Session 6	
14:00–14:30	Diego Mollá, Christopher Jones and Abeed Sarker *Impact of Citing Papers for Summarisation of Clinical Documents*
14:30–14:45	Tatyana Shmanina, Lawrence Cavedon and Ingrid Zukerman *Challenges in Information Extraction from Tables in Biomedical Research Publications: a Dataset Analysis*
14:45–15:00	Antonio Jimeno Yepes, Andrew MacKinlay, Justin Bedo, Rahil Garvani and Qiang Chen *Deep Belief Networks and Biomedical Text Categorisation*
14:30–14:45	Fumiyo Fukumoto, Shougo Ushiyama, Yoshimi Suzuki and Suguru Matsuyoshi *The Effect of Temporal-based Term Selection for Text Classification*
Session 7	
15:00–15:15	Final remarks
15:15–17:00	Poster session with ADCS

Contents

Invited talk

Deep QA: Moving beyond the hype to examine the challenges in creating a cognitive assistant for humans

Jennifer Lai
IBM Research
jlai@us.ibm.com

Abstract

According to Wikipedia, Watson is "an artificially intelligent computer system capable of answering questions posed in natural language, developed in IBM's DeepQA project by a research team". Hiding behind this fairly bland definition is a complex set of technological challenges that cover areas ranging from NLP to context management, dialogue structure, feedback loops, and personalisation. In this talk Jennifer will first introduce several key NL projects from IBM Research to give an overview of the lab's work and will then delve into the Life of Watson, what 'he' could be when he 'grows up', and the many deep research questions that need to be addressed along the way.

Jennifer Lai. 2014. Deep QA: Moving beyond the hype to examine the challenges in creating a cognitive assistant for humans. In *Proceedings of Australasian Language Technology Association Workshop*, page 2.

Full papers

The Effect of Dependency Representation Scheme on Syntactic Language Modelling

Sunghwan Mac Kim
Department of Computing
Macquarie University
Sydney, NSW 2109, Australia
sunghwan.kim@mq.edu.au

John K Pate
Department of Computing
Macquarie University
Sydney, NSW 2109, Australia
john.pate@mq.edu.au

Mark Johnson
Department of Computing
Macquarie University
Sydney, NSW 2109, Australia
mark.johnson@mq.edu.au

Abstract

There has been considerable work on syntactic language models and they have advanced greatly over the last decade. Most of them have used a probabilistic context-free grammar (PCFG) or a dependency grammar (DG). In particular, DG has attracted more and more interest in the past years since dependency parsing has achieved great success. While much work has evaluated the effects of different dependency representations in the context of parsing, there has been relatively little investigation into them on a syntactic language model. In this work, we conduct the first assessment of three dependency representations on a transition-based dependency parsing language model. We show that the choice of dependency representation has an impact on overall performance from the perspective of language modelling.

1 Introduction

Syntactic language models have been successfully applied to a wide range of domains such as speech recognition, machine translation, and disfluency detection. Although n-gram based language models are the most widely used due to their simplicity and efficacy, they suffer from a major drawback: they cannot characterise the long-range relations between words. A syntactic language model, which exploits syntactic dependencies, can incorporate richer syntactic knowledge and information through syntactic parsing. In particular, syntactic structure leads to better performance of language model compared to traditional n-gram language models (Chelba and Jelinek, 2000). Most of the syntactic language models have used a probabilistic context-free grammar (PCFG) (Roark, 2001; Charniak, 2001) or a dependency grammar (DG) (Wang and Harper, 2002; Gubbins and Vlachos, 2013) in order to capture the surface syntactic structures of sentences.

Researchers have shown an increased interest in dependency parsing and it has increasingly been recognised as an alternative to constituency parsing in the past years. Accordingly, various representations and associated parsers have been proposed with respect to DG. DG describes the syntactic structure of a sentence in terms of head-dependent relations between words. Unlike constituency models of syntax, DG directly models relationships between pairs of words, which leads to a simple framework that is easy to lexicalise and parse with. Moreover, a DG-based, particularly transition-based, parser is fast and even achieves state-of-the-art performance compared to the other grammar-based parsers. It is therefore suitable for identifying syntactic structures in incremental processing, which is a useful feature for online processing tasks such as speech recognition or machine translation.

The aim of this study is to explore different dependency representations and to investigate their effects on the language modelling task. There are publicly available converters to generate dependencies. Ivanova et al. (2013) investigated the effect of each dependency scheme in terms of parsing accuracy. Elming et al. (2013) evaluated four dependency schemes in five different natural language processing (NLP) applications. However, to our knowledge, no previous work has investigated the effect of dependency representation on a syntactic language model.

The remainder of this paper is organised as follows. Section 2 gives a brief overview of related work on dependency schemes and language modelling. In Section 3 we discuss three dependency schemes and Section 4 describes our dependency parsing language model. Then, the experimental

Sunghwan Kim, John Pate and Mark Johnson. 2014. The Effect of Dependency Representation Scheme on Syntactic Language Modelling. In *Proceedings of Australasian Language Technology Association Workshop*, pages 4−13.

settings and a series of results are presented in Section 5. Finally, conclusions and directions for future work are given in Section 6.

2 Related Work

A number of studies have been conducted on dependency representations in NLP tasks. Several constituent-to-dependency conversion schemes have been proposed as the outputs of the converters (Johansson and Nugues, 2007; de Marneffe and Manning, 2008; Choi and Palmer, 2010; Tratz and Hovy, 2011). Previous work has evaluated the effects of different dependency representations in various NLP applications (Miwa et al., 2010; Popel et al., 2013; Ivanova et al., 2013; Elming et al., 2013). A substantial literature has examined the impact of combining DG with another diverse grammar representation, particularly in the context of parsing (Sagae et al., 2007; Øvrelid et al., 2009; Farkas and Bohnet, 2012; Kim et al., 2012).

Many works on syntactic language models have been carried out using phrase structures. Chelba and Jelinek (2000) experiment with the application of syntactic structure in a language model for speech recognition. Their model builds the syntactic trees incrementally in a bottom-up strategy while processing the sentence in a left-to-right fashion and assigns a probability to every word sequence and parse. The model is very close to the arc-standard model that we investigate in this paper. Roark (2001) implements an incremental top-down and left-corner parsing model, which is used as a syntactic language model for a speech recognition task. The model effectively exploits rich syntactic regularities as features and achieves better performance than an *n*-gram model. Charniak (2001) describes a syntactic language model based on immediate-head parsing, which is called a Trihead model and empirically shows that the Trihead model is superior to both a trigram baseline and two previous syntactic language models.

Wang and Harper (2002) present a syntactic DG-based language model (SuperARV) for speech recognition. Multiple knowledge sources are tightly integrated based on their constraint DG but SuperARV does not construct explicit syntactic dependencies between words. Nonetheless, it achieves better perplexity than both a baseline trigram and other syntactic language models. Recently, Gubbins and Vlachos (2013) showed how to use unlabelled and labelled dependency grammar language models to solve the Sentence Completion Challenge set (Zweig and Burges, 2012). Their models performed substantially better than *n*-gram models.

3 Alternative Dependency Representations

Previous work has defined different dependency schemes, and provided software tools for converting the syntactic constituency annotations of existing treebanks to dependency annotations. We experiment with the following three schemes for the language modelling task.

- LTH: The LTH dependency scheme is extracted from the automatic conversion of Penn Treebank using the LTH converter (Johansson and Nugues, 2007).[1] The converter has a lot of options that generate linguistic variations in dependency structures and it was configured to produce a functional rather than lexical DG in this study.

- P2M: The P2M scheme is obtained by running the Penn2Malt converter (Nivre, 2006)[2] based on a standard set of head rules. This converter was deprecated by the LTH converter but it is still used to make a comparison with previous results.

- STD: The STD scheme is used in the Stanford parser (de Marneffe and Manning, 2008)[3], which comes with a converter. In this study, the Penn Treebank was converted to Stanford basic dependencies for projective dependency parsing.

The syntactic representations differ in systematic ways as shown in Figure 1. For instance, auxiliaries take the lexical verb as a dependent in all schemes except for STD, where the lexical verb is the head of a VP. In addition to the typological differences, there is rich variation in dependency labels with respect to the schemes. The STD scheme has 49 dependency labels, which is the largest set

[1] http://nlp.cs.lth.se/software/treebank_converter/

[2] http://w3.msi.vxu.se/~nivre/research/Penn2Malt.html

[3] http://nlp.stanford.edu/software/lex-parser.shtml

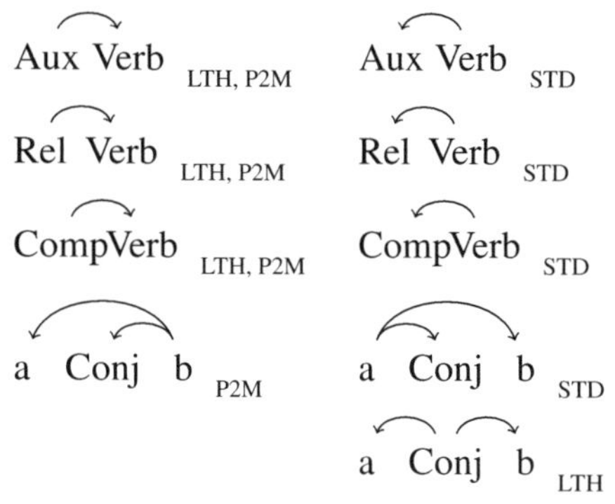

Figure 1: Auxiliaries, relative/subordinate clauses and coordination in the DG schemes.

of dependency labels used here. The LTH dependencies are defined by 22 label types, whereas the P2M scheme employs 12 labels. The fine-grained set of dependency labels in STD allows a more precise expression of grammatical relations. For instance, the label *adv* (unclassified adverbial) in LTH can be expressed using either *advcl* (adverbial clause modier) or *advmod* (adverbial modier) in STD. We evaluate the dependency schemes by incorporating them into a language model architecture in the experiments.

4 A Dependency Parsing Language Model

In this section we describe our syntactic language model in terms of parsing and language modelling. Using the theoretical framework for generative transition-based dependency parsing introduced by Cohen et al. (2011), we propose a generative version of the arc-standard model that defines probability distributions over transitions and finds the most probable ones given stack features.

4.1 Generative Dependency Parsing Model

Following Nivre (2008), a transition-based dependency parsing model is defined as a tuple $S = (C, T, I, C_t)$, where C is a set of configurations, T is a set of permissible transitions, I is an initialisation function, and C_t is a set of terminal configurations. A transition sequence for a sentence is a sequence of configurations where each non-initial configuration is obtained by applying a transition to a previous configuration. A configuration is a triple (α, β, A), where α is stack, β is queue and A is a set of dependency arcs. The stack α stores partially processed words and the queue β records the remaining input words, respectively. The function I maps a sentence to an initial configuration with empty α and A, and β containing the words of the sentence. The set C_t has a terminal configuration, where α contains a single word and β is empty.

The arc-standard model has three distinct types of transitions as follows:

- $Shift_{pw}(SH_{pw})$: move the first item i in the queue onto the stack and predict POS p and word w for the item
- $Left\text{-}Arc_l(LA_l)$: combine the top two items i, j on the stack and predict a dependency label l over an arc $j \rightarrow i$
- $Right\text{-}Arc_l(RA_l)$: combine the top two items i, j on the stack and predict a dependency label l over an arc $i \rightarrow j$

This model processes the input sentence from left to right in a bottom-up fashion using three transitions. A parse tree is incrementally derived through the transition sequence. In particular, *Shift* predicts the next POS p and word w in the queue with a probability $P(Shift, p, w)$, which is a probability both of the *Shift* transition and the POS/word prediction.

The probability of a parse tree is defined as the product of the probabilities of transitions in Eq (1).

$$P(\pi) = \prod_{i=1}^{2n-1} P(t^i|\alpha^{i-1}, A^{i-1}) \qquad (1)$$

where π is a parse tree, n is the number of words in a sentence and t is a transition such that $t \in T$.

More specifically, transitions are conditioned on topmost stack items and in particular, the probability of *Shift* is defined as follows:

$$\begin{aligned} &P(Shift_{pw}|\alpha, A) \\ &\quad = P(Shift|\alpha, A) \cdot P(p|Shift, \alpha, A) \\ &\quad\quad \cdot P(w|p, Shift, \alpha, A) \end{aligned} \qquad (2)$$

This factored generative approach alleviates the effect of sparsity. More specifically, first a relatively coarse-grained *Shift* is predicted given stack features and then we predict a fine-grained POS tag for the transition. Then a more fine-grained prediction of a word is made for the POS to further decompose the *Shift* prediction.

For labelled dependency parsing, we simultaneously generate the dependency and its label. In contrast, *Left-Arc* and *Right-Arc* are predicted in unlabelled dependency parsing without considering the dependency label. For instance, as explained in Section 3, 22 dependency labels are in the LTH scheme and thus 45 combinations of transitions and labels are jointly learned and predicted including the *Shift* transition, which does not have a label, in the labelled parsing model. Note that the probability of *Shift* transition is estimated in a factored fashion as described above.

The above probabilities are subject to the following normalisation condition, namely the sum of all transition probabilities should be one:

$$\sum_{p \in P} \sum_{w \in W} P(Shift_{pw}|\alpha, A) + \sum_{l \in L} P(Left\text{-}Arc_l|\alpha, A) + \sum_{l \in L} P(Right\text{-}Arc_l|\alpha, A) = 1$$

where P and W stand for predefined POS tag and word vocabularies, respectively. L is a set of dependency labels corresponding to each dependency scheme.

4.2 Beam Search

Our parsing model maintains a beam containing multiple configurations. To allow the parser to consider configurations with expensive early moves but cheap late moves, we sort our configurations by a figure-of-merit (FOM) that adjusts a configuration's probability with heuristics about. The beam search runs in each word position using a separate priority queue. A priority queue contains configurations that have been constructed by the same numbers of *Shift*, and the same or different numbers of *Left-Arc* or *Right-Arc* transitions. An initial configuration is inserted into the first priority queue corresponding to the first word position and then the algorithm loops until all configurations have terminal conditions. Each configuration is populated off the queue and updated by applying each of permissible transitions to the current configuration. The updated configuration is pushed onto the corresponding queue with respect to the number of *Shift*. The configurations in each priority queue are ranked according to the FOMs. The ranked configurations are discarded if they fall outside the beam. Looping continues for the current word position until the queue is empty. For the configurations in the final queue, we compute the probability of an input sentence by summing over all their probabilities.

Configurations in the same queue cover different amounts of the input string since they could have different numbers of *Left-Arc* or *Right-Arc*. The configurations are not comparable to each other in terms of their probabilities. For this reason, we propose a FOM to penalise the case where the stack has more items. To this end, the FOM incorporates the probability cost of the reductions that will be required to reduce all the items on the stack. An estimate of the probability of reductions uses a rough approximation $1/(4L)^m$, L is the number of labels (if the scheme is unlabelled, L=1) and m is the number of stack items. The FOM is estimated by multiplying the probability of a configuration by the predicted probability of reducing every stack item.

4.3 Random Forest Model for Word Distribution

The probability of a word in Eq (2) is calculated from the word RF model. The training procedure of our RF model is similar to that of Xu and Jelinek (2007). The growing algorithm starts with a root node and a decision tree is constructed by splitting every node recursively from the root node through a two-step splitting rule. Node splitting terminates when each node triggers a stopping rule in order to avoid overfitting.

We overcome data sparsity by first observing that a decision tree essentially provides a hierarchical clustering of the data, since each node splits the data. We linearly interpolate the distributions of the leaf nodes recursively with their parents, ultimately backing off to the root node. The interpolation parameters should be sensitive to the counts in each node so that we back off only when the more specific node does not have enough observations to be reliable. However, giving each node of each decision tree its own interpolation parameter would itself introduce data sparsity problems. We instead use Chen's bucketing approach (Chen and Goodman, 1996) for each tree level, in which nodes on the same level are grouped into buckets and one interpolation parameter is estimated for each bucket. The first step is to divide up the nodes on the same level into bins based on Chen's scores. We then use the EM algorithm to find the optimal interpolation parameter for all the nodes in each bucket using heldout data.

In a RF model, the predictions of all decision trees are averaged to produce a more robust pre-

$S1_p, S2_p, S3_p$	POS
$S1_w, S2_w, S3_w$	word
$S1_{lp}, S2_{lp}$	POS of left-most child
$S1_{rp}, S2_{rp}$	POS of right-most child
$S1_{lw}, S2_{lw}$	word of left-most child
$S1_{rw}, S2_{rw}$	word of right-most child
$S1^*_{ll}, S2^*_{ll}$	Label of left-most child
$S1^*_{rl}, S2^*_{rl}$	Label of right-most child

Table 1: Conditioning stack features, where Si represents the ith item on the stack (S1 is a top-most stack item). Note that dependency label features are only used in labelled parsing.*

diction, as in Eq (3):

$$P(w|p, Shift, \alpha, A) = \frac{1}{m}\sum_{t=1}^{m} P^j(w|p, Shift, \alpha, A) \quad (3)$$

where m denotes the total number of decision trees and $P^j(w|\cdot)$ is the probability of the word w calculated by the jth decision tree.

The word probability is calculated conditioned on the stack features of the current configuration. Table 1 shows the stack features that are used in our RF model. Our unlabelled parsing model estimates the conditional probabilities of the word, given 14 different features. The labelled parsing model uses four additional label-related features.

4.4 Maximum Entropy Model for Transition/POS Distribution

Conditional ME models (Berger et al., 1996) are used as another classifier in our parsing-based language model together with RF. The probability of a transition or a POS tag in Eq (2) is calculated from the corresponding transition ME or POS ME model. For instance, the probability of *Shift* is calculated as shown in Eq (4).

$$P^{ME}(Shift|\alpha, A) = \frac{1}{Z(\alpha, A)}\exp(\lambda \cdot f(\alpha, A, Shift)) \quad (4)$$

where $f(\alpha, A, Shift)$ denotes feature functions that return non-zero values if particular stack items appear in (α, A) and the transition is *Shift*. λ is the corresponding real-valued weight vector, and more informative features receive weights further from zero. $Z(\alpha, A) = \sum_{t \in T}\exp(\lambda \cdot f(\alpha, A, t))$ is the partition function that ensures the distribution is properly normalised. The feature weights λ are tuned to maximise the regularised conditional likelihood of the training data. It is equivalent to the minimisation of the regularised negative log conditional likelihood:

$$\hat{\lambda} = \underset{\lambda}{\text{argmin}}(-\sum_i \log P_\lambda(y_i|x_i) + \sum_j \frac{\lambda_j^2}{2\sigma_j^2}) \quad (5)$$

where $\sum_j \lambda_j^2/2\sigma_j^2$ is a Gaussian prior regulariser that reduces overfitting by penalising large weights. In practice, we use a single parameter σ instead of having a different parameter σ_i for each feature.

In this work we use the limited memory BFGS (L-BFGS) algorithm (Liu and Nocedal, 1989), which is an efficient numerical optimisation algorithm, to find the optimal feature weights $\hat{\lambda}$. In the ME model, we rely on two kinds of features: (1) atomic features from Table 1, and (2) conjunctive features that are combinations of the atomic features. The feature templates are shown in Table 2.

Type	**Features**
Unigram	$S1_p, S2_p, S3_p, S1_w, S2_w, S3_w$
	$S1_{lp}, S2_{lp}, S1_{rp}, S2_{rp}$
	$S1_{lw}, S2_{lw}, S1_{rw}, S2_{rw}$
	$S1^*_{ll}, S2^*_{ll}, S1^*_{rl}, S2^*_{rl}$
Bigram	$S1_w \circ S1_p, S2_w \circ S2_p, S3_w \circ S3_p$
	$S1_w \circ S2_w, S1_p \circ S2_p$
	$S1_p \circ S1_{lp}, S2_p \circ S2_{lp}$
	$S1_p \circ S1_{rp}, S2_p \circ S2_{rp}$
	$S1_w \circ S1^*_{ll}, S1_w \circ S1^*_{rl}$
	$S1_p \circ S1^*_{ll}, S1_p \circ S1^*_{rl}$
	$S2_w \circ S2^*_{ll}, S2_w \circ S2^*_{rl}$
	$S2_p \circ S2^*_{ll}, S2_p \circ S2^*_{rl}$
Trigram	$S1_p \circ S2_p \circ S3_p, S1_p \circ S2_w \circ S2_p$
	$S1_w \circ S2_w \circ S2_p, S1_w \circ S1_p \circ S2_p$
	$S1_w \circ S1_p \circ S2_w, S2_p \circ S2_{lp} \circ S1_p$
	$S2_p \circ S2_{rp} \circ S1_p, S2_p \circ S1_p \circ S1_{lp}$
	$S2_p \circ S1_p \circ S1_{rp}, S2_p \circ S2_{lp} \circ S1_w$
	$S2_p \circ S2_{rp} \circ S1_w, S2_p \circ S1_w \circ S1_{lp}$
Fourgram	$S1_w \circ S1_p \circ S2_w \circ S2_p$

Table 2: Stack feature templates of the ME model.

4.5 Language Model

A generative parsing model assigns a joint probability$P(\pi, s)$ for a parse tree π and an input sentence s. The probability of a sentence $P(s)$ is computed by summing over all parse trees, $P(s) = \sum_\pi P(\pi, s)$. Therefore, our generative parser can be used as a language model, which assigns a probability $P(s)$ to a sentence s, using the probabilities of parse trees from Eq (1).

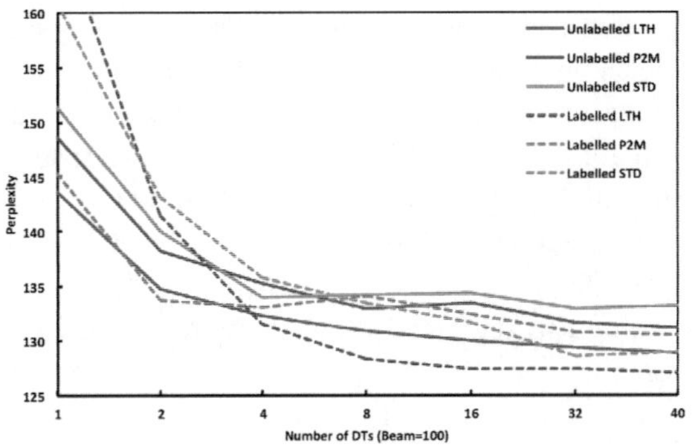

(a) a fixed beam size 100

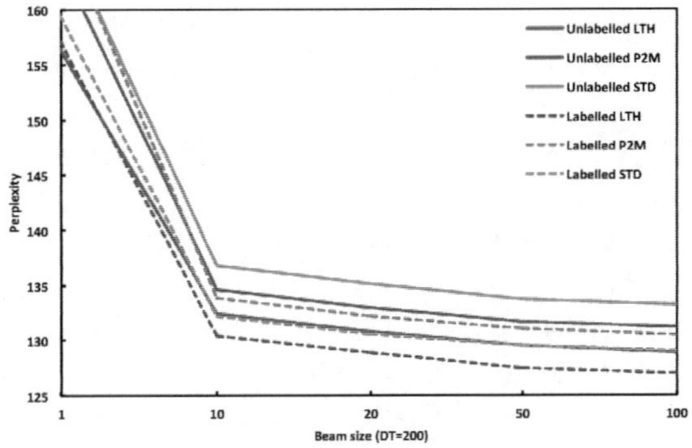

(b) a fixed number of decision trees 40

Figure 2: Perplexity results trained and tested on WSJ.

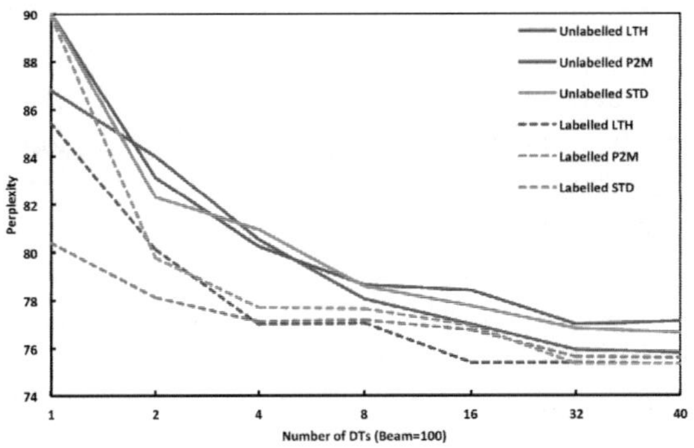

(a) a fixed beam size 100

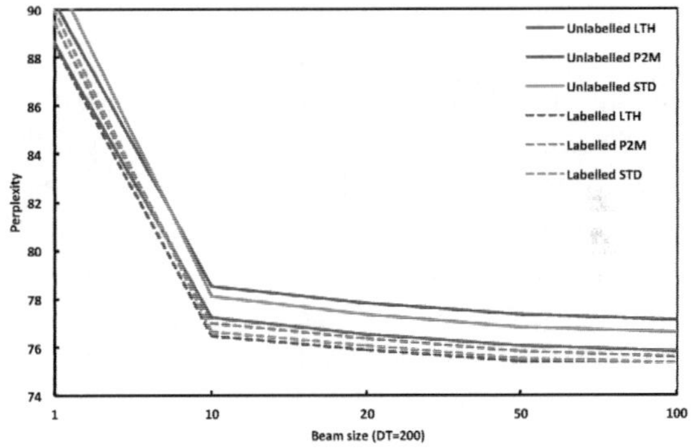

(b) a fixed number of decision trees 40

Figure 3: Perplexity results trained and tested on Switchboard.

5 Experiments

5.1 Experimental Settings

We empirically evaluate the effects of three dependency schemes (LTH, P2M, STD) on our dependency language models in terms of perplexity and word error rate (WER). Several experiments are conducted varying the number of decision trees and the beam size on each dependency scheme. Each dependency language model uses a maximum beam size of 100, and up to 40 decision trees are generated for the RF classifier. We train the transition/POS ME classifiers using 400 iterations with no frequency cutoff for features and σ for the Gaussian prior is set to 1. Our experiments use three evaluation datasets for unlabelled and labelled dependency language models.

Perplexity Results trained and tested on WSJ: Most of the syntactic language models (Roark, 2001; Charniak, 2001; Xu and Jelinek, 2007; Wang and Harper, 2002) were evaluated on the Wall Street Journal (WSJ) section of the Penn Treebank (Marcus et al., 1993) in terms of perplexity. The WSJ is speechified by following the conventions of previous work. All punctuation is removed, words are lowercased, and numbers are replaced by a symbol N. All words outside the vocabulary limit (10,000 words) are mapped to a special UNK symbol. Sections 0-20 are used as the training set, sections 21-22 as the heldout set, and sections 23-24 for testing.

Perplexity Results trained and tested on Switchboard: We ran experiments on the Switchboard part of the Penn Treebank. Following Johnson and Charniak (2004), both sections 2 and 3 were used for a training set (sw2005.mrg-sw3993.mrg). We split section 4 into a held-out set (sw4519.mrg-sw4936.mrg) and a test set (sw4004.mrg-sw4153.mrg). The Switchboard corpus was preprocessed so that all disfluencies are removed from constituent trees prior to converting to dependency structure. We applied three converters on the cleaned version of Switchboard to obtain three dependency schemes. The vocabulary consists of all the words in the training data and contains 13,706 word types.

WER Results trained on WSJ and tested on HUB1: We performed a small speech recognition evaluation on *n*-best lists from the DARPA '93 HUB1 test setup. A real task-based evaluation would be worthwhile besides perplexity since previous studies found that lower perplexity does not necessarily mean lower WER in their models (Roark, 2001; Wang and Harper, 2002; Xu and Jelinek, 2007). The HUB1 corpus consists of 213 sentences taken from the WSJ with a total of 3,446 words. The corpus is provided along with a lattice trigram model, which is trained on approximately 40 million words with a vocabulary of 20 thousand words. We used the A* decoding algorithm of SRILM to extract 50-best lists from the lattices measuring the lattice trigram and acoustic scores. The average number of candidates is roughly 21.7 in the lists. The WER of the lattice trigram model is 13.7% and the oracle WER, which is the lowest WER to the references, is 7.9% for the 50-best lists. There are token discrepancies between the Penn Treebank and the HUB1 lattices for contractions, possessives and numbers.[4] For simplicity, we do not speechify the numbers (i.e., not expand them into text), whereas we follow previous work in dealing with the discrepancies of contractions or possessives. We use the Penn Treebank tokenisation, which separates clitics from their base word (i.e. '*can't*' is represented as '*ca n't*'), for training and running our models. Two tokens of treebank format are then combined into one to be aligned with gold standard word sequences for the WER evaluation. Our trained models were used with the same training data (1 million words) and vocabulary as in the above perplexity experiments on WSJ. We followed Roark (2001) in multiplying the language model scores by 15 before interpolating them with the acoustic model scores.

5.2 Experimental Results

The Effects of Decision Trees and Beam Search: To illustrate the effects of decision trees and beam size, we plot perplexity that corresponds to each scheme. As can be seen from Figure 2a, the perplexities are improved for all schemes using more decision trees. Perplexity reductions of two labelled schemes (LTH, STD) are relatively large except for labelled P2M, and particularly the perplexities drop sharply up to random forests of size 8 for labelled LTH. On the other hand, the perplexities of unlabelled schemes are decreased at a sluggish pace and they are more insensitive to the number of decision trees. As Figure 2b illustrates, the general shape of the perplexity curves drops quickly as beam size increases from 1 to 10, and then to flatten as beam size increases further. We do not obtain much benefit if the beam size is larger than 10. Figure 3 shows the perplexity results on Switchboard for different numbers of decision trees and variable beam sizes as on WSJ. We can observe the positive effects of these two parameters (random forest size and beam search) with respect to perplexity. Figure 3b shows similar trends to the WSJ perplexities, which are dramatically reduced up to a beam size of 10, and then level out. The perplexity trends in Figure 3a are quite different, showing that unlabelled schemes have a gentle slope over numbers of decision trees. The number of decision trees has a relatively high impact on the performance of unlabelled schemes on Switchboard.

Performance Comparison: Table 3 presents the perplexity and WER results of unlabelled and labelled schemes for LTH, P2M and STD. We can see that labelled LTH achieves the lowest perplexities, whereas unlabelled P2M and STD perform the worst overall. For labelled schemes we observe their superior performance compared to unlabelled schemes in terms of perplexity. The perplexity results indicate that dependency labels improve the performance of a dependency language model. In particular, labelled STD has the largest perplexity reduction (3.2%) compared to unlabelled STD, which yields the worst perplexity on WSJ. Overall, LTH outperforms both P2M and STD regardless of unlabelled or labelled scheme in terms of perplexity. Although the WERs are not significantly different across the different methods, unlabelled P2M leads to the best performance (14.6%), whereas labelled P2M is the worst performing scheme (15.1%).[5] Labelled LTH and

[4]For instance, "**Bill 's** car **isn 't** worth **$100**" vs. "**Bill's** car **isn't** worth **one hundred dollars**".

[5]All results of statistical significance tests are presented with $p < 0.05$ level using the SCLITE toolkit with the option MAPSSWE, which stands for Matched Pairs Sentence Segment Word Error.

Models	WSJ Perplexity	SWBD Perplexity	HUB1 WER
Unlabelled LTH	128.84	75.81	14.8
Unlabelled P2M	131.12	77.09	14.6
Unlabelled STD	133.18	76.61	14.7
Labelled LTH	126.97	75.33	14.9
Labelled P2M	130.45	75.59	15.1
Labelled STD	128.96	75.34	14.7

Table 3: Perplexities and WERs of unlabelled and labelled LTH, P2M and STD schemes. We measured their performance on WSJ, Switchboard and HUB1 datasets.

STD perform roughly on par with unlabelled LTH and STD, respectively.

Analysis and Discussion: Our results indicate that the choice of dependency representation affects the performance of the syntactic language model. One thing to note is that it is hard to tell what scheme is overall best in our experiments. An interesting observation is that the dependency labels are somewhat ineffective for the speech recognition task in contrast to perplexity evaluation. The results demonstrate that each evaluation measure tends to have its own preferred scheme. For instance, the LTH scheme is preferred for the perplexity evaluation, whereas STD is preferred under WER. Our finding is in line with previous work, which claims that a task-based evaluation does not correlate well with a theoretical evaluation (Rosenfeld, 2000; Jonson, 2006; Och et al., 2004; Miwa et al., 2010; Elming et al., 2013; Smith, 2012). They commonly claim that lower perplexity does not necessarily mean lower WER, and the relation between two measures is clearly not transparent. Miwa et al. (2010) found that STD performs better for event extraction, whereas LTH outperforms STD in terms of parsing accuracy.

5.3 Comparison with Previous Work

In this section, we compare our model to previous work discussed in the literature. As baselines, we use two influential models, namely a modified Kneser-Ney (mKN) trigram model (Chen and Goodman, 1998) and Charniak's Trihead language model (Charniak, 2001).[6] The two models were trained with the same training data and vocabulary on WSJ as mentioned in Section 5.1. The SRILM toolkit (Stolcke, 2002) was used to build the trigram mKN smoothed language model.

[6]The mKN is still considered one of the best smoothing methods for *n*-gram language models and the Trihead model achieves the better perplexity and WER compared to Chelba's and Roark's models (Lease et al., 2005). Moreover, there is no significant difference between Chelba's SLM and Wang's SuperARV in terms of WER although the SuperARV even obtains a much lower perplexity (Wang and Harper, 2002). For these reasons, we think that Charniak's model is the strongest competitor among syntactic language models.

Models	Perplexity	WER
mKN trigram	148.65	17.2
Trihead	131.40	15.0
Unlabelled LTH	128.84	14.8
Labelled LTH	126.97	14.9

Table 4: Perplexity and WER comparisons with previous work.

The performance of the two baselines in Table 4 was measured conducting the same test procedures on WSJ and HUB1. Our perplexities and WERs were selected from the previous sections for the LTH scheme, which performs well uniformly. It is shown that both unlabelled and labelled LTH schemes significantly improve upon the mKN baseline in terms of WER. The WER improvement of LTH over the Trihead model is not statistically significant, although the LTH scheme achieves better perplexity than Trihead regardless of dependency labels.

6 Conclusion and Future Work

We explored three different dependency schemes using a dependency parsing language model. Our study indicates that the choice of scheme has an impact on overall performance. However, no dependency scheme is uniformly better than the others in terms of both perplexity and WER. Nevertheless, there are some generalisations we can make. When evaluated on WSJ and Switchboard, unlabelled and labelled LTHs are generally better than the others in terms of perplexity. In contrast, unlabelled and labelled STDs yield the best overall performance in the HUB1 WER evaluation. It is interesting to see that perplexity has a weak correlation with WER in dependency parsing language models. We note that it is hard to figure out from our results which dependency directions are preferred in structures such as prepositional phrase attachment. For instance, "Is the rightmost noun favoured? or Is the leftmost noun favoured?" as a head in noun sequences in the context of language modelling. As future work, we plan to carry out further investigation of the effect of each structure and explore what is the most or least preferable combination of structures on a syntactic language model.

Acknowledgments

We would like to thank the reviewers for their thoughtful comments and suggestions.

References

Adam L. Berger, Vincent J. Della Pietra, and Stephen A. Della Pietra. 1996. A Maximum Entropy Approach to Natural Language Processing. *Computational Linguistics*, 22(1):39–71.

Eugene Charniak. 2001. Immediate-Head Parsing for Language Models. In *Proceedings of 39th Annual Meeting of the Association for Computational Linguistics*, pages 124–131, Toulouse, France.

Ciprian Chelba and Frederick Jelinek. 2000. Structured language modeling. *Computer Speech & Language*, 14(4):283–332.

Stanley F. Chen and Joshua Goodman. 1996. An Empirical Study of Smoothing Techniques for Language Modeling. In Arivind Joshi and Martha Palmer, editors, *Proceedings of the Thirty-Fourth Annual Meeting of the Association for Computational Linguistics*, pages 310–318, San Francisco. Morgan Kaufmann Publishers.

Stanley F. Chen and Joshua Goodman. 1998. An Empirical Study of Smoothing Techniques for Language Modeling. Technical Report TR-10-98, Center for Research in Computing Technology, Harvard University.

Jinho D Choi and Martha Palmer. 2010. Robust constituent-to-dependency conversion for English. In *Proceedings of 9th Treebanks and Linguistic Theories Workshop (TLT)*, pages 55–66.

Shay B. Cohen, Carlos Gómez-Rodríguez, and Giorgio Satta. 2011. Exact Inference for Generative Probabilistic Non-Projective Dependency Parsing. In *Proceedings of the 2011 Conference on Empirical Methods in Natural Language Processing*, pages 1234–1245, Edinburgh, Scotland, UK, July. Association for Computational Linguistics.

Marie-Catherine de Marneffe and Christopher D. Manning. 2008. The Stanford Typed Dependencies Representation. In *Coling 2008: Proceedings of the workshop on Cross-Framework and Cross-Domain Parser Evaluation*, pages 1–8, Manchester, UK, August.

Jakob Elming, Anders Johannsen, Sigrid Klerke, Emanuele Lapponi, Hector Martinez Alonso, and Anders Søgaard. 2013. Down-stream effects of tree-to-dependency conversions. In *Proceedings of the 2013 Conference of the North American Chapter of the Association for Computational Linguistics: Human Language Technologies*, pages 617–626, Atlanta, Georgia, June. Association for Computational Linguistics.

Richárd Farkas and Bernd Bohnet. 2012. Stacking of Dependency and Phrase Structure Parsers. In *Proceedings of COLING 2012*, pages 849–866, Mumbai, India, December. The COLING 2012 Organizing Committee.

Joseph Gubbins and Andreas Vlachos. 2013. Dependency Language Models for Sentence Completion. In *Proceedings of the 2013 Conference on Empirical Methods in Natural Language Processing*, pages 1405–1410, Seattle, Washington, USA, October. Association for Computational Linguistics.

Angelina Ivanova, Stephan Oepen, and Lilja Øvrelid. 2013. Survey on parsing three dependency representations for English. In *51st Annual Meeting of the Association for Computational Linguistics Proceedings of the Student Research Workshop*, pages 31–37, Sofia, Bulgaria, August. Association for Computational Linguistics.

Richard Johansson and Pierre Nugues. 2007. Extended constituent-to-dependency conversion for English. In *Proceedings of the 16th Nordic Conference on Computational Linguistics (NODALIDA)*.

Mark Johnson and Eugene Charniak. 2004. A TAG-based noisy channel model of speech repairs. In *Proceedings of the 42nd Annual Meeting of the Association for Computational Linguistics*, pages 33–39.

Rebecca Jonson. 2006. Generating Statistical Language Models from Interpretation Grammars in Dialogue Systems. In *Proceedings of 11th Conference of the European Association of Computational Linguistics*, pages 57–65. The Association for Computer Linguistics.

Sunghwan Mac Kim, Dominick Ng, Mark Johnson, and James Curran. 2012. Improving Combinatory Categorial Grammar Parse Reranking with Dependency Grammar Features. In *Proceedings of COLING 2012*, pages 1441–1458, Mumbai, India, December. The COLING 2012 Organizing Committee.

Matthew Lease, Eugene Charniak, and Mark Johnson. 2005. Parsing and its Applications for Conversational Speech. In *IEEE International Conference on Acoustics, Speech, and Signal Processing (ICASSP)*, volume 5, pages 961–964.

Dong C. Liu and Jorge Nocedal. 1989. On the Limited Memory BFGS Method for Large Scale Optimization. *Math. Program.*, 45(3):503–528, December.

Michell P. Marcus, Mary A. Marcinkiewicz, and Beatrice Santorini. 1993. Building a large annotated corpus of English: The Penn Treebank. *Computational linguistics*, 19(2):313–330.

Makoto Miwa, Sampo Pyysalo, Tadayoshi Hara, and Jun'ichi Tsujii. 2010. Evaluating Dependency Representations for Event Extraction. In *Proceedings of the 23rd International Conference on Computational Linguistics (Coling 2010)*, pages 779–787, Beijing, China, August. Coling 2010 Organizing Committee.

Joakim Nivre. 2006. *Inductive dependency parsing*. Springer.

Joakim Nivre. 2008. Algorithms for Deterministic Incremental Dependency Parsing. *Computational Linguistics*, 34(4):513–553.

Franz Josef Och, Daniel Gildea, Sanjeev Khudanpur, Anoop Sarkar, Kenji Yamada, Alex Fraser, Shankar Kumar, Libin Shen, David Smith, Katherine Eng, Viren Jain, Zhen Jin, and Dragomir Radev. 2004. A Smorgasbord of Features for Statistical Machine Translation. In Daniel Marcu Susan Dumais and Salim Roukos, editors, *HLT-NAACL 2004: Main Proceedings*, pages 161–168, Boston, Massachusetts, USA, May 2 - May 7. Association for Computational Linguistics.

Lilja Øvrelid, Jonas Kuhn, and Kathrin Spreyer. 2009. Cross-framework parser stacking for data-driven dependency parsing. *Traitement Automatique des Langues (TAL) Special Issue on Machine Learning for NLP*, 50(3):109–138.

Martin Popel, David Mareček, Jan Štpánek, Daniel Zeman, and Zdnk Žabokrtský. 2013. Coordination Structures in Dependency Treebanks. In *Proceedings of the 51st Annual Meeting of the Association for Computational Linguistics (Volume 1: Long Papers)*, pages 517–527, Sofia, Bulgaria, August. Association for Computational Linguistics.

Brian Roark. 2001. Probabilistic top-down parsing and language modeling. *Computational Linguistics*, 27(2):249–276.

Ronald Rosenfeld. 2000. Two decades of statistical language modeling: where do we go from here? *Proceedings of the IEEE*, 88(8):1270–1278, Aug.

Kenji Sagae, Yusuke Miyao, and Jun'ichi Tsujii. 2007. HPSG Parsing with Shallow Dependency Constraints. In *Proceedings of the 45th Annual Meeting of the Association of Computational Linguistics*, pages 624–631, Prague, Czech Republic, June. Association for Computational Linguistics.

Noah A. Smith. 2012. Adversarial Evaluation for Models of Natural Language. *CoRR*, abs/1207.0245.

Andreas Stolcke. 2002. SRILM - an extensible language modeling toolkit. In *Proceedings of the International Conference on Spoken Language Processing*, pages 901–904.

Stephen Tratz and Eduard Hovy. 2011. A Fast, Accurate, Non-Projective, Semantically-Enriched Parser. In *Proceedings of the 2011 Conference on Empirical Methods in Natural Language Processing*, pages 1257–1268, Edinburgh, Scotland, UK, July.

Wen Wang and Mary P. Harper. 2002. The SuperARV Language Model: Investigating the Effectiveness of Tightly Integrating Multiple Knowledge Sources. In *Proceedings of the 2002 Conference on Empirical Methods in Natural Language Processing*, pages 238–247. Association for Computational Linguistics, July.

Peng Xu and Frederick Jelinek. 2007. Random forests and the data sparseness problem in language modeling. *Computer Speech & Language*, 21(1):105–152.

Geoffrey Zweig and Chris J.C. Burges. 2012. A Challenge Set for Advancing Language Modeling. In *Proceedings of the NAACL-HLT 2012 Workshop: Will We Ever Really Replace the N-gram Model? On the Future of Language Modeling for HLT*, pages 29–36, Montréal, Canada, June. Association for Computational Linguistics.

Multilingual lexical resources to detect cognates in non-aligned texts

Haoxing Wang
Queensland University of Technology
2 George St, Brisbane, 4000
haoxing.wang@hdr.qut.edu.au

Laurianne Sitbon
Queensland University of Technology
2 George St, Brisbane, 4000
l.sitbon@qut.edu.au

Abstract

The identification of cognates between two distinct languages has recently started to attract the attention of NLP research, but there has been little research into using semantic evidence to detect cognates. The approach presented in this paper aims to detect English-French cognates within monolingual texts (texts that are not accompanied by aligned translated equivalents), by integrating word shape similarity approaches with word sense disambiguation techniques in order to account for context. Our implementation is based on BabelNet, a semantic network that incorporates a multilingual encyclopedic dictionary. Our approach is evaluated on two manually annotated datasets. The first one shows that across different types of natural text, our method can identify the cognates with an overall accuracy of 80%. The second one, consisting of control sentences with semi-cognates acting as either true cognates or false friends, shows that our method can identify 80% of semi-cognates acting as cognates but also identifies 75% of the semi-cognates acting as false friends.

1 Introduction

Estimating the difficulty of a text for non-native speakers, or learners of a second language, is gaining interest in natural language processing, information retrieval and education communities. So far measures and models to predict readability in a cross-lingual context have used mainly text features used in monolingual readability contexts (such as word shapes, grammatical features and individual word frequency features). These features have been tested when estimating readability levels for K-12 (primary to high school) readers. As word frequency can be partially estimated by word length, it remains the principal feature for estimation second language learners with the assumption that less frequent words are less likely to have been encountered and therefore accessible in the memory of the learnt language by readers. However such features are not entirely adapted to existing reading abilities of learners with a different language background. In particular, for a number of reasons, many languages have identical words in their vocabulary, which opens a secondary access to the meaning of such words as an alternative to memory in the learnt language. For example, English and French languages belong to different branches of the Indo-European family of languages, and additionally European history of mixed cultures has led their vocabularies to share a great number of similar and identical words. These words are called cognates.

Cognates have often slightly changed their orthography (especially in derived forms), and quite often meaning as well in the years and centuries following the transfer. Because of these changes, cognates are generally of one of three different types. First of all, true cognates are English-French word pairs that are viewed as similar and are mutual translations. The spelling could be identical or not, e.g., *prison* and *prison*, *ceramic* and *céramique*. False cognates are pairs of words that have similar spellings but have totally unrelated meanings. For example, *main* in French means *hand*, while in English it means *principal* or *essential*. Lastly, semi-cognates are pairs of words that have similar spellings but only share meanings in some contexts. One way to understand it in a practical setting is that they behave as true cognates or false cognates depending on their sense in a given context.

In this paper, we present a method to identify the words in a text in a given target language and that could acceptably be translated by a true cognate in a given source language (native language of a reader learning the target language). Accept-

Haoxing Wang and Laurianne Sitbon. 2014. Multilingual lexical resources to detect cognates in non-aligned texts. In *Proceedings of Australasian Language Technology Association Workshop*, pages 14–22.

ability in this context does not necessarily mean that a translator (human or automatic) would chose the true cognate as the preferred translation, but rather that the true cognate is indeed a synonym of the preferred translation. The method we present takes into account both characteristics of true cognates, which are similar spelling and similar meaning.

Most of the previous work in cognate identification has been operating with bilingual (aligned) corpora by using orthographic and phonetic measurements only. In such settings, the similarity of meaning is measured by the alignment of sentences in parallel texts. Basically, all the words in a parallel sentence become candidates that are then evaluated for orthographic similarity.

In the absence of aligned linguistic context, we propose that candidates with similar meaning can be proposed by a disambiguation system coupled with multilingual sense based lexicon where each word is associated to a set of senses, and senses are shared by all languages. A multilingual version of WordNet is an example of such lexicons. In this paper, we use BabelNet, which is an open resource and freely accessible semantic network that connects concepts and named entities in a very large network of semantic relations built from WordNet, Wikipedia and some other thesauri. Furthermore, it is also a multilingual encyclopedic dictionary, with lexicographic and encyclopedic coverage of terms in different languages. In order to disambiguate the word sense, BabelNet provides an independent Java tool that is called Babelfy. It employs a unified approach connecting Entity Linking (EL) and Word Sense Disambiguation (WSD) together. Moro et al. (2014) believe that the lexicographic knowledge used in WSD is useful for tackling EL task, and vice versa, that the encyclopedic information utilized in EL helps disambiguate nominal mentions in a WSD setting. Given an English sentence, Babelfy can disambiguate the meaning of each named entity or concept. For example, "You will get more <volume when beating egg whites if you first bring them to room <temperature." The words with bracket in front are cognates. *Volume* has been disambiguated as "The amount of 3-dimensional space occupied by an object", and *temperature* refers to "The degree of hotness or coldness of a body or environment". After the English word has been processed, it will search the words in other languages that contain this particular sense as candidates. The English word in the source is then compared to the candidates in the target language to establish orthographic/phonetic similarity. Formula 1 shows how we measure the cognateness C of an English word W based on the word shape similarity WSS of all its possible translations CW, and will motivated further in sections 3 and 4.

$$C(W) \approx Max_{CW}(WSS(CW)) \quad (1)$$

Because there are several types of orthographic and phonetic similarities used in the literature, we first establish which is most discriminative of cognates. We then evaluate a threshold-based approach and machine learning based approach to leverage orthographic/phonetic similarity to discriminate cognates from non cognates.

The first evaluation focuses on the performance of our method on a cognate detection task in natural data. The natural dataset contains 6 different genres of text. A second evaluation focuses specifically on semi-cognates classification in controlled sentences, where 20 semi-cognates were each presented in a sentence where they would translate as a cognate and a sentence where they would not.

The paper is organized as follows. Section 2 presents related research on cognate identification and introduces word sense disambiguation with Babelfy. Section 3 describes a general approach to tackle the cognate identification work, while section 4 specifically presents our implementation process. Finally, section 5 focuses on the evaluation and experiment results. Discussion, conclusion and future work are presented in section 6 and 7 respectively.

2 Related Work

2.1 Identifying cognates using orthographic/phonetic similarity

The most well-known approach to measuring how similar two words look to a reader is to measure the Edit Distance (ED) (Levenshtein, 1966). The ED returns a value corresponding to the minimum number of deletions, insertions and substitutions needed to transform the source language word into the target language word. The Dice coefficient measurement (Brew and McKelvie, 1996) is defined as the ratio of the number of n-grams that are shared by two strings and the total number of n-grams in both strings. The Dice coefficient with bi-grams (DICE) is a particularly popular word similarity measure. In their work, Brew and McKelvie looked only at pairs of verbs in English and French, pairs that are extracted from aligned sentences in a parallel corpus. Melamed (1999) used another popular technique, the Longest Common Subsequence Ratio (LCSR), that is the ratio of the length of the longest (not necessarily contiguous) common subsequence (LCS) and the length of the longer word. Simard, Foster and Isabelle (1992) use cognates to align sentences in bi-texts. They only employed the first four characters of the English-French word pairs to determine whether the word pairs are cognates or not.

ALINE (Kondrak, 2000), is an example of a phonetic approach. It was originally designed to align phonetic sequences, but since it chooses the optimal alignment based on the similarity score, it could also be used for computing word shape similarity between word pairs. Kondrak believed that ALINE provides a more accurate result than a pure orthographic method. Kondrak and Dorr (2004) reported that a simple average of several orthographic similarity measures outperforms all the measures on the task of the identification of cognates for drug names. Kondrak proposed the n-gram method (Kondrak, 2005) a year later. In this work, he developed a notion of n-gram similarity and distance, which revealed that original Levenshtein distance and LCSR are special cases of n-gram distance and similarity respectively. He successfully evaluated his new measurement on deciding if pairs of given words were genetic cognates, translational cognates or drug names cognates respectively. The results indicated that Bi gram distance and similarity are more effective than Tri gram methods. Bi gram methods outperform Levenshtein, LCSR and Dice coefficient as well. Rama (2014) combines subsequence feature with the system developed by Hauer and Kondrak, which employs a number of word shape similarity scores as features to train a SVM model. Rama stated, "The subsequences generated from his formula weigh the similarity between two words based on the number of dropped characters and combine vowels and consonants seamlessly". He concludes that using the Hauer and Kondrak's system with a sequence length of 2 could maximize the accuracy. However, none of the work mentioned above has taken the word context to account.

2.2 Identifying cognates using semantic similarity

Kondrak (2001) proposed COGIT, a cognate-identification system that combines ALINE with semantic similarity. Given two vocabulary lists (L1, L2) in distinct languages, his system first calculates the phonetic similarities between each pair of entries (i, j) ∈ (L1 × L2). The semantic similarity of each pair of word is calculated based on the glosses information between a pair of words. The glosses are available in English for all words in both lists. The overall similarity is a linear combination of phonetic and semantic similarity, with different importance assigned to them respectively. The final outcome of this system is a list vocabulary-entry pair, sorted according to the estimated likelihood of their cognateness. Although their evaluation suggested that their methods employing semantic information from glosses perform better than methods based on word shape (phonetic and orthographic), they only focus on finding cognates between different Native American languages.

Frunza (2006) focuses on different machine learning techniques to classify word pairs as true cognates, false cognates or unrelated. She designed two classes called "orthographically similar" and "not orthographically similar" to separate these three types of cognates. However, since the cognate and false cognate are likely to have a high orthographical similarity, their features also include one form of semantic similarity that is whether the words are translations of each other. As a result, this third class - "translation of each other" allows the classifiers to make a decision when a false cognate has a high orthographical similarity. Similar to Kondrak who uses Wordnet and European Wordnet to fetch the glosses, Frunza employs bilingual dictionaries to retrieve the translations.

The method proposed by Mulloni, Pekar, Mitkov and Blagoev (2007) also combines orthographic similarity and semantic similarity. They first extract candidate cognate pairs from comparable bilingual corpora using LCSR, followed by the refinement process using corpus evidence about their semantic similarity. In terms of the semantic similarity, they believe that if two words have similar meanings – and are therefore cognates – they should be semantically close to roughly the same set of words in both (or more) languages. For example, for English *article* and French *article*, their method first finds a set of ten most similar words in the representative language respectively. Then, the method uses a bilingual dictionary to find the correspondence between the two sets of words. Thirdly, a collision set is created between two sets of neighbors, saving words that have at least one translation in the counterpart set. Lastly, The Dice coefficient is used to determine the similarity of the two sets which becomes the semantic similarity of the two original words.

2.3 Word Sense Disambiguation

Unlike all the previous methods which take semantic similarity into consideration, our proposed approach is based on word sense disambiguation (WSD) within monolingual texts, as we aim to use the sense of words as a pivot to identify candidate cognates. There are two mainstream approaches to word sense disambiguation. One is supervised WSD, which uses machine learning methods to learn a classifier for all target words from labeled training sets. Navigli (2012) asserts that memory-based learning and SVM approaches proved to be most effective. The other approach is Knowledge-based WSD, which exploits knowledge resources such as semantic networks to determine the senses of words in context. Such approaches use network features to identify which interpretation of the words in a sentence leads to the most connected representation with the words (as a semantic graph). The application we employ in this paper is called Babelfy which is powered by BabelNet.

2.4 BabelNet

BabelNet follows the structure of a traditional lexical knowledge base and accordingly consists of a labeled directed graph where nodes represent concepts and named entities, while edges express semantic relations between them. The network contains data available in WordNet and also incorporates new nodes and relationships extracted from the Wikipedia (Navigli and Ponzetto, 2012).

Each node in BabelNet is called a Babel synsets. Navigli (2013) explains that each Babel synset represents a given meaning and contains all the synonyms that express that meaning in a range of different languages. More precisely, a Babel synset contains (1) a synset ID; (2) the source of the synset (such as WIKI or WordNet); (3) the corresponding WordNet synset offset; (4) the number of senses in all languages and their full list; (5) the number of translations of the sense and their full list. For example, when the English word *bank* means a financial institution, its translations in other languages as (German *bank*), (Italian *banca*), and (French *banque*); (6) the number of semantic pointers such as relations to other Babel synsets and their full list; (7) its corresponding glosses (possibly available in many languages).

The early version of BabelNet can disambiguate verbs, nouns, adverbs and adjectives, but only provides French synonyms for nouns. The newly released Babelfy tool, which is fully supported by BabelNet, can disambiguate all nominal and named entity mentions within a text, and access French synonyms for all types of words (verbs, nouns, adverbs and adjectives). According to the description from Moro et al. (2014), the WSD and entity linking is achieved in three steps: (1) associating each vertex such as concept or named entity to generate a semantic signature of a given lexicalized semantic network. The semantic network refers to Babelnet; (2) extracting all linkable fragments from a given text and list possible meanings based on semantic network for each of them; (3) creating a graph-based semantic interpretation of the whole input text by linking candidate meanings of extracted fragments using the previously-generated semantic signature, followed by a dense sub-graph of this representation to select the best candidate meaning of each fragment.

Babelfy has been evaluated on various datasets and compared with different systems, and has been shown to achieve a better disambiguating performance among all the participating systems by using the selected datasets.

3 General Framework

We first present a general framework for cognate detection supported by disambiguation and multilingual resources. This framework provides a score of "cognateness" with regards to a source language for every word in text written a target language. Such a score can be interpreted as the likelihood that a reader learns the target language would be assisted by their native language (the source language) to understand the meaning of the word.

To calculate the score of a word W, the main steps in our framework are as follows:

- Identify the likelihood of each possible sense of W (semantic similarity score (SS))
- For each sense, all the translations of the sense in the source language become candidate cognates CW
- For each candidate cognate (CW), calculate its word shape similarity score (WSS), its orthographic similarity with W.
- Determine the cognateness of W as the maximum combined SS and WSS score, that is:

$$C(W) = Max_{CW}\big(x.SS(CW) + (1-x).WSS(CW)\big)$$

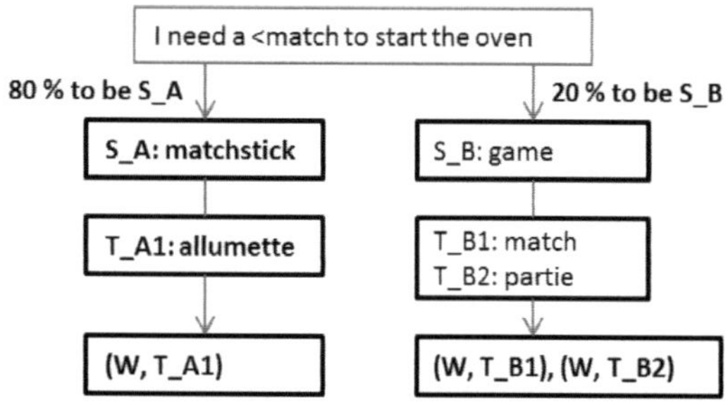

Figure 1 Process of general framework

For example, there are two possible meanings for the word *match* after disambiguation, which are S_A *matchstick* and S_B *game*, with 80% and 20% of sense likelihood respectively (this then becomes the (SS) score between the possible translations of each sense and the initial word). In the second step, all the possible translations of each sense in French will be retrieved according the multilingual resource. Finally, the retrieved translation will be paired with the word *match*. As shown in the figure 1, the final pairs under sense *A* would be (W, T_A1), similarly, pairs generated under sense *B*, which are (W, T_B1), (W, T_B2) and so on. For each of the candidate pair, the possible translation leads to the WSS score by applying orthographic/phonetic distance between the translation and the initial word (e.g., between *match* and *allumette, match* and *partie*). We then determine the cognateness of the word *match* by using the maximum combined SS and WSS score.

4 Methodology

The general approach presented in section 3 would be suited to the early version of BabelNet (version 1.0.1). Babelfy has a much higher accuracy for disambiguating; it does not provide sense likelihood for several candidate senses but only a single candidate sense. This is taken into account in our implementation by providing a simplified approach that does not use sense similarity. Indeed, in this paper we are assuming that the semantic similarity score is a static value which is always 1 and leave the combined formula for future work. As a result, the cognateness of a word W is now estimated by:

$$C(W) \approx Max_{CW}\big(WSS(CW)\big)$$

While scores are suited to applications that will not directly need a decision (such as used as a feature in readability measure, or used with graded colours in a visual interface), many will require a binary interpretation, including our evaluation framework. The binary decision is whether a word is a potential cognate of at least one of its likely translations. Such a decision can be based on a threshold for the cognate score presented above, or can be modeled using a panel of scores with a machine learning approach.

The implementation process is depicted in Figure 2 and the steps described as follows.

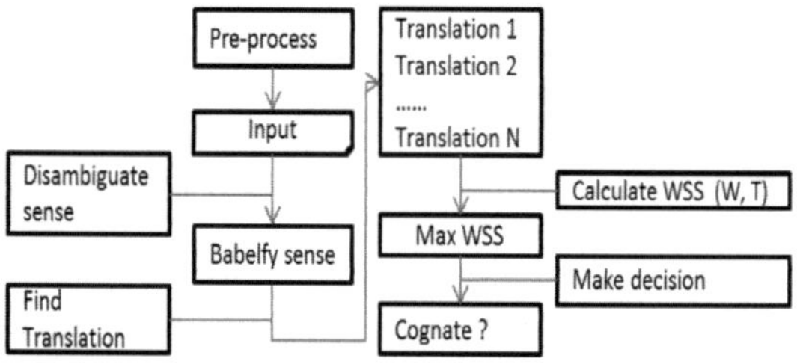

Figure 2 Process of implementation

Pre-Processing: The document is split in sentences; then each word within the sentence is stemmed using Krovetz Stemmer algorithm.

Disambiguate Sense: The stemmed sentence is disambiguated by Babelfy, with a specified "Exact" matching level. This matching level was empirically found to provide more accurate results than other options. For each word W in the sentence, we obtain a Babel Sense S.

Find Translations: query BabelNet based on the Babel Sense id of S. This provides a list of translations [T1, T2, …] of sense S.

Calculate WSS Score: Several measures can be used to calculate WSS score between word W and its translations. For example, we could get WSS1 as the score between (W, T1) and WSS2 for (W, T2) by using DICE. In the end, the Max [WSS1, WSS2] is selected as the final WSS score under sense S for word W with DICE.

Make Decision: We propose two approaches to decide whether or not a word W is cognate. The threshold approach states that true cognates are likely to have higher scores than non-cognates (Mulloni et Al., 2007). As a result, we build a training and a testing set for both cognate pairs (known cognates) and non-cognate pairs (random word pairs), and estimate the threshold that best separates cognates from non-cognates in the training set. The second approach proposes that several orthographic similarity measures can be retained, and the decision can be made using machine learning. A model is learnt from all W and all similarity measures in a training set of natural annotated data. For example, if a word W has 2 translations [T1, T2]; list_a which is [WSS1a, WSS2a, WSS3a, WSS4a, WSS5a] would be the WSS scores of T1, similarly, list_b ([WSS1b, WSS2b, WSS3b, WSS4b, WSS5b]) for T2. The 5 WSS scores in each list are calculated from Levenshtein, Bi Distance, LCSR, Dice and Soundex respectively. By finding the biggest value of (WSS1a, WSS1b), (WSS2a, WSS2b), (WSS3a, WSS3b) and so on, we generate a best value list which is Max [WSS1, WSS2, WSS3, WSS4, WSS5] for a word W.

5 Evaluation

5.1 Tuning the decision models

For the threshold approach, the training set contains 600 English French true cognate pairs and 600 English French non cognate pairs. The testing set contains 300 English French true cognate pairs and 300 English French non-cognate pairs. True cognate pairs were collected from various online resources. Non-cognate pairs were compiled by randomly selecting English words and French words from news websites[1].

While most cognate pairs on existing lists are of exactly identical words, this does not reflect the reality so we purposely included one third of non-identical cognate pairs in the training set. We have compared Bi Distance, Dice coefficient, Soundex, Levenshtein, and LCSR.

Measure	Threshold	Accuracy
BI distance	0.4	0.911
LCSR	0.444	0.898
Dice Coefficient	0.235	0.895
Levenshtein	0.428	0.882
Soundex	0.675	0.871

Table 1 Threshold and Accuracy of each orthographic measure.

Table 1 shows the accuracy of each measure used as a threshold on the testing set. In future evaluation, we will use the BI Distance to generate WSS score, but also Soundex. The reason we still employ Soundex despite its lowest accuracy is that it is a popular phonetic measure, so it is interesting to make comparisons with the BI distance.

For the machine learning approach, two models are trained from different training corpus described in the following section, one using Support Vector Machines (SVM) and Naïve Bayes (NB).

5.2 Cognate detection in natural data

The first experiment aims to evaluate our approach on natural language texts.

A corpus has been collected from web sources based on 6 different genres: cooking recipes (cook), political news (politics), sports news (sport), technical documentation (tech), novel (novel) and subtitles (sub). For each genre, we have collected 5 documents of roughly 500 words, resulting in a total 30 documents. A bilingual English/French speaker has manually annotated this training corpus to identify the true cognates[1]. Recent borrowings (such as *croissant* in English or *weekend* in French) were also annotated as cognates. The annotator reported that while some true cognates are very obvious as they have exactly the same spelling, there were cases where the words in French and English obviously shared some etymology and had some similarity (i.e. *juice* vs. *jus* or *spice* vs. *épice*), but it was difficult to decide if they would support a reader's understanding. Some words had a different spelling but very similar pronunciation and were therefore considered as cognates in this annotation process.

Table 2 lists the total numbers of cognates (C), non-cognates (N), stop words (S) and non-word characters (NW) for both the testing and training set. In brackets we show the number of cognates and non cognates that are actually processed by Balelfy and considered in the evaluation.

	Training	Testing
S	5,503	6,711
NW	585	752
C	1,623 (1,441)	2,138 (1,978)
N	3,368 (2896)	3,736 (2,008)
Total	11,709 (4,337)	13,337 (3,986)

Table 2 Natural Data corpus characteristics.

When testing our approaches on this dataset, we are interested in the overall accuracy, but also more specifically in the capacity of our system to identify the cognates and only the cognates. We

[1]Datasets presented in this paper are all available here: https://sourceforge.net/projects/cognates/files/?source=navbar

therefore use 3 measures of evaluation, Namely Accuracy (A), Recall (R) and Precision (P).

	BI Distance			Soundex		
	A	P	R	A	P	R
cook	0.81	0.73	0.81	0.79	0.71	0.8
politics	0.80	0.82	0.76	0.77	0.78	0.77
tech	0.80	0.78	0.78	0.8	0.77	0.8
sport	0.79	0.68	0.64	0.74	0.64	0.67
novel	0.81	0.56	0.76	0.8	0.54	0.77
sub	0.81	0.51	0.78	0.81	0.49	0.76
avg	0.80	0.72	0.75	0.78	0.69	0.77

Table 3 Results from decisions made by the thresholds approach with BI and Soundex

Table 3 shows the results of the threshold method, using either the BI distance or the Soundex similarity, for each genre and the average (avg). These results show that BI Distance has a higher overall detecting accuracy than Soundex, with average 0.8 compared with 0.78. It is interesting to observe that Soundex has a better recall rate than BI, which is to be expected given our definition of cognates as being words supported via a source language, rather than purely orthographically similar. There are no major differences across genres between Soundex and BI Distance. Both measures have higher precision and recall rate in cooking recipe (cook), political news (politics) and technology (tech), but lower results in sport news (sport), novel (novel) and subtitles (sub).

Table 4 shows the results for the two trained models. NB improves the precision across all genres but reduce the recall rate compared with SVM, which provides a completely reversed trend. The largest difference is observed for the sport news, novels and subtitles. NB dramatically improves their precision and still provides acceptable recall values, while SVM has lower precision but similar recall rate. The results also suggest that in addition to having an overall higher accuracy, NB is more robust across genres as there are smaller variations in precision and comparable variations in recall. For example, the precision range of SVM is between [0.47, 0.82] but [0.63, 0.85] for NB. If we compare the results between machine learning and threshold approaches, the BI distance, which is the best threshold approach exhibits variations of a similar order and range as those from SVM across the genres. As a result, the NB model is more likely to provide a balanced precision, recall and overall accuracy rate.

	SVM			NB		
	A	P	R	A	P	R
cook	0.82	0.75	0.81	0.8	0.77	0.73
politics	0.81	0.82	0.78	0.79	0.85	0.70
tech	0.82	0.78	0.82	0.83	0.84	0.76
sport	0.76	0.65	0.74	0.78	0.73	0.62
novel	0.79	0.53	0.78	0.85	0.65	0.74
sub	0.78	0.47	0.77	0.87	0.63	0.74
avg	0.80	0.70	0.78	0.82	0.77	0.71

Table 4 Results from decisions made by the machine learning approach

Finally, we establish 2 baselines to situate our results. The first baseline model (BL1) assumes that all words in the testing set are non cognates. To establish the second baseline (BL2), we employ an English/French cognate word list provided by Frunza (2006), and apply a simple decision rule that every word in the text that is present in the list should be returned as a cognate.

The results from two baselines are in the table 5. Because novel and subtitles contain less cognates, this results in the overall accuracy of BL1 and BL2 on these two genres being almost as good as the rates calculated from SVM. Precision and recall are not applied to BL1, and there is a huge variation between precision and recall values in BL2 across all the genres. This highlights the limits of a list-based approach.

	BL1	BL2		
	A	A	P	R
cook	0.58	0.64	0.95	0.14
politics	0.44	0.52	0.92	0.15
tech	0.52	0.58	0.86	0.14
sport	0.59	0.64	0.88	0.12
novel	0.77	0.78	0.61	0.13
sub	0.8	0.83	0.69	0.24
avg	0.6	0.65	0.85	0.15

Table 5 Results from decisions made by a naïve (BL1) and a list-based (BL2) baseline.

5.3 Testing semi-cognates in controlled sentences

Our second evaluation aims to test the robustness of our approach specifically for semi-cognates. For example, the English word *address* is a true cognate when it means "mailing, email" or "deftness, skill, dexterity". However, it is a false cognate when it refers to "discourse". This task is highly dependent on the quality of the disambiguation.

20 semi-cognates are used to create controlled sentences where they appear in either as a true cognate or a false cognate. For each semi-cognate, we created 2 sentences, one where it is a true cognate and one where it is a false cognate. Additionally, we ensured that the other words in the sentences were neither true nor false cognates. Using *address* as an example again, the sentences created were "What is your <address?" and "His keynote <address is very insightful."

In this evaluation we use the NB model to make decisions since it provided the best accuracy in the previous evaluation.

True Cognate		F. Cognate	
C	N	C	N
15	4	14	5

Table 6 Results from NB model.

Table 6 shows the confusion matrix when the model is applied to the 20 sentences containing true cognates and the 20 sentences containing false cognates. The confusion matrices first show that 2 semi-cognates fail to be annotated or that BabelNet did not contain translation for the disambiguated sense. On the 4 errors made on recognizing the true cognates, 2 of them are due to an error in disambiguation, and for the other 2 Babelfy fails to give provide the correct translations because the extracted text fragment is a combination of two words or more. For example, "I like action movie", the sense of word *action* is correct but mapped to *action_movie* instead of *action* itself. Of the 14 errors made on recognizing false cognates, 6 were due to errors in the disambiguation, 7 were due to erroneous translations of the sense, and only 2 were due to an error of the model (word *organ* and *orgue* were considered cognates). For example, the word *assume* in sentence "I <assume full duty in this matter" was disambiguated as "Take to be the case or to be true and accept without verification or proof." It has translations such as *assumer*, *supposer*. Since we will only take the translation that has the highest WSS score, the *assumer* is selected instead of *supposer*.

6 Discussion

While the performance of our approach show improvements over a baseline using a dictionary based approach, there are a number of errors that could be avoided by integrating a probabilistic disambiguation approach as proposed in section 3. The issue of the quality of the disambiguation system, even though we selected a system with high performances, has been highlighted in section 5.3 on the semi-cognate evaluation, but has also been observed on natural data.

Another issue that is that Babelfy is not able to process all the words that should be disambiguated. For example, "You can bring egg whites to room <temperature by setting the eggs out on the counter at least 30 <minutes in <<advance of your preparation", and the *advance* was ignored. Table 2 shows how many such missing words are occurring in the natural dataset. The number of missing words varies across genres, for example, subtitles may only have 9 missing words out of 2,000 while sport news may have 55. Non cognate words are more likely to be ignored compared with true cognates; especially the cooking recipes and political news may include lots of low frequency word and name entities.

Additionally, there are several cases where an identified sense does not have a French translation in BabelNet (although we verified that the language has some). For instance, "Place the egg whites in a <bowl in a pan of warm water", although Babelfy successfully disambiguates *bowl* as "A round vessel that is open at the top; mainly used for holding food or liquids", BabelNet simply does not have a French translation *bol* under this specific sense in its network. Furthermore, some errors come from erroneous translations provided by BabelNet, even though we filter the translation sources to only use open multilingual wordnet (omwn), wiki, wikidata, wiki translation (wikitr). For instance, *marshmallow* shows French translation *marshmallow* instead of *chamallow*, and *soccer* shows French translation *soccer* instead of *football*, thus impacting on the precision. Finally, annotations are sometime subjective for similar but non identical words, or close but non identical meanings.

7 Conclusion and Future work

We presented a methodology to identify potential cognates in English sentences for a French reader. The accuracy is around 80%, and it is high enough to successfully be used in sentence selection schemes to support learners to get better understanding before tackling the hard texts, which has been proposed an alternative learning method for English Learners (Uitdenbogerd, 2005).

As implied earlier, our proposed approach is highly dependent on the sources used; our future work will first try to develop a strategy to minimize the noise and analyze how much the performance can be improved with ideal settings. Future work will also focus on integrating the decision model, or directly the cognateness score, into readability measures. In a pilot study, we found that word level criteria such as frequency or length are indeed not applicable when the word is a cognate (that is, very difficult words such as word *disambiguation* can actually be very transparent and therefore easy in the context of a multilingual reader). Thirdly, more work is needed to more accurately detect usages of semi-cognates, and integrating the SS score with WSS score, so that the actual readability measure to balance the impact from semantic and word shape feature and possibly alleviate errors made by a disambiguation system.

References

Brew, C., and McKelvie, D. (1996). Word-pair extraction for lexicography. *Proceedings of the second International conference on new methods in language processing,* Ankara, Turkey, 45-55.

Frunza, O.M. (2006). Automatic identification of cognates, false friends, and partial cognates. *Masters Abstracts International, 45,* 2520.

Kondrak, G. (2000). A new algorithm for the alignment of phonetic sequences. *Proceedings of the 1st North American chapter of the Association for Computational Linguistics,* Seattle, Washington, 288-295.

Kondrak, G. (2001). Identifying cognates by phonetic and semantic similarity. Proceedings of the second meeting of the North American Chapter of the Association for Computational Linguistics on Language technologies, Pittsburgh, Pennsylvania, USA, 1-8. doi: 10.3115/1073336.1073350.

Kondrak, G. (2005). N-gram similarity and distance. *String processing and information retrieval, 3772,* 115-126, Springer Berlin Heidelberg.

Kondrak, G., and Dorr, B. (2004). Identification of confusable drug names: A new approach and evaluation methodology. *Proceedings of the 20th international conference on Computational Linguistics,* 952-958. doi: 10.3115/1220355.1220492.

Levenshtein, V.I. (1966). Binary codes capable of correcting deletions, insertions and reversals. *Soviet physics doklady, 10,* 707.

Melamed, I.D. (1999). Bitext maps and alignment via pattern recognition. *Comput Linguist., 25*(1), 107-130.

Moro, Andrea, Alessandro Raganato, and Roberto Navigli. (2014). Entity Linking meets Word Sense Disambiguation: A Unified Approach. *Transactions of the Association for Computational Linguistics,* 2.

Mulloni, A., Pekar, V., Mitkov, R., & Blagoev, D. (2007). Semantic evidence for automatic identification of cognates. *Proceedings of the 2007 workshop of the RANLP: Acquisition and management of multilingual lexicons,* Borovets, Bulgaria , 49-54.

Navigli, R. (2012). A quick tour of word sense disambiguation, induction and related approaches. *Proceedings of the 38th international conference on Current Trends in Theory and Practice of Computer Science,* Czech Republic, 115-129. doi: 10.1007/978-3-642-27660-6_10

Navigli, R. (2013). A quick tour of babelnet 1.1. Proceedings of the 14th international conference on Computational Linguistics and Intelligent Text Processing, Samos, Greece, I, 25-37. doi: 10.1007/978-3-642-37247-6_3

Navigli, R., and Ponzetto, S.P. (2012). Joining forces pays off: Multilingual joint word sense disambiguation. Proceedings of the 2012 Joint Conference on Empirical Methods in Natural Language Processing and Computational Natural Language Learning, Jeju Island, Korea, 1399-1410.

Rama, T. (2014). Gap-weighted subsequences for automatic cognate identification and phylogenetic inference. arXiv: 1408.2359.

Simard, M., Foster, G.F., and Isabelle, P. (1993). Using cognates to align sentences in bilingual corpora. *Proceedings of the 1993 conference of the Centre for Advanced Studies on Collaborative research: distributed computing,* Toronto, Ontario, Canada, *2.*

Uitdenbogerd, S. (2005). Readability of French as a foreign language and its uses. *Proceedings of the Australian Document Computing Symposium,* 19-25.

Automated Generation of Test Suites for Error Analysis of Concept Recognition Systems

Tudor Groza[1,2]
[1]School of ITEE
The University of Queensland
[2]Garvan Institute of Medical Research
Australia
tudor.groza@uq.edu.au

Karin Verspoor
Dept of Computing and Information Systems
The University of Melbourne
Australia
karin.verspoor@unimelb.edu.au

Abstract

We present an architecture and implementation of a system that builds structured test suites for concept recognition systems. The system applies provided test case definitions to a target concept vocabulary, to generate test cases organised according to those definitions. Test case definitions capture particular characteristics, or produce regular transformations, of concept terms. The test suites produced by the system enable detailed, systematic, error analysis of the performance of concept recognition systems.

1 Introduction

In this paper, we introduce a framework to automate development of test suites for ontology concept recognition systems. The objective of the work is to enable the assessment of system competence and performance, by organising test cases into groups based on carefully defined characteristics. While failure analysis is often done in terms of such characteristics, it is generally done in an unsystematic manner. By providing a framework for automatically building test suites, we aim to enable more systematic investigation of errors.

We focus in this initial work on ontology concept recognition systems, that is, systems that aim to detect concepts defined in an ontology in natural language text. Prior work has demonstrated substantial differences in the performance of such systems, due to linguistic variability in the expression of ontology concepts (Funk et al., 2014). The use of *structured test suites* has been shown to enable identification of performance errors of such systems (Cohen et al., 2010), as well as being useful for finding bugs (Cohen et al., 2008). Structured test suites enable systematic evaluation, exhaustivity, inclusion of negative data, and control over data (Oepen et al., 1998). They can focus on specific linguistic phenomena, that can be presented in isolation and in controlled combinations.

Evaluation of the performance of NLP methods is typically done with respect to annotated training data. Methods are assessed based on their ability to reproduce human performance on a task, as measured in terms of the standard metrics of *precision*, *recall*, and *F-score*. Such metrics provide a quantitative basis for comparing performance of different methods. However, they are by their nature aggregative, considering all annotations in the corpus as equal for evaluation purposes. Furthermore, such metrics do not provide insight into the nature of errors made by the methods. As stated by (Cohen et al., 2004), testing a system on an annotated corpus "tells you how often the system failed, but not what it failed at; it tells you how often the system succeeds, but not where its strengths are." Yet investigation of the strengths and failures of a system can reveal information meaningful for improving system performance, and is a critical component of error analysis. This approach is commonly applied in software testing. The methodology of *equivalence partitioning* (Myers, 1979) explicitly involves partitioning the input into equivalence classes that are representative of a range of possible test cases.

This paper introduces a framework for supporting automatic generation of test suites, with the goal of supporting more rigorous testing and evaluation of ontology concept recognition system. Concept recognition (CR) aims to link ontological concepts, defined in a specified ontology, to free text spans denoting entities of interest. CR is a natural evolution of the more traditional Named Entity Recognition (NER) task, which focuses only on detecting the mentions of entities of interest within unstructured textual sources, without aligning them to ontological terms. Well-studies CR tasks include, in particular, gene and protein nor-

Tudor Groza and Karin Verspoor. 2014. Automated Generation of Test Suites for Error Analysis of Concept Recognition Systems. In *Proceedings of Australasian Language Technology Association Workshop*, pages 23−31.

malisation (Lu et al., 2011), which involves entity linking of gene/protein mentions to biological data bases. In the context of large structured vocabularies, the CR task involves mapping of terms to specific vocabulary identifiers. The set of NER categories in CR is therefore effectively as large as the number of primary terms in the vocabulary.

Our test suite generation framework consists of 3 main components:

1. **An Input Wrapper** that loads terminology from an ontology, controlled vocabulary, or other target resource.
2. **Test Case Definitions** that specify characteristics of target terms to be incorporated as cases into the test suite.
3. **A Test Suite Factory** that produces a structured test suite for the input ontology, from the test case definitions.

Together, these components support automatic creation of a structured test suite, that can be used to systematically assess the performance of a concept recognition system. Each test case defines an equivalence class of terms, along a defined dimension. The framework is available at `https://github.com/tudorgroza/cr_testsuites`. We welcome contributions of new test case definitions and input wrappers.

2 Background

2.1 Concept Recognition Systems

The class of NLP system that we are primarily concerned with testing is the *concept recognition system*. These are systems that aim to detect mentions of terms corresponding to concepts from an ontology or controlled vocabulary in natural language text. These could be named entity recognition systems, where the set of named entities is defined by a target resource (e.g., the set of all registered US corporations, or the set of all genes in GenBank[1]).

In the biomedical domain, ontology concept recognition systems have been a recent focus of development, due to a proliferation of biomedical ontologies[2]. A number of systems have recently been developed, or deployed, to address this domain, including the US National Library of Medicine's MetaMap tool (Aronson and Lang, 2010), the NCBO Annotator (Jonquet et al., 2009), ConceptMapper (Tanenblatt et al., 2010; Funk et al., 2014), WhatIzIt (Rebholz-Schuhmann and others, 2008) and Neji (Campos et al., 2013).

These systems could equally make use of machine learning, or rule-based methods. Rule-based systems have the advantage of being flexibly redeployable to new ontologies or vocabularies that might be defined, as they do not require training data. Furthermore, in a normalisation context in which specific vocabulary items must be detected and normalised to an identifier (e.g., not just recognising a US corporation mention, but mapping that mention to a specific register ID), the number of target classes is effectively the number of concept classes. This can be prohibitive for an effective machine learning technique.

2.2 Use of Test Suites in NLP

A structured test suite consists of a set of carefully selected test cases that are designed to test specific functionality or the performance of an algorithm on a controlled input. In the development of software systems, test suites are used for acceptance and regression testing, to ensure that the software satisfies a given set of requirements and that a change to the code does not inadvertently break a given required functionality. In NLP, a test suite can be used to automatically verify the performance of an algorithm on specific linguistic phenomena. Test suites rely on *controlled variation* of the linguistic inputs, and allow analysis to be performed along particular dimensions of variation. This is in stark contrast to standard annotated corpora that reflect natural linguistic variation and natural distribution of entities, which is dependent on the collection strategy for the corpus. In error analysis of a task using an annotated corpus, the categorisation of annotations and errors into coherent groups is typically done in *post-hoc* analysis. It has been demonstrated that this can be both challenging to implement and insightful with regards to the generalisability of algorithms (Stoyanov et al., 2009; Kummerfeld et al., 2012; Kummerfeld and Klein, 2013). Using a test suite, it is done *a priori* through the test suite construction.

The use of test suites has long benefited development of NLP systems for syntactic analysis

[1] `http://www.ncbi.nlm.nih.gov/genbank`

[2] There are 384 ontologies, containing close to 6 million concept classes in total, listed in the US National Center for Biomedical Ontology's BioPortal, `http://bioportal.bioontology.org` (Whetzel et al., 2011).

(Oepen et al., 1998; Oepen, 1999), as well as from systematic organisation of grammatical phenomena along typological dimensions. The LinGO Grammar Matrix (Bender et al., 2010; Bender et al., 2002) captures linguistic variation along a number of defined dimensions, and enables creation of an initial grammar based on a library of syntactic structures. One of the key elements of the Matrix is support for regression testing via automated tests, such that any change to a grammar or the linguistic phenomena captured in the system can be automatically assessed for impact to the performance on previously existing phenomena. Such test suites are used for validation and exploration of changes to a grammar, during grammar engineering (Bender et al., 2008).

However, the approach has had limited adoption beyond analysis of deep parsing systems. A methodology and data resources was introduced to support feature-based evaluation of molecular biology entity recognition systems (Cohen et al., 2004). The data resources included examples of entity names across four categories of variation, orthographic (length, token "shape", presence of Greek letters, etc.), morphosyntactic (prefixes, suffixes, presence function words, etc.), source (e.g., a dictionary or a database), and lexical (e.g., status with respect to a language model or vocabulary). That work demonstrated that a test suite can be a good predictor of performance on named entities with particular typographic characteristics.

The approach was later applied to ontology concept recognition systems (Cohen et al., 2010). That work identifies a core set of terminological features that was common to the ontology concept recognition context and the named entity recognition context: *a*) Length *b*) Numerals *c*) Punctuation *d*) Function/stopwords *e*) Source or authority *f*) Canonical form in source (e.g., ontology or database); and *g*) Syntactic context.

In each case of this prior work, the test suites have been generated manually and contain a limited number of examples.

Other frameworks supporting evaluation of NLP systems, including ontology concept recognition systems, have been developed. U-compare (Kano et al., 2009) provides a sophisticated evaluation environment, specifically targeting evaluation and comparison of workflows for document annotation, including syntactic annotation, NER, and information extraction of events. The framework allows multiple systems to be compared over the same data, producing quantitative results in terms of precision, recall, and F-score, as well as supports visual inspection of annotations and annotation differences (Kano et al., 2011). However, there is no direct support for quantitative error analysis.

3 A Framework for Ontology Test Suite generation

We propose a framework to automate development of test suites for ontology concept recognition systems. Given an ontology definition file, and a set of specifications of the typological dimensions of interest, the framework generates a test suite. This test suite organises the ontology terms and any synonyms defined in the ontology according to the typological dimensions of interest.

Figure 1 depicts the high-level architecture of the framework. This comprises three major components: (i) the Input Wrapper – handling the processing of a given ontology or term resource, according to a specification file; (ii) the Test Case – defining specific characteristics along a dimension of interest; and (iii) the Test Case Factory – generating a test suite from a given input according to a set of defined test cases. In the following sections we describe each of these components.

3.1 Input Wrapper

The Input Wrapper processes a given terminological input resource, according to a provided *specification*, and provides an iterator over the *entity profiles* defined by the dataset. Generically, the InputWrapper does not rely on any assumptions about the input resource, but rather delegates these assumptions to the underlying implementation. This means that the input resource could be an explicitly structured ontology or dictionary, as well as an annotated (gold standard) corpus, for which the target vocabulary for a particular set of entities or concepts can be inferred from the annotations.

An Entity Profile captures the terminological representation of an individual concept or named entity, and is expected to include the following properties: (i) a unique identifier – i.e., the URI of a concept in the case of an ontology, or a plain identifier in the case of an annotated corpus; (ii) the list of labels – i.e., preferred and/or alternative labels for ontological concepts, or a canonical

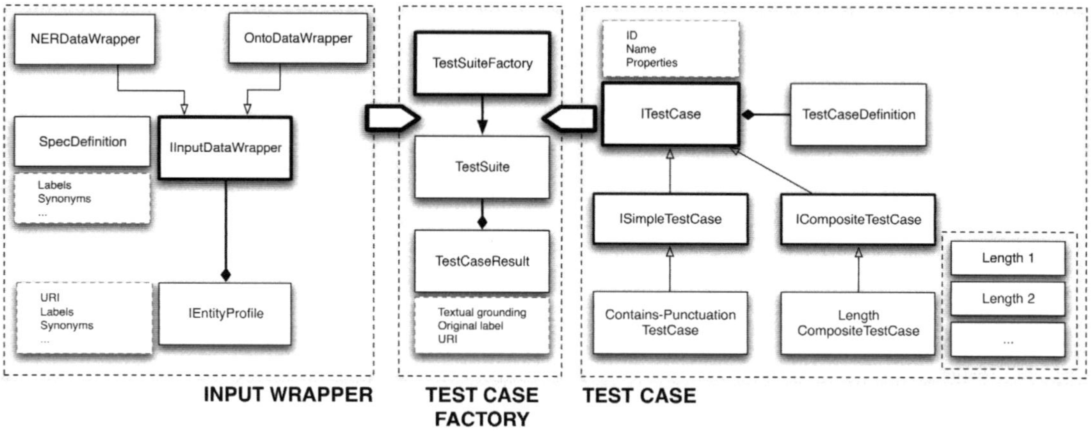

Figure 1: High-level overview of the test suite framework and its three major components: Input Wrapper – handling the input and producing Entity Profiles; Test Case – defining specific test case scenarios; Test Case Factory – bridging the provided input and a set of defined test cases.

textual representation for a concept or entity derived from a corpus annotation; and (iii) the list of synonyms – i.e., exact, related, broader or narrower synonyms for ontological concepts, or alternative textual representations for a concept or entity, as inferred from an annotated corpus.

3.1.1 Ontology term resources

The underlying Input Wrapper implementation is also responsible for defining the structure of the specification, according to which the processing is done. The current implementation of the framework provides an Ontology Data Wrapper that is able to perform the above-listed steps for a given ontology. The format of the ontology should be one of the formats supported by the OWL Api (Horridge and Bechhofer, 2011) – e.g., OWL, OBO, or RDF/XML. The resulting entity profiles will correspond to ontological concepts described via their URIs and the labels or synonyms defined in the specification. The actual specification is independent of the ontology, the ontology format or the implementation of the ontology processing mechanism within the OntoDataWrapper and it is defined using a simple JSON configuration file. This enables one to create and process the same ontology using different configurations.

The structure of the configuration file specifies:

- `conceptTypes`, the types of concepts to be processed
- `labelProperties`, the label properties to be considered
- `synonymProperties`, the synonyms properties to be considered, including a possible filtering based on the synonym type
- `uriPatterns`, URI patterns that should be included or excluded from the processing

Below we provide an example of an ontology specification (for an `OntoDataWrapper`) that will process only classes and will use the standard `dfs:label` and `skos:prefLabel` properties, in addition to any exact synonyms, defined by the pair `ono:synonym` – `ono:synonym type`. Furthermore, the specification excludes from processing three particular URIs (HP:0000001, HP:0000004 and HP:0000005). Please note that for brevity purposes, we do not list the complete URI of the properties.

```
{
  "conceptTypes": ["CLASS"],

  "labelProperties":{
    "http://.../rdf-schema#label":{},
    "http://.../skos#prefLabel":{},
  },

  "synonymProperties":{
    "http://.../obo/synonym":{
      "http://.../obo/synonymtype":["EXACT"]}
  },

  "uriPatterns":{
    "http://.../obo":[
      "*",
      "~HP_0000001",
      "~HP_0000005",
      "~HP_0000004"]
  }
}
```

3.1.2 Annotated corpus resources

We can straightforwardly extend the basic framework developed for ontology concepts to standard text corpora with annotations of ontology concepts or named entities over naturalistic text data. The framework enables organisation of annotated examples according to typological characteristics.

At a minimum, all that is required to achieve this at the basic technical level is to define an appropriate `InputDataWrapper`, e.g. `NERDataWrapper` in Figure 1. This Input Wrapper must know how to parse the relevant corpus representation. It would iterate through each annotation in the corpus, and either generate a new Entity Profile, or augment an existing Entity Profile when a new synonym or alternate form of an existing Entity is encountered.

3.2 Test Case Definitions

Test cases have the role of selecting or manipulating entity profiles characterised by certain properties of interest. As exemplified in (Cohen et al., 2010), the equivalence relations captured in such test cases may focus on length-based properties, lexical composition, lexical variation, etc. In principle, we can classify test cases into two categories: simple and composite. Simple test cases have a non-parametric form and analyse a particular property of entity profiles – e.g., if they contain punctuation. Composite test cases consist of a series of simple test cases concentrated on a single property, but which can be parametrized. For example, the process of verifying the existence of a given stop word (e.g., "of", "by", "from") in an entity profile is independent of the actual stop word. Hence, a test case targeting treatment of terms containing stop words can take the stop word as a parameter. We consider this type of test case to be composite.

Our framework supports both types of test cases. In general, a Test Case includes high-level metadata (i.e., an identifier and a name, to improve human readability) and the set of properties that can be configured – as per the listing below.

```
public interface ITestCase {

  public String getId();

  public String getName();

  public List<String> getAcceptedProperties();

  public void addEntity(IEntityProfile profile);
}

public interface ISimpleTestCase extends ITestCase {

  public void runTestCases(Properties properties);

  public List<ITestCaseResult> retrieveTestCases();
}
```

The properties supported by the Test Case might include the number of entries to be generated in the test suite for this test case (this would apply to both test case types), or parameter values (which would be particular to a composite test case), e.g., the set of stop words to be analysed. The runtime values for these properties are transferred to the test case via a TestCaseDefinition, or in a programmatic manner, subject to the deployment settings.

Running a Test Case involves three steps: (i) populating the Test Case with Entity Profiles, (ii) generating Test Case Results according to the specified properties values, and (iii) retrieving the Test Case Results. The last two steps are dependent on the test category, as shown in the definition of the Simple Test Case interface in the listing above.

The results are currently provided as a set of objects that contain the resulting `textual grounding` (to be used as input in validation), the `original lexical representation` and the `identifier` of the associated entity. For example, let's consider a lexical variation Test Case applied to the Gene Ontology[3] (Gene Ontology Consortium, 2000) concept GO:0070170 (*regulation of tooth mineralization*). The process result consists of:

- `textual grounding`: *regulated* tooth mineralization
- `original lexical representation`: regulation of tooth mineralization
- `concept identifier`: GO:0070170

Currently, the framework contains three simple test cases:

- Contains Arabic numeral – generates candidates that contain isolated Arabic numerals (e.g., 1, 2, ...)
- Contains Roman numeral – generates candidates that contain isolated Roman numerals (e.g., I, IX, ...)
- Contains punctuation – generates candidates that contain punctuation tokens

and two parametric composite test cases

[3]The Gene Ontology is an ontology capturing concepts related to gene function and biological processes.

- Contains stop word – generates candidates that contain user-specified stop words (e.g., OF, FROM, BY, ...)
- Length – generates candidates that have lexical groundings with a length in tokens equal to the list of user-specified lengths.

All test cases generate results in a randomised manner. That is, except for the core test case functionality, no particular heuristics or rules are used when selecting the resulting concepts.

3.3 Test Suite Factory

The Test Suite Factory connects the Input Wrapper to the existing Test Case implementations. Its role is to generate sets of Test Cases – a Test Suite – according to a provided definition on a given input. The implementation of the Test Suite Factory allows it to be used both in a continuous pipeline manner, as well as in a batch process. In the pipeline setting, the factory accepts dynamic creation and alteration of Test Suite definitions, while in the batch process setting the definitions need to be provided via a simple configuration file. Subject to the deployment setting, the resulting Test Suite can be used directly in evaluation experiments, or serialised for offline processing.

There are a few technical aspects that are worth mentioning in the context of the Test Suite Factory. The current implementation forces a generic Test Case to ingest one Entity Profile at-a-time (provided by the Input Wrapper Entity Profile iterator) – see the Test Case interface definition in the listing above. The actual processing of this Entity Profile is then delegated to the specific Test Case implementation (independently of its category). The rationale behind this decision was to maintain the memory footprint of the Input Wrapper at a reasonable level. This enables, for example, the processing of the 110MB SNOMED-CT clinical vocabulary (in its tabulated format, containing 398K concepts and 1.19M descriptions) on a standard machine without the need of a large memory allocation. Yet in order to take advantage of a multi-core architecture, where this is available, the test suite generation process introduces two parallelisation points. A first parallelisation point is created when iterating over the Entity Profiles, with each Entity Profile being provided at the same time to all instantiated Test Cases. The second parallelisation point is delegated to the Test Case implementation, which may take advantage of it when generating the Test Case Results.

4 Use of the generated Test Suite for evaluation

The framework we have developed provides the critical scaffolding for designing and creating Test Suites. It can be applied for concept recognition evaluation using the following workflow:

1. Given an ontology of interest, define the desired Input Wrapper specification – see the example discussed above;
2. Specify a desired Test Suite definition – using existing Test Cases and/or implementing additional ones;
3. Generate Test Case Results (via the Test Case Factory) and serialise them on disk.

To allow for an easy and versatile creation of Test Suite definitions, the Test Case Factory is able to instantiate Test Suites based on a configuration file that specifies the list of Test Cases and the properties to be used at runtime. Below we list an example of such a configuration file using all existing Test Case implementations (introduced above). Each Test Case is specified using its unique identifier, followed by a set of values for the properties it requires. The number of entries to be generated (by both simple and composite test cases) is specified via the `NO_ENTRIES` property. In addition, the composite Test Case Contains-STOP requires the actual stop words to be analysed (here TO, FROM and OF). A similar configuration could be provided also to the Length composite Test Case. The current implementation provides, however, the option of generating tests on all available lengths represented in the input terminology (ontology or corpus annotations), as shown in the listing below.

```
testcase[0].id=Contains-Arabic
testcase[0].property[NO_ENTRIES]=6

testcase[1].id=Contains-Arabic
testcase[1].property[NO_ENTRIES]=6

testcase[2].id=Contains-Punctuation
testcase[2].property[NO_ENTRIES]=4

testcase[3].id=Contains-STOP
testcase[3].set[TO].property[STOP_WORD]=to
testcase[3].set[TO].property[NO_ENTRIES]=10
testcase[3].set[FROM].property[STOP_WORD]=from
testcase[3].set[FROM].property[NO_ENTRIES]=6
testcase[3].set[OF].property[STOP_WORD]=of
testcase[3].set[OF].property[NO_ENTRIES]=5

testcase[4].id=Length
testcase[4].set[ALL].property[LENGTH]=ALL
```

An excerpt from the application of this Test Suite to the Gene Ontology is listed below.

```
#Contains-Arabic

T-helper 1 cell differentiation | GO:0045063
RNA cap 4 binding | GO:0000342

#Contains-Roman

transcription from RNA polymerase
   III type 2 promoter | GO:0001009
mitochondrial respiratory chain complex
   III assembly | GO:0034551

#Contains-Punctuation

21U-RNA binding | GO:0034583
6-deoxy-6-sulfofructose-1-phosphate
   aldolase activity | GO:0061595

#Contains-STOP-OF

establishment of neuroblast polarity | GO:0045200
regulation of tooth mineralization | GO:0070170

#Contains-STOP-TO

response to cortisone | GO:0051413
glutamate catabolic process to 4-hydroxybutyrate |
 GO:0036241

#Contains-STOP-FROM

calcitriol biosynthetic process from calciol |
 GO:0036378
positive regulation of exit from mitosis | GO:0031536

#Length-1

costamere | GO:0043034
amicyanin | GO:0009488
plasmodesma | GO:0009506

#Length-2

spermidine transport | GO:0015848
lobed nucleus | GO:0098537

#Length-3

energy transducer activity | GO:0031992
sinoatrial valve morphogenesis | GO:0003185
```

A specific concept recognition system evaluation process can ingest this serialisation, parse it into strings and annotations (identifier labels), and apply the concept recognition system directly to the test suite. Standard evaluation metrics (e.g., Precision, Recall, F-Score) can be computed directly on this data. Furthermore, by taking advantage of the intrinsic structure of the test suite, with individual test case strings grouped together, the Test Suite can be used to compute evaluation metrics per-category basis. This provides a more informative view of the strengths and weaknesses of the system under scrutiny, on the basis of the test cases. Coupled with a standardised error analysis framework, the test suite can be used to create comparative overviews across multiple concept recognition systems.

5 Discussion

5.1 Towards an end-to-end test suite-based evaluation system

The current implementation focuses on the test suite generation framework. We assume that a test suite generated with the framework will be used in a separate evaluation process, as described in Section 4.

Future developments of the framework will include an integrated evaluation pipeline, which will realise the required steps, notably parsing of the test suite, submission of each test string in turn to a concept recognition system, tracking of matches (TP/FP/FN), and category-based calculation of quantitative evaluation metrics.

Moreover, for ontology-based concept recognition, we intend to provide a library of generated Test Suites using ontologies from the BioPortal (Whetzel et al., 2011), in addition to a series of baselines, created using off-the-shelf systems, such as the NCBO Annotator (Jonquet et al., 2009) or ConceptMapper (Tanenblatt et al., 2010).

5.2 Generation of term variants

The sample test cases implemented to date address particular characteristics of concept terms. They involve matching of existing ontology terms and synonyms in the input source to these characteristics, and result in the organisation and grouping of those terms according to those characteristics. However, test cases can also be defined that manipulate terms in controlled ways to produce term variants for testing. This allows testing of the robustness of concept recognition in the face of particular types of changes to the input.

Several such changes were explored in the Gene Ontology test suite of (Cohen et al., 2010), including generation of plural variants of singular terms, and manipulation of word order of a multi-word term (which could either be expected to be tolerated by a concept recognition system, or an explicit error case that should be avoided).

Variants might be generated in which words of a multi-word term are separated, e.g. with a particular type of intervening text. An adjective might be inserted in a noun phrase (e.g., *regulation of exit from mitosis* → *regulation of* ***rapid*** *exit from mitosis*), or a quantifier added (e.g., *ensheathment of neurons* → *ensheathment of* ***some*** *neurons*).

Alternative syntactic realisations such as nominalisations or adjectival forms (e.g., *nucleus* →

nuclear), or linguistic alternations (e.g., *regulation of X $\rightarrow$ X regulation*) can be generated. Semantic variation can also be captured, such as substitution of a phrase within a synonym, e.g., *positive regulation $\rightarrow$ up-regulation* (as a substring of a longer term). Similarly, variants that involve abstraction or manipulation of terms with other terms embedded within them (i.e., recursive structure) can be generated to measure structural impacts (Verspoor et al., 2009; Ogren et al., 2005).

To the extent that such changes are systematic and generalisable, they can be represented programmatically and used to generate test cases within the test suite. This is planned for the next phase of system development.

5.3 Sentential contexts

The current framework focuses on generating test suites that consist of target vocabulary terms, or controlled variants of those terms. However, it has been previously pointed out that the performance of a concept recognition system may be dependent on the complexity of linguistic environment in which a concept is mentioned, rather than (or in combination with) the characteristics of the concept term itself (Cohen et al., 2004). Indeed, many methods for named entity recognition depend on the availability of meaningful (or at least syntactically correct) linguistic contexts in which term mentions occur; conditional random field models that are trained on naturally occurring data, for instance, are explicitly defined to make use of sentential context in their models.

Therefore, we aim to provide Test Case definitions that enable systematic specification of sentential contexts for the terms of the vocabulary source. This can be achieved with a Composite Test Case which combines Test Cases for concepts, with a set of sentential contexts (themselves varying according to controlled characteristics).

6 Conclusions

We have introduced a framework for automated creation of test suites for concept recognition systems. While prior work on test suites has either produced a static test suite for a particular NLP task (e.g., grammar engineering), or provided data aimed at generating specific types of test cases (Cohen et al., 2004), we have produced a software implementation that directly supports the specification of test cases, and generation of the test suite according to those test cases for a provided input terminology. The input can be extracted directly from a structured vocabulary resource such as an ontology, or inferred from annotations over a natural language corpus.

Test suites provide a powerful tool for error analysis. Following software engineering methodology, the organisation of data into explicitly defined classes provides insight into *how* a system succeeds or fails, rather than *how often*. An analysis of the performance of a concept recognition system in these terms is complementary to the standard evaluation metrics. While assessment of precision, recall, and F-score over naturalistic data clearly remains the most suitable strategy for gauging overall performance of the system, a test suite provides a more granular assessment corresponding to potential error categories.

Our initial implementation contains only a limited number of existing test case definitions. However, the framework is flexible and new test cases appropriate to particular sets of concepts, and particular corpus characteristics, can easily be added. We invite the community to contribute test cases to the framework.

Acknowledgments

Tudor Groza gracefully acknowledges the funding received from the Australian Research Council (ARC) via the Discovery Early Career Researcher Award (DECRA) [DE120100508].

References

Alan R. Aronson and Francois-Michel Lang. 2010. An overview of MetaMap: historical perspective and recent advances. *Journal of the American Medical Informatics Association*, 17:229–236.

Emily M. Bender, Dan Flickinger, and Stephan Oepen. 2002. The grammar matrix: An open-source starter-kit for the rapid development of cross-linguistically consistent broad-coverage precision grammars. In John Carroll, Nelleke Oostdijk, and Richard Sutcliffe, editors, *Proceedings of the Workshop on Grammar Engineering and Evaluation at the 19th International Conference on Computational Linguistics*, pages 8–14, Taipei, Taiwan.

Emily M. Bender, Dan Flickinger, and Stephan Oepen. 2008. Grammar engineering for linguistic hypothesis testing. In Nicholas Gaylord, Stephen Hilderbrand, Heeyoung Lyu, Alexis Palmer, and Elias Ponvert, editors, *Texas Linguistics Society 10: Computational Linguistics for Less-Studied Languages*. CSLI Publications.

Emily M. Bender, Scott Drellishak, Antske Fokkens, Laurie Poulson, and Safiyyah Saleem. 2010. Grammar customization. *Research on Language & Computation*, 8(1):23–72. 10.1007/s11168-010-9070-1.

David Campos, Sergio Matos, and Jose Luis Oliveira. 2013. A modular framework for biomedical concept recognition. *BMC Bioinformatics*, 14:281.

K. Bretonnel Cohen, Lorraine Tanabe, Shuhei Kinoshita, and Lawrence Hunter. 2004. A resource for constructing customized test suites for molecular biology entity identification systems. In *HLT-NAACL 2004 Workshop: BioLINK 2004, Linking Biological Literature, Ontologies and Databases*, pages 1–8. Association for Computational Linguistics.

K. Bretonnel Cohen, William A. Baumgartner, Jr., and Lawrence Hunter. 2008. Software testing and the naturally occurring data assumption in natural language processing. In *Software Engineering, Testing, and Quality Assurance for Natural Language Processing*, SETQA-NLP '08, pages 23–30, Stroudsburg, PA, USA. Association for Computational Linguistics.

K. Bretonnel Cohen, Christophe Roeder, William A. Baumgartner Jr., Lawrence E. Hunter, and Karin Verspoor. 2010. Test suite design for biomedical ontology concept recognition systems. In *Proceedings of the Seventh International Conference on Language Resources and Evaluation (LREC'10)*, Valletta, Malta, May. European Language Resources Association (ELRA).

Christopher Funk, William Baumgartner, Benjamin Garcia, et al. 2014. Large-scale biomedical concept recognition: an evaluation of current automatic annotators and their parameters. *BMC Bioinformatics*, 15(1):59.

Gene Ontology Consortium. 2000. Gene Ontology: tool for the unification of biology. *Nat Genet*, 25(1):25–29.

Matthew Horridge and Sean Bechhofer. 2011. The OWL API: A Java API for OWL Ontologies. *Semantic Web Journal*, 2(1):11–21.

Clement Jonquet, Nigam H Shah, and Mark A Musen. 2009. The open biomedical annotator. *Summit on translational bioinformatics*, 2009:56–60.

Yoshinobu Kano, William A. Baumgartner, Luke McCrohon, et al. 2009. U-compare. *Bioinformatics*, 25(15):1997–1998.

Y. Kano, J. Bjorne, F. Ginter, T. Salakoski, et al. 2011. U-compare bio-event meta-service: compatible bionlp event extraction services. *BMC bioinformatics*, 12(1):481.

K. Jonathan Kummerfeld and Dan Klein. 2013. Error-driven analysis of challenges in coreference resolution. In *Proceedings of the 2013 Conference on Empirical Methods in Natural Language Processing*, pages 265–277. Association for Computational Linguistics.

K. Jonathan Kummerfeld, David Hall, R. James Curran, and Dan Klein. 2012. Parser showdown at the wall street corral: An empirical investigation of error types in parser output. In *Proceedings of the 2012 Joint Conference on Empirical Methods in Natural Language Processing and Computational Natural Language Learning*, pages 1048–1059. Association for Computational Linguistics.

Zhiyong Lu, Hung-Yu Kao, Chih-Hsuan Wei, et al. 2011. The gene normalization task in BioCreative III. *BMC Bioinformatics*, 12(Suppl 8):S2.

Glenford J. Myers. 1979. *The Art of Software Testing*. John Wiley & Sons, Inc.

S. Oepen, K. Netter, and J. Klein. 1998. TSNLP - test suites for natural language processing. In John Nerbonne, editor, *Linguistic Databases*, chapter 2, pages 13–36. CSLI Publications.

Stephan Oepen. 1999. Competence and Performance Laboratory. User and Reference Manual. Technical report, Computational Linguistics, Saarland University.

P Ogren, K Cohen, and L Hunter. 2005. Implications of compositionality in the Gene Ontology for its curation and usage. In *Pacific Symposium on Biocomputing*, pages 174–185.

Dietrich Rebholz-Schuhmann et al. 2008. Text processing through Web services: calling Whatizit. *Bioinformatics*, 24(2):296–298.

Veselin Stoyanov, Nathan Gilbert, Claire Cardie, and Ellen Riloff. 2009. Conundrums in noun phrase coreference resolution: Making sense of the state-of-the-art. In *Proceedings of the Joint Conference of the 47th Annual Meeting of the ACL and the 4th International Joint Conference on Natural Language Processing of the AFNLP*, pages 656–664. Association for Computational Linguistics.

Michael Tanenblatt, Anni Coden, and Igor Sominsky. 2010. The ConceptMapper Approach to Named Entity Recognition. In *Proceedings of the Seventh International Conference on Language Resources and Evaluation (LREC'10)*, Valletta, Malta, May. European Language Resources Association (ELRA).

K. Verspoor, D. Dvorkin, K.B. Cohen, and L. Hunter. 2009. Ontology quality assurance through analysis of term transformations. *Bioinformatics*, 25(12):i77.

Patricia L Whetzel, Natalya F Noy, Nigam H Shah, Paul R Alexander, Csongor Nyulas, Tania Tudorache, and Mark A Musen. 2011. BioPortal: enhanced functionality via new Web services from the National Center for Biomedical Ontology to access and use ontologies in software applications. *Nucleic Acids Research*, 39(Web Server issue):W541–5, July.

Trading accuracy for faster entity linking

Kristy Hughes **Joel Nothman** **James R. Curran**
ə-lab, School of Information Technologies
University of Sydney
NSW 2006, Australia
{khug2372@uni.,joel.nothman@,james.r.curran@}sydney.edu.au

Abstract

Named entity linking (NEL) can be applied to documents such as financial reports, web pages and news articles, but state of the art disambiguation techniques are currently too slow for web-scale applications because of a high complexity with respect to the number of candidates. In this paper, we accelerate NEL by taking two successful disambiguation features (popularity and context comparability) and use them to reduce the number of candidates before further disambiguation takes place. Popularity is measured by in-link score, and context similarity is measured by locality sensitive hashing.

We present a novel approach to locality sensitive hashing which embeds the projection matrix into a smaller array and extracts columns of the projection matrix using feature hashing, resulting in a low-memory approximation. We run the linker on a test set in 63% of the baseline time with an accuracy loss of 0.72%.

1 Introduction

Named entity linking (NEL) (Bunescu and Pasca, 2006; Varma et al., 2009; Cucerzan, 2007) is the task of mapping mentions of named entities to their canonical reference in a knowledge base (KB). Recently, this task has been motivated by the Text Analysis Conference (TAC) Knowledge Base Population (KBP) entity linking task. In this task, systems are given queries comprising of a mention string and document ID, and return the referring entity ID from the KB (in this case, Wikipedia) or a NIL ID if the entity is not in the KB.

While large amounts of candidate data provides rich information that can be used for disambiguation, we show that data transfer and query costs comprise over 51% of running time in the unsupervised configuration of Radford (2014). Additionally, whole document approaches for disambiguation compare text using methods such as cosine similarity, but are slow for high-dimensional data such as text (Indyk and Motwani, 1998).

In this paper, we pre-filter candidates using a combination of candidate popularity and context similarity. These features are complimentary to each other, because a high in-link count suggests that the mention string refers to that entity frequently, but a high similarity measure is required for less popular candidates. Since context comparison is expensive to compute, we use LSH (Gionis et al., 1999) to produce a compact binary hash representation of each document, which can be compared using Hamming distance. This fast, informed pre-filtering reduces data communication costs and the number of similarity comparisons.

While LSH has been shown to be a good approximation to cosine similarity on image data (Lu et al., 2008), we show that it this is also the case on text data. Using a hash size of 1024 bits, LSH similarity and cosine similarity have a Spearman correlation of 0.94, with correlation increasing as hash size increases. Using a hash size of 2kB and a LSH similarity threshold of 0.56, and keeping the top 7 candidates by in-link score, we run the linker in 63% of the time with an accuracy loss of 0.72%.

We also present a new, low-memory version of LSH which embeds the projection matrix into a smaller vector and extracts rows of the projection matrix using feature hashing. This method allows for an expandable vocabulary, and only requires storing a single, smaller vector, resulting in fast generation of document hashes.

Our LSH pre-filtering method enables the task to feasibly be applied to linking longer documents (financial reports), big data (the web), and real-time or frequently updated documents (the news) with only a very small drop in accuracy.

Kristy Hughes, Joel Nothman and James R. Curran. 2014. Trading accuracy for faster named entity linking. In *Proceedings of Australasian Language Technology Association Workshop*, pages 32−40.

2 Background

Named entities (NEs) in natural language are often difficult to resolve; one entity can be referred to by many different mention strings (synonymy) or multiple distinct entities referred to by the same mention string (polysemy). While the task of resolving this ambiguity is automatically and subconsciously performed by most people when they read text, this is a much more difficult task for automated systems to perform.

The NE ambiguity problem has been approached within the field of computational linguistics as three related tasks: Cross-document Coreference Resolution (Bagga and Baldwin, 1998), Wikification (Mihalcea and Csomai, 2007), and named entity linking (NEL) (Bunescu and Pasca, 2006). NEL aims to link in-text mentions of NEs to a knowledge base (KB) using the context of the mention and the vast amount of structured and unstructured information held in the KB.

Approaches to NEL vary (Hachey et al., 2013; Ji and Grishman, 2011), however many systems share some core components. Radford et al. (2012) combines three seminal approaches (Cucerzan, 2007; Varma et al., 2009; Bunescu and Pasca, 2006) to produce the NEL system on which this paper is based. Almost all approaches can be split into 3 stages: mention extraction, candidate generation and candidate disambiguation.

The mention extraction stage involves chaining together mentions in a document that refer to the same entity, and candidate generation stage involves retrieving entities from the KB that have similar names to mentions in the query's chain. The candidate disambiguation stage compares each candidate with the query and ranks them by the aggregate of similarity scores.

Core to almost all approaches is the usefulness of the prior probability of a candidate entity, and the amount of overlap in text between the query document and candidate entity. These two features are complementary to each other.

Prior probability is a measure of the popularity of the entity. This can be calculated from a large corpus of disambiguated entities, most often using Wikipedia's internal links, and is independent from the query document, so it can be precomputed and stored. Popular entities appear in all contexts, and so they will often not require a particular context for readers to know what the mention string refers to.

Less popular entities are distinguished by readers through the context that they appear. Therefore context similarity is an important measure of the validity of a candidate. The most popular way for comparing the similarity of text is by using cosine similarity, and many of the scores in the candidate disambiguation stage use cosine similarity, some only over sentences and others over entire documents.

To compute cosine similarity over a document, text is mapped to a bag of words (BOW) vector containing the count of each word in the document, and the dot product of these vectors represents their similarity. For a BOW, the dimensionality of the vector is number of words in the vocabulary, v. Cosine similarity can also be applied more broadly using any textual feature as a dimension of the vector. Since these vectors are generally sparse (you do not have every word in the vocabulary appear in one document), it is are often fast to compute. However, due to the high number of comparisons needed (every document-candidate pair), it can become an expensive measure to use.

Dimensionality reduction of these BOW vectors before computing cosine similarity further decreases its computational complexity and the cost of data transfer (as lower dimensional forms can be precomputed and stored). Popular methods of dimensionality reduction are singular value decomposition and principle component analysis (Muflikhah and Baharudin, 2009; Lin et al., 2011), however these are expensive to compute and adds skew to the data, so they don't correlate well with cosine similarity.

Dimensionality reduction through random projections removes much of this pre-computational work, while also not introducing significant skew (Lu et al., 2008). BOW vectors are mapped to lower dimensions by pre-computing some randomly generated hyperplanes called the projection matrix, and computing the matrix multiplication of the vector and the projection matrix.

Locality sensitive hashing (LSH) makes the comparison process in the projected space more efficient by binarising the embedded vectors into a hash (Gionis et al., 1999), approximating cosine similarity of the BOWs as the Jaccard similarity of the hashes. While LSH is faster to compute, it still requires a large projection matrix to be stored, and there needs to be a way of dealing with new words that appear, which we discuss in section 5.

Step	Approx Time (%)	Substep	Approx Time (%)
Initialisation and output	0.9		0.9
Mention Extraction	2.5	C&C NER	1.6
		Chaining	0.9
Candidate Generation	31.0	Build query	0
		Expand query	0.9
		Retrieve candidate ID s	5.7
		Retrieve processed candidates	20.6
		Compile in-memory structure	3.8
Candidate Disambiguation	65.6	In-link prior probability	0.1
		Reference probability	13.1
		Alias cosine	10.6
		Category score	6.2
		Context score	29.5
		In-link overlap	3.2
		Sentence context	2.3
		Rank and determine NIL	0.6
Total Time	100.0		100.0

Table 1: A profile of the TAC 11 dataset reveals that both the candidate generation and candidate disambiguation phases are slow

3 NEL Profile

This paper extends the unsupervised NEL system introduced by Radford (2014) with the aim of increasing its speed while maintaining comparable accuracy. In order to do this, it is important to first discover which stages are computationally expensive. The system consists of three main stages: mention extraction, candidate generation and candidate disambiguation.

The mention extraction stage aims to find all mentions of named entities in a document in order to find aliases for the mention string. It begins by preprocessing the document with a part of speech tagger and performing named entity recognition. Similar to the task of word sense disambiguation, we assume that mention strings have one sense per discourse. Thus, they are clustered into chains that refer to the same entity using limited coreference resolution rules such as acronym expansion and substring name matching.

The candidate generation stage produces a list of candidate entities (Wikipedia articles) for each chain in the document. We take the longest mention string in a chain to be the canonical mention and use this to search the database for suitable matches. Candidates are returned from a Solr database (limited to 100 candidates) if the canonical mention matches matches a Wikipedia pages' title, redirect titles or apposition stripped title. This stage aims to ensure that the correct entity is returned as a candidate, while minimising the size of the candidate set for feasible disambiguation. Once a list of candidate names is obtained from Solr, the data associated with each candidate is retrieved from a Hypertable database.

While these first two stages aim to maximise recall, the candidate disambiguation stage aims to distinguish the correct entity from the rest of the candidates by ranking them according to a score. The final score is the sum of the in-link prior probability, reference probability, alias cosine similarity, category score, context score, in-link overlap and sentence context. A more detailed description of each can be found in Radford (2014).

We profiled (Radford, 2014) to discover linking bottlenecks. It is often difficult to judge timing of systems due to the variability caused by differing hardware and loads, so we ran all our experiments over the TAC 11 dataset and queries 10 times to get an average run-time of 1778.39 seconds with a standard error of 9.5 seconds. Our experiments were run on an unloaded machine with two 2.30GHz Intel(R) Xeon(R) E5-2470 CPUs and 62GiB RAM. The full break-down of this profile can be seen in Table 1, which shows that both the candidate generation and candidate disambiguation steps are expensive.

The candidate generation step is expensive due to an external database query which retrieves candidate information such as Wikipedia pages. The run-time of this step is linear to the number of candidates retrieved, as well as linear to the amount of data associated with each candidate.

The candidate disambiguation stage takes 65.6% of run-time. The most expensive score to compute is the context score, which take context information from the candidate, such as the disambiguating term in each candidate's Wikipedia title, anchor text from links within the first paragraph, and links to pages that link back to the candidate. These context terms are searched for within the query document using a trie. While the complexity of this step is related to the number of context terms, the dominating cost is from the number of candidates. Other expensive steps are the reference probability score and alias cosine score.

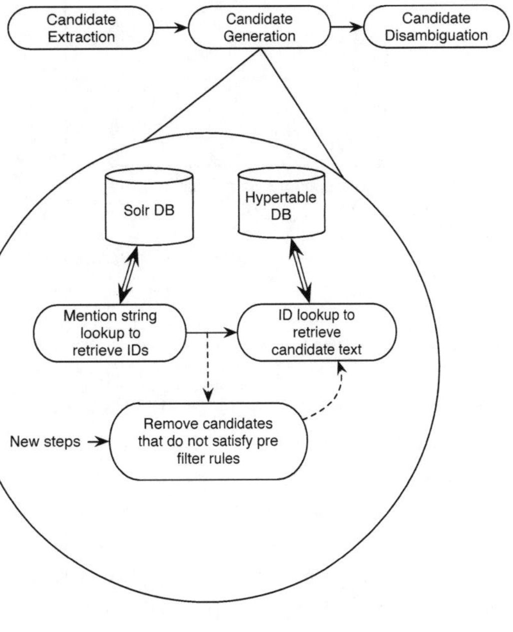

Figure 1: NEL Pipeline and our changes

4 Pre-filtering candidates

Since the expensive steps that have been identified are costly for each candidate, we consider a pre-filter which reduces the number of candidates before their full text is retrieved from the database, and before disambiguation occurs. This will trade accuracy for speed because the load is reduced for both the candidate generation and candidate disambiguation steps, at the cost of some true candidates inadvertently being eliminated. We hypothesise that correct candidates either are either contextually similar with the query document, or are popular and so do not require any contextual overlap. For example, a query document mentioning Melbourne is likely to have similar words to the Wikipedia page for Melbourne. This contextual similarity is important for capturing the correct entity because Melbourne could also refer to Melbourne, Nova Scotia or Melbourne, Quebec. However, a query document mentioning Australia is not necessarily going to share context with the page for Australia because of its notability.

Popularity is measured using an in-link score, which measures the prior probability that a particular candidate is linked to by the mention string. Since this is document insensitive, in-link scores have been precomputed for all candidates in the KB and are retrieved from the database when the name query occurs. We use the rank of candidates sorted by in-link score because it is more meaningful than their raw score, which may vary greatly between candidates. Since Solr returns candidates sorted by this score in the existing system, using their rank is not an expensive step.

Context between documents is generally measured using cosine similarity. For our purposes, we compute the cosine similarity of the BOW of the document (a vector containing the count of each word in the document). We use these raw counts, rather than TF-IDF because some initial experiments suggested that it did not change the spread of correct candidates and it was expensive to retrieve IDF scores. While we found in-link rank to be a very fast pre-filtering method, cosine similarity has to be computed for each candidate of a given document, making it slow when there is a high number of candidates.

For each query, we retain the top i candidates by in-link count. For any remaining candidates, we calculate the similarity between the query document and each candidate's Wikipedia page text, retaining those with a similarity above ℓ. This fits within the candidate generation stage. We store candidate data needed for these thresholds in the Solr database, so that filtering occurs after the Solr query, but before the Hypertable query (Figure 1). In order for this to be an effective pre-filter, it must be fast with respect to the number of candidates, otherwise it defeats the purpose. Since cosine similarity is slow, we use locality sensitive hashing to approximate cosine similarity.

$$\underbrace{\begin{bmatrix} r_{1,1} & r_{1,2} & \cdots & r_{1,v} \\ \vdots & \ddots & & \vdots \\ \vdots & & \ddots & \vdots \\ r_{b,1} & \cdots & \cdots & r_{b,v} \end{bmatrix}}_{\substack{b\times v \text{ random hyperplanes matrix} \\ H}} \times \underbrace{\begin{bmatrix} c_1 \\ c_2 \\ \vdots \\ c_v \end{bmatrix}}_{\text{BOW}} = \underbrace{\begin{bmatrix} x_1 \\ x_2 \\ \vdots \\ x_b \end{bmatrix}}_{\text{Projected vector}} \rightarrow \begin{matrix} x_i \geq 0 \mapsto 1 \\ x_i < 0 \mapsto 0 \end{matrix} \rightarrow \underbrace{\begin{bmatrix} 1 \\ 0 \\ \vdots \\ 1 \end{bmatrix}}_{\text{Hash}}$$

Figure 2: Creating a document hash representation using LSH

5 Low memory LSH

Locality sensitive hashing (LSH) (Broder, 1997; Indyk and Motwani, 1998) is generally used for grouping similar objects from a large data set by mapping them to buckets based on the bits in their lower-dimensional hash (Ravichandran et al., 2005). Since the number of candidates per document is relatively small, this approach is unnecessary, but we use it to compute an extremely efficient approximate similarity function. This is done by counting the number of bits that are the same between the document and query hash. Since hashes are binary, this can be done taking the XOR of the hashes, and counting the 0's which is very fast using the popcount CPU instruction. While the similarity function is very fast, we also need the hashing technique to be very fast, since documents are unseen and their hashes must be calculated in real-time. To do this, we present a new method of generating hashes which is different from the traditional method.

Traditionally, cosine LSH projects the document vectors, or bags of words (BOWs), of dimension v to a lower dimensional (b) binary hash. A BOW document representation is a real valued vector where each element corresponds to the count of each word in the combined vocabulary of all the documents, excluding stop words. BOWs are projected by computing their dot product with a projection matrix (M) of normally distributed random numbers (r_i). The result of this operation, a low-dimensional vector, is then binarised into a hash by mapping non-negative numbers to 1, and negative numbers to a 0 (Figure 2).

This method of LSH requires the vocabulary to be precomputed, which is not suitable for many NEL applications as unseen documents often contain unseen words that must be dealt with. If unseen words are discarded, the hashes no longer become a true representation of the document. Conversely, adding a row to the projection matrix every time a new word is discovered, which is frequent under Zipf's Law, incurs a runtime cost, and results in unbounded memory consumption. Additionally, query documents are unseen so their hash representation cannot be pre-computed, requiring M to be loaded into memory. This can be expensive with a large vocabulary and high number of bits, as $|M| = b \times v$.

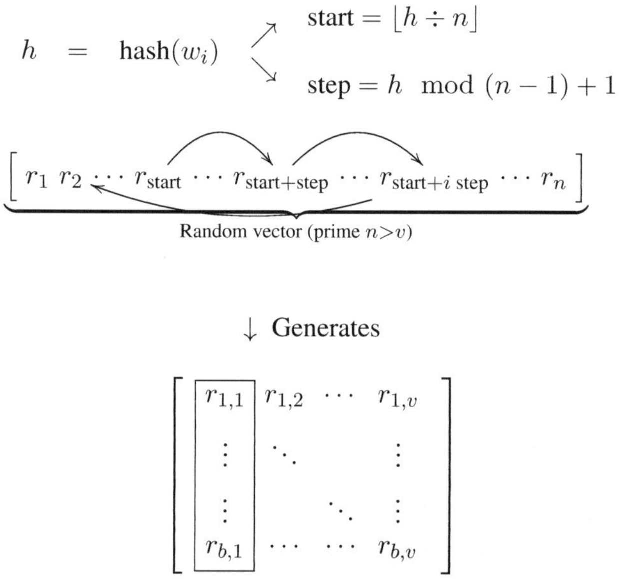

Figure 3: Low-memory LSH generates rows of the hyperplane matrix

We present a low-memory LSH technique which embeds M in a single, fixed-length array, M', and artificially generates rows of M by stepping through M' (Figure 3). To find the start and step for a particular row, the word associated with that row is hashed into a 32-bit integer using a string hash function, xxhash. We divide the integer by the length of M', with the quotient being the starting place in M' and the remainder being the step size. We step through the M' until we have produced a b length row and multiply it by the value corresponding to that word. This is done for each word in the document and the resulting rows are added together and binarised to produce the hash. This effectively mimics the normal matrix multiplication.

The theoretical basis for this method relies on the idea that each word in the document will correspond to a unique start and step, which produces a unique row of the projection matrix. To ensure that no repeating occurs in the generated row, we need the step length to be co-prime to $|M'|$. Thus we choose $|M'|$ to be prime, so that all step lengths are co-prime to $|M'|$. This method allows us to embed an $|M'|(|M'|-1) \times |M'|$ dimension random matrix in M' without substantially affecting LSH, provided that $|M'|$ is prime and larger than the true size of the vocabulary (which is unknown), and $b < |M'|$. This new LSH method only needs to generate and store $|M'|$ random numbers, rather than $b \times v$ random numbers, and thus is more space-efficient than traditional LSH.

6 Experiments and Evaluation

Our first experiment determines the correlation of LSH with cosine similarity to confirm that it correlates well in text data, and to find a suitable hash size. To show the correlation between cosine and LSH, we graphed the cosine similarity and LSH similarity between all query-candidate pairs for the TAC 11 dataset. We calculated both Pearson and Spearman correlation as to not make incorrect distributional assumptions that may affect its validity.

We evaluate our system in terms of both run time and accuracy and measure it as a trade-off, since speed increases usually come at a cost to accuracy. We judge a good trade-off between the time and accuracy as one where the time taken to run the NEL system is significantly shorter without significantly impacting the speed. We use TAC 11 data as a training set, and then test our best configuration on the held-out TAC 12 dataset.

We pre-filter candidates retrieved from the Solr search using the similarity of their hash with the document's hash. This relies on the assumption that candidates with low similarity between documents are likely not to be a correct link. We determine the time-accuracy trade-off when filtering by a similarity threshold. We use in-link score which is retrieved from the Solr database as a baseline pre-filtering method. We also combine both in-link score and LSH similarity to test how they work together. This is under the assumption that in-link score is a measure of entity popularity, and so will retrieve different candidates to LSH similarity, which is an approximation of context similarity.

We precomputed the 2kB hashes for all TAC 11 candidates and stored them in the Solr database. Our pre-filtering experiments retrieved the hashes of all candidates during the Solr search (Figure 1), cut-down the hash to the number of dimensions we were experimenting with, and pre-filtered them according to their hash similarity with the query's hash for various thresholds (i.e. hash similarity $>$ threshold). This meant that extra time was added to the candidate generation step by retrieving hashes from Solr and calculating hash similarity, but time was taken away from the candidate generation step also because fewer candidates had to be retrieved from Hypertable. The candidate disambiguation phase is where most of the time gain occurs, as whole document linking has fewer candidates to disambiguate.

The accuracy of the NEL system is the macro-averaged accuracy over the entities, as to align with the TAC task measures. Our experiments are all run over the TAC 11 dataset, and the NIL baseline (linking all queries as NIL) is 51.84. We use the unsupervised configuration of the Radford (2014) system for all of our linking experiments. This configuration took an average of **1778.39** seconds to run (Table 1) and achieved an accuracy **87.16%**. We use this configuration as out baseline for time-accuracy trade-offs that occur when filtering candidates at differing thresholds.

7 Results and Analysis

Our results show that low-memory LSH requires a high number of bits to correlate well with cosine similarity (Figure 4). With 512 bits we can see a linear trend between cosie similarity ane low-memory LSH, however Pearson correlation exceeds 0.9 for hash sizes larger than 2^{13}.

We notice some particularly high hash similarity when the cosine similarity is 0, and after some investigation, we discovered that these similarity scores were for candidates with no text. If a candidate has no text, their default LSH hash is a string of 0's, so their similarity measure with the document is effectively counting the proportion of 0's in the document hash. We expected LSH similarity

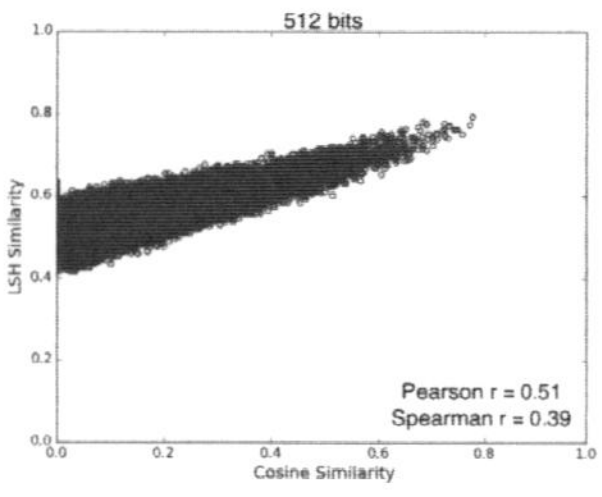

(a) 2^9 bits

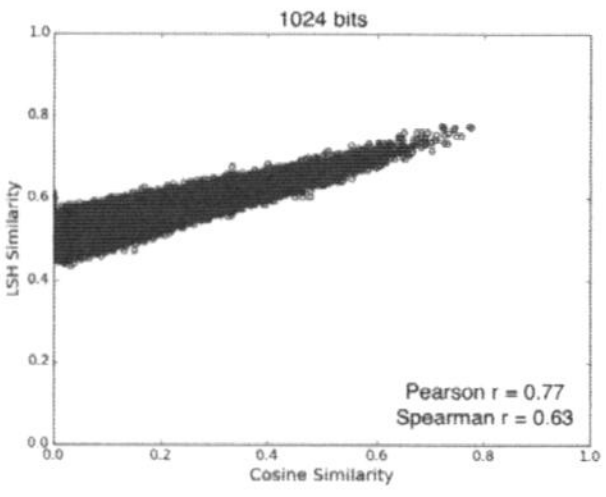

(b) 2^{10} bits

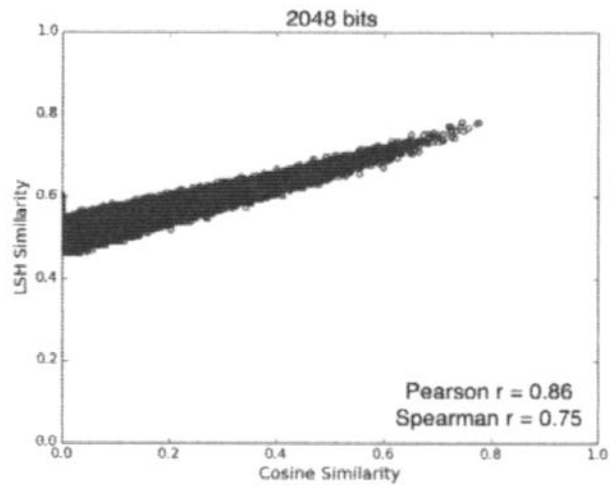

(c) 2^{11} bits

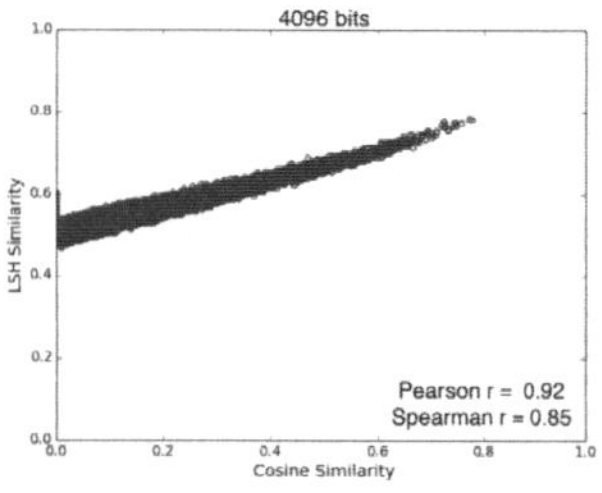

(d) 2^{12} bits

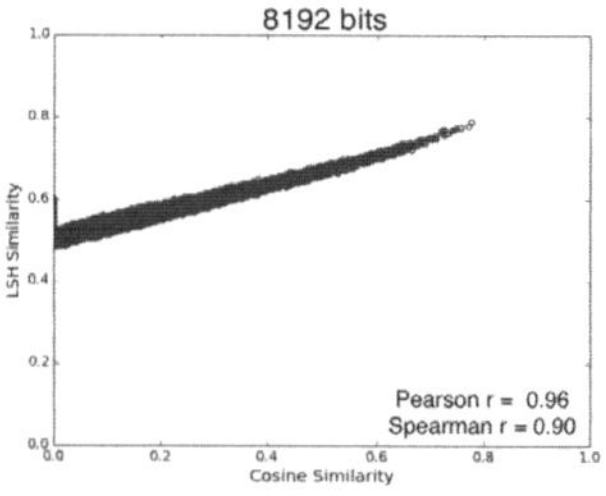

(e) 2^{13} bits

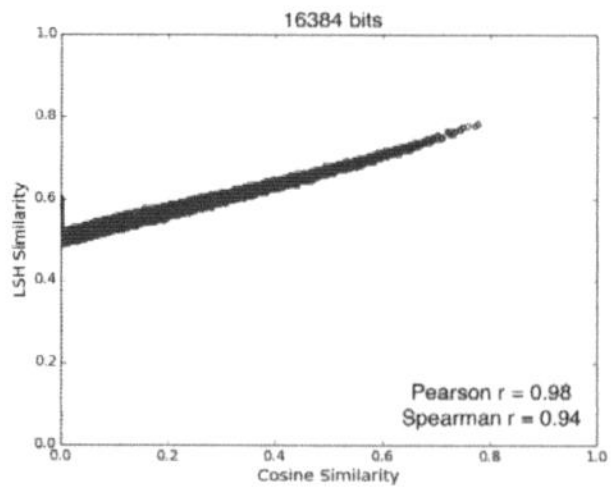

(f) 2^{14} bits

Figure 4: LSH and Cosine correlation increases as hash dimensionality increases.

to be 0.5 for non-correlated documents, since this is the expected value that any two bits are equal. One possible explaination for this relates to the small size of the projection array, M'. With low-memory LSH, each row of M is generated by effectively sampling from a sample (M') rather than the population ($\mathcal{N}$) and so any bias that the sample may have is magnified in the full matrix. This may result in the proportion of 1's having a slight skew away from the theoretical mean of 0.5. Figure 5 shows that the distribution of M' is reasonably centered at 0 for an array of $16\,411$ random numbers. The results of a t-test to see if the mean was significantly different to 0 was inconclusive, with a p-value of 0.18. However, when we use only 2053 random numbers in M' we see a significant bias. We are not yet sure whether this is the cause of the anomalous points, and whether this theoretical flaw has any practical effect. We have a proposed solution to this problem of the sample mean, which we will discuss later in future work.

In order for the pre-filtering mechanism to be valid, we need the filter method to be very fast and not scale badly with the number of candidates. To use LSH instead of cosine, we need the cost of hashing each document plus the cost of computing the LSH similarity for each document-candidate pair to be faster than the cosine of each document-candidate pair. Our experiments show that LSH similarity performs at 38.1% of the time of cosine

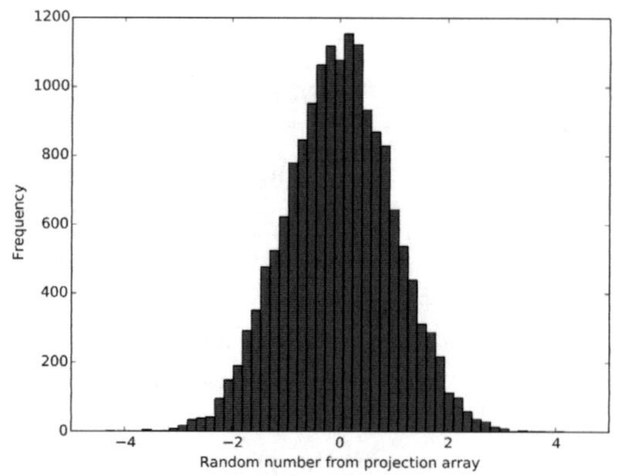

Figure 5: Distribution of M' is not centered at 0. This could be the cause of anomalous LSH similarity scores where cosine similarity is 0

similarity for a hash size of 2^{14} bits. This cost decreases as hash size decreases, however so does the correlation coefficient.

Our time-accuracy trade-offs are shown in Table 2. We notice that there is a general trend with accuracy increasing as the number of top-inlinks increases and as LSH similarity threshold decreases, at the cost of speed. This is also shown visually in Figure 6. This shows us that our best time-accuracy trade-off is when $\ell = 0.56$ and $i = 7$, since only a slight amount of accuracy is lost for a large gain in speed.

Threshold for ℓ	Threshold for i											
	No in-links		1		2		5		7		11	
	Time	Acc	Time	Acc	Time	Acc	Time	Acc	Time	Acc	Time	Acc
No LSH	–	–	42.89	81.33	45.6	84.84	55.53	86.04	58.37	86.53	62.5	86.89
0.53	68.2	84.22	69.76	86.67	71.4	87.2	74.58	87.29	80.27	87.42	79.64	87.47
0.54	56.58	79.87	64.16	86.09	62.61	86.93	66.98	87.07	72.85	87.38	73.76	87.56
0.55	48.78	74.62	55.45	85.38	57.2	86.49	65.66	86.8	69.05	87.16	70.14	87.47
0.56	41.93	68.93	51.98	84.62	54.8	86.36	60.05	86.8	63.91	87.11	67.78	87.47
0.57	37.59	64.8	49.41	83.78	54.16	85.87	58.31	86.62	64.15	86.98	67.58	87.38
0.58	34.97	62.36	49.07	83.47	51.61	85.78	58.1	86.58	63.25	86.98	66.39	87.29
0.59	33.77	59.82	48.19	82.98	51.22	85.51	57.25	86.53	63.06	86.89	66.22	87.2
0.6	32.16	58.13	47.63	82.84	51.75	85.42	56.98	86.49	63.48	86.84	65.91	87.16

Table 2: Time-accuracy trade-off for different in-link ranks and LSH similarity thresholds. Time is measured in percentage of original system (1778.39 seconds) and accuracy is the total accuracy of the system with that configuration

Configuration	Accuracy	Time (s)	Average Time (% of baseline)	Standard Error (%)
Baseline	74.35	2293	100	0.02
$i = 7$ $\ell = 0.56$	73.63	1455	63	0.01
$i = 2$ $\ell = 0.56$	71.52	1179	53	–

Table 3: Results for three chosen thresholds shows that this method is robust across unseen datasets.

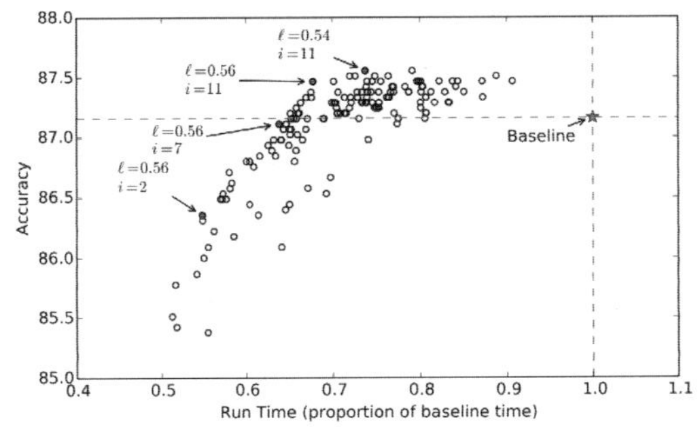

Figure 6: Candidate filtering time for different configurations. Top in-links is fast, while the combined LSH configurations take more time

We choose $\ell = 0.56$ and $i = 7$ to test on an unseen dataset, with results shown in Table 3. We see that results are robust to an unseen dataset, with accuracy decreasing by 0.42 while running at 63.4% of the baseline time.

8 Conclusion

In this paper, we used pre-filtering of candidates to achieve faster time in linking without substantial loss of accuracy. Using a LSH similarity threshold of 0.54 and keeping the top 3 in-links, we decreased the speed by 20% with no loss of accuracy.

We also presented a new method for calculating LSH which runs much faster than regular LSH, requires significantly less storage space than regular LSH and also allows for an expanding vocabulary. We show that this method correlates well with cosine similarity, with a hash size of 1024 bits having a Spearman correlation score of 0.94.

The system we presented uses relatively simple heuristics to decrease the number of candidates that need to be processed in the disambiguation phase. This enables supervised models with large feature sets to be feasibly trained. Our low-memory LSH method can be applied elsewhere in NEL, such as in the disambiguation phase. Features that were previously too expensive in the original vector space can be hashed and their similarity approximated. This is particular useful for features that have a high complexity with regard to candidate size.

Acknowledgments

This work was supported by ARC Discovery grant DP1097291. The authors thank the anonymous reviewers and the ə-lab researchers for their helpful feedback.

References

Amit Bagga and Breck Baldwin. 1998. Entity-based cross-document coreferencing using the vector space model. In *Proceedings of the 36th Annual Meeting of the Association for Computational Linguistics and 17th International Conference on Computational Linguistics - Volume 1*, ACL '98, pages 79–85.

Andrei Broder. 1997. On the resemblance and containment of documents. In *Proceedings of the Compression and Complexity of Sequences 1997*, pages 21–29.

Razvan Bunescu and Marius Pasca. 2006. Using encyclopedic knowledge for named entity disambiguation. In *Proceedings of the 11th Conference of the European Chapter of the Association for Computational Linguistics (EACL-06), Trento, Italy*, pages 9–16, April.

Silviu Cucerzan. 2007. Large-scale named entity disambiguation based on Wikipedia data. In *Proceedings of EMNLP-CoNLL 2007*, pages 708–716.

Aristides Gionis, Piotr Indyk, and Rajeev Motwani. 1999. Similarity search in high dimensions via hashing. In *Proceedings of the 25th International Conference on Very Large Data Bases*, VLDB '99, pages 518–529.

Ben Hachey, Will Radford, Joel Nothman, Matthew Honnibal, and James R. Curran. 2013. Evaluating entity linking with Wikipedia. *Artificial Intelligence*, 194:130–150, January.

Piotr Indyk and Rajeev Motwani. 1998. Approximate nearest neighbors: Towards removing the curse of dimensionality. In *Proceedings of the Thirtieth Annual ACM Symposium on Theory of Computing*, STOC '98, pages 604–613.

Heng Ji and Ralph Grishman. 2011. Knowledge base population: Successful approaches and challenges. In *Proceedings of the 49th Annual Meeting of the Association for Computational Linguistics: Human Language Technologies - Volume 1*, HLT '11, pages 1148–1158, Stroudsburg, PA, USA. Association for Computational Linguistics.

Lin Lin, Chao Chen, Mei-Ling Shyu, and Shu-Ching Chen. 2011. Weighted subspace filtering and ranking algorithms for video concept retrieval. *IEEE Multimedia*, 18(3):32–43.

Yu-En Lu, Pietro Lió, and Steven Hand. 2008. On low dimensional random projections and similarity search. In *Proceedings of the 17th ACM Conference on Information and Knowledge Management*, CIKM '08, pages 749–758.

Rada Mihalcea and Andras Csomai. 2007. Wikify!: Linking documents to encyclopedic knowledge. In *Proceedings of the Sixteenth ACM Conference on Conference on Information and Knowledge Management*, CIKM '07, pages 233–242.

Lailil Muflikhah and Baharum Baharudin. 2009. Document clustering using concept space and cosine similarity measurement. In *Proceedings of the 2009 International Conference on Computer Technology and Development - Volume 01*, ICCTD '09, pages 58–62.

Will Radford, Will Cannings, Andrew Naoum, Joel Nothman, Glen Pink, Daniel Tse, and James R. Curran. 2012. (Almost) Total recall. In *Proc. Text Analysis Conference (TAC2012)*.

Will Radford. 2014. *Linking Named Entities to Wikipedia*. Ph.D. thesis, University of Sydney.

Deepak Ravichandran, Patrick Pantel, and Eduard Hovy. 2005. Randomized algorithms and nlp: Using locality sensitive hash function for high speed noun clustering. In *Proceedings of the 43rd Annual Meeting on Association for Computational Linguistics*, ACL '05, pages 622–629.

Vasudeva Varma, Praveen Bysani, and Kranthi Reddy. 2009. IIT Hyderabad at TAC 2009. In *Proc. Text Analysis Conference (TAC2009)*.

Unsupervised Biographical Event Extraction Using Wikipedia Traffic

Alexander Hogue **Joel Nothman** **James R. Curran**
ə-lab, School of Information Technologies
University of Sydney
NSW 2006, Australia
{ahog5691@uni.,joel.nothman@,james.r.curran@}sydney.edu.au

Abstract

Biographical summarisation can provide succinct and meaningful answers to the question "Who is X?". Current supervised summarisation approaches extract sentences from documents using features from textual context.

In this paper, we explore a novel approach to biographical summarisation, by extracting important sentences from an entity's Wikipedia page based on internet traffic to the page over time. Using a pilot data set, we found that it is feasible to extract key sentences about people's notability without the need for a large annotated corpus.

1 Introduction

"What is Julian Assange known for?" is a question which can be answered in many ways. Previous computational approaches to answering questions like these have focused on summarisation: selecting a subset of sentences from a group of documents relating to a person and ordering them (Biadsy et al., 2008; Zhou et al., 2004). Full text summaries do provide some insight into the notability of their subject, but can also contain superfluous information. To pinpoint the notoriety of individuals, we aim to extract the sentences from a document which show how the document's subject is notable.

We provide an alternate, unsupervised approach to the broader task of biography abstraction, which exploits external information about text, rather then extracting textual features directly.

In this paper, we respond to "What is Julian Assange known for?" with sentences mentioning important events which have occurred in his life. It is the breadth of possible reasons for which one could be notable that make supervised approaches to this task difficult — the creation of a corpus large enough to cover the range of notable events would require a prohibitive amount of annotation. Furthermore, this task would be tedious for annotators, since sentences expressing notability are sparse among documents, and some high-level understanding of the notability of the page subject is required to judge each sentence's notability.

We hypothesise that when a notable event happens to a person, traffic to their Wikipedia page peaks abruptly, and an edit is made to their page describing the event.

To explore this hypothesis, a simple outlier-based method is applied to extract peaks (short periods of sudden activity) from Wikipedia page traffic data, which are used to locate page edits which align to sentences contributing to the notability of the page subject. Event reference identification is a difficult task (Nothman, 2014), and errors in event extraction may mask the performance of our system, so in our initial approach we choose the sentence as our unit of event description.

We evaluate by creating a corpus of Wikipedia pages about people. Each sentence annotated with its human-judged significance to the person's notability. We then measure how reliably page traffic data can be used to identify these most notable events. Our initial investigation into extracting key sentences has shown that it is feasible to approach the task in this unsupervised manner.

Exploring the relationship between Wikipedia traffic, page edits, and the occurrence of notable events can provide us with a deeper understanding of how the public respond to events, and an extrinsic source of information on the importance of sentences in Wikipedia articles.

2 Background

The goal of many approaches to biography abstraction is to provide some distilled knowledge on the notability of a person. A simple approach to biographical abstraction is to summarise exist-

Alexander Hogue, Joel Nothman and James R. Curran. 2014. Unsupervised Biographical Event Extraction Using Wikipedia Traffic. In *Proceedings of Australasian Language Technology Association Workshop*, pages 41−49.

ing documents about an entity, selecting the most representative content of the text while adhering to length constraints.

Early approaches to the task train a sentence classifier (Teufel and Moens, 1997) on a corpus of sentences which are in some way biographical. This corpus is typically existing biographies, or manually selected sentences from a larger corpus. Previous work has used Wikipedia as large, alternate source of biographical sentences (Biadsy et al., 2008), hypothesising that most sentences in Wikipedia's articles about people are biographical.

Zhou et al. (2004) experiment with non-binary sentence classification, requiring a summary to have at least one sentence of each category in a "biographical checklist", with categories such as work, scandal, and nationality. Training a classifier to categorise sentences into these classes requires costly manual annotation. A similar effort would be required for a supervised learning approach to extract important biographical sentences.

Biographical abstraction has also been approached as a relation extraction task. DIPRE (Brin, 1999) has been an influential pattern extraction system which bootstraps using a small set of seed facts to extract not only the patterns they represent, (e.g.@ [person] WORKS_FOR [organisation]) but also to extract additional patterns. Liu et al. (2010) presented BIOSNOWBALL for the biographical fact extraction domain, which extracts biographical key-value pairs. It is the wide range of reasons for notoriety (which would require a large number of potential patterns to fill) motivating our novel source of measures of importance — Wikipedia page traffic over time.

Rather than the traditional approach of classifying sentences via textual features (Schiffman et al., 2001) or locating events (Filatova and Hatzivassiloglou, 2004), we explore the use of an extrinsic source of information indicating what is interesting. Motivating this approach is our hypothesis that many people are most well-known for the events they were involved in. These events have previously been ordered temporally by supervised learning from textual features, (Filatova and Hovy, 2001), and our extrinsic information may assist with the temporal location of events with little temporal information mentioned in text.

Various features of Wikipedia have been previously exploited in NLP, since they provide a massive source of human-written semi-structured information. Plain text has been used to assist named entity recognition (Nothman et al., 2013), page categories have been used to create an ontology (Suchanek et al., 2007) and infoboxes (key-value pairs of facts) have been used to provide additional context to information in text (Wu and Weld, 2010). Wikipedia's revision history is exploited less frequently, but has proven useful to train a model of sentence compression (Yamangil and Nelken, 2008). We know of no prior work that aligns page traffic to text in Wikipedia.

2.1 Timeseries Analysis

To exploit the Wikipedia page traffic data, we need to extract peaks from timeseries data. There are many definitions of *peaks* in the literature on timeseries peak extraction, and many approaches to detecting them. Motivating much of this research is the need to automatically detect spikes in Electroencephalography results (EEG) (Wilson and Emerson, 2002). EEG peaks are typically moderate in amplitude, whereas spikes in page traffic are often several standard deviations above the mean, so our peaks are easier to detect.

A simple approach is to keep a moving average over some window of previous points, comparing each point to the average of the window of previous points. Vlachos et al. (2004) employ this approach using only two window sizes (short term and long term) to detect high traffic periods for the MSN search engine. Their results show instances where a peak in search traffic appears at the time notable events occur to some entities (for instance, the death of a famous British actor), which has also been observed in both page traffic and edits by Nunes et al. (2008). This approach suits our task since the peaks we wish to detect are so prominent.

Through peak extraction techniques, we extract the date on which important events happened to people. By extracting edits to Wikipedia articles near the time of these peaks, we can find the single sentence in the current version of the article which is most similar, and associate it with the important event which happened at the time of the peak.

By providing a sentence-level summary of key events which occur to a person, we pinpoint the notoriety of individuals without the need for a hand-annotated training corpus.

3 Edits and Events

Before considering page traffic data, we performed a preliminary manual analysis of the relationship between the occurrence of real-world events and views and edits to the relevant Wikipedia pages.

Wikipedia includes yearly summaries of key events, their date of occurrence and main participants. We randomly sampled people from these pages for the years 2008–2013,[1] and inspected edits made to those people's Wikipedia entries around the event's date. Findings from our analysis follow:

Editors are quick to respond We manually investigated the typical delay between an event happening and a person's Wikipedia page being updated to reflect the event. The time difference between the recorded date of the event and the date of the page edit mentioning the event was manually recorded, and we found that the typical delay was less that 1 day in 19 of 20 cases. Note that this experiment only considered events notable enough to appear in a short summary of the year, so this result may not generalise to less notable people.

Edits occur in bursts We observed a pattern in the distribution of page edits in response to popular events. Before the day of the event, edits are sparse and mostly minor. On the day of the event, the earliest edit tends to briefly describe the event (e.g. On May 31, he was shot). This edit is followed by a burst of edits soon after, with the volume and frequency of edits correlated with to the notability of the event.

Edits are iteratively mutated Within a burst of edits, consecutive edits consist of modifications to the original edit, new information as the story unfolds, vandalism, reversion of vandalism, updates to outdated sections of the article, and elaboration on sections of the article unrelated to the event. Nunes et al. (2008) have also observed this phenomenon, noting that when a burst of edits occurs, editors tend to contribute "updates on the specific event and generic revisions to the whole topic".

The text introduced at the time of the event may have been heavily modified, or even removed completely as the page is updated over time. Often the original edit is lengthened, and this property has been previously used to create a training corpus for sentence compression (Yamangil and Nelken, 2008). For instance, for a candidate edit of George Tiller was shot on May 31, 2009, we might extract from the current-day article On May 31, 2009, Tiller was shot through the eye and killed by anti-abortion activist Scott Roeder.

Our overall method in the following section builds on these findings, but additionally relies on mapping page view data to edit data.

4 Method

Our task is to extract sentences corresponding to biographical events from Wikipedia articles. We do this by exploring the relationship between Wikipedia page view traffic timeseries and Wikipedia page edits. Specifically, we detect peaks in the page traffic timeseries data for each page, and search the edit history at the time of those peaks for an edit mentioning the event. Since the important sentences we identify are in a snapshot of Wikipedia substantially later than the edit, an alignment step is required, as the originally-inserted text may well be edited further.

4.1 Our Hypothesis

There are three related timeseries we explore in this paper: real-world events occurring to people, visits to their Wikipedia pages, and edits to those pages. Figure 1 shows the relationship between page view spikes and sentences in the article text mentioning the real-world events that caused them. We hypothesise that these timeseries relate such that when a notable event happens to a person, it is reported in the media, traffic to their Wikipedia page increases, and an edit is made to the page adding the occurrence of the event.

4.2 Wikipedia traffic

Wikipedia[2] provides hourly pageview counts[3] (the number of times each article was visited in each hour) for every article on the `wikipedia.org` domain[4] since December 2007. We import each year's worth of data into an instance of WiredTiger[5], a space-efficient key-value store.

Motivated by our experiment measuring the delay between an event occurring and an edit reflecting it being made (see Section 6), we combined

[1] 2008–2013 have coverage in Wikipedia traffic data.

[2] Also https://stats.grok.se/

[3] As well as the URL suffix from each HTTP request, regardless of status.

[4] https://dumps.wikimedia.org/pagecounts-raw/

[5] https://wiredtiger.org/

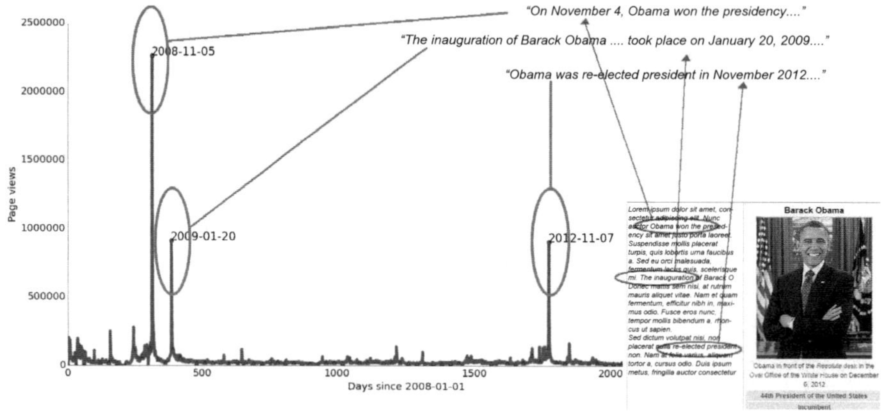

Figure 1: System overview. Peaks in the timeseries of page traffic data are used to find sentences in Wikipedia articles which express the notability of the page subject.

the hourly page view counts into daily counts. This also smooths our timeseries, averaging out the sinusoidal patterns at the hourly level which reflect the day/night cycle of the timezone which has the most Wikipedia readers. We also filter out any namespace modifiers (e.g. Category:People), and no longer existing articles as of 2014. There are some caveats — for instance, we cannot detect events which happened to an individual before their Wikipedia page was created. Most critically, since Wikipedia's page traffic statistics were first recorded in December 2007, much of the (timestamped) edit history for some pages does not have corresponding page view data.

4.3 Peak Detection

Once we have extracted the timeseries for a particular Wikipedia article, we then locate the dates on which the article received a spike in traffic. We use a simple standard deviation-based method to locate peaks in the timeseries data, computing the weighted average of previous points. For each point, the weights for each previous point decay exponentially.

Specifically, μ_i is defined for the ith point of the timeseries p_i by:

$$\mu_0 = p_0$$

$$\mu_i = dp_i + (1-d)\mu_{i-1}$$

Where $0 < d < 1$ is a dampening constant. For a timeseries with standard deviation σ, the ith point p_i is a peak if:

1. p_i is a local maximum
2. $p_i > \mu_i + \theta\sigma$

for a constant $\theta > 0$ determining the extent to which detected peaks differ from the mean, and where local maxima are defined simply as points larger than their immediate neighbours. So our peaks are maxima which are also outliers. Figure 2 shows the effects of varying θ on spike detection. Increasing θ linearly increases the magnitude a maximum must have to be considered a spike. Since our data forms a timeseries, each peak corresponds to a date. We can search Wikipedia's edit history at that time for edits potentially mentioning an event that may have caused the peak.

4.4 Edit Extraction and Selection

Given the date at which a spike in page traffic occurred, we next search for an edit to the page potentially mentioning this event. All edits to a particular page are stored in the page's revision history, and each edit is represented as additions and removals from the previous version of the page. Since we are searching for new information, we consider an edit as one or more additions to the page text (removal of text is ignored). There is a wide range of potential ways a page can be edited. Edits typically contain (a) new information (b) corrections to false information (c) vandalism (d) reversal of vandalism (e) spelling and grammar corrections. We observed that both long additions and elaborations as well as spelling/grammar edits tend to appear in the days after the announcement of a notable event as the increased page traffic prompts editors to update the article.

Motivated by this, we extract all edits within a

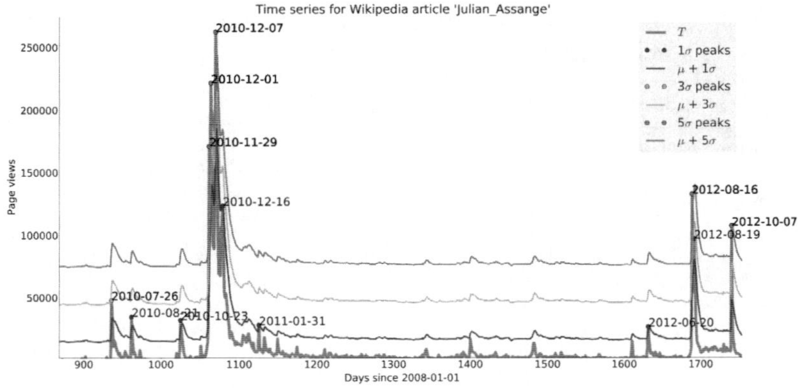

Figure 2: The effect of variation in σ on peak detection. In this image, T is the timeseries, σ is the T's standard deviation and μ is T's weighted moving average. ($d = 0.25$)

window spanning W days on either side from the reported date of the peak, and filter out additions within them which do not have between 5 and 100 words to create our set of candidate edits. The minimum size restriction is to account for small spelling/grammar edits or categorisation edits (e.g. the addition of `Category:Footballer`), and the maximum size restriction helps ignore vandalism (which often deletes the entire article) and its reversion, as well as rewrites which are much broader than the statement of a particular fact.

From this list of candidate edits, we associate the earliest edit within the window to our detected peak. Motivating this approach is the distribution of Wikipedia edits over time which we have observed when a notable event happens to someone, as discussed in Section 3. We observed that this edit is most likely to contain new information on the recent occurrence of a notable event.

Once we have obtained a candidate edit for each spike, we attempt to find the sentence in the current-day Wikipedia article which corresponds to the edit. Aware of the iterative mutation which occurs to edits from our analysis in Section 3, we associate with the edits around the time of a peak the most similar sentence in the current-day Wikipedia article. For each traffic peak we associate at most one important sentence. We measure the cosine similarity of bag-of-word representations of the edit and candidate sentence. To vectorise both the article sentences and our edit, we first remove stop words[6], and convert all text to lower-case. Non-alphanumeric tokens are then removed, and tokens are stemmed by the Porter stemming algorithm (Porter, 1980). Frequency-weighted cosine similarity scores $\in [0, 1]$ are computed between our candidate edit and each sentence in the current-day Wikipedia article, and the most similar sentence is returned.

5 Annotated Corpus

To evaluate our system, we created a manually-annotated test set comprising of a random sample of Wikipedia articles that (a) had less than 100 sentences (b) had the most frequently mentioned year[7] in the range $[2007, 2014]$ (c) had the most frequently mentioned year occuring at least twice (d) was categorised within Wikipedia's Category:1950 births to Category:2001 births.

We chose these restrictions to find Wikipedia articles about people who have had notable events occur within the time period for which we have page traffic data (2008–2013). The sentence restriction was made in order to control the amount of annotation work to be done, but has the side effect of choosing at most moderately notable people, since Wikipedia articles on popular people are substantially longer than 100 sentences. We note that key events relating to people of great fame are well documented, and it is extracting events for the long tail of less notable people which is more difficult.

[6]We use the English stop word list provided in NLTK (Bird, 2006).

[7]Any token that is a number from 1900 to 2020 is considered a year.

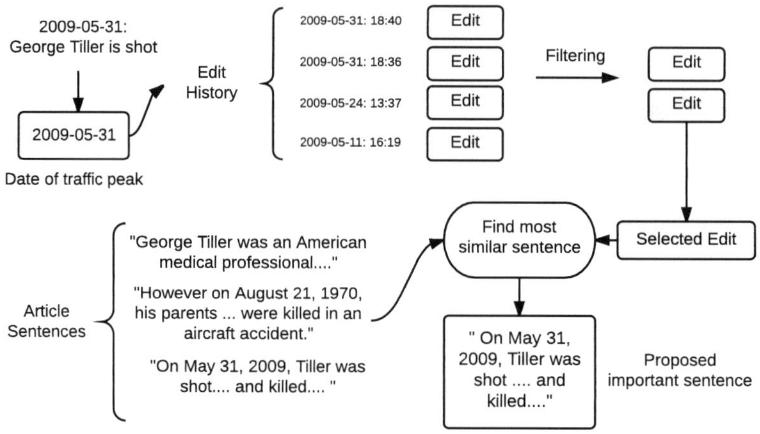

Figure 3: Process taken to align edits to sentences in the current-day Wikipedia article.

5.1 Annotation Procedure

To obtain only the sentences in Wikipedia articles, we parsed the Wikipedia[8] article markup to extract body paragraph text, and used Punkt (Kiss and Strunk, 2006) unsupervised sentence boundary detection trained on a collection of Wikipedia articles, as in Nothman et al. (2013). The sentences were imported into a web-based annotation tool, where 10 native English speakers were tasked with annotating sentences all from 10 Wikipedia articles with scores from 1 to 5 (or X) based on the contribution of the sentence to the notability of the page entity, with the X category for sentences which do not mention the page entity (e.g. facts about their family). We chose this numerical scheme since articles may differ in the number of important sentences, and a multi-category annotation (rather than binary) task allows annotators to calibrate and distinguish between major and minor notable events. We also asked annotators not to distinguish between the page subject, and groups of people the page subject is part of (for instance, Kurt Cobain and his band Nirvana). Example annotations are presented in Table 3.

An initial experiment on a single page suggested that annotators had difficulty distinguishing between facts and events. For instance, the sentence She joined the Labour party in 2006 could be interpreted as containing a fact (being *in* the Labour Party) or an event (*joining* the Labour Party). To allow annotators to focus on interpreting the contributions sentences had to notability, we did not ask annotators to differentiate between facts and events. Due to the redundancy in our annotation (10 annotators annotated each sentence), and the difficulty of the annotation task, we use a consensus-based method to interpret which sentences are important to the notability of the page entity. A sentence is important if 80% or more of its annotations are 4 or 5.

5.2 Corpus Analysis

In total, 261 sentences were annotated over 10 articles, once by all annotators[9]. This is a difficult task, and in this section we explore some of the difficulties annotators experience.

Table 1 lists statistics about our created corpus. We are most interested in the sentences annotators rate as important, rather than the distribution of low scores. We see that annotators had difficulty reaching consensus, with about two thirds of sentences having entropy greater than one bit. On average once per article, annotators also had difficulty determining if a sentence was about the page subject, with there being a mid-range number of Xs, rather than agreement on whether the sentence merits an X or not (the X category marks sentences not about the page subject). An example of a difficult sentence to annotate as such is The album debuted at #2 on the Swedish albums chart and stayed at this position for a second week. Annotators had difficulty reaching consensus on whether this sentence pertained to the page subject. 13% of sentences were considered important according to our criteria (at least 80% 4s and 5s). We see in Table 2 the distribution of all annotations for our task. The most frequently assigned scores were 2 and 3, suggesting that the most frequent variety of

[8]The current version as of 2014-04-01.

[9]With a small number of exceptions

Criteria on sentence s	Sentences
s is important	35
$H(s) > 1$	176
$H(s) > 2$	23
$33\% < X(s) < 66\%$	15

Table 1: Annotated corpus statistics, where H is entropy, and $X(s)$ is the percentage of Xs assigned to s. Sentences to which 4 or 5 were assigned by at least 80% of annotators are considered important.

Score	Annotations	Sentences
1	356	100
2	541	166
3	536	181
4	416	154
5	278	78
Total	2404	261

Table 2: For each score, the total number of times it was assigned, and the number of sentences which received the score at least once.

sentence annotated was of minor notability. Annotators were reserved in assigning 5s to sentences (with 11% of annotations assigned being 5s), but did not necessarily agree on which sentences to annotate as 5 — less than half of sentences with at least one 5 also had 80% or more 4s and 5s.

6 Results and Analysis

6.1 Peak detection

We set $\theta = 5$ in our experiments in order to detect the maximum number of spikes in our timeseries which were sufficiently many standard deviations above the (weighted) mean. We saw that as θ increased, the number of peaks detected dropped off rapidly. So, our approach is robust to parameter variation, and peaks are easy enough to detect that we can set θ to be large. We also set d to 0.25.

6.2 Important Sentence Extraction

From our result in Section 3 measuring the typical delay between events and edits reflecting them, (1 day) we chose a window size W of 5 (2 days either side of the peak) to account for additional delays which may occur for less notable people.

Dev	P	R	$F_{\beta=1}$
First sentence baseline	27%	80%	40%
Peaks only	7%	20%	10%
Combined	33%	50%	40%

Table 4: Baseline set-based comparison of our preliminary system on our development data

Test	P	R	$F_{\beta=1}$
First sentence baseline	13%	50%	21%
Peaks only	7%	33%	11%
Combined	13%	33%	19%

Table 5: Baseline comparison of our preliminary system on test data)

	Important	Unimportant
Important	1	13
Unimportant	4	100

Table 6: Baseline Confusion Matrix. Rows show the gold standard sentence classifications and columns show our system's classifications

Tables 4 and 5 lists our set-based precision, recall, and f-score for our corpus of 10 articles, (5 development, 5 test) comparing the sentences marked as important by our system and by annotators. By convention, the first sentence of each Wikipedia article tends to be the most informative. For instance, Caroline Lind (born October 11, 1982) is an American rower, and is a two-time Olympic gold medalist.. The information contained in this sentence is often repeated later in the article. Since it is so informative, our annotators ranked this sentence highly for all articles in our corpus. This inspired the development of a simple baseline: A system which returns only the first sentence for every article. This is similar to the typical (hard to beat) baseline for summarisation of news articles — the first 2-3 sentences of the article.

We configured our system to additionally return the first sentence of each article, and saw an increase in f-score from 11% to 19% on our development set, but decrease in overall f-score compared to the first sentence only baseline. Table 6 shows our baseline system's confusion matrix. We see that the majority of errors are in recall — our system does not extract 13 of the 14 gold-standard sentences. We see in Table 7 that returning the first sentence of each article helps with these recall errors.

There are many stages in our pipeline where errors can occur. Annotators can tag a sentence as important which has no spike associated with it, due to lack of timeseries data coverage (before 2008), a lack of spike associated with the sentence, or due to the page traffic increase being too small to be detected as a spike. The most frequent cause of these recall errors is during the edit detection phase, when there are co-incidental edits

Person	Sentence	Score (1 - 5 or X)
Caroline Lind	In her Olympic debut at the 2008 Summer Olympics in Beijing, Lind won a gold medal as a member of the women's eight team.	5
Ed Stoppard	In 2007, he played the title role in the BBC's drama-documentary Tchaikovsky: Fortune and Tragedy.	4
Charlie Webster	This lasted for just a few months and she moved on to present the Red Bull Air Race worldwide for ITV4.	3
Charlie Webster	In April 2009, Webster ran in the London Marathon raising money for the Bobby Moore Fund for Cancer Research UK.	2
Caroline Lind	Lind pursued an M.B. A. with an Accounting Concentration at Rider University, in Lawrenceville, New Jersey.	1
Charlie Day	His father, Dr. Thomas Charles Day, is retired and was a professor of Music History and Music Theory at Salve Regina University in Newport, Rhode Island.	X

Table 3: Sample annotations of sentences from several Wikipedia articles. Each sentence is scored from 1 to 5 or with X, with 5 being a sentence critical to the fame of the page subject, 1 being a sentence which is about the page subject, but does not contain an event or fact, and X being a sentence which is not about the page subject.

	Important	Unimportant
Important	5	9
Unimportant	5	99

Table 7: Confusion Matrix — Baseline system + first sentence of each article always returned. Rows show the gold standard classifications and columns show our system's classifications

to the page in the days leading to a notable event, and when the first edit to a page on the day of a notable event does not mention the event (for instance, vandalism inspired by the notable event).

Errors in the alignment phase can occur because some edits correspond to multiple sentences in the final document. For instance, a revision listing several films in which an actor appeared is later split into several sentences, one for each film. This results in several similar candidate sentences for the edit, our system can choose only one. Furthermore, in a number of cases the iterative updating of the page as a story unfolds causes the text from the original edit to be missing entirely from the final version of the article.

A peak can also be detected for which there is no corresponding page edit, nor a corresponding sentence in the current article. For instance, a spike appears in singer Jimmy Barnes' page view timeseries in 2012, at the same time his daughter first appears on a popular television program.

7 Conclusion

In this paper, we have proposed a novel approach for summarising the notability of a person, and explored the relationship between Wikipedia traffic, page edits, and the occurrence of notable events.

Our experiments have been limited by our small sample of annotated data. A critical next step will be developing a larger sample of annotated data, which will help us understand the task better, and allow exploration into ordering sentences by the amplitude of their associated spike. Two stages that require further exploration are the selection of edits, and their alignment to the current page.

Extracting edits corresponding to page traffic peaks need not limit the source of corresponding sentences to the Wikipedia article text itself. The extracted edits may also bear comparison to other biographies of the same entity, or to sentences in the corpus of news articles about them. It may be interesting to use a similar approach in an entity-centred long-term news retrieval query.

The page traffic data need not be the only source of information indicating interestingness. Other work could use the appearence of the entity in media or in query logs to identify key edits to their Wikipedia page.

We have provided insight into which parts of this task are easy and which are difficult. Our initial exploration into exploiting this timeseries data to detect any of the wide variety of reasons one might be famous has set the stage for further exploration of this new, free, extrinsic source of information about what is interesting.

8 Acknowledgements

This work was supported by ARC Discovery grant DP1097291. The authors thank the anonymous reviewers and the ə-lab researchers for their helpful feedback.

References

Fadi Biadsy, Julia Hirschberg, Elena Filatova, and LLC InforSense. 2008. An Unsupervised Approach to Biography Production Using Wikipedia. In *Proceedings of the 46th Annual Meeting of the Association for Computational Linguisitics: Human Language Technologies*, pages 807–815.

Steven Bird. 2006. NLTK: the natural language toolkit. In *Proceedings of the COLING/ACL on Interactive presentation sessions*, pages 69–72. Association for Computational Linguistics.

Sergey Brin. 1999. Extracting patterns and relations from the world wide web. In *The World Wide Web and Databases*, pages 172–183. Springer.

Elena Filatova and Vasileios Hatzivassiloglou. 2004. Event-based extractive summarization.

Elena Filatova and Eduard Hovy. 2001. Assigning time-stamps to event-clauses. In *Proceedings of the workshop on Temporal and spatial information processing-Volume 13*, page 13. Association for Computational Linguistics.

Tibor Kiss and Jan Strunk. 2006. Unsupervised multilingual sentence boundary detection. *Computational Linguistics*, 32(4):485–525.

Xiaojiang Liu, Zaiqing Nie, Nenghai Yu, and Ji-Rong Wen. 2010. BioSnowball: automated population of Wikis. In *Proceedings of the 16th ACM SIGKDD International Conference on Knowledge Discovery and Data Mining*, pages 969–978.

Joel Nothman, Nicky Ringland, Will Radford, Tara Murphy, and James R. Curran. 2013. Learning multilingual named entity recognition from wikipedia. *Artificial Intelligence*, 194:151–175.

Joel Nothman. 2014. *Grounding event references in news*. Ph.D. thesis, School of Information Technologies, University of Sydney.

Sérgio Nunes, Cristina Ribeiro, and Gabriel David. 2008. Wikichanges: exposing wikipedia revision activity. In *Proceedings of the 4th International Symposium on Wikis*, page 25. ACM.

Martin F Porter. 1980. An algorithm for suffix stripping. *Program: electronic library and information systems*, 14(3):130–137.

Barry Schiffman, Inderjeet Mani, and Kristian J Concepcion. 2001. Producing biographical summaries: Combining linguistic knowledge with corpus statistics. In *Proceedings of the 39th Annual Meeting on Association for Computational Linguistics*, pages 458–465. Association for Computational Linguistics.

Fabian M Suchanek, Gjergji Kasneci, and Gerhard Weikum. 2007. Yago: a core of semantic knowledge. In *Proceedings of the 16th International Conference on World Wide Web*, pages 697–706. ACM.

Simone Teufel and Marc Moens. 1997. Sentence extraction as a classification task. In *Proceedings of the ACL*, volume 97, pages 58–65.

Michail Vlachos, Christopher Meek, Zografoula Vagena, and Dimitrios Gunopulos. 2004. Identifying similarities, periodicities and bursts for online search queries. In *Proceedings of the 2004 ACM SIGMOD international conference on Management of data*, pages 131–142. ACM.

Scott B Wilson and Ronald Emerson. 2002. Spike detection: a review and comparison of algorithms. *Clinical Neurophysiology*, 113(12):1873–1881.

Fei Wu and Daniel S Weld. 2010. Open information extraction using Wikipedia. In *Proceedings of the 48th Annual Meeting of the Association for Computational Linguistics*, pages 118–127. Association for Computational Linguistics.

Elif Yamangil and Rani Nelken. 2008. Mining wikipedia revision histories for improving sentence compression. In *Proceedings of the 46th Annual Meeting of the Association for Computational Linguistics on Human Language Technologies: Short Papers*, pages 137–140. Association for Computational Linguistics.

Liang Zhou, Miruna Ticrea, and Eduard H Hovy. 2004. Multi-Document Biography Summarization. In *Proceedings of the Conference of the European Chapter of the Association for Computational Linguistics*, pages 434–441.

A Comparative Study of Weighting Schemes for the Interpretation of Spoken Referring Expressions

Su Nam Kim, Ingrid Zukerman, Thomas Kleinbauer and **Masud Moshtaghi**
Clayton School of Information Technology, Monash University
Clayton, Victoria 3800, Australia
`firstname.lastname@monash.edu`

Abstract

This paper empirically explores the influence of two types of factors on the interpretation of spoken object descriptions: (1) descriptive attributes, e.g., colour and size; and (2) interpretation stages, e.g., syntax and pragmatics. We also investigate two schemes for combining attributes when estimating the goodness of an interpretation: Multiplicative and Additive. Our results show that the former scheme outperforms the latter, and that the weights assigned to the attributes of a description and the stages of an interpretation influence interpretation accuracy.

1 Introduction

Referring expressions have been the topic of considerable research in *Natural Language Generation* (*NLG*) and psychology. In particular, attention has been paid to the usage of descriptive attributes, such as lexical item, colour, size, location and orientation (Section 2).

In this paper, we present an empirical study that examines the contribution of two types of factors to the understanding of spoken descriptions: (1) *descriptive attributes*, such as colour and size; and (2) *stages of an interpretation*, e.g., syntax and pragmatics. Our study was conducted in the context of *Scusi?*, a *Spoken Language Understanding* (*SLU*) system that interprets descriptions of household objects (Zukerman et al., 2008) (Section 3). Given a description such as "the *large blue* mug", where the descriptive attributes pertain to colour and size, in the absence of such a mug, should an SLU system prefer a large pink mug or a small blue mug? A preference for the former favours size over colour, while preferring the latter has the opposite effect. Similarly, considering the stages of an interpretation, if an *Automatic Speech Recognizer* (*ASR*) produces the text "the *played* inside the microwave" when a speaker says "the *plate* inside the microwave", should an SLU system prefer interpretations comprising objects inside the microwave or interpretations where "played" is considered a verb? A preference for the former favours pragmatics, while a preference for the latter favours the heard text.

We represent the contribution of a factor by assigning it a weight — factors with a higher weight are more influential than those with a lower weight; and investigate two methods for learning the weights of the factors pertaining to descriptive attributes and to interpretation stages: steepest ascent hill climbing and a genetic algorithm (Section 4). In addition, we consider two schemes for combining descriptive attributes, viz *Multiplicative* and *Additive* (Section 3.1). Our contribution pertains to the idea of empirically determining the influence of different factors on the interpretation accuracy of an SLU module, the methods for doing so, and the analysis of our results.

The rest of this paper is organized as follows. Next, we discuss related work. In Section 3, we outline our SLU system and the schemes for combining descriptive attributes. The learning algorithms appear in Section 4, and the results of our evaluation experiments in Section 5, followed by concluding remarks.

2 Related Work

The use and importance of different attributes in object descriptions has been studied both in psychology and in *NLG* (Krahmer and van Deemter, 2012), but there is little related research in *Natural Language Understanding* (*NLU*). Further, we have found no work on the relative importance of the different interpretation stages, e.g., is pragmatics more important than parsing?

Several studies have found that people tend

Su Nam Kim, Ingrid Zukerman, Thomas Kleinbauer and Masud Moshtaghi. 2014. A Comparative Study of Weighting Schemes for the Interpretation of Spoken Referring Expressions. In *Proceedings of Australasian Language Technology Association Workshop*, pages 50−58.

to include in their descriptions attributes that do not add discriminative power, e.g., (Dale and Reiter, 1995; Levelt, 1989, p. 129–134), which can be partly explained by the incremental nature of human language production and understanding (Pechmann, 1989; Kruijff et al., 2007). The incrementality of human speech was also considered by van der Sluis and Krahmer (**?**), in combination with object salience, when generating multimodal object references; while van Deemter (2006) and Mitchell *et al.* (2011) studied the generation of descriptions that employ gradable attributes, obtained from numerical data, focusing on size-related modifiers.

Gatt *et al.* (2007) compared the performance of several generation algorithms with respect to a combination of features, viz colour, position (restricted to placement in a grid), orientation and size. Their algorithm produced descriptions similar to those generated by people when the priority order of the attributes was *colour* $\succ$ *orientation* $\succ$ *size*. In contrast, Herrmann and Deutsch (1976) found that the choice of discriminative attributes is perceptually driven, but posited that there is no universally applicable priority ordering of attributes. This view was extended by Dale and Reiter (1995, p. 20), who suggested investigations to determine the priority order of attributes for different domains.

In this paper, we apply Dale and Reiter's suggestion to the understanding of spoken descriptions. However, rather than finding a priority order of attributes like Gatt *et al.* (2007), we learn weights that reflect the importance of descriptive attributes, and consider two schemes for combining these attributes. In addition, we extend this idea to the processing stages employed when interpreting descriptions.

3 SLU Systems and Case Study

The study described in this paper was conducted in the context of our SLU system *Scusi?* (Zukerman et al., 2008). However, what is important is not the specifics of a particular system, but the features of SLU systems to which our study is relevant. Specifically, the systems in question must have several processing stages, e.g., ASR, syntax, semantics and pragmatics; each processing stage must produce an N-best list of outputs (interpretations), e.g., N parse trees; and each interpretation generated at each stage must be assigned a score

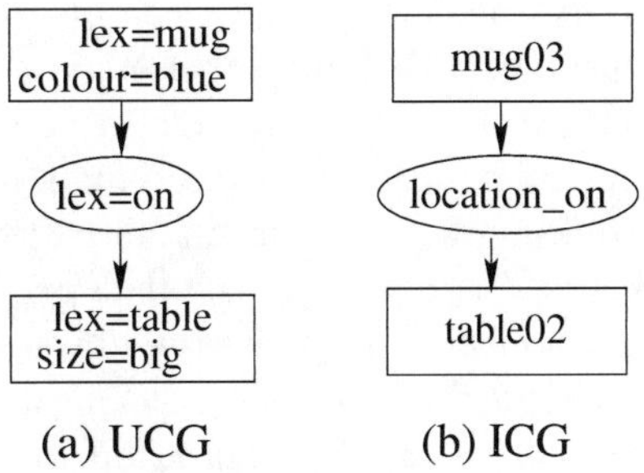

Figure 1: Sample UCG and ICG for "the blue mug on the big table".

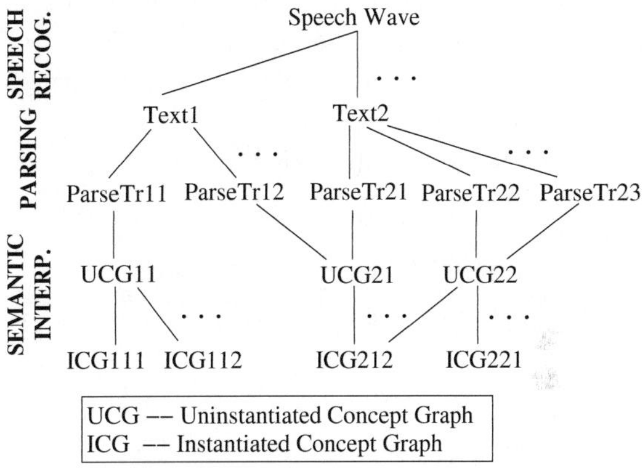

Figure 2: *Scusi?*'s processing stages.

or probability that reflects its goodness.

Scusi? has four interpretation stages: ASR (Microsoft Speech SDK 6.1) produces candidate texts from a speech wave; Syntax (Charniak's probabilistic parser) generates parse trees; Semantics produces *uninstantiated Concept Graphs* (*UCGs*) (Sowa, 1984); and Pragmatics generates *instantiated Concept Graphs* (*ICGs*). Each of these outputs is assigned a probability. A UCG contains descriptive attributes (lexical item, colour and size of concepts, and positional relations between concepts) extracted from its "parent" parse tree. An ICG contains candidate objects within the current context (e.g., a room) and positional relations that reflect those specified in its parent UCG. For instance, Figure 1(a) shows one of the UCGs returned for the description "the blue mug on the big table", and Figure 1(b) displays one of the ICGs generated for this UCG. Note that the concepts in the UCG have generic names, e.g., `mug`, while the ICG contains specific objects, e.g., `mug03`, which is a candidate match for `lex=mug, colour=blue`.

Most interpretation stages can produce multiple outputs for a given input, e.g., up to 50 parse trees for a given ASR output. The graph of all possible interpretations (Figure 2) is usually too large to explore exhaustively in a practical spoken dialogue system. Therefore, *Scusi?* initially generates a promising ICG by selecting the top-ranked interpretation for each stage, and then performs a prescribed number of iterations as follows: in each iteration, an interpretation type (speech wave, text, parse tree or UCG) is selected probabilistically for further processing, giving preference to types produced by later interpretation stages in order to increase the specificity of the generated interpretations. An interpretation of the selected type is then probabilistically chosen for expansion, giving preference to more promising (higher scoring) interpretations, e.g., if a text is chosen, then a new parse tree for this text is added to the list of available parse trees.

3.1 Probability of an interpretation

The scores produced by *Scusi?* are in the $[0, 1]$ range, allowing them to be interpreted as *subjective probabilities* (Pearl, 1988). After making conditional independence assumptions, the probability of an ICG is estimated as follows (Zukerman et al., 2008):

$$\begin{aligned} \Pr(I|S,\mathcal{C}) \;=\; & \Pr(T|S)^{W_t}\Pr(P|T)^{W_p} \\ & \Pr(U|P)^{W_u}\Pr(I|U,\mathcal{C})^{W_i} \end{aligned} \quad (1)$$

where S, T, P, U and I denote speech wave, textual interpretation, parse tree, UCG and ICG respectively, and $\mathcal{C}$ denotes the current context (e.g., a room). The weights W_t, W_p, W_u and W_i reflect the importance of the outcome of each interpretation stage, i.e., ASR (text), Syntax (parse tree), Semantics (UCG) and Pragmatics (ICG).

The first two probabilities in Equation 1 are obtained from the ASR and the parser. The third probability, which reflects the complexity of a semantic interpretation, is estimated as the reciprocal of the number of nodes in a UCG. The last probability, viz the probability of an ICG I given UCG U and context $\mathcal{C}$, reflects the goodness of the match between ICG I and its parent UCG U in context $\mathcal{C}$. Specifically, the probability of I is estimated by a combination of functions that calculate how well the actual attributes of the objects in I (lexical item, colour, size and positional relation) match those specified in its parent UCG U.

We studied two schemes for combining these functions: *Multiplicative* and *Additive*.

Multiplicative scheme. This scheme is similar to that used in Equation 1:

$$\begin{aligned} \mathrm{SC}_{\mathrm{MULT}}(I|U,\mathcal{C}) = & \prod_{i=1}^{N}\prod_{j=1}^{N}\Pr(\mathrm{loc}(k_i,k_j))^{W_{loc}} \times \quad (2) \\ & \prod_{i=1}^{N}\Pr(u_{i,lex}|k_i)^{W_{lex}}\Pr(u_{i,col}|k_i)^{W_{col}}\Pr(u_{i,siz}|k_i)^{W_{siz}}, \end{aligned}$$

where N is the number of objects in ICG I, and the weights W_{lex}, W_{col}, W_{siz} and W_{loc} reflect the importance of lexical item, colour, size and location respectively. The second line in Equation 2 represents how well each object k_i in ICG I matches the lexical item, colour and size specified in its parent concept u_i in UCG U; and the first line represents how well the relative locations of two objects k_i and k_j in context $\mathcal{C}$ (e.g., a room) match their specified locations in U (e.g., $on(k_i, k_j)$). For instance, given the ICG in Figure 1(b), the second line in Equation 2 estimates the probability that `mug03` could be called "mug" and its colour could be called "blue" (no size was specified), and the probability that `table02` could be called "table" and considered "big" (no colour was specified). The first line estimates the probability that `mug03` could be said to be on `table02` (if the mug is elsewhere, this probability is low).

This scheme is rather unforgiving of partial matches or mismatches, e.g., the probability of a lexical match between "mug" and `cup01`, which is less than 1, is substantially reduced when raised to an exponent greater than 1; and a mismatch of a single attribute in an ICG significantly lowers the probability of the ICG.

Additive scheme. This more forgiving scheme employs the following formulation to estimate the probability of an ICG I given its parent UCG U and context $\mathcal{C}$:

$$\begin{aligned} \mathrm{SC}_{\mathrm{ADD}}(I|U,\mathcal{C}) = & \sum_{i=1}^{N}\sum_{j=1}^{N}\Pr(\mathrm{loc}(k_i,k_j))W_{loc} + \quad (3) \\ & \sum_{i=1}^{N}\{\Pr(u_{i,lex}|k_i)W_{lex} + \Pr(u_{i,col}|k_i)W_{col} + \\ & \Pr(u_{i,siz}|k_i)W_{siz}\}\,. \end{aligned}$$

In principle, this scheme could also be applied to combining the probabilities of the interpretation stages. However, we did not explore this option owing to its inferior performance with respect to descriptive attributes (Section 5).

Probabilities from different sources

There are large variations in the probabilities returned by the different interpretation stages. In particular, the probabilities returned by the parser are several orders of magnitude smaller than those returned by the other stages. To facilitate the learning of weights, we adjust the probabilities returned by the different interpretation stages so that they are of a similar magnitude. To this effect, we adopt two approaches: (1) adjusting the probabilities returned by the parser by calculating their standardized score z_i, and (2) normalizing the probabilities of the ICGs by introducing a factor that depends on the weights assigned to different descriptive attributes. The second approach takes advantage of specific information about ICGs, which is not available about parse trees.

Adjusting parse-tree probabilities. Given a probability p_i returned by the parser, we calculate its z-score z_i for an input value x_i as follows: $z_i = (x_i - \mu)/\sigma$, where μ is the mean and σ the standard deviation of the probabilities returned by the parser for our development corpus (Section 5.2). The z_i scores are then transformed to the $[0, 1]$ range using a sigmoid function $z_i^{Norm} = \frac{1}{1+e^{-z_i}}$.

Normalizing ICG probabilities. The ICG scores obtained by the Multiplicative scheme are often in a small band in a very low range, while the ICG scores obtained by the Additive scheme are typically greater than 1. In order to expand the range of the former, and map the latter into the $[0, 1]$ range, we incorporate the following normalizing factor φ into their formulation:

$$\varphi = \sum_{i=1}^{M}\sum_{j=1}^{M} W_{loc} + \sum_{i=1}^{M}\{W_{lex} + W_{col} + W_{siz}\},$$

where the weights correspond to the descriptive attributes that were mentioned.

This factor is incorporated into the Multiplicative and Additive schemes as follows:

- **Multiplicative scheme.**

$$\mathrm{Pr}_{\mathrm{MULT}}(I|U, \mathcal{C}) = \mathrm{SC}_{\mathrm{MULT}}(I|U, \mathcal{C})^{1/\varphi} \quad (4)$$

- **Additive scheme.**

$$\mathrm{Pr}_{\mathrm{ADD}}(I|U, \mathcal{C}) = \frac{1}{\varphi}\mathrm{SC}_{\mathrm{ADD}}(I|U, \mathcal{C}) \quad (5)$$

4 Learning Weights

In this section, we describe the algorithms used to learn the weights for the interpretation stages (W_t, W_p, W_u, W_i) and the descriptive attributes (W_{lex}, W_{col}, W_{siz}, W_{loc}), and our evaluation metrics.

4.1 Learning algorithms

In order to learn the values of the weights, an SLU system must be run on the entire training corpus each time a set of weights is tried. To control the search time, *Scusi?* was set to perform 150 iterations. In addition, we investigated only irrevocable search strategies: steepest ascent hill climbing and a genetic algorithm, employing two ranges of integer weights: a small range of $[1, 4]$ for our cross-validation experiment (Section 5), and a larger range of $[1, 20]$ for our development-dataset experiment (Section 5.2). In general, the algorithms produced low weights, except for the genetic algorithm in the development-dataset experiment, where it generated high weights for most descriptive attributes.

The fitness function for both search strategies is the system's average performance on a training corpus using the *NDCG*@10 metric. This metric, which is described in Section 4.2, was chosen due to its expressiveness, and the value 10 was selected because a response generation system may plausibly inspect the top 10 interpretations returned by an SLU module.

Steepest ascent hill climbing (SA). All weights are initially set to 1. In each iteration, a weight is increased by 1 while keeping the other weights at their previous value;[1] the weight configuration that yields the best performance is retained. This process is repeated until performance no longer improves after one round of changes.

Genetic algorithm (GA). One set of weights is considered a gene. Owing to the relatively long processing time for training corpus runs, we restrict the gene population size to 15, initialized with random values for all weights. In each iteration, the 10 best performing genes are kept, and the other five genes are replaced with offspring of the retained genes. Offspring are generated by selecting two genes probabilistically, with better genes having a higher selection probability, and probabilistically choosing between mutation and

[1]In preliminary experiments, we considered increments of 0.5, but this did not affect the results.

crossover, and between the parent weights to be retained in a crossover operation. This process is repeated until the performance of the population does not improve four times in a row.

4.2 Evaluation metrics

Scusi?'s performance is evaluated using two measures: *Fractional Recall* $@K$ (*FRecall*$@K$) and *Normalized Discounted Cumulative Gain* $@K$ (*NDCG*$@K$) (Järvelin and Kekäläinen, 2002).

FRecall$@K$ is a variant of Recall that accounts for the fact that an N-best system ranks equiprobable interpretations arbitrarily:

$$FRecall@K(d) = \frac{\sum_{j=1}^{K} fc(I_j)}{|C(d)|},$$

where $C(d)$ is the set of correct interpretations for description d, I_j is a candidate interpretation for d, and fc is the fraction of correct interpretations among those with the same probability as I_j (it is a proxy for the probability that I_j is correct).

DCG$@K$ is similar to *FRecall*, but provides a finer-grained account of rank by discounting interpretations with higher (worse) ranks. This is done by dividing $fc(I_j)$ by a logarithmic penalty that reflects I_j's rank:

$$DCG@K(d) = fc(I_1) + \sum_{j=2}^{K} \frac{fc(I_j)}{\log_2 j}.$$

DCG$@K$ is normalized to the $[0, 1]$ range by dividing it by the *DCG*$@K$ score of an ideal N-best result, where the $|C(d)|$ correct interpretations of description d are ranked in the first $|C(d)|$ places:

$$NDCG@K(d) = \frac{DCG@K(d)}{1 + \sum_{j=2}^{\min\{|C(d)|,K\}} \frac{1}{\log_2 j}}.$$

5 Evaluation

In this section, we describe two experiments where we compare the performance of three versions of *Scusi?*: (1) with weights learned by SA, (2) with weights learned by GA, and (3) with Unity weights (all descriptive attributes and interpretation stages have a weight of 1).

As mentioned in Section 4.1, the entire training corpus must be processed for each weight configuration, resulting in long training times, in particular for GA. To reduce these times, rather than trying to learn all the weights at once, we first learned the weights of descriptive attributes, and then used the results of this experiment to learn the weights of the interpretation stages. Further, the former weights were learned from manually transcribed texts, while the latter were learned from actual ASR outputs. This was done because descriptive attributes in head nouns (lexical item, colour and size) were often mis-heard by the ASR, which hampers a learning system's ability to determine their contribution to the performance of an SLU module.

Table 1: Distribution of descriptive attributes over the 341-dataset.

Attribute	Number (%)
Lexicon, Colour	14 (4.11%)
Lexicon, Colour, Position	150 (43.99%)
Lexicon, Colour, Size	3 (0.88%)
Lexicon, Colour, Position, Size	20 (5.87%)
Lexicon, Position	152 (44.57%)
Lexicon, Position, Size	2 (0.59%)
Lexicon, Size	0 (0.00%)
Total	341 (100%)

The resultant versions of *Scusi?* were evaluated using the corpus described in (Kleinbauer et al., 2013), denoted *341-dataset*, which consists of 341 free-form, spoken descriptions generated by 26 trial subjects for 12 objects within four diverse scenes (three objects per scene, where a scene contains between 9 and 17 objects). The descriptions are annotated with Gold standard ICGs. Table 1 displays the details of the descriptions and their attributes.

5.1 Experiment 1 – Cross-validation

Owing to run-time restrictions, we performed only three-fold cross validation, where the search algorithms were trained on 120 descriptions and tested on 221 descriptions. Both the training set and the test set were selected by stratified sampling according to the distribution of the descriptive attributes. Note that the training corpora comprise 360 descriptions in total, i.e., there are 19 extra descriptions in the training data because, as seen in Table1, descriptions containing size, e.g., "the *large* brown desk", were quite rare, and hence were included in more than one training set.

Each algorithm learned weight configurations for the interpretation stages and the descriptive attributes for each validation fold. The weights learned by SA generally differed from those learned by GA, and there were some differences in

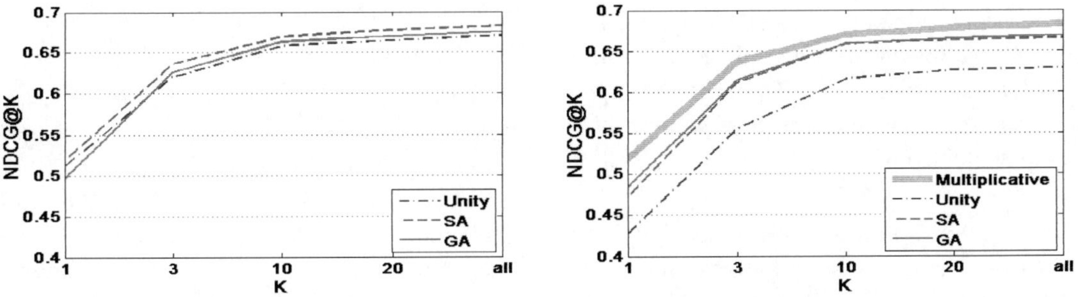

(a) Multiplicative scheme

(b) Additive scheme

Figure 3: Average *NDCG@K* obtained over three-fold cross validation (scale 0.4-0.7).

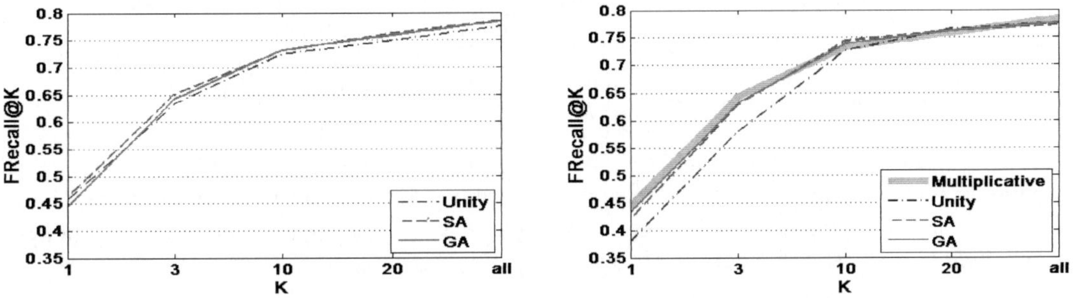

(a) Multiplicative scheme

(b) Additive scheme

Figure 4: Average *FRecall@K* obtained over three-fold cross validation (scale 0.35-0.8).

the weights learned for each fold. Both algorithms assigned a weight of 1 to the ASR stage under the Additive attribute-combination scheme, and a higher weight under the Multiplicative scheme; the Syntax stage mostly received a weight of 1; and the Semantics and Pragmatics stages were assigned higher weights. GA tended to assign higher weights than SA to descriptive attributes, while SA consistently ascribed a weight of 1 to size and location. Despite these differences, both algorithms outperformed the Unity baseline on the training set, with GA achieving the best results, and the Multiplicative scheme outperforming the Additive scheme.

Results

Figures 3 and 4 display the average of *NDCG@K* and *FRecall@K* respectively for the three validation folds for $K \in \{1, 3, 10, 20, \text{all}\}$ under the Multiplicative and the Additive attribute-combination schemes (the grey shadow in Figures 3b and 4b represents the best performance obtained under the Multiplicative scheme for ease of comparison). Note that owing to the small number of folds, statistical significance cannot be calculated.

Performance across attribute-combination schemes – the Multiplicative scheme outperforms the Additive scheme in terms of *NDCG@K* for all values of K, and performs slightly better than the Additive scheme in terms of *FRecall@K* for $K \in \{1, 3, \text{all}\}$ (the schemes perform similarly for $K \in \{10, 20\}$).

Comparison with Unity – in terms of *NDCG@K*, SA outperforms Unity for all values of K under both attribute-combination schemes; and GA outperforms Unity for all values of K under the Additive scheme, and for $K \geq 3$ under the Multiplicative scheme. In terms of *FRecall@K*, SA outperforms Unity for all values of K under the Multiplicative scheme; GA performs better than Unity under the Multiplicative scheme for $K \geq 3$; and both SA and GA outperform Unity for $K \leq 10$ under the Additive scheme (all the schemes perform similarly for $K \in \{20, \text{all}\}$). It is worth noting the influence of the Additive scheme on Unity's performance in terms of *NDCG@K*, suggesting that Unity fails to find the correct interpretation more often than the other schemes or finds it at worse (higher) ranks.

SA versus GA – GA outperforms SA under the Additive scheme in terms of both performance metrics for $K = 1$, while SA outperforms GA in terms of *FRecall@*10. Under the Multiplicative scheme, SA performs better than GA in terms of *NDCG*@K for all values of K, and in terms of *FRecall*@K for $K \leq 3$. The algorithms perform similarly for the other values of K under both attribute-combination schemes.

Summary – SA's superior performance in terms of *NDCG*@K indicates that it finds the correct interpretations at lower (better) ranks than Unity and GA. GA's good performance on the training data, together with its slightly worse performance on the test data, suggests that GA over-fits the training data.

5.2 Experiment 2 – Development Set

The results of our first experiment show that the proposed weight-learning scheme for descriptive attributes and interpretation stages improves *Scusi?*'s performance. However, as seen in Table 1, speakers in this dataset used positional attributes in the vast majority of the descriptions, rarely using size. This influences the weights that were learned, in particular W_{siz}, as size had little effect on performance.

To address this issue, we conducted an experiment where we learned the weights on a handcrafted development dataset, and tested the performance of the three versions of our SLU system on the entire 341-dataset. The development dataset, denoted *62-dataset*, was designed to facilitate learning the influence of descriptive attributes on an SLU system's performance (assuming consistent ASR performance, the influence of the interpretation stages should be largely invariant across corpora). Thus, the descriptive attributes and combinations thereof are more evenly distributed in the development corpus than in the 341-dataset, but positional attributes still have a relatively high frequency. Table 2 displays the details of the descriptions in the 62-dataset and their attributes.

Despite the wider range of values considered for this experiment ($[1, 20]$), the weights learned by SA from the 62-dataset were only slightly different from those learned from the three training folds in the 341-dataset. In contrast, several of the weights learned by GA were in the high end of the range. This is partly explained by the fact that the genes in GA are randomly initialized from the entire range.

Table 2: Distribution of descriptive attributes over the 62-dataset.

Attribute	**Number (%)**
Lexicon, Colour	5 (8.06%)
Lexicon, Colour, Position	8 (12.90%)
Lexicon, Colour, Size	7 (11.30%)
Lexicon, Colour, Position, Size	8 (12.90%)
Lexicon, Position	20 (32.26%)
Lexicon, Position, Size	10 (16.13%)
Lexicon, Size	4 (6.45%)
Total	62 (100%)

Results

Figures 5 and 6 respectively display the average of *NDCG*@K and *FRecall*@K for $K \in \{1, 3, 10, 20, \text{all}\}$ under the Multiplicative and the Additive attribute-combination schemes. Statistical significance was calculated using the two-tailed Wilcoxon signed rank test, and reported for *p-value* ≤ 0.05.

Performance across attribute-combination schemes – the Multiplicative scheme outperforms the Additive scheme in terms of *NDCG*@K for all values of K (statistically significant with *p-value* $\ll 0.01$ for SA and Unity, and only for $K = 1$ for GA). In terms of *FRecall*@K, the Multiplicative scheme outperforms the Additive scheme for all values of K for SA (statistically significant for $K \leq 10$), for $K \leq 3$ for Unity (statistically significant), and for $K \in \{1, 3, \text{all}\}$ for GA (statistically significant for $K = 1$).

Comparison with Unity – SA outperforms Unity under the Multiplicative attribute-combination scheme (statistically significant for *NDCG*@K for $K \geq 3$ and for *FRecall*@3). Under the Additive scheme, SA outperforms Unity in terms of *NDCG*@K (statistically significant for $K \in \{1, 3, 10, \text{all}\}$), but in terms of *FRecall*@K, SA outperforms Unity only for $K \leq 3$ (statistically significant for $K = 1$). In contrast to SA, GA's performance was rather disappointing, with Unity outperforming GA under the Multiplicative scheme (statistically significant for *NDCG*@20), and GA slightly outperforming Unity under the Additive scheme only for $K \leq 3$.

SA versus GA – SA consistently outperforms GA under both attribute-combination schemes for both performance metrics (statistically significant for all values of K in terms of *NDCG*@K and for $K \leq 20$ in terms of *FRecall*@K under the Multi-

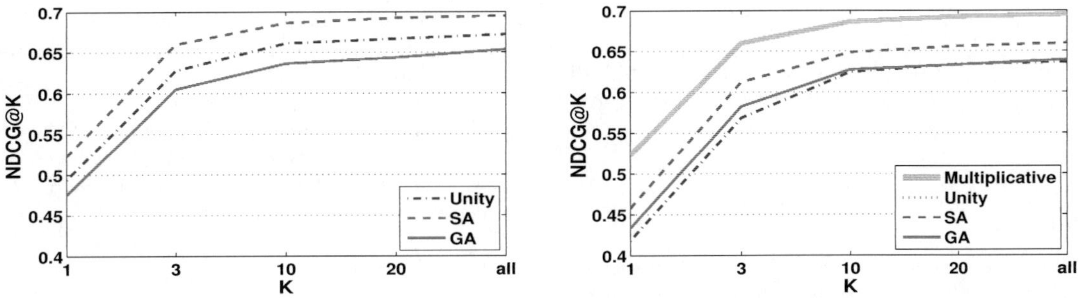

(a) Multiplicative scheme (b) Additive scheme

Figure 5: Average *NDCG*@K obtained from training on the 62-dataset (scale 0.4-0.7).

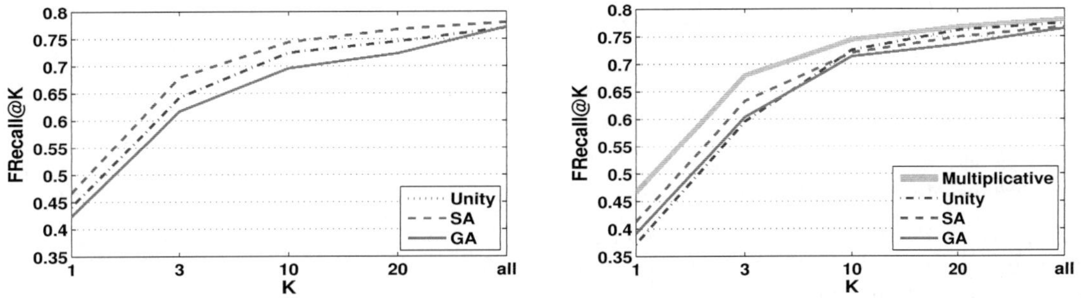

(a) Multiplicative scheme (b) Additive scheme

Figure 6: Average *FRecall*@K obtained from training on the 62-dataset (scale 0.35-0.8).

plicative scheme, and in terms of *NDCG*@K for $K \in \{3, 10, 20\}$ under the Additive scheme).

Summary – the results of this experiment are consistent with those of the cross-validation experiment in the superior performance of the Multiplicative attribute-combination scheme, and of SA under this scheme. However, in this experiment, SA consistently outperforms GA under the Additive scheme, Unity outperforms GA under the Multiplicative scheme, and GA and Unity perform similarly under the Additive scheme.

6 Conclusion

We have offered an approach for learning the weights associated with descriptive attributes and the stages of an interpretation for an N-best, probabilistic SLU system that understands referring expressions in a household context. In addition, we have compared two schemes for combining descriptive attributes: Multiplicative and Additive.

Our results show that in the context of our application, interpretation performance can be improved by assigning different weights to different interpretation stages and descriptive attributes. Specifically, the best performance was obtained using weights learned with SA under the Multiplicative attribute-combination scheme. However, the fact that different weights were obtained for each validation fold and for the development dataset indicates that the weights are sensitive to the training corpus, and a larger training corpus is required. Nonetheless, despite the differences in the learned weights, SA performed similarly across both datasets/training-regimes, as did Unity. In contrast, GA exhibited larger differences between the weights and results obtained for the two datasets/training-regimes, in particular for the Additive attribute-combination scheme. This, together with GA's excellent performance on the training data, especially in the cross-validation experiment, compared to its performance on the test data, suggests that GA may be over-fitting the training data.

We also found that performance was sensitive to the values of tunable system parameters, such as the number of interpretations generated per description (*Scusi?* was set to generate only 150 interpretations to reduce the run time of the learning algorithms). The effect of these values on performance requires further investigation, e.g., learning the values of the system's parameters together with the weights of the descriptive attributes and the interpretation stages, which in turn would pose additional challenges for the learning process.

Acknowledgments

This research was supported in part by grant DP110100500 from the Australian Research Council.

References

R. Dale and E. Reiter. 1995. Computational interpretations of the Gricean maxims in the generation of referring expressions. *Cognitive Science*, 18(2):233–263.

A. Gatt, I. van der Sluis, and K. van Deemter. 2007. Evaluating algorithms for the generation of referring expressions using a balanced corpus. In *ENLG07 – Proceedings of the 11th European Workshop on Natural Language Generation*, pages 49–56, Saarbrücken, Germany.

T. Herrmann and W. Deutsch. 1976. *Psychologie der Objektbenennung*. Hans Huber.

K. Järvelin and J. Kekäläinen. 2002. Cumulated gain-based evaluation of IR techniques. *ACM Transactions on Information Systems (TOIS)*, 20(4):422–446.

Th. Kleinbauer, I. Zukerman, and S.N. Kim. 2013. Evaluation of the *Scusi?* spoken language interpretation system – A case study. In *IJCNLP2013 – Proceedings of the 6th International Joint Conference on Natural Language Processing*, pages 225–233, Nagoya, Japan.

E. Krahmer and K. van Deemter. 2012. Computational generation of referring expressions: A survey. *Computational Linguistics*, 38(1):173–218.

G.-J. Kruijff, P. Lison, T. Benjamin, H. Jacobsson, and N. Hawes. 2007. Incremental, multi-level processing for comprehending situated dialogue in human-robot interaction. In *LangRo'2007 – Proceedings from the Symposium on Language and Robots*, pages 509–514, Aveiro, Portugal.

W.J.M. Levelt. 1989. *Speaking: from Intention to Articulation*. MIT Press.

M. Mitchell, K. van Deemter, and E. Reiter. 2011. Two approaches for generating size modifiers. In *ENLG2011 – Proceedings of the 13th European Workshop on Natural Language Generation*, pages 63–70, Nancy, France.

J. Pearl. 1988. *Probabilistic Reasoning in Intelligent Systems*. Morgan Kaufmann Publishers, San Mateo, California.

T. Pechmann. 1989. Incremental speech production and referential overspecification. *Linguistics*, 27:89–110.

J.F. Sowa. 1984. *Conceptual Structures: Information Processing in Mind and Machine*. Addison-Wesley, Reading, MA.

K. van Deemter. 2006. Generating referring expressions that involve gradable properties. *Computational Linguistics*, 32(2):195–222.

I. Zukerman, E. Makalic, M. Niemann, and S. George. 2008. A probabilistic approach to the interpretation of spoken utterances. In *PRICAI 2008 – Proceedings of the 10th Pacific Rim International Conference on Artificial Intelligence*, pages 581–592, Hanoi, Vietnam.

Developing a Sina Weibo Incident Monitor for Disasters

Bella Robinson* bella.robinson@csiro.au
Hua Bai*,** hua.bai@csiro.au
Robert Power* robert.power@csiro.au
Xunguo Lin* xunguo.lin@csiro.au

* CSIRO Digital Productivity Flagship
G.P.O. Box 664
Canberra, ACT 2601, Australia

** School of Management
Harbin Institute of Technology
92 Xidazhi Street, Harbin,
Heilongjiang, China, 150001

Abstract

This paper presents ongoing work to develop an earthquake detector based on near-real-time microblog messages from China. The system filters earthquake related keywords from Sina Weibo messages available on the public timeline and uses a classifier to determine if the messages correspond to people experiencing an earthquake. We describe how the classifier has been established and report preliminary results of successfully using it as a detector for earthquake events in China.

We also provide an overview of how we have accessed messages in Chinese from Sina Weibo, including a summary of their structure and content. We note our experience of processing this text with Natural Language Processing packages and describe a preliminary web site for users to view the processed messages.

Our long term aim is to develop a general alert and monitoring system for various disaster event types in China reported by the public on Sina Weibo. This first case study provides a working example from which an 'all hazards' system can be developed over time.

1 Introduction

Natural disasters are a major cause of loss and damage to both lives and properties around the world. Many disasters impact regions and populations with little warning which is made worse by the projected impacts of climate change and increasing urbanization of the world's population. For these reasons, it is important to enhance the ability and effectiveness of emergency management.

One of the pressing challenges while managing an emergency or crisis event is the collection and communication of reliable, relevant and up to date information. Timely, accurate and effective messages play a vital role for disaster response. For emergencies, a rapid response is needed to make effective decisions and to mitigate serious damage. Losses can be reduced by providing information to both rescue organizations and potential victims.

Microblogging services have proven to be a useful source of information to emergency managers to gain first hand information about disaster events from the community experiencing them (Abel et al., 2012; Cameron et al., 2012; Chowdhury et al., 2013; Zhou et al., 2013). This new source of information can be used by emergency coordinators and responders to provide appropriate services to the affected area. It can also be used by the wider community to seek timely information about the event and as a means of engaging with the unfolding situation from a safe distance.

Work to date has focused predominantly on Twitter as the social media microblogging source. This service is not available in China and we wanted to explore processing techniques using messages from Sina Weibo, the Chinese equivalent to Twitter. Our initial task is to identify earthquake events and this investigation is the first step in developing a general alert and monitoring system for disaster events in China.

The rest of the paper is organised as follows. First (§2) background material is provided to motivate this investigation with a focus on China. This includes how emergency events are currently managed in China, the current use of social media services there and Sina Weibo in particular. We then provide an overview of the issues of processing Chinese text (§3) and present related work (§4). This is followed by a description of the problem (§5) and details of building the classifier (§6). We conclude with a discussion of building a prototype

Bella Robinson, Hua Bai, Robert Power and Xunguo Lin. 2014. Developing a Sina Weibo Incident Monitor for Disasters. In *Proceedings of Australasian Language Technology Association Workshop*, pages 59−68.

earthquake detection web site and planned future work (§7) and a discussion of our findings (§8).

2 Background

2.1 Motivation

As social media, especially microblogging services, become more pervasive, information can be produced, retrieved and spread more quickly and conveniently than ever before. The importance of advanced information and communication technologies has been verified by recent disaster events. For example, during the Asian Tsunami that devastated many coastal regions of Thailand and other countries in 2004, first-hand information came from online services, including news reports, rescue efforts, victims experience and emotional responses (Leidner et al., 2009).

In October 2013, hurricane 'Fitow' was accompanied by heavy rain resulting in flash flooding in Yuyao City, China causing communication blackouts and the destruction of traffic infrastructure. This resulted in rescuers not being able to access flooded areas with several towns becoming 'lonely islands'[1]. With landline communication disconnected, online social media provided an important medium for information dissemination. According to a report from the organisation Kdnet Cloud Intelligence System (KCIS), who report on Chinese Internet usage, there were more than 300,000 queries for the phrase 'Yuyao flood' on the Sina Weibo platform during the week of the event[2]. This Chinese microblogging platform was used by many people to send messages and spread information asking for help and noting their trapped location by commenting on the government's Weibo account @YuyaoPublication. This information was helpful for the rescue workers.

More generally, research from the American Red Cross (2012) showed that 20% of American citizens obtained emergency information from a mobile application, 76% would expect help to arrive in less than three hours of posting a request on social media and 40% would inform friends and loved ones they were safe if impacted by an emergency event. Similar findings (Thelwall and Stuart, 2007) note that Web 2.0 technologies were used world wide as a source of information to determine the status of an unfolding emergency situation. For example, if loved ones are safe, what the ongoing risks are, the official response activities and to emotionally connect to the event.

[1] http://www.guancha.cn/local/2013_10_09_177085.shtml

[2] http://www.kcis.cn/4409

2.2 Emergency Management in China

The Chinese central government established the Emergency Management Office (EMO) in December 2005 (Bai, 2008) to provide integrated emergency management. It was established, along with associated laws, after the 2003 SARS epidemic and is responsible for emergency planning, natural disasters, technological accidents, public sanitation issues, security concerns, and recovery and reconstruction activities.

The EMO has a coordination role between many government agencies such as the Ministry of Civil Affairs, State Administration of Work Safety, Ministry of Public Security, Ministry of Health and other related agencies. Under the central government, all local governments follow the same structure to establish a province or city level EMO. This local level EMO has authority to coordinate between corresponding local government agencies to coordinate the emergency response, disaster relief and recovery activities as required.

In China, emergency events are classified into four levels corresponding to the required government involvement:

- Level 4, small case, less than 3 fatalities, manage at the local level.
- Level 3, major incident, 3 to 10 fatalities, escalate to city level.
- Level 2, serious, between 10 and 30 fatalities, escalate to province level.
- Level 1, extremely serious, over 30 fatalities, escalate to the state council.

2.3 Use of Social Media in China

China is the world's most populous country and second largest by land area after Russia. Recent rapid economic and technological developments have resulted in more Chinese people having access to computers or mobile phones which are used increasingly to exchange information via microblogging services. By the end of 2013, the number of users of microblogging services in China reached 281 million, with nearly 70% of users (approximately 196 million people) accessing their accounts via mobile phone (China Internet Network Information Centre, 2014). This large user group provides an opportunity to study Chinese microblogging for the purposes of situation awareness of disaster events.

2.4 Sina Weibo

Sina Weibo (now trading as the Weibo Corporation) is the most influential Chinese microblogging service (Wang et al., 2014). It was established in August 2009 by the Sina Company, one of the largest news web portal and blog services in China, in response to the government blocking access to popular social media sites such as Twitter and Facebook in July 2009, due to riots in Ürümqi.

Sina Weibo has more than 156 million active users per month and more than 69 million active users per day[3]. Sina Weibo is similar to Twitter, providing user services to create content and manage their accounts with access available from mobile devices. An Application Programming Interface (API) exists as a number of Restful Web Service endpoints to access content by providing query parameters with results returned as JSON.

3 Processing Chinese Text

3.1 Segmentation

The main difficulty with processing Chinese text is the lack of whitespace between words. Automatic word segmentation on Chinese text has been an active research topic for many years (Sproat and Shih, 1990; Chen and Liu, 1992; Nie et al., 1996; Foo and Li, 2004; Gao et al., 2005) resulting in numerous software tools. Examples include the Stanford Word Segmenter, the IK Analyzer and Microsoft's S-MSRSeg. For our classification experiments we used the ansj_seg [4] tool which is a Java implementation of the hierarchical hidden Markov model based Chinese lexical analyzer ICTCLAS (Zhang et al., 2003).

3.2 Traditional and Simplified Chinese

In mainland China, Simplified Chinese replaced Traditional Chinese in 1964 with Traditional Chinese still used in Taiwan, Hong Kong and Macau. The difference is mostly with the characters, with, as the name suggests, the Simplified Chinese characters being simpler. The same grammar and sentence structure are used for both. The main method of dealing with Traditional Chinese text is to initially convert it to Simplified Chinese. For example, 'injured' in Simplified Chinese is 伤 while in Traditional Chinese it is 傷.

3.3 Word Difficulties

Polysemous words, synonyms and variant words are particularly difficult to handle when processing Chinese text.

Polysemous words are where one word has multiple meanings which can only be resolved by context. Word sense disambiguation should be able to address this issue however this has been difficult for Chinese text due to a lack of large scale and high quality Chinese word sense annotated corpus. Similarly, synonyms are also an issue where many Chinese words are different in terms of sound and written text, but they have the same meaning.

There are numerous Chinese words that are written differently but they have the same pronunciation and meaning. For example, 唯 and 惟 are pronounced the same and both mean 'unique'. These variant words can be considered the same as synonyms and treated similarly.

Chinese synonym lists have been compiled (Jiaju, 1986; Zhendong and Qiang, 1998) which are useful however in practice auto-identification algorithms are preferred, such as the Pattern Matching Algorithm (Yong and Yanqing, 2006), Link Structure and Co-occurrence Analysis (Fang et al., 2009), and Multiple Hybrid Strategies (Lu et al., 2009).

3.4 Stop Word Lists

Stop word removal is a common pre-processing step for text analysis where stop word lists can be predefined or learned. Zou et al. (2006) describe an automatic Chinese stop word extraction method based on statistic and information theory and Hao and Hao (2008) define a weighted Chi-squared statistic based on $2 * p$ contingency table measure in order to automatically identify potential stop words for a Chinese corpus. The downside to these automatic methods is that they are computationally expensive and reliant on a specific training corpus, and so predefined stop word lists are often used instead.

There are five popular Chinese stop words lists predominantly in use (Tingting et al., 2012): Harbin Institute of Technology (includes 263 symbols/punctuation characters and 504 Chinese words); Baidu (includes 263 symbols/punctuations, 547 English words and 842

[3] http://ir.weibo.com/phoenix.zhtml?c=253076&p=irol-newsArticle&ID=1958713

[4] https://github.com/ansjsun/ansj_seg

Chinese words); Sichuan University Machine Intelligent Lab (includes 975 Chinese words); Chinese stop word list (a combination of the previous three mentioned above, includes 73 symbols/punctuations, 1113 Chinese words and 9 numbers); Kevin Bouge Chinese (includes 125 Chinese words). These lists have different features with none considered authoritative. For our work we have used the fourth list mentioned above[5], a combination of the first three.

4 Related Work

4.1 Emergency Event Detection

With the popularity of the Internet, many countries have developed disaster event detection systems. For example, earthquake detectors such as 'Did You Feel It?'[6] and 'Toretter' (Sakaki et al., 2013; Sakaki et al., 2010), make use of Web 2.0 technologies and can detect earthquakes via user reports, media news and other official information.

'Twitcident' (Abel et al., 2012) monitors Tweets targeting large gatherings of people for purposes of crowd management by focusing on specific locations and incident types. 'Tweet4act' (Chowdhury et al., 2013) performs a similar function by using keyword search to identify relevant Tweets which are then filtered using text classification techniques to categorise them into pre-incident, during-incident and post-incident classes.

There are other systems as well, 'CrisisTracker' (Rogstadius et al., 2013), the Ushahidi platform (used by volunteers during the Haiti earthquake (Heinzelman and Waters, 2010) and Hurricane Sandy[7]) and the Emergency Situation Awareness system (Power et al., 2014) which provides all-hazard situation awareness information for emergency managers from Twitter.

Since the Wenchuan earthquake in China on 12 September 2008, also known as the 2008 Sichuan earthquake, researchers began to pay more attention to Twitter's role during disaster events. Sakaki et al have developed and improved a real-time report and early warning management system using Twitter (Sakaki et al., 2013; Sakaki et al., 2010). The U.S. Geological Survey (USGS) have designed the Twitter Earthquake Detector (Earle et al., 2012) based on the ratio of the short term average of word frequencies to their long term average, referred to as the STA/LTA algorithm. In Australia, a Twitter based earthquake detector has been developed and is used by the Joint Australian Tsunami Warning Centre (JATWC) (Robinson et al., 2013b; Robinson et al., 2013a). Similarly, the Earthquake Alert and Report System (EARS) (Avvenuti et al., 2014) also uses Twitter to detect earthquake events and determine damage assessments of earthquakes in Italy.

All of these systems focus on Twitter with little attention paid to messages originating from China. Two notable exceptions are described below.

4.2 Emergency Event Detection in China

Qu et al. (2011) examined Sina Weibo messages posted after the 2010 Yushu earthquake. They collected and analysed 94,101 microblog posts and 41,817 re-posts during the 48-day period immediately after the earthquake. Two keyword search queries were used to gather the data: 玉树+地震 (Yushu AND earthquake) and 青海+地震 (Qinghai AND earthquake). They then performed three types of analysis: content analysis where they categorised the messages into four groups of informational, action-related, opinion-related and emotion-related; trend analysis where they examined the distribution of different message categories over time; and information spread analysis where they examined the reposting paths of disaster related messages.

Zhou et al. (2013) also analysed Sina Weibo messages related to the Yushu earthquake. They used a naive Bayes classifier to partition messages into five groups: 'fire brigade', 'police force', 'ambulance services', 'government' and 'other', aiming to help emergency organisations respond more efficiently during an emergency. They do not, however, provide methods for event detection.

5 The Problem

5.1 Overview

The task is to filter messages published on Sina Weibo that include earthquake related keywords or phrases and refine them using a classifier to identify those that relate to actual earthquake events being felt. There are a number of secondary aims also, mainly around reliably accessing and processing messages published on Sina Weibo. There are differences between Chinese and English for the purposes of Natural Language Processing and

[5] http://www.datatang.com/data/19300

[6] http://earthquake.usgs.gov/earthquakes/dyfi/

[7] https://sandydc.crowdmap.com/

we want to explore these in detail. While there are studies of Chinese text classification (Luo et al., 2011; Yen et al., 2010; He et al., 2000), few of them focus on short text microblog messages, especially supporting disaster response.

Our long term aim is to assess the utility of Sina Weibo as a new and relevant source of information for emergency managers to help with disaster response for different kinds of disaster events.

5.2 Preliminary Work

A user account is needed to obtain messages from the public timeline using the Open Weibo API. We had to register using a smart phone app since web browsers on a desktop failed to render the web site correctly, making user interactions ineffective. The Open Weibo API[8] provides instructions in Chinese on using the API. The 'Translate to English' feature of the Chrome web browser was used since information available on their English pages appeared to be out of date.

The API has a number of endpoints but some are not available to 'default' users. To obtain content relating to earthquakes from Sina Weibo, the search/topics endpoint could be used to get messages containing certain keywords, but this is restricted. Similarly, the place/nearby_timeline also appeared useful, but it has a maximum search radius of 11,132 metres and only returns geotagged messages. Note that this search radius limit appears to be arbitrary.

The public timeline endpoint appeared the most useful[9]. It returns the most recent 200 public messages. With a rate limit of 150 requests per hour, this endpoint is polled every 24 seconds. Our system was implemented as a Java program and the Weibo4J[10] library was used for calling the Open Weibo API. Weibo4J has a simple interface and handles the OAuth authentication required to interact with the API.

The JSON message structure is similar to that from Twitter. Each message has a unique identifier, user information (user_id, a picture, thumbnail, name, description, URL, gender), a timestamp of when the message was created, the message text, the source (application) used to send the message, the user's location (province, city, location and coordinates when provided), the user's language setting (over 98% of our messages retrieved have the ISO-639 code zh-cn, which indicates simplified Chinese characters) and so on.

[8] http://open.weibo.com/wiki/%E5%BE%AE%E5%8D%9AAPI

[9] http://open.weibo.com/wiki/2/statuses/public_timeline

[10] https://code.google.com/p/weibo4j/

5.3 Message Summary

After initial experimentation, our system has been continuously retrieving messages from the public timeline since 29 August 2014 at a rate of around 470 messages per minute, or around 28,000 per hour as shown in Figure 1. Note the dips which were due to Internet outages. By the end of October 2014, over 42 million messages have been processed.

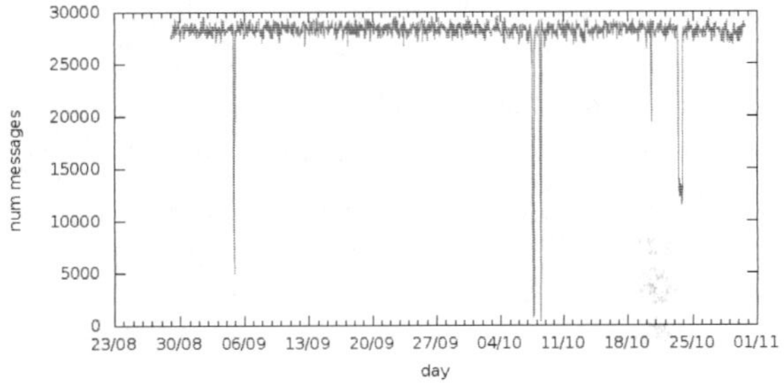

Figure 1: Hourly message counts.

Assuming there are around 90 million messages posted each day[11], this means the default rate limitations for accessing the public timeline is only providing approximately 0.8% of all messages posted. While this is only a small fraction of the content available, it is enough to detect events reported by users, as will be demonstrated below.

6 Building the Earthquake Classifier

We used the Support Vector Machine (SVM) (Joachims, 1998) method for text classification to help identify Sina Weibo messages that report feeling an earthquake. The LIBSVM (Chang and Lin, 2011) software, configured with the linear kernel function, was used to perform C-support vector classification (C-SVC) for this purpose. In this section, we describe the method used to train an SVM classifier. Relevant training data was collected and labelled (§6.1) and a range of message features to use was explored (§6.2) using ten-fold cross validation to find the most accurate feature combination.

[11] http://ir.weibo.com/phoenix.zhtml?c=253076&p=irol-products

(+)	地震地震！	Earthquake, earthquake!
(+)	原来大家都感觉到地震啦！……瞬间头好晕	Everyone felt the earthquake! Feel dizzy ......
(+)	哪里地震了？	Where is the earthquake?
(-)	2010年全球地震一览http://sinaurl.cn/hEQH1	2010 Global Earthquakes List: `http://sinaurl.cn/hEQH1`
(-)	那地震带会改变吗？ //@薛蛮子: 科普	Will the seismic zone move? @ Xue Manzi: science
(-)	唐山地震碑林 24万人啊[泪]	Tangshan Earthquake Memorial, 240,000 people perished [tears]

Table 1: Example positive (+) and negative (-) Messages containing the phrase 'earthquake' (地震).

6.1 Training Data

The first task was to assemble a training dataset. Up to 1,000 messages from around 50,000 high scoring users were obtained. Sina Weibo attributes a user score based on their activity: the number of messages posted, comments made, friends and followers, reposted messages and so on. Not all of these users had 1,000 messages available and so a total of around 25 million were obtained. The date range for this data was February 2012 to July 2013 which was collected by a colleague with a higher level of Sina Weibo access than we do.

The messages were then filtered to those containing the word earthquake: 地震, reducing the number of messages to 21,396. To find positive examples, these messages were further filtered by only including those posted an hour after the time of known earthquake events in 2012 and 2013[12], as listed in Table 2, reducing the number to 3,549.

Location	Date/Time	Mag	Messages
Pingtung, Taiwan	26/2/12 10:34	6.0	8
Yilan, Taiwan	10/6/12 05:00	5.7	6
Xinyuan, Xinjiang	30/6/12 05:07	6.6	9
Dengta, Liaoning	23/1/13 12:18	5.1	50
Nantou, Taiwan	27/3/13 10:03	6.4	61
Lushan, Sichuan	20/4/13 08:02	7.0	228
Tongliao, Inner Mongolia	22/4/13 17:11	5.3	24
Nantou, Taiwan	02/6/13 13:43	6.7	56
Minxian, Gansu	22/7/13 07:45	6.7	25

Table 2: Earthquake events.

Next, the messages were manually examined to find positive examples of someone experiencing an earthquake. This task was performed by the two Chinese speaking authors with their individual results compared and mutual agreement reached. 467 such messages were found and the events they are associated with are indicated in Table 2. Then a collection of the same size (467) of negative messages was similarly assembled. Note that there were numerous repeated messages (reposts) such as news reports and shared prayers. For these messages only a single representative example was included with the others excluded. A sample of positive and negative messages can be seen in Table 1 where the original message in Chinese is shown, followed by a translation.

[12]`http://www.csi.ac.cn/manage/eqDown/`

6.2 Feature Selection

A range of message features were explored when developing the earthquake classifier: character count, word count, user mention count, hash tag count, hyperlink count, question mark count, exclamation mark count and unigrams (word n-grams of size 1).

In order to generate the SVM feature vector for each message the following steps were carried out:

1. Count the number of characters, user mentions, hash tags, hyperlinks, question marks and exclamation marks in the message.

2. Remove punctuation and replace hashtags, user mentions and hyperlinks with a constant string value (e.g. 'TAG').

3. Perform text segmentation, again using ansj_seg [4], recording the number of tokens produced; the 'word count'.

4. Remove stop words and tokens introduced at step 2 to produce the final set of unigrams, which includes the original hashtag tokens, but not user mentions or hyperlinks.

By examining the training messages, the positive ones seemed shorter, frequently contained exclamation marks and keywords such as 'shake' (摇, 摇动) 'felt' (感, 感觉) and 'scared' (惊, 惊慌). To be certain that we didn't miss an important but less obvious feature we ran an exhaustive ten-fold cross validation process using all possible combinations of features; $2^8 - 1 = 255$ iterations in total. A selection of the results are shown in Table 3. The simple accuracy measure, which is the percentage of correct classifications, and the F_1, precision and recall scores have all been calculated. The best combination of features, indicated by the dagger† and in bold in Table 3, was char count, link count, question mark count, exclamation mark count and unigrams. However the accuracy for this combination is only marginally better than unigrams by themselves.

Features	Accuracy	F_1 Score	Precision	Recall
unigrams	87.4%	0.876	0.862	0.893
exclamation	54.5%	0.418	0.580	0.334
question	49.6%	0.661	0.498	0.983
hyperlink	49.9%	0.445	0.498	0.573
hashtag	50.1%	0.608	0.549	0.891
user mention	50.6%	0.519	0.546	0.728
char count	64.7%	0.688	0.615	0.782
word count	63.2%	0.680	0.601	0.784
all features	88.0%	0.881	0.874	0.891
best combo†	**88.9%**	**0.890**	**0.881**	**0.902**

Table 3: Feature combination results.

6.3 Training Set Size

While the best F_1 and accuracy measures appear to be very good, we were unsure whether we had used enough training data for this process. In order to see the effect of different training set sizes we ran an experiment where the size of the training set was adjusted. For this experiment, we performed ten-fold cross validation on incrementally larger sets of training data, from 10% (84 messages) to 100% (934 messages). The results are shown in Figure 2. The features used for this experiment were the best combination identified by the feature selection process.

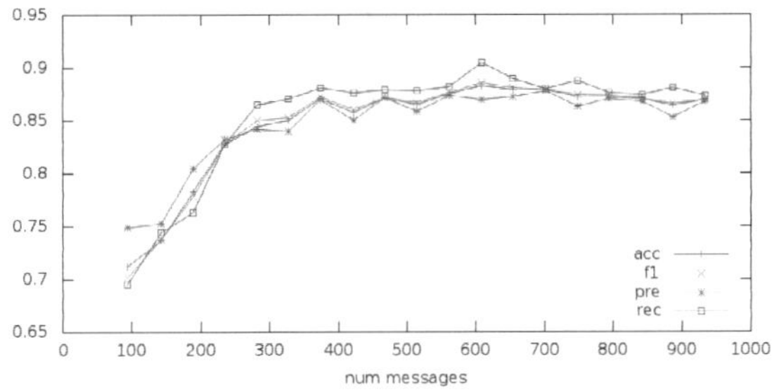

Figure 2: Adjusting the training set size.

While improvement is achieved up to the 300 message mark, only small gains are achieved after that. The maximum accuracy measure is reached at the 600 message mark, although that has a slightly larger variation between the precision and recall than the results achieved with larger training sets. It appears that the results have plateaued, which likely indicates that additional data would not improve the classifier's accuracy with the feature set we have chosen.

7 Developing an Incident Monitor

7.1 The SWIM Web Application

In order to easily view the Sina Weibo messages a web application was developed[13]. Recent messages from a selected city or province can be viewed as well as messages containing the earthquake keyword 地震. The classifier is used on the earthquake messages to highlight the positive messages, including the probability (as calculated by LIBSVM) that the message is positive. A 7-day timeline chart is also included for the earthquake messages to show if there have been any recent spikes in earthquake activity.

Figure 3 shows the web application displaying earthquake messages. The spike in the timeline chart corresponds to a 4.3M earthquake which occurred about 100km from Beijing at 18:37:41 on 6 September 2014[14]. The first positively classified message related to this event has the timestamp 18:38:24, a delay of 43 seconds. This message is followed by 55 positively (all true) and 3 negatively (1 false) classified earthquake messages in the next five minutes. Note that the messages are in reverse chronological order so the older messages are at the bottom of the page. Also, the 'Translate to English' feature of the Chrome browser has been used to translate the messages and user identifying features have been redacted.

7.2 Further Work

China is affected by a variety of natural disasters, not only earthquakes. We would like to repeat our earthquake classifier experiments to analyse messages relating to typhoon and flooding events in particular.

An earthquake detector will be developed triggered by a burst of messages containing the keyword 地震 (earthquake) which are positively classified and originate from the same geographic region. Very few messages are geotagged with exact coordinates, so we will need to approximate most message locations based on their user profile location settings (city, province and location). When an earthquake is detected, the Sina Weibo message collector can be 'zoomed' to gather messages from the affected region providing more information about the severity and impact of the earthquake.

[13]http://swim.csiro.au/

[14]http://www.csndmc.ac.cn/newweb/secondpage.jsp?id=1471

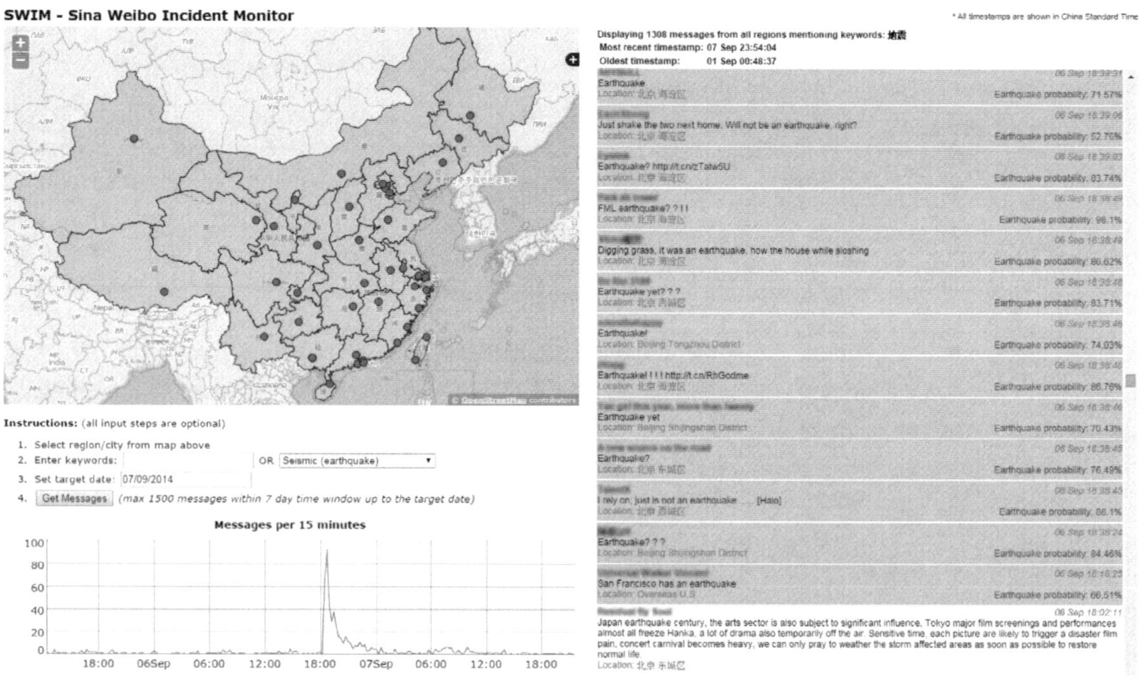

Figure 3: The Sina Weibo Incident Monitor (SWIM) Web Application

8 Conclusion

We have conducted a focused experiment to examine the feasibility of using messages from Sina Weibo to detect earthquake events. This was done by sampling messages provided on the public timeline, filtering messages that contain the keyword 'earthquake' (地震) and using a classifier to determine if messages are reports from users experiencing an earthquake.

The classifier was trained using a sample of 934 messages with an even split of positive and negative messages obtained from 'high scoring' Sina Weibo users posted soon after actual earthquake events. A comprehensive feature set was explored, with the best combination being character count, link count, question mark count, exclamation mark count and unigrams resulting in an accuracy of 88.9% and an F_1 score of 0.890.

A web site has been developed to prototype our earthquake detector. This allows users to focus on a particular province or city of interest in China or to show all messages recently posted on the public timeline. Messages containing the keyword 'earthquake' (地震) can be filtered on the display with those being positively classified highlighted in red along with an indication of the classification confidence. By correctly classifying a burst of positive messages related to the 4.3 magnitude earthquake on 6 September 2014 in Zhangjiakou City in Hebei Province, we believe that timely earthquake detection is feasible.

Future work will include setting up a notification system to report detected earthquake events; exploring the use of different training datasets with a view to improving classification accuracy; ranking messages based on a classifier's prediction of confidence to improve how notifications are interpreted; including further natural language processing techniques such as named entity recognisers, word sense disambiguation and part of speech tagging; and extending the type of events detected to include other emergency management scenarios, such as fires, typhoons and floods.

Acknowledgements

The second author, Hua Bai, thanks the China Scholarship Council for financial support and CSIRO for hosting the research project. Thanks also go to Prof. Guang Yu (School of Management Harbin Institute of Technology) and Xianyun Tian (PhD student of School of Management Harbin Institute of Technology) for providing the Sina Weibo datasets used for training the classifiers.

Hua Bai is a joint PhD student of the Harbin Institute of Technology and CSIRO.

References

Fabian Abel, Claudia Hauff, Geert-Jan Houben, Richard Stronkman, and Ke Tao. 2012. Twitcident: Fighting fire with information from social web streams. In *Proceedings of the 21st International Conference Companion on World Wide Web*, WWW '12 Companion, pages 305–308, Lyon, France. ACM.

American Red Cross. 2012. More Americans using mobile apps in emergencies. `http://www.redcross.org/news/press-release/More-Americans-Using-Mobile-Apps-in-Emergencies`, August. Accessed: 2 September 2014.

Marco Avvenuti, Stefano Cresci, Andrea Marchetti, Carlo Meletti, and Maurizio Tesconi. 2014. Ears (Earthquake Alert and Report System): A real time decision support system for earthquake crisis management. In *Proceedings of the 20th ACM SIGKDD International Conference on Knowledge Discovery and Data Mining*, KDD '14, pages 1749–1758, New York, New York, USA. ACM.

Victor Bai. 2008. Emergency management in China. `http://www.training.fema.gov/EMIWeb/edu/Comparative%20EM%20Book%20-%20Chapter%20-%20Emergency%20Management%20in%20China.doc`. Accessed: 5 September 2014.

Mark A. Cameron, Robert Power, Bella Robinson, and Jie Yin. 2012. Emergency situation awareness from Twitter for crisis management. In *Proceedings of the 21st International Conference Companion on World Wide Web*, WWW '12 Companion, pages 695–698, Lyon, France. ACM.

Chih-Chung Chang and Chih-Jen Lin. 2011. LIBSVM: A library for support vector machines. *ACM Transactions on Intelligent Systems and Technology*, 2:27:1–27:27. Software available at `http://www.csie.ntu.edu.tw/~cjlin/libsvm`.

Keh-Jiann Chen and Shing-Huan Liu. 1992. Word identification for Mandarin Chinese sentences. In *Proceedings of the 14th Conference on Computational Linguistics - Volume 1*, COLING '92, pages 101–107, Nantes, France. Association for Computational Linguistics.

China Internet Network Information Centre. 2014. The 33rd statistical report on internet development in China. `http://www.redcross.org/news/press-release/More-Americans-Using-Mobile-Apps-in-Emergencies`, January. Accessed: 29 August 2014.

Soudip Roy Chowdhury, Muhammad Imran, Muhammad Rizwan Asghar, Sihem Amer-Yahia, and Carlos Castillo. 2013. Tweet4act: Using incident-specific profiles for classifying crisis-related messages. In *The 10th International Conference on Information Systems for Crisis Response and Management (ISCRAM)*, Baden-Baden, Germany, May.

Paul S. Earle, Daniel C. Bowden, and Michelle Guy. 2012. Twitter earthquake detection: Earthquake monitoring in a social world. *Annals of GeoPhysics*, 54(6):708–715.

Huang Fang, Liu Youhua, Zhang Kezhuang, and Li Yin. 2009. Automatic recognition of Chinese synonyms using link structure and co-occurrence analysis. *Journal of Modern Information*, 29(8):125–127.

Schubert Foo and Hui Li. 2004. Chinese word segmentation and its effect on information retrieval. *Information Processing & Management*, 40(1):161 – 190.

Jianfeng Gao, Mu Li, Andi Wu, and Chang-Ning Huang. 2005. Chinese word segmentation and named entity recognition: A pragmatic approach. *Comput. Linguist.*, 31(4):531–574, December.

Lili Hao and Lizhu Hao. 2008. Automatic identification of stop words in Chinese text classification. In *Computer Science and Software Engineering, 2008 International Conference on*, volume 1, pages 718–722. IEEE.

Ji He, Ah-Hwee Tan, and Chew Lim Tan. 2000. A comparative study on Chinese text categorization methods. In *PRICAI Workshop on Text and Web Mining*, volume 35.

Jessica Heinzelman and Carol Waters. 2010. Crowdsourcing crisis information in disaster-affected Haiti. Technical report, United States Institute of Peace, Washington DC, USA, September.

Mei Jiaju. 1986. The function and formation of semantic systems: A new Chinese thesaurus of synonyms. *Multilingua*, 5(4):205–209, December.

Thorsten Joachims. 1998. Text categorization with suport vector machines: Learning with many relevant features. In *Proceedings of the 10th European Conference on Machine Learning*, ECML '98, pages 137–142, London, UK, UK. Springer-Verlag.

Dorothy E. Leidner, Gary Pan, and Shan L. Pan. 2009. The role of IT in crisis response: Lessons from the SARS and Asian tsunami disasters. *J. Strateg. Inf. Syst.*, 18(2):80–99.

Yong Lu, Chengzhi Zhang, and Hanqing Hou. 2009. Using multiple hybrid strategies to extract Chinese synonyms from encyclopedia resource. *Innovative Computing ,Information and Control, International Conference on*, 0:1089–1093.

Xi Luo, Wataru Ohyama, Tetsushi Wakabayashi, and Fumitaka Kimura. 2011. A study on automatic Chinese text classification. In *Document Analysis and Recognition (ICDAR), 2011 International Conference on*, pages 920–924. IEEE.

Jian-Yun Nie, Martin Brisebois, and Xiaobo Ren. 1996. On Chinese text retrieval. In *Proceedings of the 19th Annual International ACM SIGIR Conference on Research and Development in Information Retrieval*, SIGIR '96, pages 225–233, Zurich, Switzerland. ACM.

Robert Power, Bella Robinson, John Colton, and Mark Cameron. 2014. Emergency situation awareness: Twitter case studies. In *Proceedings of the 1st International Conference, ISCRAM-med*, volume 196 of *LNBIP*, pages 218–231, Toulouse, France, October. Springer International Publishing.

Yan Qu, Chen Huang, Pengyi Zhang, and Jun Zhang. 2011. Microblogging after a major disaster in China: A case study of the 2010 Yushu earthquake. In *Proceedings of the ACM 2011 conference on Computer supported cooperative work*, pages 25–34. ACM.

Bella Robinson, Robert Power, and Mark Cameron. 2013a. An evidence based earthquake detector using Twitter. In *Proceedings of the Workshop on Language Processing and Crisis Information 2013*, pages 1–9, Nagoya, Japan, October. Asian Federation of Natural Language Processing.

Bella Robinson, Robert Power, and Mark Cameron. 2013b. A sensitive Twitter earthquake detector. In *Proceedings of the 22nd International Conference Companion on World Wide Web*, WWW '13 Companion, pages 999–1002, Rio de Janeiro, Brazil. International World Wide Web Conferences Steering Committee.

Jakob Rogstadius, Maja Vukovic, Claudio Teixeira, Vassilis Kostakos, Evangelos Karapanos, and Jim Laredo. 2013. Crisistracker: Crowdsourced social media curation for disaster awareness. *IBM Journal of Research and Development*, 57(5):4:1–4:13, Sept.

Takeshi Sakaki, Makoto Okazaki, and Yutaka Matsuo. 2010. Earthquake shakes Twitter users: Real-time event detection by social sensors. In *Proceedings of the 19th International Conference Companion on World Wide Web*, WWW '10 Companion, pages 851–860, Raleigh, North Carolina, USA. ACM.

Takeshi Sakaki, Makoto Okazaki, and Yutaka Matsuo. 2013. Tweet analysis for real-time event detection and earthquake reporting system development. *IEEE Transactions on Knowledge and Data Engineering*, 25(4):919–931.

Richard Sproat and Chilin Shih. 1990. A statistical method for finding word boundaries in Chinese text. *Computer Processing of Chinese and Oriental Languages*, 4(4):336–351.

Mike Thelwall and David Stuart. 2007. RUOK? Blogging communication technologies during crises. *J. Computer-Mediated Communication*, 12(2):523–548.

Zhuang Tingting, Wang Ping, and Cheng Qikai. 2012. Temporal related topic detection approach on microblog. *Journal of Information Resources Management*, 3:40–46.

Ning Wang, James She, and Junting Chen. 2014. How "Big vs" dominate Chinese microblog: A comparison of verified and unverified users on Sina Weibo. In *Proceedings of the 2014 ACM Conference on Web Science*, WebSci '14, pages 182–186, Bloomington, Indiana, USA. ACM.

Show-Jane Yen, Yue-Shi Lee, Yu-Chieh Wu, Jia-Ching Ying, and Vincent S Tseng. 2010. Automatic Chinese text classification using n-gram model. In *Computational Science and Its Applications–ICCSA 2010*, pages 458–471. Springer.

Lu Yong and Hou Yanqing. 2006. Automatic recognition of Chinese synonyms based on pattern matching algorithm. *Journal of the China Society for Scientific and Technical Information*, 25(6):720–724.

Hua-Ping Zhang, Hong-Kui Yu, De-Yi Xiong, and Qun Liu. 2003. HHMM-based Chinese lexical analyzer ICTCLAS. In *Proceedings of the Second SIGHAN Workshop on Chinese Language Processing - Volume 17*, SIGHAN '03, pages 184–187, Sapporo, Japan. Association for Computational Linguistics.

Dong Zhendong and Dong Qiang. 1998. HowNet Knowledge Database. `http://www.keenage.com`, August. Accessed: 22 August 2014.

Yanquan Zhou, Lili Yang, Bartel Van de Walle, and Chong Han. 2013. Classification of microblogs for support emergency responses: Case study Yushu earthquake in China. *2013 46th Hawaii International Conference on System Sciences*, pages 1553–1562.

Feng Zou, Fu Lee Wang, Xiaotie Deng, Song Han, and Lu Sheng Wang. 2006. Automatic construction of Chinese stop word list. In *Proceedings of the 5th WSEAS International Conference on Applied Computer Science*, ACOS'06, pages 1009–1014, Hangzhou, China. World Scientific and Engineering Academy and Society (WSEAS).

Finding expertise using online community dialogue and the Duality of Expertise

Michael Niemann
Faculty of Information Technology,
Monash University
Melbourne, AUSTRALIA
michael.niemann@monash.edu

Abstract

The Duality of Expertise considers the "Expert" to be a social role dependent on an individual's expertise claims and the opinion of their community towards those claims. These are the internal and external aspects of a person's expertise. My Expertise Model incorporates this duality in a process designed for expertise finding software in an online community forum. In this model, a posting's term usage is evidence of expertise claims. The dialogue acts in replies to those postings are evidence of the community's opinion. The model's preprocessing element uses a bricolage of linguistic and IR tools and methods in a novel way to construct each author's expertise profile. For any topic query, the profiles are ranked to determine the Community Topic Expert. A series of experiments demonstrate the advantage of utilising the Duality of Expertise when ranking experts rather than just the internal or external aspects of expertise.

1 Introduction

The Internet provides people and organisations with access to new resources for problem solving and guidance. While there are skillful staff or friends within their own networks, sometimes they need to look outside their own group to find the required knowledge. Specialised online communities are one such source of expertise.

Traditionally, expertise is treated as a combination of knowledge, training and experience (Ericsson, 2000; Gould, 1999). However, expertise is also relative to the context in which it is sought (Mieg, 2006). Who is regarded as a suitable topic expert depends on who is available and the depth and breadth of their expertise. Any local resident may be able to tell you where the local train station is, but you may need a railway employee if you want know how regular the trains are.

Likewise, it is not enough to simply determine who in an online community knows something about a topic. Many "know-it-alls" profess to be experts but do not have much expertise. For guidance, we look to others in the community for advice on who they consider to be Community Topic Experts. This "Expert" label is a social role bestowed by the community (Mieg, 2006). It is relative to the community's knowledge on the topic and the expertise they have encountered when interacting with members. Who is a suitable expert depends on the community's opinion of the relative expertise of its members.

My research looks at modelling and identifying someone's expertise by considering both their expertise claims and their community's opinion towards those claims. This Duality of Expertise is investigated by examining the linguistic interactions within an online community's forum. The content of a forum author's postings is evidence of their expertise claims. The dialogue acts of the community's replies to those postings is evidence of the community's opinion.

My Expertise Model utilises the Duality of Expertise in such a way that the model is easily incorporated within expertise finding software for such a forum. This is evaluated through experiments based on the TREC2006 Expert Search task and the related forum postings from the W3C corpus.

This paper is structured as follows. Section 2 discusses previous research relating to expertise and expertise finding technology. The approach and model used in my research is outlined in Section 3. Section 4 explains the experiments run to evaluate the model. Their outcomes are discussed in Section 5. The conclusion in Section 6 summarises my research.

Michael Niemann. 2014. Finding expertise using online community dialogue and the Duality of Expertise. In *Proceedings of Australasian Language Technology Association Workshop*, pages 69−78.

2 Related research

Research has identified various aspects of what makes up an expert. An expert is traditionally seen as someone who is knowledgeable. However, Ericsson (2000) argues that an expert learns how to use that knowledge through deliberate practise. This expertise is only related to one topic or field (Gould, 1999) but every expert is different as their experience and reflections of their actions are unique (Bellot, 2006; Schön, 1983), as is the manner in which they utilise those skills (Rolfe, 1997). For this reason, a person's expertise cannot be simply defined by labels or fields e.g., *'law'*.

Simple "yellow pages" software systems try to use such labels to declare the expertise of an organisation's staff (Ackerman and Halverson, 2003). People searching for expertise (expertise seekers) can use simple search engines to search through related databases or staff web-pages for possible experts (Yimam-Seid and Kobsa, 2003), but these systems rely on staff to update them and are often incomplete or inaccurate with little quality control (Lemons and Trees, 2013).

More specialised expert finding systems have been developed to form expert profiles based on evidence of people's expertise. This evidence ranges from authoring academic and company papers (Richards et al., 2008; Yan et al., 2006), being mentioned on web-pages (Balog et al., 2006; Campbell et al., 2003; Liu et al., 2012) or social media and email communications (Guy et al., 2013; Kautz et al., 1997; Kumar and Ahmad, 2012). The survey by Balog et al. (2012) shows that expertise finding is often treated very much as an information retrieval (IR) problem. The relevance of a person's expertise to the specific topic is commonly evaluated based on simple term usage, ranking candidate experts using a probabilistic or vector-based model.

Some early researchers have considered the social network of experts. Schwartz and Wood (1993) formed specialization subgraphs (SSG) based on emails between people. They found each author's Aggregate Specialisation Graph (ASG) was particular to them, supporting the concept of expertise being particular to the individual. The graphs can be used to refer an expertise seeker to someone they know, who may then refer them to someone they consider to be an expert based on previous interactions. Similarly, the Referral Web system described by Kautz et al. (1997) links people to experts through the co-occurrence of their names in a document, like an email, research article or web-page. This relies on the social network associations being related to particular areas of expertise, yet the manner in which the associated graph is constructed is very ad-hoc.

More recently, Guy et al. (2013) investigated using social media for expertise finding and found that feedback to social media messages can be a good indication of people's expertise. The ComEx Miner system (Kumar and Ahmad, 2012) attempted to identify the sentiment in feedback to blog entries using lists of adverbs and positive, negative and neutral adjectives. However, a blog provides very one-sided discussions as the opening post is always by the same author and it is not always clear whether comments are replying to the blog or other comments. Therefore a blog may not be a good example of community interaction.

Weigand considers dialogue to be a dialogic act "to negotiate our purposes" (Weigand, 2010, p. 509) through language. Part of that purpose is to be accepted in the community through interaction. Dialogue acts represent the intentions of speakers (Austin, 1975; Searle, 1969; Searle, 1975).[1] Traditionally these are applied to utterances but researchers have attempted to classify the dialogue acts of email sentences (Cohen et al., 2004; Jeong et al., 2009) and entire emails (Carvalho and Cohen, 2005; Feng et al., 2006) and forum messages (Bhatia et al., 2012; Kim et al., 2010). To Weigand, each dialogue act has a corresponding reactive action. Socially, the dialogue act is a claim, such that the claimant desires the suitable reaction to fulfill this claim (Weigand, 2010). Thus dialogue is a negotiation between participants who respond to each other's dialogue acts whilst trying to achieve their own objectives, including social acceptance within the community.

Likewise McDonald and Ackerman (1998) and Hytönen et al. (2014) found that when seeking assistance from experts, people often had to consider various psychological costs like a potential loss of status, expected reciprocity and social equity. Through the sharing of knowledge and the use and recognition of expertise during the interaction, dialogue participants negotiate an outcome that meets their personal objectives (Mieg, 2001). This may include establishing the value of the exchange and nature of the truth. Similarly, in an online fo-

[1] The term *'dialogue act'* is used in this paper rather than *'speech act'* due to the absence of speech in my data.

rum the dialogue acts of the replies are responses to the content and intent of the previous posting and are indicative of the forum community's opinion towards the author's proposals. Therefore, the group's opinion of an author's claims and thus their expertise can be judged by examining the dialogue acts in the group's replies to the author.

3 Model

My Expertise Model is a process that enables the incorporation of the Duality of Expertise in an expertise finding system (Figure 1). The Duality of Expertise is a relationship between an expert and their community, based on their expertise claims and the community's opinion of those claims.

A person's expertise claims are their representation of the topics about which they assert to be knowledgeable. An internal aspect of expertise, it relates to how an individual presents themselves to others. The claim demonstrates their topics of interest, but does not judge the accuracy of the claim nor whether they are an expert on the topic.

The external aspect of expertise is the community's opinion towards the relative expertise of the member claiming expertise. Based on the claims as well as other interactions and expertise within the community, the community judges whether the person is the Community Topic Expert, or whether they are not as knowledgeable on the topic as others in the community.

The Expertise Model is designed to evaluate and find expertise within online communities by examining forum postings. Each discussion thread is a linguistic interaction between community members with each posting being an author's contribution to the community's knowledge. Term usage in postings is evidence of the author's expertise claims. It is assumed authors claim expertise on what they write about. The community's opinion is recognised through the responses to a member's postings and expertise claims. The dialogue acts in reply postings are evidence of this opinion.

The Expertise Model uses a combination of these internal and external aspects of expertise to construct expertise profiles for each author then evaluate the relevance of their profile to the topic of expertise being sought. The outcome is a list of authors ranked according to whether they are the Community Topic Expert.

There are four main stages in the model: preprocessing, profiling, topic querying and ranking.

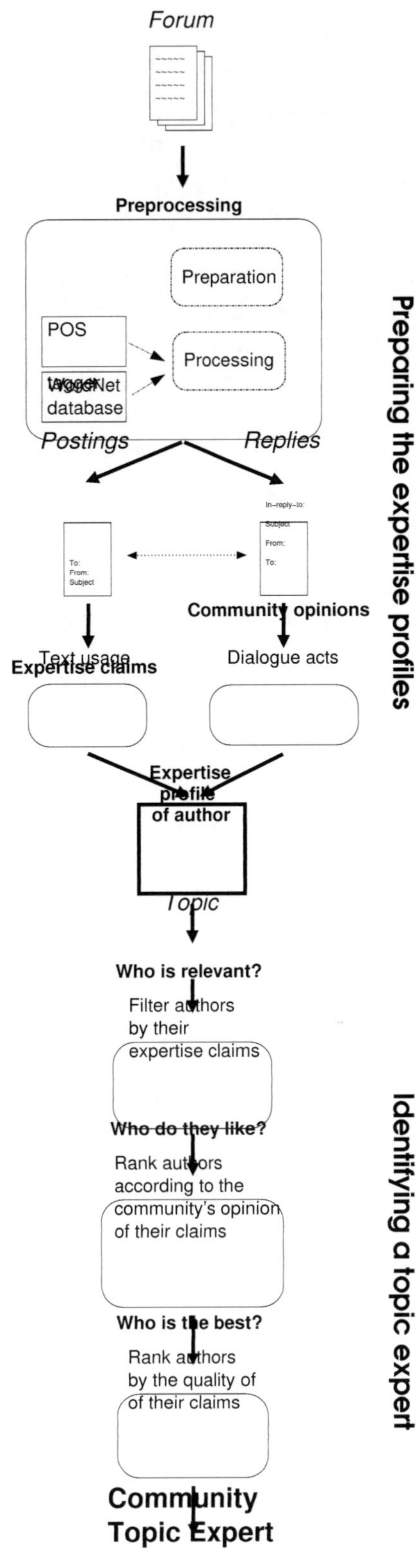

Figure 1: Expertise Model

3.1 Preprocessing

For a given forum, the preprocessing prepares the data to a standardised format and processes it according to various linguistic criteria. The preparation includes extracting postings from their source files (e.g., web-pages or digests), standardising the form of the metadata, and identifying quotations and non-dialogue lines in the postings. The linguistic processing includes sentence segmentation, term tokenisation, part-of-speech tagging, lemmatisation, and identification of the semantic concepts associated with the terms. These tasks can be completed using third-party software like a part-of-speech tagger and the WORDNET lexical database, but many expertise finding systems I have reviewed did not include such preprocessing.

The preprocessing also identifies the dialogue acts in the reply postings. The dialogue acts used (Table 1) were based on those used in the Verbmobil, TRAINS and DAMSL research (Alexandersson et al., 1995; Core, 1998; Ferguson et al., 1996). The decision to simplify the number of acts to six was made after reviewing the dialogue in the 20 NEWSGROUPS corpus (Rennie, 2008) and the CORVUS corpus which I collected from five professional and semi-professional mailing lists. These acts were broadly related to the historical attributes of experts, e.g., supplying and seeking information and reflection, the community's attitude when responding, e.g., support, rejection or enquiry, and other acts not related to expertise. The dialogue studied was found to be more a discussion than questions and answers so less focus was given to related acts (e.g., *Answer, Clarification*). The six acts used subsumed these acts.

Dialogue act	Example sub-categories subsumed
Inform	Inform, Answer, Clarification, Suggestion, Explanation, Order, Instruction, Statement, Opinion, Signal Not Understanding,
Positive	Agreement, Acceptance, Acknowledgement, Support, Thanks
Negative	Disagreement, Rejection, Criticism
Question	Yes/No, Rhetorical Query, Request Query
Reflection	Reflection, Correction, Experience
Other	Greeting, Bye, Coding, Graphic, Numeric, Quotation, Signature

Table 1: The dialogue acts

3.2 Profiling

For the profiling, the preprocessing established metadata for forum discussions, including lists of each author's postings and the reply postings. This enables the profiling to be divided into the data relating to the internal aspect of expertise, being the term and semantic concept usage of each author, and the external aspect of expertise, namely the dialogue acts in the replies to each author's postings. This data is indexed per author and can be updated whenever new postings appear in a forum.

3.3 Topic querying

Any expertise finding system needs to interface with an expertise seeker to determine what expertise is sought. For my Expertise Model, the expertise topic is indicated by one or more query terms. There are no restrictions on how many terms or which particular terms can be given as the topic. Just as the profiling does not represent expertise topics by a finite set of labels, neither is there any restriction on the topic query terms. While the interface is presumed to be part of any expertise finding system that may incorporate my Expertise Model, any topic terms still undergo the same linguistic processing as the posting content.

3.4 Ranking

Various ranking methods are used to identify the Community Topic Expert that best meets the user's needs. This ranking utilises existing IR methods in novel ways. The relevance of the term usage is ranked through a combination of the vector space model with the term frequency-inverse document frequency (tf-idf) measure to identify the specialised usage of terms. This allows the filtering of authors not relevant to the topic as well as ranking their topic relevance when there is ambiguity as to who claims to have greater expertise.

For the community opinion, each author has an opinion vector based on the dialogue acts used in their postings' replies. For each act, two dimensions were added to the vector:

1. Number of replies with at least one instance of the dialogue act
2. Average number of instances of the dialogue act per reply

	Gold Replies	Bad Replies
Reply postings	378	531
Reply authors	169	241
Average postings per author	2.2	2.2
Postings replied to	304	386
Authors replied to	92	199
Average replies per author	4.1	2.7
Annotated Postings	378	531
Annotated Sentences	6731	11908
Postings with at least one		
- Positive DA	121 (32%)	178 (33%)
- Negative DA	20 (5%)	79 (15%)
- Question DA	126 (33%)	179 (34%)
- Reflection DA	6 (2%)	10 (2%)
- Inform DA	338 (89%)	498 (94%)
- Other DA	361 (96%)	499 (94%)
- Positive & Negative DAs	13 (3%)	39 (7%)
- Positive & Question DAs	46 (12%)	83 (16%)
- Negative & Question DAs	12 (3%)	45 (8%)
- Negative, Positive & Question DAs	11 (3%)	30 (6%)
Average quantity in a posting		
- Positive DA	1.9	2.1
- Negative DA	1.6	1.6
- Question DA	2.1	2.3
- Reflection DA	1.1	1.6
- Inform DA	9.3	10.9
- Other DA	8.4	11.0

Table 2: Statistics of the annotated reply postings

The community opinion of an author's expertise on a topic was scored using the Expertise Opinion Measure (EOM, Equation 1), where $v(q, a)$ is an opinion vector for author a, topic query q and constant α. This formula is similar to Rocchio's Algorithm in the use of weighted comparisons of an author's vector to the centroid vectors of relevant and irrelevant results (Manning et al., 2008). The GOLD centroid is formed from the opinion vectors of known experts on the topic q. The BAD centroid is formed from the vectors of non-experts on the topic. The similarity measure (*sim*) uses a method like cosine comparison.

Expertise Opinion Measure (EOM)

$$EOM(a,q) = \alpha \times sim(v(q,a), centroid(q, GOLD)) - ((1-\alpha) \times sim(v(q,a), centroid(q, BAD)) \quad (1)$$

Through these measures, the Expertise Model

1. filters out authors whose expertise claims are not relevant to the topic,
2. determines which authors the community thinks highly of, and
3. determines the best of the topic experts.

Thus the linguistic interaction is used to determine the community's expert on a required topic on the basis of the author's claims and the forum community's opinion towards those claims.

4 Experiments

The Expertise Model was evaluated through a series of experiments, each examining an aspect of how the Duality of Expertise is represented. This evaluation was conducted using a preprocessor and the Lemur INDRI IR system,[2] modified to act as an expertise finding system. The preprocessor utilised a novel combination of scripts written by me based on established linguistic and IR

[2] http://www.lemurproject.org/indri.php

technologies and methodologies. The preprocessor also made use of the C&C Tools POSTAGGER[3] and WORDNET 3.0 for the lemmatisation and semantic relationships.

The test-set was based on the TREC2006 Expertise Search task in the Enterprise track (Soboroff et al., 2006). This task had participants identify experts from a corpus of W3C website files. My test-set only included the pages containing forum postings from W3C mailing lists, about 60% of the original corpus documents (Craswell et al., 2005). Personal homepages and other documents were ignored as they do not relate to the linguistic interactions within the W3C community.

The 49 TREC2006 queries were used, each set of terms referring to a topic of expertise, e.g., *'SOAP security considerations'*. TREC supplied a list of candidate experts that linked identification numbers to names and email addresses, e.g., *candidate-0025 Judy Brewer jbrewer@w3.org*. This was based on a list of people involved in the W3C (Soboroff et al., 2006). TREC2006 gave a "goldlist" for each topic query of who were judged to be relevant experts and who were not experts. This judgement did not consider all candidate experts but was based on the top 20 responses from TREC2006 participants and human judgement, given a review of documents related to the candidates. For my evaluation I increased the list from 1092 to 1844 candidate experts by including any unlisted forum authors and included heuristics in the preprocessor to recognise when an author used a nickname or alternate email address. This allowed each author's postings to be better identified.

For each topic, the top 50 ranked authors were evaluated using the *trec_eval* software[4] from TREC . This tool evaluates TREC results in various ways but I focused on the Mean Average Precision (MAP)[5] and the Interpolated Precision at Recall 0.0. MAP is commonly used as the main measure for TREC participants. The interpolated precision represents the highest precision for any recall level above 0.0 (Buckley and Voorhees, 2005; Manning et al., 2008). If the rank 1 author for a topic is a known expert, the recall may be low but the precision will be 1.0. If no known expert for the topic is rank 1, then the interpolated precision at recall 0.0 will be lower, due to the lower rank of the known experts. Therefore, the interpolated precision at recall 0.0 can be considered a measure of the degree to which known experts are given the highest ranks in the results.

The evaluation was divided into three stages (Table 3). First the internal aspect of the Expertise Model (the Knowledge Model or KM) was examined, using only it to determine the community's experts. Then only the external aspect of the Expertise Model (the Community Model or CM) was utilised for the expertise finding process. Finally, all aspects of the Expertise Model were evaluated in combination. This allowed comparisons to be made between when the aspects are used individually, as is commonly done by other researchers, and when the expertise ranking is conducted based on the Duality of Expertise.

The vector space model IR method provided the baseline for these evaluations. This used the raw, unaltered forms of the topic query terms and sought perfect matches in the postings, the contents of which were indexed according to the posting, not the author. The topic expert was the author of the most relevant posting. No consideration was made of what else each author had posted about outside the posting being ranked.

For the Knowledge Model, there were three main experiments:

- **KM1: Raw terms by author** – The baseline method was modified with all of an author's postings being indexed together, so their contributions to the forum were examined as a set when considering their expertise claims.
- **KM2: Lemmatised terms by author** – Before indexing, terms were tagged as a noun, verb, adjective, adverb or other, then lemmatised, e.g., *'antennas'* becomes *'antenna#n'*. This utilises the linguistic processing from the preprocessing and considers the linguistic context of the term usage.
- **KM3: Semantic data by author** – Each lemmatised term was indexed as their corresponding WORDNET synsets, e.g., *'antenna#n'* is indexed as synsets *02715229*, *04843270* and *02584915* because it has three senses in WORDNET . The hyponyms and hypernyms of these synsets were also indexed, e.g., *'03204955 directional antenna'*

[3] http://svn.ask.it.usyd.edu.au/trac/candc/wiki/POSTagger

[4] http://trec.nist.gov/trec_eval/trec_eval_latest.tar.gz

[5] precision = number of relevant experts returned ÷ number of candidate experts returned
recall = number of relevant experts returned ÷ total number of relevant experts

Experiment	MAP	Interpolated Precision at Recall 0.0
Baseline: Raw terms by Post	*0.0785*	*0.5539*
KM1: Raw Terms by Author	0.1348	0.7065
KM2: Lemmatised Terms by Author	0.1344	0.7355
KM3: Semantic Data by Author	0.1302	0.7113
CM1: Generalised EOM ($\alpha = 0.6$)	0.1156	0.6061
CM2: Non-author EOM ($\alpha = 1.0$)	0.0990	0.6061
CM3: Topic-specific EOM ($\alpha = 0.75$)	0.1250	0.7834
Expertise Model ($\alpha = 0.5$)	**0.1461**	**0.8682**

Table 3: Experimental results

and *'03269401 electrical device'*. This extends the idea of terms being evidence of an author's expertise claims by making each term represent the broader semantic concepts that the claims relate to, not just words.

The experiments for the Community Model utilised the dialogue acts in the replies to the top 50 postings from the baseline experiment. I hand-annotated the dialogue acts using the six acts in Table 1. While other research has attempted to automate similar annotation using a classifier (Cohen et al., 2004; Jeong et al., 2009), my research focused on the effectiveness of the data and the model, not designing a classifier. The Expertise Opinion Measure used the dialogue acts to evaluate community's opinion of each author's expertise. After reviewing the spread of annotated dialogue acts (Table 2), I omitted the *Inform*, *Reflection* and *Other* acts from the EOM as they were either too rare or too general. In contrast, the use of *Positive*, *Negative* and *Question* acts seemed to differ depending on whether they were in response to an expert or not. It was hoped that this would aid the Community Model.

Three main experiments were conducted, each training the centroids on different sets of postings.

- **CM1: Generalised EOM** – These centroids used the opinion vectors for experts and non-experts of any query other than the current topic query and excluding the opinion vectors of the expert being ranked.
- **CM2: Non-author EOM** – The opinion vectors of any author relevant to any topic contributed to the centroids, still excluding the current author's vector.
- **CM3: Topic-specific EOM** – The centroids were formed only from the replies to authors relevant to the current topic query, including the author being ranked.

The opinion vector of the author being ranked only used dialogue acts from the replies to their topic-related postings. These experiments examined whether the community opinion should be considered as dependent on the topic or whether there can be a single opinion of each author.

Finally, the relevance scores from the Knowledge Model and the Expertise Opinion Measure from the Community Model were used together as shown in Figure 1. The relevance score is used to filter out non-relevant authors, based on each author's lemmatised term usage and treating their postings as a collection. Authors are then ranked based on the community's responses to their postings, using the EOM with topic-based centroids. Finally, any tied rankings are resolved using the relevance scores. The top ranked author is judged to be the Community Topic Expert, according to the linguistic evidence of the internal and external aspects of their expertise.

5 Discussion

As shown on Table 3, the Expertise Model achieved the best results but lessons can be learnt from the experiments with the Knowledge and Community Models.

The experiments with the Knowledge Model made it clear that the contents of single documents in isolation cannot be considered good evidence of someone's expertise. Their expertise claims are better recognised through an examination of all their postings, treating them as a body of alleged knowledge. Further processing like lemmatisation allows the lexical evidence to be better associated with the context in which it was used. While the MAP value for the lemmatisation experiment

(KM2) was similar to that without lemmatisation (KM1), there was a marked improvement in the interpolated precision. This indicates that lemmatisation gave higher ranks to the top experts. Conceptualising the term usage further through the use of WORDNET synsets, hyponyms and hypernyms was not as successful. This was mainly due to ambiguity caused by the multiple senses in WORDNET for each term, as no sense disambiguation was included in the preprocessing because it was not a focus area of my research. However, early experiments tested using synsets alone. The results improved when only each term's first WORDNET sense was used. When the hypernyms and hyponyms were also considered, the results improved further but the best results (as shown for KM3 on Table 3) occurred when hypernyms and hyponyms for only a single sense were considered per term. This suggests that with improved sense handling, the internal aspect of the Expertise Model is best represented by considering all of an expert's lexical contributions to the community and how they are associated with each other through hypernyms and hyponyms.

The experiments with the Community Model were not as successful as those for the Knowledge Model. Various α values were tried for each run with the most successful indicated on Table 3. While no single α value was best for all experiments, there was a general preference for $\alpha > 0.5$. This indicates the importance of an author having a similar opinion vector to that of known experts. However, the results also indicate that with the EOM, the community opinion is best represented when centroids are related to opinion vectors for authors of topic-relevant postings. This was supported by earlier experiments that ranked authors using opinion vectors based on responses to any of their postings, not just relevant ones. These experiments were far less successful with MAP values below 0.1. Therefore, the community's opinion of an author's expertise is topic-specific. The community does not simply consider an expert at one topic to be an expert at all fields, regardless of the specialised nature of the community. This supports the concept of expertise being particular to each individual and dependent on the context in which expertise is sought.

The best results were achieved when the internal and external aspects of expertise are combined in the Expertise Model. The MAP and the interpolated precision for the Expertise Model were clearly better than those for any of the previous experiments. Furthermore, the best results occurred when $\alpha = 0.5$. This differed from the results for the Community Model in the equal weight given to what the EOM considers to be standard community responses to experts and those of non-experts. Therefore, knowing information about non-experts is just as vital as knowing experts.

This demonstrates how the Duality of Expertise can be incorporated in the Expertise Model and automatically identify Community Topic Experts in an online forum. Using a bricolage of freely available linguistic and IR resources and methods, the model processes forum postings in a novel way, enabling the ranking of authors' expertise through the community's linguistic interaction.

In future research, the definitions and choice of the dialogue acts will be reviewed before further annotations. The automated classification of the acts and sense disambiguation will be trialled. Further experiments will use deeper hypernyms and hyponyms to increase the number of synsets associated with each author's expertise. The expertise and dialogue in social media like LinkedIn and Facebook groups will be examined.

6 Conclusion

This research examined the presence of the Duality of Expertise in online community forums. This duality is used within my Expertise Model to determine the Community Topic Expert, considering the expertise claims in their postings and the community's opinion towards these postings and claims. This is achieved through use of the term usage in the postings and the dialogue acts in the replies. Experiments showed that the best representation for the expertise claims is achieved when all of an expert's contributions are considered together and the terms are lemmatised. Results when linking terms to semantic concepts are encouraging. The Expertise Opinion Measure is used to score the community's opinion of each expert based on the similarity of their opinion vector to those of other experts and non-experts. The experiments also showed that the community has a different opinion about every forum author for each topic of expertise sought. This and the Duality of Expertise supports the concept of expertise being relative to the context in which it is found, such that it has internal and external aspects.

Acknowledgments

The usage of data from public online forums was approved by the Monash University Human Research Ethics Committee (MUHREC Project Number CF10/2626 - 2010001463). This research was partly supported by funding from an Australian Postgraduate Award and the Monash University Faculty of Information Technology. Thank you to the reviewers of this paper for their comments.

References

Mark S. Ackerman and Christine Halverson. 2003. Sharing expertise: The next step for knowledge management. *Social Capital and Information Technology*, pages 273–299.

Jan Alexandersson, Elisabeth Maier, and Norbert Reithinger. 1995. A robust and efficient three-layered dialogue component for a speech-to-speech translation system. In *Proceedings of the seventh conference on European chapter of the Association for Computational Linguistics*, EACL '95, pages 188–193, San Francisco, U.S.A. Morgan Kaufmann Publishers Inc.

John L. Austin. 1975. *How to do things with words*. Clarendon Press, Oxford, England, 2nd edition.

Krisztian Balog, Leif Azzopardi, and Maarten de Rijke. 2006. Formal models for expert finding in enterprise corpora. In *Proceedings of the 29th annual international ACM SIGIR conference on Research and development in information retrieval*, SIGIR, pages 43–50, New York, U.S.A. ACM.

Krisztian Balog, Yi Fang, Maarten de Rijke, Pavel Serdyukov, and Luo Si. 2012. Expertise retrieval. *Foundations and Trends in Information Retrieval*, 6(2-3):127–256, February.

Andrea Bellot. 2006. Advanced practioners' use of reflexivity in decision-making. *Nursing Times*, 102(45):33, December.

Sumit Bhatia, Prakhar Biyani, and Prasenjit Mitra. 2012. Classifying user messages for managing web forum data. In *Fifteenth International Workshop on the Web and Databases (WebDB 2012)*, WebDB, pages 13–18, Scottsdale, U.S.A.,.

Chris Buckley and Ellen Voorhees, 2005. *TREC: Experiment and Evaluation in Information Retrieval*, chapter 3. MIT Press.

Christopher S. Campbell, Paul P. Maglio, Alex Cozzi, and Byron Dom. 2003. Expertise identification using email communications. In *Proceedings of the twelfth international conference on Information and knowledge management*, CIKM, pages 528–531, New York, U.S.A. ACM.

Vitor R. Carvalho and William W. Cohen. 2005. On the collective classification of email speech acts. In *SIGIR '05: Proceedings of the 28th annual international ACM SIGIR conference on Research and development in information retrieval*, SIGIR, pages 345–352.

William W. Cohen, Vitor R. Carvalho, and Tom M. Mitchell. 2004. Learning to classify email into "speech acts". In Dekang Lin and Dekai Wu, editors, *Proceedings of EMNLP 2004*, EMNLP, pages 309–316, Barcelona, Spain, July. Association for Computational Linguistics.

Mark G. Core. 1998. Analyzing and predicting patterns of DAMSL utterance tags. Technical report, AAAI Technical Report SS-98-01.

Nick Craswell, Arjen P. de Vries, and Ian Soboroff. 2005. Overview of the TREC-2005 enterprise track. In *The Fourteenth Text REtrieval Conference (TREC 2005) Proceedings*.

K. Anders Ericsson. 2000. How experts attain and maintain superior performance: Implications for the enhancement of skilled performance in older individuals. *Journal of Aging and Physical Activity*, 8(4):346–352.

Donghui Feng, Erin Shaw, Jihie Kim, and Eduard Hovy. 2006. Learning to detect conversation focus of threaded discussions. In *Proceedings of HLT-NAACL 2006*, HLTNAACL, pages 208–215.

George Ferguson, James Allen, and Brad Miller. 1996. TRAINS-95: Towards a mixed-initiative planning assistant. In *Proceedings of the 3rd Conference on AI Planning Systems*, AIPS-95, pages 70–77.

Nick Gould. 1999. Qualitive practice evaluation. *Evaluation and Social Work Practice*, pages 63–80.

Ido Guy, Uri Avraham, David Carmel, Sigalit Ur, Michal Jacovi, and Inbal Ronen. 2013. Mining expertise and interests from social media. In *Proceedings of the 22nd International Conference on World Wide Web*, WWW '13, pages 515–526, Republic and Canton of Geneva, Switzerland. International World Wide Web Conferences Steering Committee.

Kaisa Hytönen, Tuire Palonen, and Kai Hakkarainen. 2014. Cognitively central actors and their personal networks in an energy efficiency training program. *Frontline Learning Research*, 2(2):15–37.

Minwoo Jeong, Chin-Yew Lin, and Gary Geunbae Lee. 2009. Semi-supervised speech act recognition in emails and forums. In *Proceedings of the 2009 Conference on Empirical Methods in Natural Language Processing*, EMNLP, pages 1250–1259, Singapore, August. Association for Computational Linguistics.

Henry Kautz, Bart Selman, and Mehul Shah. 1997. ReferralWeb: Combining social networks and collaborative filtering. *Communications of the ACM*, 40(3):63–65, March.

Su Nam Kim, Li Wang, and Timothy Baldwin. 2010. Tagging and linking web forum posts. In *Proceedings of the Fourteenth Conference on Computational Natural Language Learning*, pages 192–202, Uppsala, Sweden, 15-16 July.

Akshi Kumar and Nazia Ahmad. 2012. Comex miner: Expert mining in virtual communities. *International Journal of Advanced Computer Science & Applications*, 3(6):54–65.

Darcy Lemons and Lauren Trees. 2013. Expertise location in the social media age. In *Presentations from APQC's 2013 Knowledge Management Conference*, Houston, U.S.A. APQC. `http://www.apqc.org/knowledge-base/documents/expertise-location-social-media-age`. Accessed on 29/07/2014.

Xiaomo Liu, G. Alan Wang, Aditya Johri, Mi Zhou, and Weiguo Fan. 2012. Harnessing global expertise: A comparative study of expertise profiling methods for online communities. *Information Systems Frontiers*, pages 1–13, September.

Christopher D. Manning, Prabhakar Raghavan, and Hinrich Schtüze. 2008. *Introduction to Information Retrieval*. Cambridge University Press, New York, U.S.A.

David W. McDonald and Mark S. Ackerman. 1998. Just talk to me: A field study of expertise location. In *Proceedings of the 1998 ACM conference on Computer supported cooperative work*, CSCW, pages 315–324, Seattle, U.S.A.

Harald A. Mieg. 2001. *The Social Psychology of Expertise: Case Studies in Research, Professional Domains, and Expert Roles*. Expertise Series. Lawrence Erlbaum Associates.

Harald A. Mieg. 2006. Social and sociological factors in the development of expertise. *The Cambridge Handbook of Expertise and Expert Performance*, (Chapter 41):743–760.

Jason Rennie. 2008. 20 Newsgroups. `http://people.csail.mit.edu/jrennie/20Newsgroups/`. Accessed 26/06/2009.

Debbie Richards, Meredith Taylor, and Peter Busch. 2008. Expertise recommendation: A two-way knowledge communication channel. In *Fourth International Conference on Autonomic and Autonomous Systems, 2008*, ICAS, pages 35–40.

Gary Rolfe. 1997. Beyond expertise: theory, practice and the reflexive practitioner. *Journal of Clinical Nursing*, 6:93–97, March.

Donald A. Schön. 1983. *The reflective practitioner: how professionals think in action*. Basic Books, New York, U.S.A.

Michael F. Schwartz and David C. M. Wood. 1993. Discovering shared interests using graph analysis. *Communications of the ACM*, 36(8):78–89.

John Searle. 1969. *Speech Acts*. Cambridge University Press.

John Searle. 1975. A taxonomy of illocutionary acts. In K. Günderson, editor, *Language, Mind and Knowledge*, pages 344–369. University of Minnesota Press.

Ian Soboroff, Arjen P. de Vries, and Nick Craswell. 2006. Overview of the TREC 2006 enterprise track. In E. M. Voorhees and Lori P. Buckland, editors, *The Fifteenth Text REtrieval Conference (TREC 2006) Proceedings*, pages 32–51. National Institute of Standards and Technology (NIST).

Edda Weigand. 2010. Language as dialogue. *Intercultural Pragmatics*, 7(3):505–515, August.

Xin Yan, Dawei Song, and Xue Li. 2006. Concept-based document readability in domain specific information retrieval. In *Proceedings of the 15th ACM international conference on Information and knowledge management*, CIKM, pages 540 – 549, Arlington, U.S.A.

Dawit Yimam-Seid and Alfred Kobsa. 2003. Expert-finding systems for organizations: Problem and domain analysis and the DEMOIR approach. *Journal of Organizational Computing and Electronic Commerce*, 13(1):1–24.

Impact of Citing Papers for Summarisation of Clinical Documents

Diego Mollá **Christopher Jones**
Macquarie University
Sydney, Australia
diego.molla-aliod@mq.edu.au
christopher.jones4@students.mq.edu.au

Abeed Sarker
Arizona State University
Tempe, AZ, USA
abeed.sarker@asu.edu

Abstract

In this paper we show that information from citing papers can help perform extractive summarisation of medical publications, especially when the amount of text available for development is limited. We used the data of the TAC 2014 biomedical summarisation task. We report several methods to find the reference paper sentences that best match the citation text from the citing papers ("citances"). We observed that methods that incorporate lexical domain information from UMLS, and methods that use extended training data, perform best. We then used these ranked sentences to perform extractive summarisation and observed a dramatic improvement of ROUGE-L scores when compared with methods that do not use information from citing papers.

1 Introduction

Text-based summarisation is a well-established area of research that aims to automatically produce condensed text representations of the original text. Text-based summarisation is useful in an increasing number of application domains where people cannot afford to spend time to read all the relevant information. This is certainly the case in the medical domain, and several approaches for the automated summarisation of medical text have been proposed, e.g. as surveyed by Afantenos *et al.* (2005).

Information from citing texts has been used in decades-old studies (Garfield et al., 1964). More recently, Nakov *et al.* (2004) proposed the use of citations for the semantic interpretation of bioscience text. They used the text surrounding the citations, which they named "citances", to summarise the original text. Further research focused on the extraction of the citances and surrounding text (Qazvinian and Radev, 2010) and on the use of these citances to gather information about the original text, which could be used as a surrogate of, or in addition to, a summary of the text (Mohammad et al., 2009; Abu-Jbara and Radev, 2011).

The Biomedical Summarization Track of the 2014 Text Analysis Conference (TAC 2014 BiomedSumm Track)[1] was designed as a set of shared tasks that focus on the use of the citances to build summaries of biomedical documents. The track organisers provided a small data set of 20 biomedical documents for training and fine-tuning. Each paper of the data set (henceforth "reference paper") has 10 citing papers, and the data are annotated with the citances found in the citing papers. For each citance, four annotators appointed by the National Institute of Standards and Technology (NIST) identified various pieces of information related to the track tasks. Three tasks were defined:

Task 1a Identify the text spans from the reference paper that most accurately reflect the text from the citance.

Task 1b Classify what facet of the paper a text span belongs to. There are 6 fixed facets: *hypothesis*, *method*, *results*, *implication*, *discussion*, and *data-set-used*.

Task 2 Generate a structured summary of the reference paper and all of the community discussion of the paper represented in the citances.

We have used the data from the TAC 2014 BiomedSumm Track to explore the hypothesis that using the information from citing papers can improve the results of an extractive summarisation

[1] http://www.nist.gov/tac/2014/BiomedSumm/

Diego Molla, Christopher Jones and Abeed Sarker. 2014. Impact of Citing Papers for Summarisation of Clinical Documents. In *Proceedings of Australasian Language Technology Association Workshop*, pages 79−87.

system. Whereas in prior work the information from the citing papers is presented as the summary of the reference paper to form what has been called citation-based summarisation, in this paper we will use the information from the citing papers as a step to select the most important sentences from the reference paper. This way the resulting summaries are directly comparable with standard extractive summarisation methods, and they suffer less from problems of balance, coherence and readability that typically affect summarisation systems based on multiple papers.

In this paper we present experiments with several settings to address task 1a of the TAC 2014 BiomedSumm track, and how these can help for task 2 and build extractive summaries. We have not explored yet how to incorporate the facet of the citances (task 1b) into task 2 and therefore we will not discuss task 1b in the remaining of this paper.

2 Finding the Best Fit to a Citance

Task 1a of the TAC 2014 BiomedSumm track assumes that the citances are known, and the goal is to identify the text spans from the reference paper that most accurately reflect the text from the citance. Figure 1 shows an example of the data for one citance.

To identify the sentences in the reference paper that best fit a citance we have tried several methods, all of which are based on computing the similarity between a sentence in the reference paper and the citance text. In all cases we have modelled each sentence as a vector, and used cosine similarity as the means to determine the closest match. Our methods vary on how the sentence vectors have been built, and how the similarity scores have been used to select the final sentences.

In our initial experiments we obtained best results after lowercasing, but without removing stop words or stemming, so all experiments conducted in this paper preprocess the text in this manner.

2.1 Oracle

We tried an oracle approach in order to have an upper bound. The oracle consists of the output given by one of the four annotators. The evaluation of the oracle was based on comparing each annotator against the other three annotators. The evaluation results are technically not an upper bound because the evaluation method is slightly different for two reasons: first, the annotator that is being used to select the target sentences is dropped from the gold data; and second, each original run is converted into multiple oracle runs, one per annotator, and the final result is the average among these runs. But it gives an idea of how much room for improvement is left by the automatic methods.

2.2 *tf.idf* and SVD

A straightforward method to build the sentence vectors is to compute the *tf.idf* scores of the sentence words. For each reference paper we computed a separate *tf.idf* matrix where the rows are the set of all sentences in the reference paper plus all sentences that appear in the citance text.

We also applied a variant that performs Singular Value Decomposition (SVD) on the *tf.idf* matrix, with the aim to reduce the size of the matrix and hopefully detect possible latent word relations. We tried with 100, 500, and 1000 components. In this paper we show the results for 500 components since it obtained the best results in our preliminary experiments.

2.3 Additional Data

Traditional uses of *tf.idf* rely on relatively large corpora. Given the very small amount of text used to compute *tf.idf* in our scenario (just the reference paper sentences and the set of citances for that reference paper), we expanded the data as follows.

Topics. Given a reference paper, we used the paper sentences plus all sentences of all documents that cite the reference paper, not just the sentences in the citance text. In the TAC data set, each reference paper had 10 citing papers.

Documents. In each reference paper we used all sentences of all documents of the TAC2014 set. This included the documents citing the reference paper, and all other documents.

Abstracts. We added the sentences of a separate collection of 2,657 abstracts extracted from PubMed and made available by Mollá and Santiago-Martínez (2011).[2] There was no guarantee that these abstracts were from any topic related to the reference paper. The resulting dataset may therefore contain noise but the additional text may help determine the important words of a document.

[2] `http://sourceforge.net/projects/ebmsumcorpus/`

Reference article: Voorhoeve.txt

Citance text: In this context, while the development of TGCTs would be allowed by a partial functional inactivation of p53 (see [53], [54]), such mechanism would be insufficient to counteract the pro-apoptotic function of p53 induced by a persistent damage, causing a rapid cell death

Target reference text: These miRNAs neutralize p53-mediated CDK inhibition, possibly through direct inhibition of the expression of the tumor-suppressor LATS2. We provide evidence that these miRNAs are potential novel oncogenes participating in the development of human testicular germ cell tumors by numbing the p53 pathway, thus allowing tumorigenic growth in the presence of wild-type p53 ... Altogether, these results strongly suggest that the expression of miR-372/3 suppresses the p53 pathway to an extent sufficient to allow oncogenic mutations to accumulate in TGCTs ... However, whereas in the majority of the cases neoplastic transformation will require inactivation of p53 (for example by expression of HPV E6, HDM2, or mutant p53), miR372&3 uniquely allowed transformation to occur while p53 was active

Figure 1: Extract of the data for task 1a. The goal is to identify the target reference text, which is an extract of the reference article. In this example, three extracts are indicated in the target reference text, separated with "...".

2.4 Additional Context

Conventional methods for the calculation of *tf.idf* assume that each document contains a reasonable amount of words. In our case we use sentences, not full documents, and therefore the information is much sparser. It is conceivable that better results may be achieved by expanding each sentence. In our experiments, we expanded each sentence by adding text from neighbouring sentences. A context window of n sentences centred on the original sentence was used. We experimented with context windows of 5, 10, 20 and 50 sentences. In our preliminary experiments we observed best results for a context window of 50 sentences but it was marginally better than 20 sentences and at the expense of computation time so in this paper we use a context window of 20.

2.5 Maximal Marginal Relevance

Maximal Marginal Relevance (Carbonell and Goldstein, 1998) uses a greedy algorithm to approximate the selection of sentences that maximises the similarity between the sentences and a query, while at the same time penalising similarity among the chosen sentences. The algorithm uses a parameter λ that adjusts the contribution of each of these two optimisation criteria, giving the definition shown in Figure 2.

For the experiments reported here we use $\lambda = 0.97$ since it gave the best results in our preliminary experiments.

2.6 UMLS and WordNet

As mentioned above, we used SVD as a means to detect latent word relations. In addition we used domain knowledge to detect explicit word relations. In particular, for every word we used all of its synsets as defined by WordNet (Fellbaum, 1998) to leverage synonymy information. We also used each word's most salient Unified Medical Language System (UMLS) concept ID and corresponding semantic types by means of the MetaMap tool (Aronson, 2001), using MetaMap's default word-sense disambiguation process. We tried several ways of using WordNet and UMLS, including the following:

1. Replace the word with the WordNet or UMLS IDs or semantic types, and apply *tf.idf* as before.

2. Keep the word and add the WordNet or UMLS IDs or semantic types and apply *tf.idf* as before. This way the data contain specific word information, plus information about word relations.

3. Apply the *tf.idf* similarity metrics separately for each information type and return a linear combination of all. We tried several combinations and settled with this one:

$$0.5 \times w + 0.2 \times c + 0.3 \times s$$

where w stands for the *tf.idf* of the original words, c stands for the *tf.idf* of the UMLS

$$\text{MMR} = \arg \max_{D_i \in R \setminus S} \left[\lambda(\text{sim}(D_i, Q)) - (1 - \lambda) \max_{D_j \in S} \text{sim}(D_i, D_j) \right]$$

Where:

- Q is the question sentence. In this paper, we used the citance text as Q.
- R is the set of sentences in the reference paper.
- S is the set of sentences that haven been chosen in the summary so far.

Figure 2: Maximal Marginal Relevance (MMR)

concepts, and s stands for the *tf.idf* of the UMLS semantic types. We did not observe any improvement of the results when incorporating the WordNet synsets in our preliminary experiments and therefore we did not use them in the experiments reported in this paper.

2.7 Results

To evaluate the methods we have used the ROUGE-L F1 score. ROUGE (Lin, 2004) is a popular evaluation method for summarisation systems that compares the output of the system against a set of target summaries. For each citance, we used the target reference text provided by the annotators, except for the Oracle setting, as described above, where the reference text of one annotator was compared against the reference text of the other three annotators.

Table 1 summarises the results of our experiments. The results of the oracle approach are relatively poor. This indicates relatively low agreement among the annotators.

We can observe an improvement of the results when using additional text to compute the *tf.idf* scores. When adding related documents (the 10 citing papers) the results clearly improved. When using a fairly large set of unrelated abstracts alone the results worsened dramatically, but when using the unrelated abstracts *in addition* to the related documents the results improved marginally *wrt.* using related documents. This seems to point that adding more data to form the *tf.idf* models helps up to a point. Ideally, we should add data that are on the topic of the reference paper.

There was also a small improvement of the results when the original sentences were extended within a context window.

The approaches giving the best results have overlapping confidence intervals. This is not surprising, given that prior work has observed that it is very difficult for two different extractive summarisation systems to produce ROUGE F1 scores with non-overlapping confidence intervals due to the long-tailed nature of the distribution of ROUGE F1 scores among different systems (Ceylan et al., 2010). In our case, in addition, the amount of data is fairly small. Nevertheless, it appears that using UMLS improves the results, and whereas MMR gives better results than UMLS, the difference is so small that it might not be worth incorporating MMR. SVD appears to improve the results over plain *tf.idf*, but again the improvement is small and the computation time increased dramatically. None of the methods approached the results of the oracle, so there is room for improvement. Still, as we will show below, these techniques are useful for extractive summarisation.

Note that the best result overall is plain *tf.idf* where the data have been expanded with the citing papers and the sentences have been expanded with a large context window (50, instead of 20). The computation time of this approach far exceeded that of the other approaches in the table, so there is still room for further exploring the use of UMLS, or smart forms to determine the related documents and extending the sentence context.

3 Building the Final Summary

Whereas the goal of task 1a of the TAC 2014 BiomedSumm track was to find the text from the reference paper that most accurately reflects the text from the citances, the goal of task 2 was to build a summary of the reference paper and all of the community discussion of the paper represented in the citances. This task was set as tentative by the organisers of the track. Figure 3 shows the target summary produced by one of the annotators.

It is reasonable to accept that information from the citances will help produce a community-based summary such as the one in Figure 3. It is not

System	R	P	F1	F1 95% CI
Abstracts	0.190	0.230	0.193	0.179 - 0.208
tf.idf	0.331	0.290	0.290	0.276 - 0.303
MMR $\lambda = 0.97$	0.334	0.293	0.293	0.279 - 0.307
SVD with 500 components	0.334	0.295	0.295	0.281 - 0.308
Topics	0.344	0.311	*0.307*	0.293 - 0.321
$0.2c + 0.3s + 0.5w$	0.364	0.294	*0.309*	0.297 - 0.320
MMR $\lambda = 0.97$ on topics	0.345	0.314	*0.311*	0.296 - 0.325
Topics + context 20	0.333	0.334	*0.312*	0.297 - 0.326
$0.2c + 0.3s + 0.5w$ on topics + context 20	0.356	0.307	*0.312*	0.299 - 0.325
Documents + context 20	0.334	0.336	*0.314*	0.299 - 0.327
Documents	0.347	0.325	*0.316*	0.303 - 0.330
Documents + abstracts	0.347	0.327	*0.317*	0.302 - 0.332
MMR $\lambda = 0.97$ on topics + context 20	0.336	0.340	*0.317*	0.303 - 0.331
Topics + context 50	0.341	0.336	**0.318**	0.302 - 0.332
Oracle	0.442	0.484	0.413	0.404 - 0.421

Table 1: ROUGE-L results of TAC task 1a, sorted by F1. The best result is in **boldface**, and all results within the 95% confidence interval range of the best result are in *italics*.

In the article A genetic screen implicates miRNA-372 and miRNA-373 as oncogenes in testicular germ cell tumors, Voorhoeve et al., performed genetic screens of miRNA to investigate its novel functions; which has implicated two of them as oncogenes. They demonstrated that miRNA-372&3 participate in proliferation and tumorigenesis of primary human cells along with oncogenic RAS and active wild-type p53 by numbing the p53 pathway.

The authors created expression library by cloning most annotated human miRNAs into their vector and made a corresponding microarray for barcode detection. Guo et al, contradicted this by stating that bead-based platform is more flexible and cost-effective for detecting barcode changes.

Voorhoeve et al., observed that in response to mitogenic signals like RAS primary human cells undergo growth arrest; in contrast cells lacking p53 overcame this arrest. They demonstrated that expression of miRNA-372&3 enabled cells to continue proliferating thus causing a selective growth advantage.

Voorhoeve et al., established that miRNA 371-3 cluster suppresses an inhibitor of CDK activity which is essential for development of TGCTs. On further investigation they observed that 3UTR of LATS2 is indeed the direct target of miRNA-372&3.

This article has a huge impact on society as Voorhoeve et al., have indicated that deregulated expression of miRNA-372&3 predisposes cells to carcinogenic events and these miRNA expressions must be carefully controlled during differentiation to prevent progression to cancer. Their expression library has helped in the functional annotation of miRNA encompassing other regulatory functions that result in DNA damage response, differentiation, sensitivity to growth factors, resistance to anti-cancer drugs etc. It remains to be seen how widespread oncogenic miRNAs are; nevertheless, their study has provided a system for uncovering the roles of other miRNAs in tumorigenesis.

Figure 3: Sample target summary for task 2 as given by an annotator

so straightforward to accept that such information would help produce a summary that does not explicitly incorporate the contribution from the citing papers. To test whether information from citing papers is useful even for a standard, non-community-based summary, we altered the data from TAC as follows: We removed the abstract from the reference paper, and used the abstract from the reference paper as the target summary. In other words, we produced training and test data such as is often done in standard text summarisation settings. Figure 4 shows the target summary for the reference paper in our example.

One of the 20 papers from the training set did not include an abstract and it was removed for the modified task.

Below we described our approaches to solve task 2 and its modified version.

3.1 Oracle

The oracle version compared the data of one annotator against that of the other annotators. Again, by building this oracle we have an idea of the difficulty of the task. The oracle was used for the unmodified task 2 but it was not possible for the modified task because only one target abstract was available for each reference paper.

3.2 Using Reference Text Alone

Our first set of experiments used the reference text alone. These methods basically used some of the most common single-document summarisation techniques. In particular we tried the following extractive summarisation techniques, which calculated a score of sentence importance and selected the top sentences:

1. *tf.idf*, SVD: compute the sum of the *tf.idf*, or *tf.idf*+SVD values of the candidate sentence.
2. Additional data, additional context: extend the data or sentence context prior to the computation of *tf.idf* as described in Section 2.
3. UMLS, WordNet: incorporate UMLS and WordNet information as described in Section 2.

3.3 Using Citing Text

We incorporated the citing text in a very straightforward way. For every citance, we used the methods described in Section 2 to rank the sentences. We then scored each sentence i by using rank(i,c), which has values between 0 (first sentence) and n (last sentence) and represents the rank of sentence i in citance c:

$$\text{score}(i) = \sum_{c \in \text{citances}} 1 - \frac{\text{rank}(i,c)}{n}$$

3.4 Results

Table 2 shows the result of the unmodified task 2, and Table 3 shows the results of the modified version. For the unmodified version we set an upper limit of 250 words per summary, as originally specified in the shared task. For the revised data set we kept the same upper limit of 250 words because it appeared to give the best results.

We observe that the confidence intervals of the best results of the version that uses the TAC data approached the results of the oracle, which is very encouraging, especially given the relatively simple approaches tried in this paper. Overall, we observed that using the scores of task 1a produced much better results than using the information from the reference paper alone. The difference was statistically significant, and given the above mentioned observation that it is generally difficult to obtain ROUGE F1 scores that have a difference that is statistically significant among different extractive summarisers (Ceylan et al., 2010), we have good evidence to the validity of approaches that leverage human knowledge of the paper through the exploitation of the citation links between papers.

Of the traditional methods, that is, the methods that did not incorporate the data of task1a, we observed no significant improvements over a simple *tf.idf* approach. Even adding additional context or documents did not help. This was the case both for the version that used the TAC data and the version that used the abstracts as the target summaries.

We can also observe that the ROUGE scores are higher for the original TAC task than for our modified task. This is compatible with the original goal of the TAC shared task, since the annotators were instructed to build sample summaries that incorporate the information from the citances. In contrast, the target summaries for our modified task were written before the citing papers.

It was interesting to observe that parameters that led to better results in Section 2 did not necessarily achieve best results now. This might be due to random effects, since the results among those settings

Endogenous small RNAs (miRNAs) regulate gene expression by mechanisms conserved across metazoans. While the number of verified human miRNAs is still expanding, only few have been functionally annotated. To perform genetic screens for novel functions of miRNAs, we developed a library of vectors expressing the majority of cloned human miRNAs and created corresponding DNA barcode arrays. In a screen for miRNAs that cooperate with oncogenes in cellular transformation, we identified miR-372 and miR-373, each permitting proliferation and tumorigenesis of primary human cells that harbor both oncogenic RAS and active wild-type p53. These miRNAs neutralize p53-mediated CDK inhibition, possibly through direct inhibition of the expression of the tumor-suppressor LATS2. We provide evidence that these miRNAs are potential novel oncogenes participating in the development of human testicular germ cell tumors by numbing the p53 pathway, thus allowing tumorigenic growth in the presence of wild-type p53.

Figure 4: Original abstract as the new sample target summary

System	R	P	F1	F1 95% CI
Oracle	0.459	0.461	0.458	0.446 - 0.470
tf.idf	0.260	0.264	0.260	0.226 - 0.290
SVD with 500 components	0.264	0.247	0.254	0.236 - 0.272
Topics	0.260	0.265	0.261	0.226 - 0.292
Documents	0.259	0.265	0.260	0.224 - 0.290
Topics + context 5	0.259	0.265	0.261	0.226 - 0.291
Topics + context 20	0.252	0.261	0.255	0.220 - 0.285
task1a (*tf.idf*)	0.384	0.375	0.378	0.350 - 0.408
task1a (MMR $\lambda = 0.97$ on topics)	0.398	0.396	*0.396*	0.372 - 0.421
task1a (MMR $\lambda = 0.97$ on topics + context 20)	0.420	0.407	**0.412**	0.385 - 0.438
task1a ($0.2c + 0.3s + 0.5w$)	0.398	0.392	*0.394*	0.369 - 0.419
task1a ($0.2c + 0.3s + 0.5w$ on topics)	0.405	0.399	*0.401*	0.378 - 0.423
task1a ($0.2c + 0.3s + 0.5w$ on topics + context 20)	0.417	0.404	*0.409*	0.387 - 0.431

Table 2: Rouge-L results of task 2 using the TAC 2014 data. The summary size was constrained to 250 words. In **boldface** is the best result. In *italics* are the results within the 95% confidence intervals of the best result.

System	R	P	F1	F1 95% CI
tfidf	0.293	0.192	0.227	0.190 - 0.261
SVD with 500 components	0.291	0.181	0.218	0.197 - 0.239
Documents	0.289	0.192	0.226	0.188 - 0.260
$0.2c + 0.3s + 0.5w$	0.314	0.210	0.247	0.207 - 0.284
task1a (tfidf)	0.425	0.264	*0.320*	0.293 - 0.353
task1a (MMR $\lambda = 0.97$)	0.418	0.275	*0.324*	0.299 - 0.351
task1a (MMR $\lambda = 0.97$ on topics)	0.436	0.272	*0.330*	0.300 - 0.363
task1a ($0.2c + 0.3s + 0.5w$)	0.439	0.276	*0.333*	0.308 - 0.358
task1a ($0.2c + 0.3s + 0.5w$ on topics)	0.428	0.276	*0.330*	0.304 - 0.357
task1a ($0.2c + 0.3s + 0.5w$ on topics + context 20)	0.451	0.279	**0.338**	0.312 - 0.366

Table 3: Rouge-L results of task 2 using the document abstracts as the target summaries. The summary size was constrained to 250 words. In **boldface** is the best result. In *italics* are the results within the 95% confidence intervals of the best result.

were within confidence intervals.

4 Summary and Conclusions

We have experimented with approaches to incorporate information from the citing papers in an extractive summarisation system. We observed that ranking the sentences of the reference paper by comparing them against the citances improved results over methods that did not incorporate such information. In other words, the information introduced by the community of authors citing a paper is useful to produce an extractive summary of the reference paper. The improvement of results was considerable, and it suggests that a good strategy to build summaries is to focus on finding citing papers and use that information in the summariser.

Given the small amount of data available we did not try supervised methods. It is conceivable that, if further data are available, better results might be achieved by applying classification-based approaches. It would be interesting to test whether supervised methods that rely on larger volumes of annotated training data would also benefit from information from the citing papers. Alternatively, the additional data could be used to produce an additional development set to fine-tune the parameters in the approaches that we have explored in this paper.

Further research includes performing a new evaluation that uses as target summaries annotations from people who have not read the abstract, since it is conceivable that authors of citing papers used text from the abstract of the original paper, and that could explain our comparatively good results.

We observed a general improvement of results when we included additional information at the stage when the underlying models for *tf.idf* were created. Both adding additional sentences, and expanding the existing sentences by adding a context window, helped produce better results. This suggests an additional strategy to improve the quality of summarisation systems: find related documents, and use their information to create better-informed language models of the reference paper.

At the time of submission of this paper the results of the TAC 2014 BiomedSumm track were not available. The organisers of TAC 2014 proposed a different approach to evaluate task 1a, based on a direct comparison of the string offsets of the extracts from the reference papers. We anticipate that such evaluation metrics is probably too strict since it does not accommodate cases where the extract has similar information to the annotated text span. It will be interesting to contrast the TAC evaluation results with our evaluation and observe whether the same conclusions still apply.

5 Acknowledgements

This research was possible thanks to a winter internship by the second author funded by the Department of Computing at Macquarie University.

References

Amjad Abu-Jbara and Dragomir Radev. 2011. Coherent Citation-Based Summarization of Scientific Papers. In *Proceedings of the 49th Annual Meeting of the Association for Computational Linguistics: Human Language Technologies*, pages 500–509.

Stergos Afantenos, Vangelis Karkaletsis, and Panagiotis Stamatopoulos. 2005. Summarization from Medical Documents: a survey. *Artificial Intelligence in Medicine*, 33(2):157–177.

A R Aronson. 2001. Effective mapping of biomedical text to the UMLS Metathesaurus: the MetaMap program. *Proceedings / AMIA ... Annual Symposium. AMIA Symposium*, pages 17–21, January.

Jaime Carbonell and Jade Goldstein. 1998. The use of MMR, diversity-based reranking for reordering documents and producing summaries. In *Proceedings of the 21st annual international ACM SIGIR conference on Research and development in information retrieval - SIGIR '98*, pages 335–336, New York, New York, USA. ACM Press.

Hakan Ceylan, Rada Mihalcea, Umut Özertem, Elena Lloret, and Manuel Palomar. 2010. Quantifying the Limits and Success of Extractive Summarization Systems Across Domains. In *Human Language Technologies: The 2010 Annual Conference of the North American Chapter of the Association for Computational Linguistics*, number June, pages 903–911. Association for Computational Linguistics.

Christiane Fellbaum, editor. 1998. *WordNet: an electronic lexical database*. Language, Speech, and Communication. MIT Press, Cambrige, MA.

Eugene Garfield, Irving H Sher, and Richard J Torpie. 1964. The Use of Citation Data in Writing the History of Science. Technical Report 64, Institute for Scientific Information, Philadelphia, PA, USA.

Chin-Yew Lin. 2004. {ROUGE}: A Package for Automatic Evaluation of Summaries. In *ACL Workshop on Tech Summarisation Branches Out*.

Saif Mohammad, Bonnie Dorr, and Melissa Egan. 2009. Using citations to generate surveys of scientific paradigms. *Proceedings of Human Language Technologies: The 2009 Annual Conference of the North American Chapter of the Association for Computational Linguistics*, (June):584–592.

Diego Mollá and Maria Elena Santiago-Martínez. 2011. Development of a Corpus for Evidence Based Medicine Summarisation. In *Proceedings of the Australasian Language Technology Workshop*.

Preslav I Nakov, Ariel S Schwartz, and Marti A Hearst. 2004. Citances : Citation Sentences for Semantic Analysis of Bioscience Text. In *SIGIR 2004*.

Vahed Qazvinian and Dragomir R Radev. 2010. Identifying Non-explicit Citing Sentences for Citation-based Summarization. In *Proceedings of the 48th Annual Meeting of the Association for Computational Linguistics*, number 1996.

The Effect of Temporal-based Term Selection for Text Classification

Fumiyo Fukumoto[1], **Shogo Ushiyama**[2], **Yoshimi Suzuki**[1] and **Suguru Matsuyoshi**[1]
[1]Interdisciplinary Graduate School of Medicine and Engineering, University of Yamanashi
[2]Faculty of Engineering, University of Yamanashi
Kofu, 400-8511, JAPAN
{fukumoto, t08kg006, ysuzuki, sugurum}@yamanashi.ac.jp

Abstract

This paper addresses the text classification problem that training data may derive from a different time period from the test data. We present a method of temporal-based term selection for timeline adaptation. We selected two types of informative terms according to corpus statistics. One is temporal independent terms that are salient regardless of the timeline. Another is temporal dependent terms which are important for a specific period of time. For temporal dependent terms extracted from the training documents, we applied weighting function that weights terms according to the temporal distance between training and test data in the process of training classifiers. The results using Mainichi Japanese newspaper documents showed improvement over the three baselines.

1 Introduction

Text classification supports and improves several tasks such as automated topic tagging, building topic directory, spam filtering, creating digital libraries, sentiment analysis in user reviews, Information Retrieval, and even helping users to interact with search engines (Mourao et al., 2008). A growing number of machine learning techniques have been applied to text classification (Xue et al., 2008; Gopal and Yang, 2010). The common approach is the use of term selection. Each document is represented using a vector of selected terms (Yang and Pedersen, 1997; Hassan et al., 2007). Then, they used training documents with category label to train classifiers. Once category models are trained, each document of the test data is classified by using these models. Terms in the documents may be considered more important to build the classification model according to the timelines, while the majority of supervised classification methods consider that each term provides equally information regardless to a period. For instance, as shown in Figure 1, the term "earthquake" appeared more frequently in the category "Science" than "International" early in 1995. However, it appeared frequently in the category "International" than "Science" since Sumatra earthquake occurred just off the southern coast of Sumatra, Indonesia in 2005. Similarly, the term "Alcindo" frequently appeared in the documents tagged "Sports" in 1994, since Alcindo is a Brazilian soccer player and he was one of the most loved players in 1994. The term did not appear more frequently in the "Sports" category since he retired in 1997. These observations show that salient terms in the training data, are not salient in the test data when training data may derive from a different time period from the test data.

In this paper, we present a method for text classification concerned with the impact that the variation of the strength of term-class relationship over time. We selected two types of informative terms according to corpus statistics. One is temporal independent terms that are salient regardless of the timeline. Another is temporal dependent terms which are salient for a specific period of time. For temporal dependent terms extracted from the training documents, we applied weighting function that weights terms according to the temporal distance between training and test data in the process of training classifiers.

Our weighting function is based on an algorithm called temporally-aware algorithm that used a Temporal Weighting Function (TWF) developed by Salles *et al.* (Salles et al., 2010). The method incorporates temporal models to document classifiers. The weights assigned to each document depend on the notion of a temporal distance, defined as the difference between the time of creation of a training example and a reference time point, *i.e.*,

Fumiyo Fukumoto, Shougo Ushiyama, Yoshimi Suzuki and Suguru Matsuyoshi. 2014. The Effect of Temporal-based Term Selection for Text Classification. In *Proceedings of Australasian Language Technology Association Workshop*, pages 88−96.

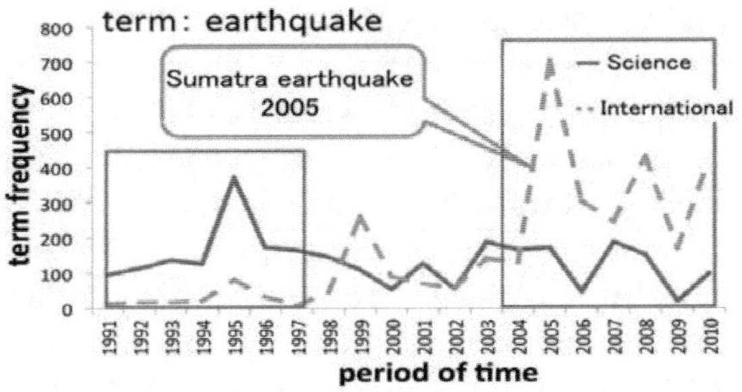

Figure 1: "earthquake" appeared in "Science" and "International" categories

temporal weighting weights training instances according to the temporal distance between training and test instances. The difference is that we applied the function to only dependent terms while a method of Salles weights all terms in the training documents. Because as illustrated in Figure 1, "earthquake" that are salient for a specific period of time and terms such as "Science" which are important regardless of the timeline in "Science" domain are both included in the training documents. These terms appearing in the training documents are equally weighted, which affect classification accuracy.

The remainder of the paper is organized as follows: Section 2 describes related work. Section 3 briefly reviews temporally-aware algorithm. Section 4 presents our framework. Finally, we report experiments and conclude our discussion with some directions for further work.

2 Related Work

The analysis of temporal aspects for text classification is a practical problem attracting more and more attention. Mourao *et al.* have shown evidence that time is an important factor in text classification (Mourao et al., 2008). More specifically, they selected training documents that are closer in time to the test document. They reported that the method has attained at 89.8% accuracy for ACM, and 87.6% for Medline. Cohen *et al.* attempted to extract context including phrases that is exploited towards better classification models (Cohen and Singer, 1999). Kim *et al.* focused on Web documents and presented a classification method using the knowledge acquisition method, Multiple Classification Ripple Down Rules (MCRDR). It enables domain users to elicit their domain knowledge incrementally and revise their knowledge base. They may then reclassify documents according to context changes (Kim et al., 2004). These techniques can be classified into adaptive document classification (Yang and Lin, 1999; Dumais and Chen, 2000; Liu and Lu, 2002; Rocha et al., 2008) where temporal aspects are considered to classification.

Several authors have attempted to capture concept or topic drift dealing with temporal effects in classification (Kelly et al., 1999; Lazarescu et al., 2004; Folino et al., 2007; Ross et al., 2012). The earliest known approach is the work of (Klinkenberg and Joachims, 2000). They attempted to handle concept changes with SVM. They used $\xi\alpha$-estimates to select the window size so that the estimated generalization error on new examples is minimized. The result which was tested on the TREC shows that the algorithm achieves a low error rate and selects appropriate window sizes. Scholz *et al.* proposed a method called knowledge-based sampling strategy (KBS) to train a classifier ensemble from data streams. They used two types of data sets, 2,608 documents of the data set of the TREC, and the satellite image dataset from the UCI library to evaluate their method. They showed that the algorithm outperformed leaning algorithms without considering concept drift (Scholz and Klinkenberg, 2007). He *et al.* attempted to find bursts, periods of elevated occurrence of events as a dynamic phenomenon instead of focusing on arrival rates (He and Parker, 2010). They used Moving Average Convergence/Divergence (MACD) histogram which was used in technical stock market analysis (Murphy, 1999) to detect bursts. They tested their method using MeSH terms and reported that the model works well for tracking topic bursts.

As mentioned above, several efforts have been made to automatically identify context changes, topic drift or topic bursts. Most of these focused just on identifying the increase of a new context, and not relating these contexts to their chronological time. In contrast, we propose a method that minimizes temporal effects to achieve high classification accuracy. In this context, Salles *et al.* proposed an approach to classify documents in scenarios where the method uses information about both the past and the future, and this information may change over time. They addressed the drawbacks of which instances to select by approximating the Temporal Weighting Function (TWF) us-

Table 1: Temporal distances against terms

	t_1	t_2	$\cdots$	t_k	D_δ
δ_1	f_{11}	f_{12}	$\cdots$	f_{1k}	$\sum_{i=1}^{k} f_{1i}$
δ_2	f_{21}	f_{22}	$\cdots$	f_{2k}	$\sum_{i=1}^{k} f_{2i}$
$\vdots$					
δ_n	f_{n1}	f_{n2}	$\cdots$	f_{nk}	$\sum_{i=1}^{k} f_{ni}$

ing a mixture of two Gaussians. They applied TWF to every training document. However, it is often the case that terms with salient for a specific period of time and important terms regardless of the timeline are both included in the training documents. We focus on the issue, and present an algorithm which weights only to the salient terms in a specific period of time.

3 Temporal Weighting Function

In this section, we briefly review Temporal Weighting Function (TWF) proposed by Salles *et al.* (Salles et al., 2010). TWF is based on the temporal distance between training and test documents creation times (Salles et al., 2010). Given a test document to be classified, the TWF sets higher weights to training documents that are more similar to the test document. The weights refer to the strength of term-class relationships. It is defined as $dominance(t, c) = \frac{N_{tc}}{\sum_{c'} N_{tc'}}$ where N_{tc} refers to the number of documents in class c that contain term t. When the dominance $dominance(t, c)$ is larger than a certain threshold value α[1], the term is judged to have a high degree of exclusivity with some class.

We note that TWF sets higher weights to training documents that temporally close to the test document. Let $S_t^{'} = \{\delta \leftarrow p_n - p_r \mid \forall r p_n \in S_{t,r}\}$ be a set of temporal distances that occur on the stability periods of term t. Here, p_n be the time of creation concerning to a training document. Stability periods of term t, referred to as $S_{t,r}$ is the largest continuous period of time, starting from the reference time point p_r in which the test document was created and growing both to the past and the future. For instance, if $S_{t,r}$ is {1999, 2000,2001}, and p_r = 2000, then $S_t^{'}$ = {-1,0,1}.

Finally, the function is determined considering the stability period of each term as a random variable where the occurrence of each possible temporal distance in its stability period is an event. The frequencies of the temporal distances δ_1 to δ_n for terms t_1 to t_k are shown in Table 1. The random variable D_δ related to the occurrences of δ, which represents the distribution of each δ_i over all terms t, is lognormally distributed if InD_δ is normally distributed. Here, InD_δ refers to log-normal distribution D_δ where D_δ stands for the distribution of temporal distance δ_i for the term t_i over all terms t. A 3-parameter Gaussian function, $F = a_i e^{-\frac{(x-b_i)^2}{2c_i^2}}$ is used to estimate the relationship between temporal distance and temporal weight, where the parameter a_i is the height of the curve's peak, b_i is the position of the center of the peak, and c_i controls the width of the curve. These parameters are estimated by using a Maximum Likelihood method.

[1]We empirically set alpha = 50% in the experiment.

4 Framework of the System

The method for temporal-based classification consists of three steps: selection of temporal independent/dependent terms, temporal weighting for dependent terms, and text classification.

4.1 Independent and dependent term selection

The first step is to select a set of independent/dependent terms from the training data. The selection is based on the use of feature selection technique. We tested different feature selection techniques, χ^2 statistics, mutual information, and information gain (Yang and Pedersen, 1997; Forman, 2003). In this paper, we report only χ^2 statistics that optimized global F-score in classification. χ^2 is given by:

$$\chi^2(t, C) = \frac{n \times (ad - bc)^2}{(a+c) \times (b+d) \times (a+b) \times (c+d)} \quad (1)$$

Using the two-way contingency table of a term t and a category C, a is the number of documents of C containing the term t, b is the number of documents of other class (not C) containing t, c is the number of documents of C not containing the term t, and d is the number of documents of other class not containing t. n is the total number of documents.

Independent terms are salient across the full temporal range of training documents. For each category C_i ($1 < i \leq n$), where n is the number of categories, we collected all documents with

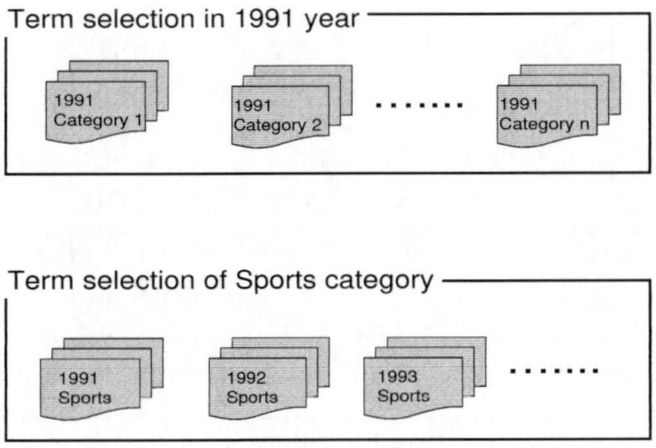

Figure 2: Term selection per year versus category

For each term $t \in D$ {
1. If t is included in the set X_{idt}, TWF is not applied to t.
// X_{idt} is a set of terms obtained by independent term selection.
2. Else if t is included in the set X_{dt}, {
// X_{dt} is a set of terms obtained by dependent term selection.
3. If t appears only in a specific year δ, t is weighted by TWF(δ).
4. Else if t occurs in several years, pick the latest year δ', t is weighted by TWF(δ').
}
}

Figure 3: Temporal weighting procedure

the same category across the full temporal range, and created a set. The number of sets equals to the number of categories. In contrast, dependent terms refer to a term that is salient for a specific period of time.

As illustrated in Figure 2, we selected dependent terms by using two methods: selection per year, and category. The former is applied to the sets of documents with different categories in the same year as illustrated in the top of Figure 2. For each category in a specific year y_j (y_j in Figure 2 refers to 1991), we collected all documents tagged in the category C_i within the year y_j, and created a set. The number of sets equals to the number of categories in the training documents. In contrast, term selection per category is applied to the sets of documents with different years in the same category shown in the bottom of Figure 2. For a specific category C_i (C_i refers to "Sports" in Figure 2), we collected all documents in the same year, and created a set. Thus, the number of sets equals to the number of different years in the training documents.

4.2 Temporal weighting

We applied χ^2 statistics and selected terms whose χ^2 value is larger than a certain threshold value. The procedure for temporal weighting of the selected term t in the training document D is shown in Figure 3. For each term t in the training document D, if t is included in a set obtained by dependent term selection, t is weighted by TWF, as the term t is salient for a specific year δ. As shown in 4 of Figure 3, if t occurs in several years, we pick up the latest year δ' and t is weighted by TWF(δ'). Because δ' is close to the year that the test document was created, and it can be considered to be reliable for accurate classification. X_{dt} in Figure 3 refers to a set of terms obtained by term selection per year (Year), or term selection per category (Cat).

4.3 Classification based on kNN

Similar to Salles's experiments (Salles et al., 2010), we tested Rocchio, kNN and NB with the TWF. As a result, we used kNN in the experiment because the result obtained by kNN was the best among them. Each training document is represented using a vector of selected independent/dependent terms. Given a test document, the system finds the k nearest neighbors among the training documents, and uses the categories of the k neighbors to weight the category candidates. The similarity score between training, and test documents collected from 1994 is illustrated in Figure 4.

The graph on the right hand side shows TWF described in Section 3. $Sim(d, d')$ indicates the similarity between training document d and the test document d'. As shown in Figure 4, we used the cosine value of two vectors to measure the similarity between the training and test documents. $f(t)$ refers to the frequency of a term t in the training/test document. t_1 in Figure 4 refers to a term that is important regardless of the timeline. In contrast, t_5 and t_7 are salient terms at a specific year, *i.e.*, 1991 and 1993. These terms are weighted by TWF, *i.e.*, the weight of t_5 is TWF(3) = TWF(1994-1991), and t_7 is TWF(1) = TWF(1994-1993). By sorting the score of candidate categories, a ranked list is obtained for the test

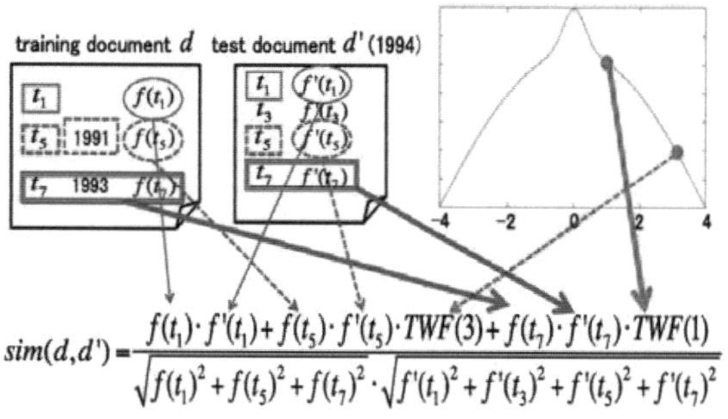

Figure 4: The similarity between training and test documents

document. The category with the highest score of the vote is assigned to the test document.

5 Experiments

We had an experiment to evaluate our method. We collected Mainichi Japanese newspaper from 1991 to 2010 and used them in the experiments[2]. Mainichi newspaper documents are classified into sixteen categories. Of these, we used six categories, "Sports", "Home", "Science", "Economy", "Arts", and "International", each of which has more than 250 documents for each year. All Japanese documents were tagged by using a morphological analyzer Chasen (Matsumoto et al., 2000). We used nouns as independent/dependent term selection.

We divided all the documents into two sets: one is to estimate the number of selected terms weighted by χ^2 statistics, 3 parameters Gaussian function, and the number of k in kNN. Another is a test data. We used the estimated parameters to classify test documents. Table 2 shows the size of data used in the experiments. "Doc" refers to the number of documents per category. As shown in Table 2, we used three types of test data to examine the effect of the method against the difference of period between the training and test data. As a result of parameter estimation, we used the number of 10,000 terms as independent terms and 3,000 for dependent terms. The estimated parameters used in a Gaussian function are shown in Table 3. The number of k in kNN was set to 12.

We evaluated text classification performance by F-score. To examine the effect of dependent term selection, we set X_{dt} in Figure 3 to three types of terms, *i.e.*, Year, Cat, and Year ∪ Cat, and compared these results. Table 4 shows the results obtained by using three types of terms. "Cat" and "Year" refer to the results obtained by term selection per category, and year, respectively. "Cat ∪ Year" refers to the results obtained by both selection methods. "Macro Avg." in Table 4 indicates macro-averaged F-score. "$*$" in Table 4 shows that "Cat" shows statistical significance t-test compared with the $*$ marked method.

As shown in Table 4, there is no significant difference among three selection methods, especially when the test and training documents are the same time period, *i.e.*, 1991 - 2000. When the test data is derived from 2001 and 2010, the macro-averaged F-score obtained by "Cat" is statistically significant compared with "Year" in some categories. These observations indicate that term selection per category is the best among other methods. Then, we used term selection per category as a dependent term selection.

We compared our method, temporal-based term selection(TTS) with three baselines: (1) SVM, (2) kNN, and (3) a method developed by Salles *et al.*

[2]http://ndk.co.jp/english/index.html

Table 2: Data used in the experiments

Parameter estimation				
Period	Training		Test	
	Doc	Total	Doc	Total
1991 - 2000	80	4,800	50	3,000
2001	–	–	500	3,000
2010	–	–	500	3,000

Training and Test				
Period	Training		Test	
	Doc	Total	Doc	Total
1991 - 2000	120	7,200	50	3,000
2001	–	–	500	3,000
2010	–	–	500	3,000

Table 3: Estimated parameters

Param.	Value
a_1	0.969
b_1	6.104×10^{-9}
c_1	7.320
a_2	0.031
b_2	-3.451×10^{-7}
c_2	0.506

Table 4: Classification Results

1991 - 2000 Test Data			
Category	Cat	Year	Cat ∪ Year
Arts	0.813	0.819	0.814
International	0.836	0.833	0.835
Economy	0.802	0.802	0.801
Home	0.747	0.751	0.751
Science	0.807	0.806	0.809
Sports	0.920	0.921	0.920
Macro Avg.	0.821	0.822	0.822

2001 Test Data			
Category	Cat	Year	Cat ∪ Year
Arts	0.799	0.791*	0.800
International	0.801	0.801	0.803
Economy	0.792	0.789	0.791
Home	0.745	0.740	0.744
Science	0.714	0.713	0.715
Sports	0.897	0.892*	0.898
Macro Avg.	0.791	0.788*	0.792

2010 Test Data			
Category	Cat	Year	Cat ∪ Year
Arts	0.330	0.323*	0.322*
International	0.718	0.714	0.718
Economy	0.694	0.698	0.695
Home	0.494	0.501	0.490
Science	0.495	0.496	0.496
Sports	0.862	0.865	0.863
Macro Avg.	0.598	0.600	0.597

* denotes statistical significance t-test, P-value ≤ 0.05

Table 5: Comparative results

1991 - 2000 Test Data				
Category	kNN	Salles	SVM	TTS
Arts	0.785*	0.795*	0.801	0.813
International	0.811*	0.810*	0.837	0.836
Economy	0.796	0.799	0.800	0.802
Home	0.715*	0.721*	0.740	0.747
Science	0.803	0.807	0.809	0.807
Sports	0.885*	0.890*	0.892*	0.920
Macro Avg.	0.799*	0.804*	0.812	0.821

2001 Test Data				
Category	kNN	Salles	SVM	TTS
Arts	0.765*	0.764*	0.780*	0.799
International	0.780*	0.783*	0.802	0.801
Economy	0.797	0.805	0.809	0.792
Home	0.717*	0.722*	0.728*	0.745
Science	0.720	0.720	0.723	0.714
Sports	0.867*	0.862*	0.870*	0.897
Macro Avg.	0.774*	0.776*	0.785	0.791

2010 Test Data				
Category	kNN	Salles	SVM	TTS
Arts	0.339	0.310*	0.340	0.330
International	0.688*	0.685*	0.687*	0.718
Economy	0.688	0.676*	0.689	0.694
Home	0.482*	0.477*	0.483*	0.494
Science	0.490	0.478	0.492	0.494
Sports	0.851*	0.850*	0.851*	0.862
Macro Avg.	0.589*	0.579*	0.590*	0.598

* denotes statistical significance t-test, P-value ≤ 0.05

(Salles et al., 2010), *i.e.*, the method applies TWF to each document. In SVM and kNN, we used the result of a simple χ^2 statistics. We used SVM-Light package for training and testing (Joachims, 1998)[3]. We used linear kernel and set all parameters to their default values. The results are shown in Table 5. "$*$" in Table 5 shows that TTS is statistical significance t-test compared with the $*$ marked methods. For instance, the performance of "Cat" in category "Arts" by using 1991-2000 test data shows significantly better to the results obtained by both kNN and Salles *et al.* methods.

As can be seen from Table 5 that macro-averaged F-score obtained by TTS was better to those obtained by kNN and Salles's methods in all of the three types of test data. When we used 1991 - 2000 and 2001 test data, the performance against the categories except for "Economy" and "Science" obtained by TTS was better to those obtained by kNN and Salles's methods. The performance obtained by TTS was better than Salles's method, especially the test data (2010) was far from the training data (1991 - 2000), as five out of six categories were statistically significant. These observations show that the algorithm which applies TWF to each term is more effective than the method applying TWF to each document in the training data. There is no significant difference between the results obtained by SVM and TTS when the test data is not far from the training data, *i.e.*,

[3]http://svmlight.joachims.org

Table 6: Sample results of term selection

Sports		International	
ind.	dep. (2000)	ind.	dep. (1997)
baseball	Sydney	president	**Tupac Amaru**
win	Toyota	premier	Lima
game	HP	army	Kinshirou
competition	hung-up	power	residence
championship	Paku	government	Hirose
entry	admission	talk	Huot
tournament	game	election	**MRTA**
player	Mita	**UN**	Topac
defeat	**Miyawaki**	politics	impression
pro	ticket	military	employment
title	ready	nation	earth
finals	Seagirls	democracy	election
league	award	minister	supplement
first game	Gaillard	**North Korea**	Eastern Europe
Olympic	attackers	chair	bankruptcy

1991 - 2000 and 2001. However, when we used 2010 test data, the result obtained by TTS is statistically significant compared with SVM. The observation shows that our method is effective when testing on data far from the training data.

Table 6 shows topmost 15 terms obtained by independent and dependent term selection. The dependent term selection is a result obtained by term selection per category. The categories are "Sports" and "International". As we can see from Table 6 that independent terms such as "baseball" and "win" are salient terms of the category "Sports" regardless to a time period. In contrast, "Miyawaki" listed in the dependent terms, is a snowboard player and he was on his first world championship title in Jan. 1998. The term often appeared in the documents from 1998 to 2000. Similarly, in the category "International", terms such as "UN" and "North Korea" often appeared in documents regardless of the timeline, while "Tupac Amaru" and "MRTA" frequently appeared in a specific year, 1997. Because in this year, Tupac Amaru Revolutionary Movement (MRTA) rebels were all killed when Peruvian troops stormed the Japanese ambassador's home where they held 72 hostages for more than four months. These observations support our basic assumption: there are two types of salient terms, *i.e.*, terms that are salient for a specific period, and terms that are important regardless of the timeline.

We recall that the overall performance obtained by four methods including our method drops when we used 2010 test data, while the performance of our method was still better than other methods in

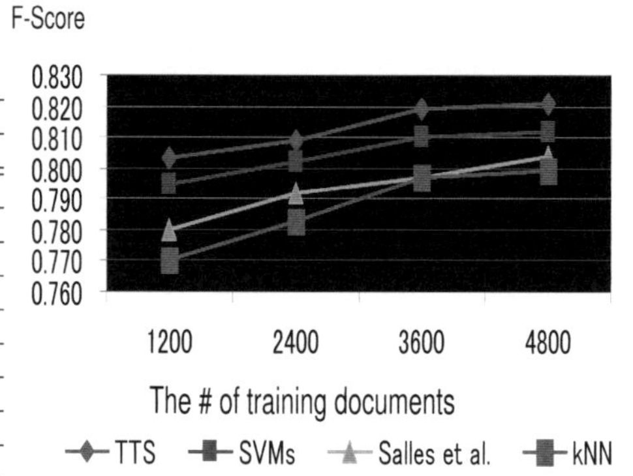

Figure 5: Performance (1991 - 2000 data)

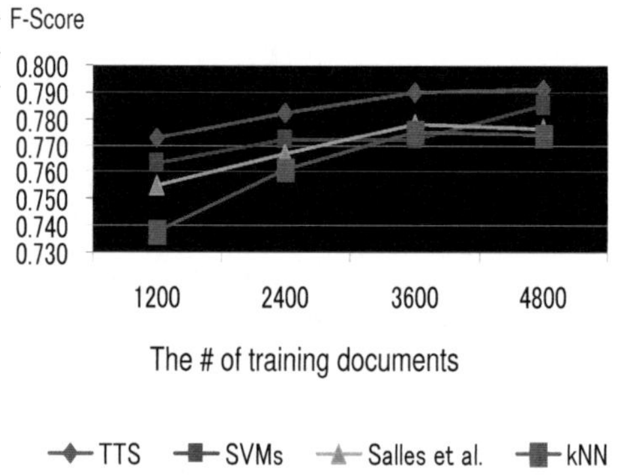

Figure 6: Performance (2001 data)

Table 5. We note that we used surface information, *i.e.*, noun words in documents as a feature of a vector. Therefore, the method ignores the sense of terms such as synonyms and antonyms. The earliest known technique for smoothing the term distributions through the use of latent classes is the Probabilistic Latent Semantic Analysis (PLSA) (Hofmann, 1999), and it has been shown to improve the performance of a number of information access including text classification (Xue et al., 2008). It is definitely worth trying with our method to achieve classification accuracy from different period of training and test data as high as that from the same time period of these data.

Finally, we evaluated the effect of the method against the number of training documents. Figures 5, 6 and 7 show the results using the test data collected from 1991 - 2000, 2001, and 2010, respectively. As we can see from Figures 5, 6 and 7, the results obtained by TTS were higher than those obtained by kNN and Salles *et al.* methods regardless of the number of training documents. Moreover, when the training and test data are the same time period, the F-score obtained by TTS using

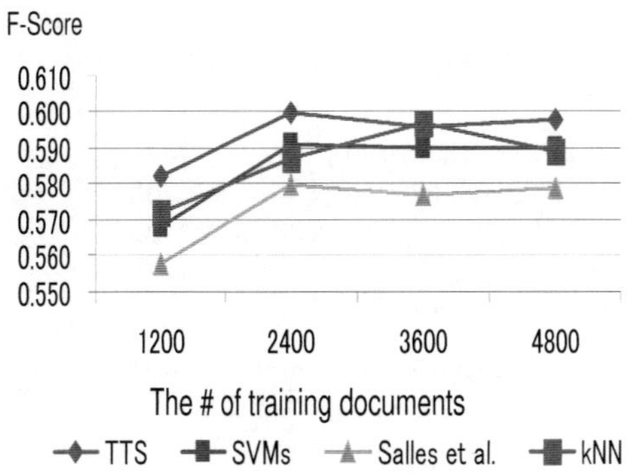

Figure 7: Performance (2010 data)

4,800 training documents and 1,200 documents were 0.821 and 0.804, respectively, and the performance was 1.7% decrease when the training data was reduced. However, those obtained by kNN and Salles *et al.* methods were 2.3% and 2.9% decreases, respectively. The behavior was similar when we used 2001 and 2010 test data. These observations support the effectiveness of our method.

6 Conclusion

We have developed an approach for text classification concerned with the impact that the variation of the strength of term-class relationship over time. We proposed a method of temporal-based term selection for timeline adaptation. The results showed that our method achieved better results than the baselines, kNN and Salles's methods in all of the three types of test data, 1991 - 2000, 2001, and 2010 test data. The result obtained by our method was statistically significant than SVM when the test data (2010) was far from the training data (1991 - 2000), while there was no significant difference between SVM and our method when the period of test data is close to the training data. Moreover, we found that the method is effective for a small number of training documents.

There are a number of interesting directions for future work. We should be able to obtain further advantages in efficacy in our approach by smoothing the term distributions through the use of latent classes in the PLSA (Hofmann, 1999; Xue et al., 2008). We used Japanese newspaper documents in the experiments. For quantitative evaluation, we need to apply our method to other data such as ACM-DL and a large, heterogeneous collection of web content. Temporal weighting function we used needs tagged corpora with long periods of time. The quantity of the training documents affects its performance. However, documents are annotated by hand, and manual annotation of documents is extremely expensive and time-consuming. In the future, we will try to extend the framework by using unsupervised methods *e.g.* Latent Dirichlet Allocation (LDA) (Blei et al., 2003; Wang and McCallum, 2006).

ACKNOWLEDGEMENTS

The authors would like to thank the referees for their valuable comments on the earlier version of this paper. This work was supposed by the Grant-in-aid for the Japan Society for the Promotion of Science (No. 25330255, 26330247).

References

D. M. Blei, A. Y. Ng, and M. I. Jordan. 2003. Latent Dirichlet Allocation. *Machine Learning*, 3:993–1022.

W. W. Cohen and Y. Singer. 1999. Context-sensitive Learning Methods for Text Categorization. *ACM Transactions of Information Systems*, 17(2):141–173.

S. Dumais and H. Chen. 2000. Hierarchical Classification of Web Contents. In *Proc. of the 23rd Annual International ACM SIGIR Conference on Research and Development in Information Retrieval*, pages 256–263.

G. Folino, C. Pizzuti, and G. Spezzano. 2007. An Adaptive Distributed Ensemble Approach to Mine Concept-drifting Data Streams. In *Proc. of the 19th IEEE International Conference on Tools with Artificial Intelligence*, pages 183–188.

G. Forman. 2003. An Extensive Empirical Study of Feature Selection Metrics for Text Classification. *Machine Learning Research*, 3:1289–1305.

S. Gopal and Y. Yang. 2010. Multilabel Classification with Meta-level Features. In *Proc. of the 33rd Annual International ACM SIGIR Conference on Research and Development in Information Retrieval*, pages 315–322.

S. Hassan, R. Mihalcea, and C. Nanea. 2007. Random-Walk Term Weighting for Improved Text Classification. In *Proc. of the IEEE International Conference on Semantic Computing*, pages 242–249.

D. He and D. S. Parker. 2010. Topic Dynamics: An Alternative Model of Bursts in Streams of Topics. In *Proc. of the 16th ACM SIGKDD Conference on Knowledge discovery and Data Mining*, pages 443–452.

T. Hofmann. 1999. Probabilistic Latent Semantic Indexing. In *Proc. of the 22nd Annual International ACM SIGIR Conference on Research and Development in Information Retrieval*, pages 35–44.

T. Joachims. 1998. SVM Light Support Vector Machine. In *Dept. of Computer Science Cornell University*.

M. G. Kelly, D. J. Hand, and N. M. Adams. 1999. The Impact of Changing Populations on Classifier Performance. In *Proc. of the fifth ACM SIGKDD International Conference on Knowledge Discovery and Data Mining*, pages 367–371.

Y. S. Kim, S. S. Park, E. Deards, and B. H. Kang. 2004. Adaptive Web Document Classification with MCRDR. In *Proc. of 2004 International Conference on Information Technology: Coding and Computing*, pages 476–480.

R. Klinkenberg and T. Joachims. 2000. Detecting Concept Drift with Support Vector Machines. In *Proc. of the 17th International Conference on Machine Learning*, pages 487–494.

M. M. Lazarescu, S. Venkatesh, and H. H. Bui. 2004. Using Multiple Windows to Track Concept Drift. *Intelligent Data Analysis*, 8(1):29–59.

R. L. Liu and Y. L. Lu. 2002. Incremental Context Mining for Adaptive Document Classification. In *Proc. of the eighth ACM SIGKDD International Conference on Knowledge Discovery and Data Mining*, pages 599–604.

Y. Matsumoto, A. Kitauchi, T. Yamashita, Y. Hirano, Y. Matsuda, K. Takaoka, and M. Asahara. 2000. *Japanese Morphological Analysis System Chasen Version 2.2.1*. In Naist Technical Report.

F. Mourao, L. Rocha, R. Araujo, T. Couto, M. Goncalves, and W. M. Jr. 2008. Understanding Temporal Aspects in Document Classification. In *Proc. of the 1st ACM International Conference on Web Search and Data Mining*, pages 159–169.

J. Murphy. 1999. *Technical Analysis of the Financial Markets*. Prentice Hall.

L. Rocha, F. Mourao, A. Pereira, M. A. Goncalves, and W. M. Jr. 2008. Exploiting Temporal Contexts in Text Classification. In *Proc. of the 17th ACM Conference on Information and Knowledge Management*, pages 26–30.

G. J. Ross, N. M. Adams, D. K. Tasoulis, and D. J. Hand. 2012. Exponentially Weighted Moving Average Charts for Detecting Concept Drift. *Pattern Recognition Letters*, 33(2):191–198.

T. Salles, L. Rocha, and G. L. Pappa. 2010. Temporally-aware Algorithms for Document Classification. In *Proc. of the 33rd Annual International ACM SIGIR Conference on Research and Development in Information Retrieval*, pages 307–314.

M. Scholz and R. Klinkenberg. 2007. Boosting Classifiers for Drifting Concepts. *Intelligent Data Analysis*, 11(1):3–28.

X. Wang and A. McCallum. 2006. Topic over Time: A Non-Markov Continuous-Time Model of Topic Trends. In *Proc. of the 12th ACM SIGKDD International Conference on Knowledge Discovery and Data Mining*, pages 424–433.

G. R. Xue, W. Dai, Q. Yang, and Y. Yu. 2008. Topic-bridged PLSA for Cross-Domain Text Classification. In *Proc. of the 31st Annual International ACM SIGIR Conference on Research and Development in Information Retrieval*, pages 627–634.

Y. Yang and X. Lin. 1999. A Re-examination of Text Categorization Methods. In *Proc. of the 22nd Annual International ACM SIGIR Conference on Research and Development in Information Retrieval*, pages 42–49.

Y. Yang and J. O. Pedersen. 1997. A Comparative Study on Feature Selection in Text Categorization. In *Proc. of the 14th International Conference on Machine Learning*, pages 412–420.

Short papers

Graph-Based Semi-Supervised Conditional Random Fields For Spoken Language Understanding Using Unaligned Data

Mohammad Aliannejadi
Amirkabir University of Technology (Tehran Polytechnic)
m.aliannejadi@aut.ac.ir

Masoud Kiaeeha
Sharif University of Technology
kiaeeha@ce.sharif.edu

Shahram Khadivi & Saeed Shiry Ghidary
Amirkabir University of Technology (Tehran Polytechnic)
{khadivi, shiry}@aut.ac.ir

Abstract

We experiment graph-based Semi-Supervised Learning (SSL) of Conditional Random Fields (CRF) for the application of Spoken Language Understanding (SLU) on unaligned data. The aligned labels for examples are obtained using IBM Model. We adapt a baseline semi-supervised CRF by defining new feature set and altering the label propagation algorithm. Our results demonstrate that our proposed approach significantly improves the performance of the supervised model by utilizing the knowledge gained from the graph.

1 Introduction

The aim of Spoken Language Understanding (SLU) is to interpret the intention of the user's utterance. More specifically, a SLU system attempts to find a mapping from user's utterance in natural language, to the limited set of concepts that is structured and meaningful for the computer. As an example, for the sample utterance:

I want to return to Dallas on Thursday

It's corresponding output would be:

```
GOAL : RETURN
TOLOC.CITY = Dallas
RETURN.DATE = Thursday.
```

SLU can be widely used in many real world applications; however, data processing costs may impede practicability of it. Thus, attempting to train a SLU model using less training data is a key issue.

The first statistical SLU system was based on hidden Markov model and modeled using a finite state semantic tagger employed in AT&T's CHRONUS system (Pieraccini et al., 1992). Their semantic representation was flat-concept; but, later He and Young (2005) extended the representation to a hierarchical structure and modeled the problem using a push-down automaton. There are other works which have dealt with SLU as a sequential labeling problem. Raymond and Riccardi (2007) and Wang and Acero (2006) have fully annotated the data and trained the model in discriminative frameworks such as CRF. CRF captures many complex dependencies and models the sequential relations between the labels; therefore, it is a powerful framework for SLU.

The Semi-Supervised Learning (SSL) approach has drawn a raft of interest among the machine learning community basically because of its practical application. Manual tagging of data can take considerable effort and time; however, in the training phase of SSL, a large amount of unlabeled data along with a small amount of labeled data is provided. This makes it more practicable and cost effective than providing a fully labeled set of training data; thus, SSL is more favorable.

Graph-based SSL, the most active area of research in SSL in the recent years, has shown to outperform other SSL methods (Chapelle et al., 2006). Graph-based SSL algorithms are generally run in two steps: graph construction and label propagation. Graph construction is the most important step in graph-based SSL; and, the fundamental approach is to assign labeled and unlabeled examples to nodes of the graph. Then, a similarity function is applied to compute similarity between pairs of nodes. The computed similarities are then assigned as the weight of the edges connecting the nodes (Zhu et al., 2003). Label propagation operates on the constructed graph. Based on the constraints or properties derived from the graph, labels are propagated from a few labeled nodes to the entire graph. These constraints include smoothness (Zhu et al., 2003; Subramanya et al., 2010; Talukdar et al., 2008; Garrette and Baldridge, 2013), and sparsity (Das and Smith, 2012; Zeng et al., 2013).

Labeling unaligned training data requires much

Mohammad Aliannejadi, Masoud Kiaeeha, Shahram Khadivi and Saeed Shiry Ghidary. 2014. Graph-Based Semi-Supervised Conditional Random Fields For Spoken Language Understanding Using Unaligned Data. In *Proceedings of Australasian Language Technology Association Workshop*, pages 98−103.

less effort compared to aligned data (He and Young, 2005). Nevertheless, unaligned data cannot be used to train a CRF model directly since CRF requires *fully-annotated* data. On the other hand, robust parameter estimation of a CRF model requires a large set of training data which is unrealistic in many practical applications. To overcome this problem, the work in this paper applies semi-supervised CRF on unlabeled data. It is motivated by the hypothesis that data is aligned to labels in a monotone manner, and words appearing in similar contexts tend to have same labels. Under these circumstances, we were able to reach 1.64% improvement on the F-score over the supervised CRF and 1.38% improvement on the F-score over the self trained CRF.

In the following section we describe the algorithm this work is based on and our proposed algorithm. In Section 3 we evaluate our work and in the final section conclusions are drawn.

2 Semi-supervised Spoken Language Understanding

The input data is unaligned and represented as a semantic tree, which is described in (He and Young, 2005). The training sentences and their corresponding semantic trees can be aligned monotonically; hence, we chose IBM Model 5 (Khadivi and Ney, 2005) to find the best alignment between the words and nodes of the semantic tree (labels). Thus, we have circumvented the problem of unaligned data. More detailed explanation about this process can be found in our previous work (Aliannejadi et al., 2014). This data is then used to train the supervised and semi-supervised CRFs.

2.1 Semi-supervised CRF

The proposed semi-supervised learning algorithm is based on (Subramanya et al., 2010). Here, we quickly review this algorithm (Algorithm 1).

In the first step, the CRF model is trained on the labeled data ($\mathcal{D}_l$) according to (1):

$$\Lambda^* = \underset{\Lambda \in \mathbb{R}^K}{\arg\min} \left[-\sum_{i=1}^{l} \log \mathrm{p}(\mathbf{y_i}|\mathbf{x_i}; \Lambda) + \gamma \|\Lambda\|^2 \right], \tag{1}$$

where Λ^* is the optimal parameter set of the base CRF model and $\|\Lambda\|^2$ is the squared ℓ_2-norm regularizer whose impact is adjusted by γ. At the first line, Λ^* is assigned to $\Lambda_{(n=0)}$ i.e. the initial parameter set of the model.

Algorithm 1 Semi-Supervised Training of CRF

1: $\Lambda_{(n=0)} = \mathrm{TrainCRF}(\mathcal{D}_l)$
2: $\mathrm{G} = \mathrm{BuildGraph}(\mathcal{D}_l \cup \mathcal{D}_u)$
3: $\{\mathrm{r}\} = \mathrm{CalcEmpiricalDistribution}(\mathcal{D}_l)$
4: **while** not converged **do**
5: $\quad \{\mathrm{m}\} = \mathrm{CalcMarginals}(\mathcal{D}_u, \Lambda_n)$
6: $\quad \{\mathrm{q}\} = \mathrm{AverageMarginals(m)}$
7: $\quad \{\hat{\mathrm{q}}\} = \mathrm{LabelPropagation(q, r)}$
8: $\quad \mathcal{D}_u^v = \mathrm{ViterbiDecode}(\{\hat{\mathrm{q}}\}, \Lambda_n)$
9: $\quad \Lambda_{n+1} = \mathrm{RetrainCRF}(\mathcal{D}_l \cup \mathcal{D}_u^v, \Lambda_n)$;
10: **end while**
11: Return final Λ_n

In the next step, the k-NN similarity graph (G) is constructed (line 2), which will discussed in more detail in Section 2.3. In the third step, the empirical label distribution (r) on the labeled data is computed. The main loop of the algorithm is then started and the execution continues until the results converge.

Marginal probability of labels (m) are then computed on the unlabeled data ($\mathcal{D}_u$) using Forward-Backward algorithm with the parameters of the previous CRF model (Λ^n), and in the next step, all the marginal label probabilities of each trigram are averaged over its occurrences (line 5 and 6).

In label propagation (line 7), trigram marginals (q) are propagated through the similarity graph using an iterative algorithm. Thus, they become smooth. Empirical label distribution (r) serves as the priori label information for labeled data and trigram marginals (q) act as the seed labels. More detailed discussion is found in Section 2.4.

Afterwards, having the results of label propagation ($\hat{\mathrm{q}}$) and previous CRF model parameters, labels of the unlabeled data are estimated by combining the interpolated label marginals and the CRF transition potentials (line 8). For every word position j for i indexing over sentences, interpolated label marginals are calculated as follows:

$$\hat{\mathrm{p}}(y_i^{(j)} = y|\mathbf{x}_i) = \alpha \mathrm{p}(y_i^{(j)} = y|\mathbf{x}_i; \Lambda_n) + (1-\alpha)\hat{\mathrm{q}}_{T(i,j)}(y), \tag{2}$$

where $T(i, j)$ is a trigram centered at position j of the ith sentence and α is the interpolation factor.

In the final step, the previous CRF model parameters are regularized using the labels estimated for the unlabeled data in the previous step (line 9)

Description	Feature
Context	$x_1\ x_2\ x_3\ x_4\ x_5$
Left Context	$x_1\ x_2$
Right Context	$x_4\ x_5$
Center Word in trigram	$\_\ x_3\ \_$
Center is Class	$IsClass(x_3)$
Center is Preposition	$IsPreposition(x_3)$
Left is Preposition	$IsPreposition(x_2)$

Table 1: Context Features used for constructing the similarity graph

as follows:

$$\Lambda_{n+1} = \underset{\Lambda \in \mathbb{R}^K}{\arg\min} \Big[-\sum_{i=1}^{l} \log p(\mathbf{y_i}|\mathbf{x_i};\Lambda_n) - \eta \sum_{i=l+1}^{u} \log p(\mathbf{y_i}|\mathbf{x_i};\Lambda_n) + \gamma\|\Lambda\|^2 \Big], \quad (3)$$

where η is a trade-off parameter whose setting is discussed later in Section 3.

2.2 CRF Features

By aligning the training data, many informative labels are saved which are omitted in other works (Wang and Acero, 2006; Raymond and Riccardi, 2007). By saving these information, the first order label dependency helps the model to predict the labels more precisely. Therefore the model manages to predict the labels using less lexical features and the feature window that was [-4,+2] in previous works is reduced to [0,+2]. Using smaller feature window improves the generalization of the model (Aliannejadi et al., 2014).

2.3 Similarity Graph

In our work we have considered trigrams as the nodes of the graph and extracted features of each trigram $x_2\ x_3\ x_4$ according to the 5-word context $x_1\ x_2\ x_3\ x_4\ x_5$ it appears in. These features are carefully selected so that nodes are correctly placed in neighborhood of the ones having similar labels. Table 1 presents the feature set that we have applied to construct the similarity graph.

$IsClass$ feature impacts the structure of the graph significantly. In the pre-processing phase specific words are marked as classes according to the corpus' accompanying database. As an example, city names such as Dallas and Baltimore are represented as *city_name* which is a class type. Since these classes play an important role in calculating similarity of the nodes, $IsClass$ feature is used to determine if a given position in a context is a class type.

Furthermore, prepositions like *from* and *between* are also important, e.g. when two trigrams like "*from Washington to*" and "*between Dallas and*" are compared. The two trigrams are totally different while both of them begin with a preposition and are continued with a class. Therefore, $IsPreposition$ feature would be particularly suitable to increase the similarity score of these two trigrams. In many cases, these features have a significant effect in assigning a better similarity score.

To define a similarity measure, we compute the Pointwise Mutual Information (PMI) between all occurrences of a trigram and each of the features. The PMI measure transforms the independence assumption into a ratio (Lin, 1998; Razmara et al., 2013). Then, the similarity between two nodes is measured as the cosine distance between their PMI vectors. We carefully examined the similarity graph on the training data and found out the head and tail trigrams of each sentence which contain *dummy* words, make the graph sparse. Hence, we have ignored those trigrams.

2.4 Label Propagation

After statistical alignment, the training data gets noisy. Hence, use of traditional label propagation algorithms causes an error propagation over the whole graph and degrades the whole system performance. Thus, we make use of the Modified Adsorption (MAD) algorithm for label propagation.

MAD algorithm controls the label propagation more strictly. This is accomplished by limiting the amount of information that passes from a node to another (Talukdar and Pereira, 2010). Soft label vectors $\hat{Y_v}$ are found by solving the unconstrained optimization problem in (4):

$$\min_{\hat{Y}} \sum_{l \in C} \Big[\mu_1 (Y_l - \hat{Y_l})^\top S\,(Y_l - \hat{Y_l}) + \mu_2 \hat{Y_l}^\top L' \hat{Y_l} + \mu_3 \big\|\hat{Y_l} - R_l\big\|^2 \Big], \quad (4)$$

where μ_i are hyper-parameters and R_l is the empirical label distribution over labels i.e. the prior belief about the labeling of a node. The first term of the summation is related to label score injection from the initial score of the node and

	% of Labeled Data		
	10	20	30
Supervised CRF	86.07	87.69	88.64
Self-trained CRF	86.34	87.73	88.64
Semi-supervised CRF	87.72	88.75	89.12

Table 2: Comparison of training results. Slot/Value F-score in %.

makes the output match the seed labels Y_l (Razmara et al., 2013). The second term is associated with label score acquisition from neighbor nodes i.e. smooths the labels according to the similarity graph. In the last term, the labels are regularized to match a priori label R_l in order to avoid false labels for high degree unlabeled nodes. A solution to the optimization problem in (4) can be found with an efficient iterative algorithm described in (Talukdar and Crammer, 2009).

Many errors of the alignment model are corrected through label propagation using the MAD algorithm; whereas, those errors are propagated in traditional label propagation algorithms such as the one mentioned in (Subramanya et al., 2010).

2.5 System Overview

We have implemented the Graph Construction in Java and the CRF is implemented by modifying the source code of CRFSuite (Okazaki, 2007). We have also modified Junto toolkit (Talukdar and Pereira, 2010) and used it for graph propagation. The whole source code of our system is available online[1]. The input utterances and their corresponding semantic trees are aligned using GIZA++ (Och and Ney, 2000); and then used to train the base CRF model. The graph is constructed using the labeled and unlabeled data and the main loop of the algorithm continues until convergence. The final parameters of the CRF are retained for decoding in the test phase.

3 Experimental Results

In this section we evaluate our results on Air Travel Information Service (ATIS) data-set (Dahl et al., 1994) which consists of 4478 training, 500 development and 896 test utterances. The development set was chosen randomly. To evaluate our work, we have compared our results with results from Supervised CRF and Self-trained CRF (Yarowsky, 1995).

For our experiments we set hyper-parameters as follows: for graph propagation, $\mu_1 = 1, \mu_2 = 0.01$, $\mu_3 = 0.01$, for Viterbi decoding, $\alpha = 0.1$, for CRF-retraining, $\eta = 0.1$, $\gamma = 0.01$. We have chosen these parameters along with graph features and graph-related parameters by evaluating the model on the development set. We employed the L-BFGS algorithm to optimize CRF objective functions; which is designed to be fast and low-memory consumer for the high-dimensional optimization problems (Bertsekas, 1999).

We have post-processed the sequence of labels to obtain the slots and their values. The slot-value pair is compared to the reference test set and the result is reported in F-score of slot classification. Table 2 demonstrates results obtained from our semi-supervised CRF algorithm compared to the supervised CRF and self-trained CRF. Experiments were carried out having 10%, 20% and 30% of data being labeled. For each of these tests, labeled set was selected randomly from the training set. This procedure was done 10 times and the reported results are the average of the results thereof. The Supervised CRF model is trained only on the labeled fraction of the data. However, the Self-trained CRF and Semi-supervised CRF have access to the rest of the data as well, which are unlabeled. Our Supervised CRF gained 91.02 F-score with 100% of the data labeled which performs better compared to 89.32% F-score of Raymond and Riccardi (2007) CRF model.

As shown in Table 2, the proposed method performs better compared to supervised CRF and self-trained CRF. The most significant improvement occurs when only 10% of training set is labeled; where we gain 1.65% improvement on F-score compared to supervised CRF and 1.38% compared to self-trained CRF.

4 Conclusion

We presented a simple algorithm to train CRF in a semi-supervised manner using unaligned data for SLU. By saving many informative labels in the alignment phase, the base model is trained using fewer features. The parameters of the CRF model are estimated using much less labeled data by regularizing the model using a nearest-neighbor graph. Results demonstrate that our proposed algorithm significantly improves the performance compared to supervised and self-trained CRF.

[1] https://github.com/maxxkia/g-ssl-crf

References

Mohammad Aliannejadi, Shahram Khadivi, Saeed-Shiry Ghidary, and MohammadHadi Bokaei. 2014. Discriminative spoken language understanding using statistical machine translation alignment models. In Ali Movaghar, Mansour Jamzad, and Hossein Asadi, editors, *Artificial Intelligence and Signal Processing*, volume 427 of *Communications in Computer and Information Science*, pages 194–202. Springer International Publishing.

Dimitri P Bertsekas. 1999. Nonlinear programming.

Olivier Chapelle, Bernhard Schölkopf, Alexander Zien, et al. 2006. *Semi-supervised learning*, volume 2. MIT press Cambridge.

Deborah A. Dahl, Madeleine Bates, Michael Brown, William Fisher, Kate Hunicke-Smith, David Pallett, Christine Pao, Alexander Rudnicky, and Elizabeth Shriberg. 1994. Expanding the scope of the atis task: The atis-3 corpus. In *Proceedings of the Workshop on Human Language Technology*, HLT '94, pages 43–48, Stroudsburg, PA, USA. Association for Computational Linguistics.

Dipanjan Das and Noah A. Smith. 2012. Graph-based lexicon expansion with sparsity-inducing penalties. In *Proceedings of the 2012 Conference of the North American Chapter of the Association for Computational Linguistics: Human Language Technologies*, NAACL HLT '12, pages 677–687, Stroudsburg, PA, USA. Association for Computational Linguistics.

Dan Garrette and Jason Baldridge. 2013. Learning a part-of-speech tagger from two hours of annotation. In *Proceedings of NAACL-HLT*, pages 138–147.

Yulan He and Steve Young. 2005. Semantic processing using the hidden vector state model. *Computer Speech & Language*, 19(1):85 – 106.

Shahram Khadivi and Hermann Ney. 2005. Automatic filtering of bilingual corpora for statistical machine translation. In Andrés Montoyo, Rafael Muńoz, and Elisabeth Métais, editors, *Natural Language Processing and Information Systems*, volume 3513 of *Lecture Notes in Computer Science*, pages 263–274. Springer Berlin Heidelberg.

Dekang Lin. 1998. Automatic retrieval and clustering of similar words. In *Proceedings of the 36th Annual Meeting of the Association for Computational Linguistics and 17th International Conference on Computational Linguistics - Volume 2*, ACL '98, pages 768–774, Stroudsburg, PA, USA. Association for Computational Linguistics.

Franz Josef Och and Hermann Ney. 2000. Giza++: Training of statistical translation models.

Naoaki Okazaki. 2007. Crfsuite: a fast implementation of conditional random fields (crfs). *URL http://www.chokkan.org/software/crfsuite.*

R. Pieraccini, E. Tzoukermann, Z. Gorelov, J. Gauvain, E. Levin, Chin-Hui Lee, and J.G. Wilpon. 1992. A speech understanding system based on statistical representation of semantics. In *Acoustics, Speech, and Signal Processing, 1992. ICASSP-92., 1992 IEEE International Conference on*, volume 1, pages 193–196 vol.1, Mar.

Christian Raymond and Giuseppe Riccardi. 2007. Generative and discriminative algorithms for spoken language understanding. In *International Conference on Speech Communication and Technologies*, pages 1605–1608, Antwerp, Belgium, August.

Majid Razmara, Maryam Siahbani, Gholamreza Haffari, and Anoop Sarkar. 2013. Graph propagation for paraphrasing out-of-vocabulary words in statistical machine translation. In *Proceedings of the Conference of the Association for Computational Linguistics (ACL).*

Amarnag Subramanya, Slav Petrov, and Fernando Pereira. 2010. Efficient graph-based semi-supervised learning of structured tagging models. In *Proceedings of the 2010 Conference on Empirical Methods in Natural Language Processing*, EMNLP '10, pages 167–176, Stroudsburg, PA, USA. Association for Computational Linguistics.

ParthaPratim Talukdar and Koby Crammer. 2009. New regularized algorithms for transductive learning. In Wray Buntine, Marko Grobelnik, Dunja Mladeni, and John Shawe-Taylor, editors, *Machine Learning and Knowledge Discovery in Databases*, volume 5782 of *Lecture Notes in Computer Science*, pages 442–457. Springer Berlin Heidelberg.

Partha Pratim Talukdar and Fernando Pereira. 2010. Experiments in graph-based semi-supervised learning methods for class-instance acquisition. In *Proceedings of the 48th Annual Meeting of the Association for Computational Linguistics*, ACL '10, pages 1473–1481, Stroudsburg, PA, USA. Association for Computational Linguistics.

Partha Pratim Talukdar, Joseph Reisinger, Marius Paşca, Deepak Ravichandran, Rahul Bhagat, and Fernando Pereira. 2008. Weakly-supervised acquisition of labeled class instances using graph random walks. In *Proceedings of the Conference on Empirical Methods in Natural Language Processing*, EMNLP '08, pages 582–590, Stroudsburg, PA, USA. Association for Computational Linguistics.

Ye-Yi Wang and Alex Acero. 2006. Discriminative models for spoken language understanding. In *International Conference on Speech Communication and Technologies.*

David Yarowsky. 1995. Unsupervised word sense disambiguation rivaling supervised methods. In *Proceedings of the 33rd Annual Meeting on Association for Computational Linguistics*, ACL '95, pages 189–196, Stroudsburg, PA, USA. Association for Computational Linguistics.

Xiaodong Zeng, Derek F Wong, Lidia S Chao, and Isabel Trancoso. 2013. Graph-based semi-supervised model for joint chinese word segmentation and part-of-speech tagging. In *ACL*, pages 770–779.

Xiaojin Zhu, Zoubin Ghahramani, John Lafferty, et al. 2003. Semi-supervised learning using gaussian fields and harmonic functions. In *ICML*, volume 3, pages 912–919.

Alveo, a Human Communication Science Virtual Laboratory

Dominique Estival
U. of Western Sydney
d.estival@uws.edu.au

Steve Cassidy
Macquarie University
steve.cassidy@mq.edu.au

Abstract

We give a hands-on demonstration of the Alveo Virtual Laboratory, a new platform for collaborative research in human communication science (HCS). Funded by the Australian Government National eResearch Collaboration Tools and Resources (NeCTAR) program, Alveo involves partners from a range of disciplines: linguistics, natural language processing, speech science, psychology, as well as music and acoustic processing. The goal of the platform is to provide easy access to a variety of databases and a range of analysis tools, in order to foster inter-disciplinary research and facilitate the discovery of new methods for solving old problems or the application of known methods to new datasets. Alveo integrates a number of tools and enables non-technical users to process communication resources (including not only text and speech corpora but also music recordings and videos) using these tools in a straightforward manner.

1 Introduction

Alveo provides easy access to a range of databases relevant to human communication science disciplines, including speech, text, audio and video, some of which would previously have been difficult for researchers to access or even know about. The system implements a uniform and secure license management system for the diverse licensing and user agreement conditions required. Browsing, searching and dataset manipulation are also functionalities which are available in a consistent manner across the data collections through the web-based Discovery Interface.

2 Alveo Tools and Corpora

The first phase of the project, from December 2012 to June 2014 (Estival et al. 2013) saw the inclusion of data collections contributed by the project partners (see the list of partners in the Acknowledgments section). Some of these were already well-known, e.g. 1, 3 and 9, but some had been difficult of access or not available, e.g. 2, 5, 6, 7, 8.

1. PARADISEC (Pacific and Regional Archive for Digital Sources in Endangered Cultures: http://paradisec.org.au): audio, video, text and image resources for Australian and Pacific Island languages (Thieberger et al. 2011).
2. AusTalk (https://austalk.edu.au): audio-visual speech corpus of Australian English (Burnham et al. 2011).
3. The Australian National Corpus (https://www.ausnc.org.au) (Cassidy et al. 2012) comprising: Australian Corpus of English (ACE); Australian Radio Talkback (ART); AustLit; Braided Channels; Corpus of Oz Early English (COOEE); Griffith Corpus of Spoken English (GCSAusE); International Corpus of English (ICE-AUS); Mitchell & Delbridge corpus; Monash Corpus of Spoken English (Musgrave and Haugh 2009).
4. AVOZES, a visual speech corpus (Goecke and Millar 2004).
5. UNSW Pixar Emotional Music Excerpts: Pixar movie theme music expressing different emotions.
6. Sydney University Room Impulse Responses: environmental audio samples which, through convolution with speech or music, can create the effect of that speech or music in that acoustic environment.
7. Macquarie University Battery of Emotional Prosody: sung sentences with different prosodic patterns.
8. Colloquial Jakartan Indonesian corpus: audio and text, recorded in Jakarta in the early 1990's (ANU).
9. ClueWeb, a dataset consisting of 733,019,372 English web pages collected between 10/02/2012 and 10/05/2012 (lemurproject.org/clueweb12).

Through the web-based Discovery interface (see Figure 2) the user can select items based on the

Dominique Estival and Steve Cassidy. 2014. Alveo, a Human Communication Science Virtual Laboratory. In *Proceedings of Australasian Language Technology Association Workshop*, pages 104–107.

results of faceted search across the collections and can organise selected data in Items Lists. Beyond browsing and searching, Alveo offers the possibility of analysing and processing the data with a range of tools. In the first phase of the project, the following tools were integrated within Alveo:

1. EOPAS (PARADISEC tool) for interlinear text and media analysis.
2. NLTK (Natural Language Toolkit) for text analytics with linguistic data (Bird, Klein, and Loper 2009).
3. EMU, for search, speech analysis and interactive labelling of spectrograms and waveforms (Cassidy and Harrington 2000).
4. AusNC Tools: KWIC, Concordance, Word Count, statistical summary and analysis.
5. Johnson-Charniak parser, to generate full parse trees for text sentences (Charniak and Johnson 2005).
6. ParseEval, to evaluate the syllabic parse of consonant clusters (Shaw and Gafos 2010).
7. HTK-modifications, a patch to HTK (Hidden Markov Model Toolkit, to enable missing data recognition. (http://htk.eng.cam.ac.uk/).
8. DeMoLib, for video analysis (http://staff.estem-uc.edu.au/roland/research/demolib-home/).
9. PsySound3, for physical and psycho-acoustical analysis of complex visual and auditory scenes (Cabrera, Ferguson, and Schubert 2007).
10. ParGram, grammar for Indonesian (Arka 2012).
11. INDRI, for information retrieval with large data sets (http://www.lemurproject.org/indri/).

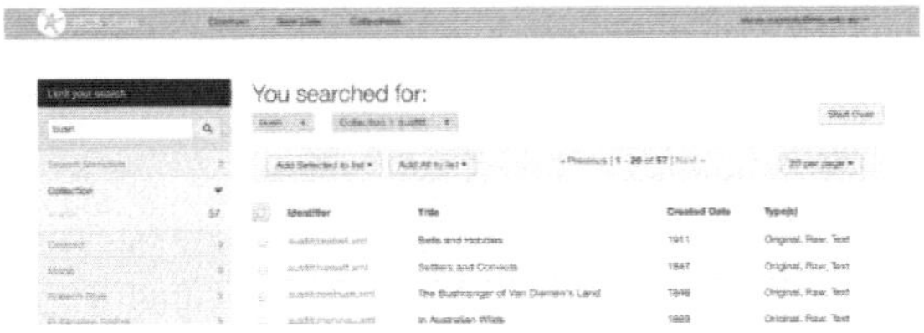

Figure 1: Screenshot of the Alveo Web interface

3 Alveo Architecture

Most of these tools require significant expertise to set up and one of the Alveo project goals is to make this easier for non-technical researchers. The Alveo Workflow Engine is built around the Galaxy open source workflow management system (Goecks et al. 2010), which was originally designed for use in the life sciences to support researchers in running pipelines of tools to manipulate data. Workflows in Galaxy can be stored, shared and published, and we hope this will also become a way for human communication science researchers to codify and exchange common analyses.

A number of the tools listed above have been packaged as Python scripts, for instance NLTK based scripts to carry out part-of-speech tagging, stemming and parsing. Other tools are implemented in R, e.g. EMU/R and ParseEval. An API is provided to mediate access to data, ensuring that permissions are respected, and providing a way to access individual items, and 'mount' datasets for fast access (Cassidy et al. 2014). An instance of the Galaxy Workflow engine is run on a virtual machine in the NeCTAR Research Cloud, a secure platform for Australian research, funded by the same government program (nectar.org.au/research-cloud). Finally, a UIMA (Unstructured Information Management Architecture) interface (Verspoor et al. 2009) has been developed to enable the conversion of Alveo items, as well as their associated annotations, into UIMA CAS documents, for analysis in a conventional UIMA pipeline. Conversely annotations from a UIMA pipeline can be associated with a document in Alveo (Estival et al. 2014). Figure 2 gives an overview of the architecture.

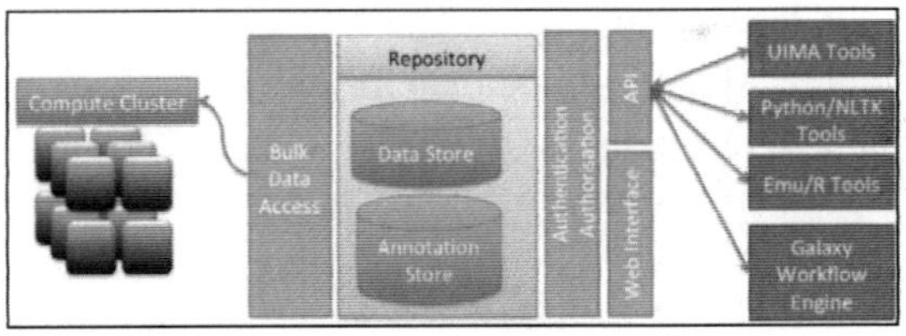

Figure 2: The architecture of the Alveo VL

4 User Acceptance Testing

Alveo was designed and implemented in partnership with Intersect, a commercial software development company specialised in the support of academic eResearch. This partnership afforded extensive professional support during development, using the Agile process (Beck et al. 2001) as well as thorough regression testing and debugging. In other projects of this type, Intersect provide User Acceptance Testing (UAT) or managed the UAT process in-house. For the Alveo project, user testing was the main way in which the academic partners were involved in the project. The central team at the lead institution oversaw the creation of the tests, distributed the tests and monitored the results.

Some testers were Linguistics students with no computing background, some were Computer Science students with limited linguistic knowledge. At some sites, the testers were Research Assistants who had worked on the tools or corpora contributed by their institutions, while others were the tool developers themselves. This variety of backgrounds and skills ensured coverage of the main domains and functionalities expected of the Alveo Virtual Lab. Some sites had undertaken to conduct large amounts of testing throughout the development, while other partners only chose to perform limited or more targeted testing, with commitments varying from 10 to 200 hours. Over 30 testers participated at various times during of the project and a total of more than 300 hours has been spent on testing during Phase I.

For each version of the system during development, a series of tests were developed. The first tests were very directive, giving very specific instructions as to what actions the user was asked to perform and what results were expected for each action. Gradually the tests became more open-ended, giving less guidance and gathering more informative feedback. The latest round of testing asked Testers to log in and to carry out a small research task. Some of the early tests, have become tutorials provided on the Alveo web page and are now available as help from within the Virtual Lab. We will use these as the basis for the hands-on demo.

5 Conclusion

One of the conditions of success of such a project is that the platform be used by researchers for their own projects and on their own data. The organisation of the User Acceptance Testing, requiring partners to contribute during the development, and providing exposure to the tools and the datasets to a large group of diverse researchers is expected to lead to a much wider uptake of Alveo as a platform for HCS research in Australia. Alveo is now open to users outside the original project partners. We will also continue to explore further interactions with complementary frameworks, such that the data and annotation storage available in Alveo can be enhanced via processing and tools from external services to supplement the functionality that is currently directly integrated.

We hope that by presenting Alveo to the Australian NLP community, we will encourage researchers to consider using Alveo as a potential repository for their data and as a platform to conduct new analysis. Alveo is already used in teaching a Computational Linguistics course at Monash University and we would encourage more instances of such educational use of the platform. Finally, we would like to invite students as well as researchers in HCS fields to propose tools and corpora which they would like to use in their own research for future inclusion in Alveo.

Acknowledgements

We thank NeCTAR for its financial support during Phase I and all the project partners (University of Western Sydney, RMIT, Macquarie University, Intersect, University of Melbourne, Australian National University, University of Western Australia, University of Sydney, University of New England, University of Canberra, Flinders University, University of New South Wales, La Trobe University, University of Tasmania, ASSTA, AusNC Inc. NICTA) for their on-going contributions to the project.

References

Arka, I. Wayan. 2012. "Developing a Deep Grammar of Indonesian within the ParGram Framework: Theoretical and Implementational Challenges " 26th Pacific Asia Conference on Language, Information and Computation.

Beck, Kent, Mike Beedle, Arie van Bennekum, Alistair Cockburn, Ward Cunningham, Martin Fowler, James Grenning, Jim Highsmith, Andrew Hunt, Ron Jeffries, Jon Kern, Brian Marick, Robert C. Martin, Steve Mellor, Ken Schwaber, Jeff Sutherland, and Dave Thomas. 2001. Manifesto for Agile Software Development. http://agilemanifesto.org/.

Bird, Steven, Ewan Klein, and Edward Loper. 2009. *Natural Language Processing with Python - Analyzing Text with the Natural Language Toolkit*: O'Reilly Media.

Burnham, Denis, Dominique Estival, Steven Fazio, Felicity Cox, Robert Dale, Jette Viethen, Steve Cassidy, Julien Epps, Roberto Togneri, Yuko Kinoshita, Roland Göcke, Joanne Arciuli, Marc Onslow, Trent Lewis, Andy Butcher, John Hajek, and Michael Wagner. 2011. "Building an audio-visual corpus of Australian English: large corpus collection with an economical portable and replicable Black Box." Interspeech 2011, Florence, Italy.

Cabrera, Densil , Sam Ferguson, and Emery Schubert. 2007. "'Psysound3': Software for Acoustical and Psychoacoustical Analysis of Sound Recordings." International Community on Auditory Display.

Cassidy, Steve, Dominique Estival, Timothy Jones, Denis Burnham, and Jared Burghold. 2014. "The Alveo Virtual Laboratory: A Web Based Repository API." 9th Language Resources and Evaluation Conference (LREC 2014), Reykjavik, Iceland, 26-31 May 2014.

Cassidy, Steve, and Jonathan Harrington. 2000. "Multi-level Annotation in the Emu Speech Database Management System." *Speech Communication* 33:61–77.

Cassidy, Steve, Michael Haugh, Pam Peters, and Mark Fallu. 2012. "The Australian National Corpus : national infrastructure for language resources." LREC.

Charniak, Eugene, and Mark Johnson. 2005. "Coarse-to-fine n-best parsing and MaxEnt discriminative reranking." 43rd Annual Meeting on Association for Computational Linguistics.

Estival, Dominique, Steve Cassidy, Peter Sefton, and Denis Burnham. 2013. "The Human Communication Science Virtual Lab." 7th eResearch Australasia Conference, Brisbane, Australia, October 2013.

Estival, Dominique, Steve Cassidy, Karin Verspoor, Andrew MacKinlay, and Denis Burnham. 2014. "Integrating UIMA with Alveo, a human communication science virtual laboratory." Workshop on Open Infrastructures and Analysis Frameworks for HLT, COLING 2014, Dublin, Ireland.

Goecke, Roland, and J.B. Millar. 2004. "The Audio-Video Australian English Speech Data Corpus AVOZES." 8th International Conference on Spoken Language Processing (INTERSPEECH 2004 - ICSLP), Jeju, Korea.

Goecks, Jeremy, Anton Nekrutenko, James Taylor, and The Galaxy Team. 2010. "Galaxy: a comprehensive approach for supporting accessible, reproducible, and transparent computational research in the life sciences." *Genome Biology* 11 (8):R86.

Musgrave, Simon, and Michael Haugh. 2009. "The AusNC Project: Plans, Progress and Implications for Language Technology." ALTA 2009, Sydney.

Shaw, Jason A., and Adamantios I. Gafos. 2010. "Quantitative evaluation of competing syllable parses." 11th Meeting of the Association for Computational Linguistics. Special Interest Group on Computational Morphology and Phonology, Uppsala, Sweden.

Thieberger, Nick, Linda Barwick, Rosey Billington, and Jill Vaughan, eds. 2011. *Sustainable data from digital research: Humanities perspectives on digital scholarship. A PARADISEC Conference*: Custom Book Centre. http://ses.library.usyd.edu.au/handle/2123/7890.

Verspoor, Karin, William Baumgartner Jr, Christophe Roeder, and Lawrence Hunter. 2009. "Abstracting the types away from a UIMA type system." *From Form to Meaning: Processing Texts Automatically*:249-256.

OCR and Automated Translation for the Navigation of non-English Handsets: A Feasibility Study with Arabic

Jennifer Biggs and Michael Broughton
Defence Science and Technology Organisation
Edinburgh, South Australia
{firstname.lastname}@dsto.defence.gov.au

Abstract

In forensics, mobile phones or handsets store potentially valuable information such as *Contact* lists, *SMS Messages*, or possibly *emails* and *Calendar* appointments. However, navigating to this content on non-English configured handsets, when the operator is untrained in the language, becomes a difficult task. We discuss a feasibility study that explored the performance of optical character recognition (OCR) systems against Arabic menus on handset LCD screens. Further, a method of automated spell correction and translation is explored considering fully automated or user-interactive workflow options. A capability technology demonstrator for non-English handset navigation was implemented based on outcomes of these studies, providing a platform for investigating workflow and usability.

1 Introduction

Some cellular exploitation tools support imaging of the handset display after the operator has navigated the handset menus to the content of interest. Such tools may support any handset type. However, navigating to this content on handsets configured for languages other than English (LOTE) is challenging for operators not trained in the language.

We undertook several feasibility studies to investigate the navigation of LOTE handsets for CELLEX purposes. The studies investigated the merits of: 1) applying Commercial-Off-The-Shelf (COTS) Optical Character Recognition (OCR) tools to photographed displays of handsets; and 2) combining LOTE OCR outputs with a method of automated translation.

1.1 OCR accuracy

COTS OCR systems are typically optimised for recognition of text at resolutions in excess of 100 dots per inch (dpi), such as scans of printed documents, newspapers or magazines, advertising accuracy rates of up to 97%. Batawi and Abulnaja (2012) report accuracy rates of between 94.8% and 97.8% for a selection of printed newspaper and magazine Arabic texts. Recognition of non-degraded printed pages may still require identification of optimal image pre-processing options (Yale University, 2008a; 2008b). Recognition accuracy for degraded documents may be expected to be significantly decreased (Herceg et al. 2005).

To utilise a COTS OCR application within a larger system architecture or workflow, where images do not meet application parameters, additional image pre-processing can be applied. Chang et al. (2007) and Chang et al. (2009) used Sakhr Automatic Reader v8.0 on photographed images of text.

1.2 Automated translation of OCR outputs

When applying Machine Translation (MT) processing to OCR output text, OCR errors are compounded. Chang et al. (2009) combined Sakhr Automatic Reader v8.0 with a statistical MT system known as PanDoRA (Zhang and Vogel, 2007), noting that word errors introduced by OCR were amplified during MT processing. For example, in translation of generated images of text from the Basic Travel Expression Corpus (BTEC) (Eck & Hori, 2005), the BLEU score of image text translation without errors was 43.12, while a 10.7% word recognition error rate severely drops the BLEU score to 28.56 (Chang et al., 2007; Chang et al. 2009).

Jennifer Biggs and Michael Broughton. 2014. OCR and Automated Translation for the Navigation of non-English Handsets: A Feasibility Study with Arabic. In *Proceedings of Australasian Language Technology Association Workshop*, pages 108−112.

2 Evaluating OCR Accuracy

The aim of this first study was to determine the feasibility of recognising Arabic text within photographed images of monochrome LCD handset displays by utilising COTS OCR applications.

A late 2003 model handset; a Nokia 2300 lv99, was selected for its backlit monochrome display of 96 x 65 pixels, with an ability to display 4 lines of text in either English and Arabic user interface languages. Image capture was performed using Samsung L200 10.2MP digital camera on a stand fixing orientation and distance with default camera settings. Two COTS OCR systems were selected for recognition of Arabic script. Each COTS system supports a range of either automated or manually determined image pre-processing and recognition settings and either automated or manual text area identification. The COTS systems will be referred to as COTS 1 and COTS 2 only.

2.1 Method

To match photographed images with image parameters expected by the COTS OCR systems, image pre-processing was performed. Images were manually cropped to the handset display area and scaled using cubic interpolation such that text heights were between supported font sizes of 6 – 20 pixels. Observation of binarised images produced by importing the cropped and scaled images into the COTS applications showed significant character erosion and background speckling. Therefore images were manually binarised using a colour threshold function in a raster graphics editor.

For the purposes of the study, manual zoning omitted screen formatting areas such as images or horizontal or vertical bars. In the case of automated zoning, OCR output lines were manually aligned with reference text lines and additional lines from non-text areas were omitted. However, additional OCR outputs from non-text symbols along the same y-axis from a ground truth text area were included.

A number of image pre-processing and recognition settings were applied per COTS OCR system in each of the Arabic and English image text recognition tasks. Accuracy was measured by line, word and character using edit distance.

A test corpus of 259 handset display images (118 Arabic and 141 English) was produced by photographing the Nokia 2300 handset during navigation of menus in both English and Arabic user interface language settings. Four font sizes were observed in the Nokia 2300 display in both English and Arabic interface languages.

Ground truth text for each image was generated containing 407 lines of Arabic and 474 lines of English in one of four font sizes.

2.2 Results

Accuracy results for each COTS system at selected levels of automation are given for Arabic and English in Table 1. Settings used for recognition of English are shown in the shaded rows. Character, word and line accuracy for recognition of English was significantly higher than equivalent settings for recognition of Arabic, except for COTS 2 where automatic settings were applied. In this case, the system output only Arabic script.

The optimal settings for the COTS 1 system provided significantly greater word and line recognition accuracy than COTS 2, although character recognition accuracy was not proportionally higher. This effect was caused by comparative distribution of recognition errors; COTS 1 system errors were clustered in groups more often than those of COTS 2.

COTS system		Character	Word	Line
1	COTS1-A4-1	75.3	43.8	34.1
	COTS1 E1-1	91.8	81.9	78.1
	COTS1-A4 Autosettings	74.4	43.2	32.9
	COTS1 E1 Autosettings	90.7	81.1	77.5
	COTS1-Autozone A1	57.5	23.7	19.2
	COTS Autozone E1	75.4	47	41.9
	COTS1 Autozone Autosettings	45.6	10.6	1.7
2	COTS2 A2-3	70.5	23.7	12.3
	COTS2 E1-3	85.6	75	74
	COTS2 Auto settings Arabic	63	11.7	7.1
	COTS2 Auto settings English	1.5	0.3	0
	COTS2 Auto zone A2	33.5	11.8	2.4
	COTS2 Autozone Autosettings	30.1	6.9	1.7

Table 1: Recognition accuracy of Arabic and English script for increasing levels of automation

3 Translation of OCR outputs

The aim of this second study was to determine the feasibility of applying automated translation to OCR output text recognised from photographed images of a Nokia 2300 handset menu LCD display. Additionally, the study aimed to identify appropriate methods for correction of recognition errors within OCR output text prior to automated translation.

The study utilised automated translation via bilingual dictionary lookup, and compares two methods for error correction of the OCR output text where an exact match is not found in the bilingual dictionary. Each error correction method generates a list of candidate matches, and is measured as fully automated, or with user-interactive selection of a correct match from the candidate list.

3.1 Method

Optimal recognition outputs as described in section 2 from the 118 images of the Arabic portion of the Nokia 2300 handset image corpus for each COTS OCR system were used.

Error correction was performed on each line of OCR output text in each of two sets of 118 text files. Error correction used spell checking based on Levenshtein string distance (or edit distance) to measure text against the spell checking dictionary. Two approaches to error correction were utilised: firstly each OCR recognition line was not tokenised, and secondly whitespace based tokenisation was performed to obtain unigram tokens from each OCR recognition line. The spell checking dictionary contained both tokenised and un-tokenised forms from the Nokia 2300 ground truth text corpus.

By comparing the original image and spell corrected text within an application interface, a user may be able to select the correct text from within spell correction options. Therefore, line accuracy was measured based on two error correction and automated translation workflow options. Firstly, accuracy of the top ranked spell checking match was measured. Secondly, line accuracy was measured where the correct recognition term was found within the top five ranked matches during spell correction.

The first error correction method tokenised each line of OCR output text, and completed word-based automated translation via the bilingual dictionary. The second error correction method used a phrase-based lookup approach based on un-tokenised OCR output lines. Error correction is completed using word n-gram segments of handset menu phrases modelled on the word-wrapped lines in handset displays.

The terminology contained within the Nokia 2300 ground truth text corpus was used as the basis for spelling correction dictionary data. Individual words from each of the n-gram phrases were added, and all menu phrases and words were translated.

A deployed application would typically be required to provide general coverage for a variety of handset makes and models. Therefore, a simulated larger corpus was developed using 1,500 terms between 1 - 4 words in length selected from an Arabic glossary of application menu terminology. The first 375 terms of each length within the glossary that did not appear in the Nokia 2300 ground truth text corpus were used. Word n-grams of length 1 – 4 were selected to simulate OCR recognition lines of word wrapped menu phrases on handset displays with varying width and display resolutions. A final corpus size of 1,665 unique n-gram expressions resulted.

3.2 Results

Line accuracy is reported for both n-gram un-tokenised and tokenised error correction methods. For both spelling correction methods, line accuracy is reported for user interactive and automated error correction. Automated error correction occurs without user interaction where only the top ranked spell checking match is used. User interactive error correction occurs where the correct term exists within the top five ranked spell checking matches.

Figure 1 shows the un-tokenised n-gram OCR recognition line method provided greater line accuracy than tokenised methods for outputs for both COTS systems outputs, regardless of user interaction. User interaction provided line accuracy increases from 85.9% to 91.1% for COTS 1 and from 80.3% to 86.5% for the un-tokenised method, and from 73% to 84.3% for COTS 1 and from 39.3% to 41.7% for COTS 2 for the tokenised method.

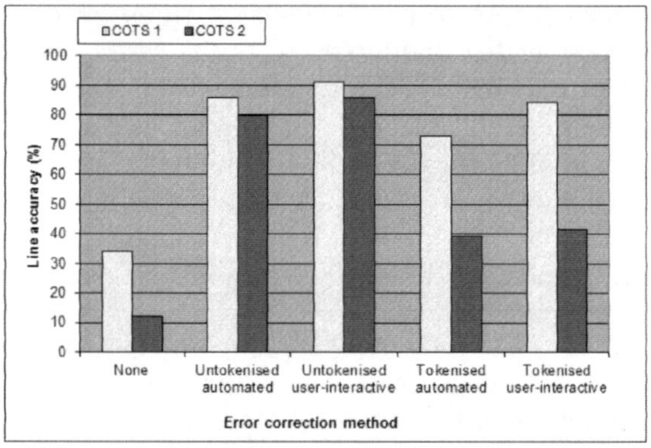

Figure 1: Line accuracy using word tokenised and line based un-tokenised error correction methods

Figure 2 illustrates the overlap between correct lines the two COTS systems following un-tokenised user-interactive error correction.

81.3% of the recognition zones were correct from both applications, while an additional 9.8% were correct from only COTS 1 recognition outputs and 5.2% were correct from only COTS 2 outputs. 3.6% of recognition zones were not correct by either application.

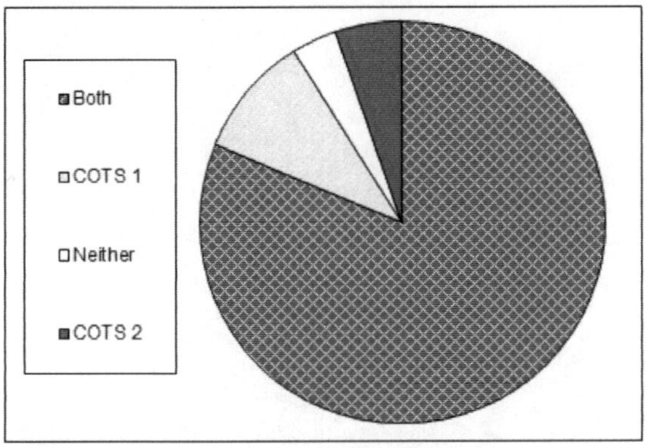

Figure 2: Lines correct following un-tokenised user-interactive error correction

4 Nokia 2300 handset study replication

A demonstrator application was developed, implementing functionalities required to complete all image OCR and translation steps from the studies. The objective in replicating previous studies was to confirm similar results could be achieved using the application and handset menu phrases rather than a simulated corpus based on software application menu phrases. A corpus of an additional 815 Arabic handset menu phrases was collected from user manuals of four handset models and compiled into a corpus suitable for spell checker and bilingual lookup dictionaries as per the method used to create the simulated corpus. This corpus was then used over the 118 Arabic images from the Nokia 2300 image corpus, using manual zone definition and the optimal application settings of the COTS 1 system. Line accuracy of 89.7% was achieved. This was comparable to the optimal line accuracy of 91.1% achieved in previously using a simulated corpus.

5 Discussion

Outcomes from these feasibility studies identified three areas in the workflow as critical to optimising OCR accuracy and overall performance; these were: 1) image interpolation and binarisation transformations; 2) delimitation of text areas in the handset display; and 3) user-interactive error correction. By using error correction on OCR lines, word segmentation errors may be eliminated and n-grams introduced in string distance based error correction.

Evaluation of the OCR and translation workflow considered only the case of a low resolution monochromatic LCD handset display in Arabic. Based on this work, recommendations could be made to improve both overall accuracy and use cases. Performance over a range of handset models, LCD display types, and recognition language should be quantified. Further OCR systems and/or customisation of OCR systems for recognition of specific handset fonts could be evaluated. A multi-OCR engine approach, such as described by Batawi and Abulnaja (2012), could also be considered.

User interactive error correction provided better outcomes than automated error correction for a given error correction approach. As no OCR system can provide 100% accuracy, text verification will be required by comparing recognised script to text in the original image, regardless of whether interactive error correction is completed. Therefore the additional time to complete user interactive error correction at LOTE text processing stages may not be considered prohibitive as the verification task is completed concurrently. However, text verification will present a challenge for those unfamiliar with the writing script, and observations from the use of the demonstrator application indicate that for such users verification is further complicated when the OCR output font differs from the image font (source).

6 Conclusion

Currently, best solutions for mobile device forensics will be either direct data extraction by a COTS solution that supports the given handset, or navigation of LOTE handset menus by a trained linguist. When these options are not available, the described studies and software implementation demonstrated a feasible workflow for navigating non-English handset menu structures by personnel untrained in the language. An outdated handset was selected due to the difference in properties of the font displayed in the low resolution monochrome LED screen to a typical COTS OCR system recognition task. Applying the technique to more current smartphones remains of interest but will also pose additional challenges.

References

Batawi, Yusof A. and Abulnaja, Osama A. (2012) Accuracy Evaluation of Arabic Optical Character Recognition Voting Technique: Experimental Study. *IJECS: International Journal of Electrical & Computer Sciences.* **12** (1) 29-33. ISSN: 2077-1231

Chang, Y., Chen, D., Zhang, Y., Yang, J. (2009) An image-based automatic Arabic translation system. In *Pattern Recognition* **42** (2009) 2127 – 2134.

Chang, Y., Zhang, Y., Vogel, S., Yang, J. (2007) Enhancing Image-based Arabic Document Translation Using a Noisy Channel Correction Model. In: In *Proceedings of MT Summit XI*, 10-14 September 2007, Copenhagen, Denmark.

Eck, M. and Hori, C. (2005) Overview of the IWSLT 2005 evaluation campaign. In: *Proceedings of International Workshop on Spoken Language Translation*, 11-17, Lisbon, Portugal

Herceg, P., Huyck, B.,Van Guilder, L., Kundu, A. (2005). Optimizing OCR Accuracy for Bi-tonal, Noisy Scans of Degraded Arabic Documents. *Visual Information Processing XIV*, edited by Zia-ur Rahman, Robert A. Schowengerdt, *Proceedings of SPIE*, Vol. 5817. pp. 179 Bellingham, WA.

Yale University (2008a) *AMEEL Digitization Manual: Part 9, OCR of Arabic Text with Sakhr*. Updated 2008 [Accessed 15 June 2012] Available from: http://www.library.yale.edu/idp/documentos/OCR_Sakhr.pdf

Yale University (2008b) *AMEEL Digitization Manual: Part 10, OCR of Arabic Text with Verus*. Updated 2008 [Accessed 15 June 2012] Available from: http://www.library.yale.edu/idp/documentos/OCR_Verus.pdf

Zhang, Y., Vogel, S. (2007) PanDoRA: A Large-scale Two-way Statistical Machine Translation System for Hand-held Devices. In: *Proceedings of MT Summit XI*, 10-14 September 2007, Copenhagen, Denmark.

Exploring Temporal Patterns in Emergency Department Triage Notes with Topic Models

Simon Kocbek[1,2], **Karin Verspoor**[2,3], **Wray Buntine**[4]
[1]Computer Science & Info Tech, RMIT University, Australia
[2]Dept of Computing and Information Systems, The University of Melbourne, Australia
[3]Health and Biomedical Informatics Centre, The University of Melbourne, Australia
[4]Faculty of IT, Monash University, Australia
skocbek@gmail.com, karin.verspoor@unimelb.edu.au, wray.buntine@monash.edu

Abstract

Topic modeling is an unsupervised machine-learning task of discovering topics, the underlying thematic structure in a text corpus. Dynamic topic models are capable of analysing the time evolution of topics. This paper explores the application of dynamic topic models on emergency department triage notes to identify particular types of disease or injury events, and to detect the temporal nature of these events.

1 Introduction

Recording of a patient's presenting complaints forms part of the standard triage procedure at most Australian hospital Emergency Departments (EDs). The complaints are typically recorded as brief notes, which capture the reason the patient has come to the ED. These notes represent the first point of contact of a patient with the hospital, and are a source of timely information about the health of the community served by the hospital. For instance, outbreaks of viruses or increased activity of spiders and snakes can be detected by monitoring ED visits.

The range of reasons for patient visits to the ED is diverse, including both accidents or injuries and disease. Topic modeling of ED triage notes provides a strategy for identifying patterns in this diverse data, i.e., for abstracting over individual patient visits to characterise trends in the health of the community. This abstraction gives a valuable snapshot of the health issues affecting the community.

Given the temporal nature of many health and injury events, including seasonal variation in viral load and day-of-the-week variation in events such as alcohol-related accidents, we expect that temporal patterns can be discerned in this data.

In this work, we explore the application of dynamic topic models on ED triage notes to identify particular types of disease or injury events, and to detect the temporal nature of these events. This analysis provides insight into the changing health needs of the community. Our findings have potential application for public health surveillance applications, where emerging issues of public concern can be detected and an appropriate response can be planned.

2 Related work

We treat each triage note is as one short document. It is known that it is very changeling for topic models to handle very short texts (Zhao et al. 2011) and various forms of tweet pooling on hashtag and/or author can be used to overcome this (Mehrotra et al 2013). For triage notes, however, its not clear what discrete variable could be used to pool on. Therefore we have not used any methods to account for the short documents.

Topic models have been only recently applied to analyse electronic health records data. Initial research suggests that the specific characteristics of the clinical language affect the methods and results of topic modeling techniques (Cohen et al, 2013). Topic modeling of Intensive Care Unit (ICU) progress notes to stratify the risk and mortality prediction for the hospital has been performed (Lehman et al., 2012). In that work, a non-parametric topic modeling method is used to discover topics as shared groups of co-occurring UMLS concepts. Salleb-Aouissi (Salleb-Aouissi

Simon Kocbek, Karin Verspoor and Wray Buntine. 2014. Exploring Temporal Patterns in Emergency Department Triage Notes with Topic Models. In *Proceedings of Australasian Language Technology Association Workshop*, pages 113–117.

et al., 2011) used topic models to show that infant colic has causes that can be illuminated by analysing a large corpus of paediatric notes.

Different models to discover topics have been used in previous work, mostly extending Latent Dirichlet Allocation (LDA) (Blei et al., 2003). LDA assumes that documents are admixtures of topics, where topics represent distributions over a fixed set of vocabularies (represented with a multinomial). Effectively, each word in a document is assigned to a topic so the word probabilities for the document become an admixture. Topic models are made dynamic by allowing time-evolution of parts of the model. An early model, the dynamic topic model (DTM) (Blei and Lafferty 2006) did this using Gaussians to represent evolution as a chain of means, and a logistic map to project vector data into probabilities. Later models used different tricks with exponential family models to extend the original LDA into the time domain (Ahmed and Xing, 2010; Xuerui and MacCallum, 2006) or non-parametric methods (Chen, Ding and Buntine, 2012).

3 Data and Methods

3.1 Data

The data for this study was obtained from the Royal Melbourne Hospital Emergency Department (ED) where triage notes for 57,984 patients over time period of 12 months (August 2010 – July 2011) were collected. We ignored 1,124 entries since they contained an empty triage note field. The average note length is 118 characters.

The triage notes are written in natural language but contain substantial numbers of abbreviations (e.g., R for right, b/c for because, ped for pedestrian), specialised clinical concepts (e.g., dementia, colonoscopy), and even patient biometric data such as blood pressure or temperature. They are also often not grammatically well-formed and often have spelling errors; they may contain a series of brief descriptive phrases and use of punctuation is inconsistent. As an example, consider the note "*alledge assault kick to head. lac to L eyebrow. ?LOC nil neck pain pupils dialated reactive ETOH tonight*". For the work described in this paper, we did not do any specialised processing of abbreviations or clinical concepts.

3.2 Dynamic topic model

The dynamic topic model we use allows components of the model to change over "epochs," where in our case epochs are month or weekend-weekday periods. Moreover, it is a first order Markov model so the components depend on that of their previous epoch. The topic model is given in graphical form in Figure 1. There are K topics, D_e documents per epoch e and each document has L_d words in it (varying per document d). Each document has topic proportions, a probability vector of $\vec{\Theta}_d$. Average topic proportions for the epoch e (a prior for $\vec{\Theta}_d$) are given by $\vec{\mu}_e$. The word vector for a topic in an epoch is given by $\vec{\phi}_{ek}$ for topic indexes $k=1,...,K$. The word vector depends on its previous counterpart, so $\vec{\phi}_{ek}$ depends on $\vec{\phi}_{(e-1)k}$. All dependencies of probability vectors on probability vectors are done with the Pitman-Yor process which allows efficient learning to be developed using blocked, collapsed Gibbs sampled data (Buntine and Mishra, 2014). The algorithm is implemented in C with a set of libraries for non-parametric topic models.

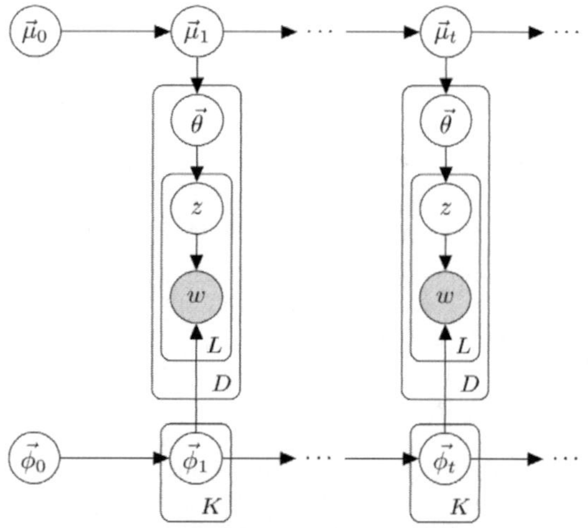

Figure 1: Graphical representation of the dynamic topic model (for epoch *1* and and *t*).

3.3 Running the experiments

For each patient we extracted their ED arrival date and the triage note assigned to the patient. The data was organised into two distinct temporal representations: by month, and by weekdays-weekends. Triage notes were then pre-processed to be in the right format for the topic modeling software. We used the Mallet (McCallum, 2002) stop list to filter out the most common words. The non-parametric dynamic topic model was applied to look for topics. Experiments for 10, 20, 30 and 40 topics were run. All the models were first initialized with 20 major Gibbs cycles of a standard topic model. We then ran the dynamic topic model with 500 (months) or 200 (weekend-weekdays) cycles.

Fewer cycles in the weekend-weekdays model were used due to time constraints.

Manual examination of topics was then performed with the goal of finding coherent and intuitively interpretable topics. Topics were presented with their top words, where we ranked the latter by fraction of their total occurrences in the topic. We also calculated normalized PMI (Han et al. 2014) to measure the coherency of each topic.

To compare topics over time, topic probabilities were calculated. Higher probability for a time period means that the topic is more likely to occur. The top ranked words for each topic were compared between epochs since different words may have different probabilities over time.

4 Results

While we measured coherence using normalised PMI, the raw results were poor, because of the large number of out of vocabulary words in the triage note content. Therefore, for the purposes of the current study we used visual inspection to evaluate topics. For month periods as epochs, 36 out of 40 topics were viewed as coherent; thus we viewed the model to be informative. We display those with interesting time structure here.

Figure 2 illustrates changes in proportions of 9 selected topics over a year. Top representative words for these topics are shown in Table 1. The topics offer a certain degree of coherence and could be interpreted as given in Table 1.

Topic	*Problem*	*Top representative words*
T1	Flu	aches, runny, chills, flu-like, fever
T2	Asthma	sentences, speaking, ventolin, talk
T3	Angina	gtn, patch, anginine, spray, aspirin
T4	Arm	foosh, rotation, shortening, rotated
T5	Insect	bite, spider, touch, burn, warm, rabies
T6	VDA	grey, code, packer, street, narcan, heroin
T7	Blood	gb, transfusion, abnormal, wcc
T8	Panic Attack	attack, panic, attacks, anxious
T9	Hernia	inguinal, hernia, testicular, hiatus

Table 1: Identified topics and representative words for the months model.

Figure 2 shows Flu and Angina peaks in Winter months. On the other hand, topics related to Arm, Insect, Drugs/Alcohol, and Hernia injuries and problems show peaks in warmer months. The Asthma topic shows a brief peak in Spring and the Panic Attacks topic increases in Autumn. The Blood topic slowly increases over time.

In Figure 3 we illustrate probabilities of 3 selected topics with interesting time structure for the weekend-weekdays model with 20 topics run. Top words for these topics appear in Table 2.

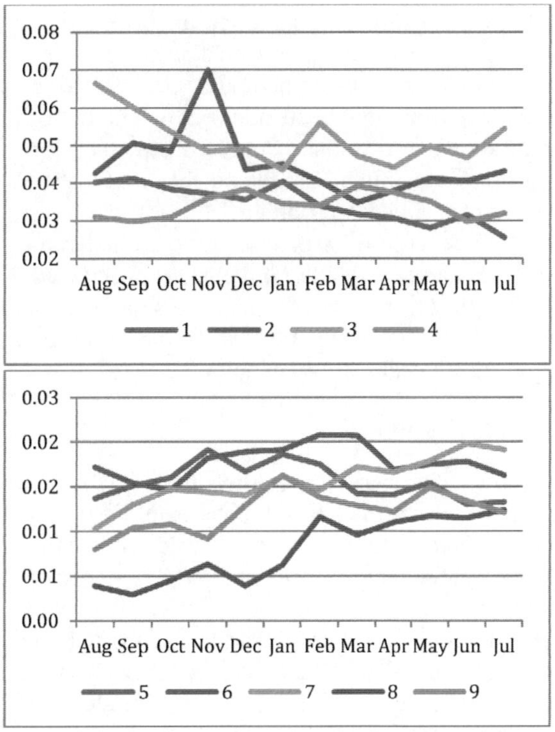

Figure 2: Probabilities of 9 topics over time (the months model). Note the scales of the top and bottom figures differ.

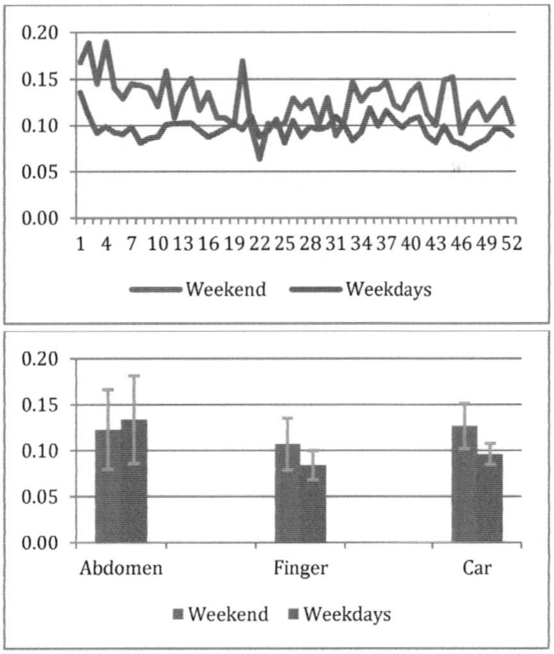

Figure 3: Probabilities of the Car topic (top), and average and standard deviation values for probabilities related to abdomen, finger and car problems (bottom).

Topic	*Top representative words*
Car	car, loc, driver, hit, speed, head
Finger	finger, cut, vasc, intact, rom, hand
Abdomen	abdo, flank, chronic, lower

Table 2: Identified topics and representative words for the weekend-weekdays model.

Figure 3 (top) shows probabilities of the car accidents topic. Each point on the x axis represents a whole week, where data is divided on weekdays (red) and weekends (blue). The bottom chart shows average and standard deviation values for probabilities for topics related to abdomen, finger and car problems. These topics were selected because their probability values demonstrate a clear division between weekends and weekdays. The Car and Finger topics have higher probabilities on weekends, while the Abdomen topic shows peaks on Weekdays.

5 Discussion

Specific characteristics of the clinical language affect the performance of topic modeling on this data. Triage notes contained considerable numbers of abbreviations, spelling mistakes, clinical concepts and multi-word phrases that the methods do not treat as a unit. Despite such problems, our analysis of ED triage notes with dynamic topic models offers some interesting conclusions.

First, we showed that topic models confirm some expected patterns in the data. For example, probability peaks in the Flu topic correspond to the influenza season in Australia (Winter). This is also the case for the Angina topic where, although the topic has a brief peak in February, we see more angina-related words in colder months and fewer in Spring/Summer. Both influenza and angina are known to be more common in Winter; this is effectively reflected in the topic models.

Several topics with peaks in warmer months also capture expected results. For example, patients seem to have more problems related to insect and animal bites in warmer months. This is expected since people spend more time outdoors, and the insects are more active, in spring and summer. The Arm and Hernia topics also peak between October and May, when people spend more time outdoors doing sports like swimming, rock climbing, volleyball, and similar. The Asthma topic has a brief peak in spring, when pollen-related problems are known to occur.

The results in Figure 2 also lead to some non-trivial conclusions. An interesting topic is VDA related to violence, and drug and alcohol problems. Looking at VDA, we can notice an increase of these issues between January and March. A more detailed analysis will be needed, but these results suggest that broader non-health related (e.g., criminal) surveillance might also be possible using this data and our methods.

Figure 2 also raises some questions. The Blood and Panic Attack topics show a constant and slow increase in probability. With current analysis of only a single year's worth of data, we are not sure about reasons for that.

Results on Figure 3 show interesting patterns when comparing weekdays and weekends. The top chart indicates that car related accidents more likely occur on weekends. Based on the Department of Infrastructure and Transport's report (BITRE, 2011), around half of all fatal crashes in Australia occur during weekends. Considering also non-fatal incidents, we view our results as informative. Peaks of finger and abdomen related problems raise questions about their meaning and further analysis will be needed.

Please note that the weekend-weekdays results should be interpreted with caution. Although the model might discover some patterns, it is not customized for analysing "periodic effects" in data. During the learning, the model tries to track things between epochs that are radically different. A weekend epoch is conditioned on the previous week, but results demonstrate essential difference, which poses challenges to the model. The models need to be adapted to deal better with such expected variation.

6 Conclusion

In this paper we have presented results of applying dynamic topic models to ED triage notes. The results should be viewed as an exploration that is indicative of the potential of the method.

In the future we plan to address several issues in this paper. We plan to address some of the specific characteristics of clinical and medical language with pre-processing techniques such as using MetaMap (Aronson and Lang, 2010) to recognise clinical concepts. We should also add periodicity modelling to the topic model, however, this is a more substantial project.

There is still substantial analysis that should be performed to more deeply explore these initial results, in particular to understand the statistical significance of the results. While the data set is not small, more years of data are required to establish any regular periodic effects. Moreover, we also need to further understand why the topic model worked quite well despite the lack of handling for short texts.

Finally, we plan to design a human evaluation to directly assess topic coherence and modify the PMI analysis to adjust for out-of-vocabulary words.

Acknowledgments

This work was partially funded by a Google Faculty Research Award. We would like to thank Theresa Vassiliou, Marie Gerdtz and Jonathan Knott from Royal Melbourne Hospital for the use of the data.

Reference

Ahmed A and Xing EP. 2010. *Timeline: A Dynamic Hierarchical Dirichlet Process Model for Recovering Birth/Death and Evolution of Topics in Text Stream*, In Proc. UAI 2010.

Aronson AR and Lang FM. 2010. *An overview of MetaMap: historical perspective and recent advances.* Journal of the American Medical Informatics Association 17:229-236.

BITRE - Bureau Of Infrastructure, Transport And Regional Economics. Australian Federal Department Of Infrastructure And Transport. 2011. *Road Deaths Australia - 2010 Statistical Summary*, https://www.bitre.gov.au/.

Blei D, Ng A, Jordan M. 2003. *Latent Dirichlet allocation.* Journal of Machine Learning Research 3: 993–1022.

Blei D and Lafferty JD. 2006. *Dynamic topic models.* In Proc. ICML, pp 113–120. ACM.

Buntine W and Mishra S. 2014. *Experiments with non-parametric topic models.* Proceedings of the 20th ACM SIGKDD international conference on Knowledge discovery and data mining. ACM.

Chen C, Ding N, Buntine W. 2012. *Dependent Hierarchical Normalized Random Measures for Dynamic Topic Modeling*, ICML 2012.

Cohen R, Elhadad M, Elhadad N. 2013. *Redundancy in electronic health record corpora: Analysis, impact on text mining performance and mitigation strategies.* BMC Bioinformatics 14: 10. doi: 10.1186/1471-2105-14-10.

Lau JH, Newman D, and Baldwin T. 2014. *Machine reading tea leaves: Automatically evaluating topic coherence and topic model quality*. Proceedings of the European Chapter of the Association for Computational Linguistics.

Lehman LW, Saeed M, Long W, Lee J, Mark R. 2012. *Risk stratification of ICU patients using topic models inferred from unstructured progress notes*. In: Proc. AMIA. 505–511.

McCallum AK. 2002. *MALLET: A Machine Learning for Language Toolkit.*, http://mallet.cs.umass.edu.

Mehrotra R, Sanner S, Buntine W, and Xie L. 2013. *Improving lda topic models for microblogs via tweet pooling and automatic labelling*. The 36th Annual ACM SIGIR Conference, 889–892.

Salleb-Aouissi A, Radeva A, Passonneau R, Tomar A, Waltz D, et al. 2011. *Diving into a large corpus of pediatric notes.* In: Proc. ICMLWorkshop on Learning from Unstructured Clinical Text.

Xuerui W, and McCallum A. 2006. *Topics over time: a non-Markov continuous-time model of topical trends.* In Proc. SIGKDD, ACM 2006.

Zhao WX, Jiang J, Weng J, He J, Lim EP, Yan H, Li X. 2011. *Comparing twitter and traditional media using topic models.* In Proceedings of ECIR'11, pages 338–349, Berlin, Heidelberg. Springer-Verlag.

Challenges in Information Extraction from Tables in Biomedical Research Publications: a Dataset Analysis

Tatyana Shmanina[1,2], **Lawrence Cavedon**[3], **Ingrid Zukerman**[1,2]
[1]Clayton School of Information Technology, Monash University, Australia
[2]NICTA Victoria Research Laboratory, Melbourne, Australia
[3]School of Computer Science and IT, RMIT University, Australia
[1]`firstname.lastname@monash.edu`, [3]`firstname.lastname@rmit.edu.au`

Abstract

We present a study of a dataset of tables from biomedical research publications. Our aim is to identify characteristics of biomedical tables that pose challenges for the task of extracting information from tables, and to determine which parts of research papers typically contain information that is useful for this task. Our results indicate that biomedical tables are hard to interpret without their source papers due to the brevity of the entries in the tables. In many cases, unstructured text segments, such as table titles, footnotes and non-table prose discussing a table, are required to interpret the table's entries.

1 Introduction

Automation of information extraction (*IE*) from biomedical literature has become an important task (Shatkay and Craven, 2012). In particular, biomedical *IE* enables the semi-automation of tasks such as document indexing (Aronson et al., 2004) and database curation, e.g., (Donaldson et al., 2003; Karamanis et al., 2008).

Most research in biomedical *IE* has concentrated on information extraction from prose. However, much important data, such as experimental results and relations between biomedical entities, often appear only in tables (Ansari et al., 2013). This insight was confirmed experimentally for the task of mutation database curation. In particular, Wong *et al.* (2009) showed that for a sample of research articles used to populate the *Mismatch Repair* database (Woods et al., 2007), tables served as a sole source of information about mutations for 59% of the documents. Yepes and Verspoor (2013) reported that a text mining tool applied to full articles and their supplementary material, used to catalogue mutations in the *COSMIC* (Bamford et al., 2004) and *InSiGHT* (Plazzer et al., 2013) databases, could recover only 3-8% of the mutations if only prose was considered. An additional 1% of the mutations was extracted from tables in the papers, with an improvement of mutation coverage to about 50% when supplementary material (mostly tables) was considered.

Information extraction from tables (*Table IE*) comprises various tasks, such as (1) classification of table entries or columns into a set of specific classes (Quercini and Reynaud, 2013; Wong et al., 2009); (2) association of table entries or columns with concepts from a domain vocabulary (Assem et al., 2010; Yosef et al., 2011); and (3) extraction of relations, defined in a vocabulary, between entities in tables – usually done with Task 2 (Hignette et al., 2009; Limaye et al., 2010; Mulwad et al., 2013; Venetis et al., 2011). These tasks are often performed by consulting external knowledge sources. However, despite the intuition that unstructured text accompanying tables often provides helpful information, little use has been made of such text. Examples of such usage are the works of Yosef *et al.* (2011), who performed collective named entity normalisation in Web texts and tables; Hignette *et al.* (2009), who employed table titles to improve relation extraction from Web tables; and Govindaraju *et al.* (2013), who improved performance in extracting a few predefined relations from papers in Economics, Geology and Petrology by processing jointly the text and tables in the papers.

This paper describes the first step of a project that aims to automatically perform Tasks 2 and 3 on biomedical tables. In this step, we manually analyse a dataset of tables from the biomedical literature to identify characteristics of biomedical tables that pose challenges for column annotation, and determine the parts of a research paper that typically contain information which is useful for interpreting tables.

Our results show that tables in biomedical research papers are generally hard to interpret without their source papers due to the brevity of the entries in the tables. Further, in many cases, un-

Tatyana Shmanina, Lawrence Cavedon and Ingrid Zukerman. 2014. Challenges in Information Extraction from Tables in Biomedical Research Publications: a Dataset Analysis. In *Proceedings of Australasian Language Technology Association Workshop*, pages 118−122.

structured text (e.g., table titles, footnotes and non-table prose discussing a table) must be considered to disambiguate table entries.

2 Analysis Design

The dataset used in our analysis comprises a set of biomedical research papers discussing genetic variation. To build the dataset, we randomly sampled five articles from each of the three datasets used in (Wong et al., 2009) and (Yepes and Verspoor, 2013). The resulting sample contains 39 tables, with a total of 280 columns.

We manually analysed the dataset to collect statistics regarding typical data types in the tables (Section 3.1). Columns in the tables were annotated with *Semantic Types* (*STs*) from the *Unified Medical Language System* (*UMLS*), which has 133 *STs* in total. To assign a label to a column in a table, the annotator first located a specific *UMLS* concept corresponding to a fine-grained type of the entities listed in the column (e.g., "[C0009221] Codon (nucleotide sequence)" for Columns 3-7 in Figure 1), after which the *ST* corresponding to the selected concept was assigned to the column (e.g., "Nucleotide Sequence [T086]"). Individual data entries were not annotated due to insufficient coverage of specific values (e.g., mutations) in *UMLS*, and the predominantly numerical nature of the data (Section 3.1).

On the basis of our annotation, we gathered statistics regarding issues that may influence the performance of an automatic Table IE system, e.g., the consistency of the data types in tables (Section 3.2), and the sources of information that are useful for concept annotation (Section 3.3). It is worth noting that the annotator (first author of the paper) had little background in biomedical science at the time of annotation, and employed external sources such as NCBI databases[1] and Wikipedia to assist with the annotation. This lack of biomedical background may have affected the accuracy of the disambiguation of biomedical entities. However, we posit that the obtained results provide more relevant insights into the use of non-table components in automatic Table IE than those obtained from expert annotation.

3 Results

3.1 Content of the Data Entries

We analysed our dataset to determine which data types are typically contained in biomedical tables. It was previously noted that, in general, table entries contain very little text, which often does not provide enough context for entity disambiguation (Limaye et al., 2010). Unlike the interpretation of noun phrases, interpreting numerical data is the biggest challenge for Table IE, because numbers are highly ambiguous (in principle they could be assigned most of the *UMLS STs*). Another significant challenge in both general and biomedical *IE* is the use of abbreviations.

In light of the above, our analysis shows that biomedical tables are very difficult to interpret:

- 42% of the columns in our sample contain numbers, and 3% contain numerical expressions (e.g., $45/290$ and 45 ± 6), both representing information such as statistical data, percentages, times, lengths, patient IDs and DNA sequences (e.g., codons 175, 176 and 179 in Column 3 in Figure 1).
- 32% of the columns comprise abbreviated entries (e.g., *MSI*, *N* and *A* in Figure 1) and symbolic representations (e.g., $\pm$ for *heterozygote*).
- 7% of the columns contain free text.
- Only 12% of the columns comprise biomedical terms as entries.
- The remaining 4% of the columns contain a mixture of abbreviations, free text, and numerical expressions.

Our study shows that numerical and abbreviated entries can be interpreted correctly if they are appropriately expanded using mentions from table titles, footnotes and prose. For example, in the table in Figure 1, the abbreviations *MSI*, *N* and *A* can be expanded using the table footnote; and codon mentions in Columns 3-7 can be expanded using the prose describing the table (highlighted).[2]

3.2 Quality of the Column Headers

We analysed our dataset to determine whether it is possible to identify types of biomedical table entries based only on the content of column headers. To do so, we first identified the number of cases where column headers were sufficient for column type identification during the manual table annotation phase (Section 2). We determined that although 97% of the columns in our sample have headers, in many cases they are too ambiguous to be used as the only evidence for the column type.

[1] http://www.ncbi.nlm.nih.gov/

[2] It was impossible to determine that Columns 3-7 in Figure 1 referred to codons without the prose.

Table 2. *p53* mutations found in 79 colorectal carcinomas

No.	Patient	EX05	EX06	EX07	EX08	EX09	Codon change	Base substitution	(type)	AA change	MSI
1	IC628				**273**		CGT → CAT	G:C → A:T	TS	Arg → His	N
2	IC630		196				CGA → TGA	G:C → A:T	TS	Arg → stop	A
3	IC634				306						
4	IC668		193								
5	IC669	**175**									
6	IC673	176									
7	IC674				285						
8	IC680		ND	255							
9	IC693	179									
10	IC694				273						
...	...	...	...	...	...	...					
20	IC812		190								
21	IC816				**273**						
22	IC819			**248**							
23	IC860				**273**						

MSI, microsatellite instability; N, negative; A, Type A MSI; TS, transition; TV, transversion; ND, not determined. Bold codon numbers indicate the acknowledged hot-spots for mutation.

examine the relationship between Type A/B instability and *p53* mutation, we sequenced the *p53* gene in our panel of 79 colorectal tumours. *p53* mutations resulting in an amino acid substitution were detected in 23 tumours (29.1%). The mutations were predominantly transitions in acknowledged hot spots; codons 175, 248 and 273 (Table 2). Of the *p53* mutations that were found in MSI tumours, all were associated with Type A MSI (Tables 2 and 3). No *p53* mutations

Figure 1: An example of a biomedical table and prose discussing the table. Source: (Oda et al., 2005)

In fact, only 34% of the columns in our sample could be annotated without referring to parts of the documents other than the column entries and their headers. In 57% of the cases, additional information was required to confirm the type of a column (e.g., Columns 3-7 in Figure 1), and in 9% of the cases, headers were not helpful in column type identification (Table 1). This finding agrees with observations in the Web domain, e.g., (Limaye et al., 2010; Venetis et al., 2011).

We then compared the labels (*STs*) assigned to table columns to the *STs* of the entities in the corresponding headers. The comparison showed that in only 53% of the cases a header was labeled with the same *ST* as the entries in the column. For instance, Columns 3-7 in Figure 1 contain entities of the class "Codon" (*ST* "Nucleotide Sequence [T086]"), while the headers, which designate exons, have the *ST* "Nucleic Acid, Nucleotide, or Nucleotide [T114]" or "Biologically Active Substance [T123]". We therefore conclude that, in general, headers in isolation are insufficient, and often misleading, for column type identification.

3.3 Sufficiency and Criticality of Information Sources for Column Annotation

We analysed the dataset to determine the contribution of different sources of information in a table and its source article to the identification of the types of biomedical table entries. To this effect, we found it useful to consider the following information sources for each column: (1) the content of the data entries in the column, (2) the header of the column, (3) the headers of other columns, (4) the title of the table, (5) table footnotes, and (6) prose describing the content of the table (referred to as "prose" for simplicity). We distinguish between two aspects of these sources: *sufficiency* and *criticality*.

- The ***sufficiency*** categories are: (1) *Sufficient*, if the source on its own was enough to identify the column label; (2) *Insufficient*, if the source allowed the formulation of a hypothesis about the column label, but required information from other sources to confirm the hypothesis; and (3) *Non-indicative*, if the source did not contribute to the column labelling.
- The ***criticality*** categories are: (1) *Critical*, if disregarding the source is very likely to lead to an annotation error; (2) *Probably Critical*, if disregarding the source may lead to an annotation error; and (3) *Non-critical*, if the source could be disregarded without causing an error.

Criticality was assigned to each information source in an incremental manner depending on the sufficiency of the source: if some "cheap" sources of information were sufficient for column type identification, more "expensive" sources were not considered to be critical. The cost of a source was based on the complexity of the methods required to locate and process this source, increasing in the following order: column header, other headers, table title, table footnotes and prose.

To illustrate these ideas, consider Column 3 (concept "Codon") in Figure 1. The other headers, table title and footnotes were classified as *Non-indicative*, and hence *Non-critical*, since they do not contain any explicit information regarding the column type ("codon" is mentioned in the footnote in a sentence about formatting, which is not considered at present). The header and prose were classified as *Insufficient*, because each merely suggests the column class, and *Critical*, because both

Information source	S	IS	NI
—	1%	18%	81%
Column header	34%	57%	9%
Other column headers	0%	22%	78%
Table title	3%	36%	61%
Table footnotes	12%	34%	54%
Prose	13%	62%	25%

Table 1: Percentages of cases where sources of information were characterised as *Sufficient* (*S*), *Insufficient* (*IS*) and *Non-indicative* (*NI*) if considered in addition to the content of the column.

Information source	C	PC	NC
Column content	19%	0%	81%
Column header	87%	4%	9%
Other column headers	8%	10%	82%
Table title	15%	16%	69%
Table footnotes	27%	10%	63%
Prose	28%	20%	52%

Table 2: Percentages of cases where sources of information were characterised as *Critical* (*C*), *Probably Critical* (*PC*) and *Non-critical* (*NC*).

were required to label the column. When annotating Column 8 ("Codon change", *ST* "Genetic Function [T045]"), the title was classified as *Probably Critical*, because there was no direct correspondence with any *UMLS* concept – the mapping was performed intuitively, and the title confirmed the chosen hypothesis.

The results of our analysis are summarised in Tables 1 and 2, which respectively show statistics regarding the sufficiency and criticality of various sources of information. The results in Table 1 indicate that none of the information sources were sufficient for each table column in our dataset when taken in isolation. However, it was possible to label every column when all the sources were considered jointly. It is worth noting that the combination of the information sources that enabled labelling all the columns of a single table varied from table to table.

As seen in Table 2, each type of unstructured text associated with tables (i.e., table titles, footnotes and prose) was characterised as critical or probably critical in a substantial number of cases. In addition, we observed that in 59.3% of the cases, a table title or prose segments were characterised as critical or probably critical; and in 70.9% of the cases a table title, footnotes or prose were critical or probably critical.

Table footnotes represent an important source of information for abbreviation expansion: 97% of the tables in our sample have footnotes in the form of unstructured text, and about 62% of the footnotes introduce at least some of the abbreviations in the tables. Further, about 72% of the footnotes contain remarks associated with column headers or data entries. No other uses of footnotes were identified.

The prose that was required to interpret the tables during annotation was found in referencing paragraphs (i.e., containing descriptors such as "(Table 4)") in 70% of the cases; in 22% of the cases the prose was found elsewhere in the sections containing referencing paragraphs; and in 8% of the cases it was found elsewhere in the source document.

Our analysis shows that table titles, footnotes and prose tend to be complementary and, in general, none of them can be disregarded during annotation (Tables 1 and 2). For example, although all the tables in our sample have titles, on average only 40% of the columns in each table are represented in the titles — column "representatives" are either not mentioned in the titles, or their entity types in the titles differ from the types of the columns.

We therefore conclude that all unstructured text associated with biomedical tables (i.e., table titles, footnotes and prose) is vital for interpreting them.

4 Conclusion

In this paper, we presented an analysis of a dataset of tables from biomedical research papers performed from the perspective of information extraction from tables. Our results show that tables in biomedical research papers are characterised by an abundance of numerical and abbreviated data, for which existing approaches to Table IE do not perform well. Further, we ascertained that in many cases, unstructured text (e.g., table titles, footnotes and non-table prose discussing a table) must be considered in order to disambiguate table entries, and determine the types of table columns.

We conclude that considering unstructured text related to tables – in particular, combining existing techniques for the interpretation of stand-alone tables with IE from unstructured text – will improve the performance of Table IE. In the near future, we propose to develop techniques for locating table descriptions in the full text of source articles, and incorporating text processing techniques into approaches to Table IE.

Acknowledgments

We would like to thank the anonymous reviewers for their very detailed and insightful comments.

NICTA is funded by the Australian Government through the Department of Communications and by the Australian Research Council through the ICT Centre of Excellence Program.

References

S. Ansari, R. E. Mercer, and P. Rogan. 2013. Automated phenotype-genotype table understanding. In *Contemporary Challenges and Solutions in Applied Artificial Intelligence*, pages 47–52. Springer.

A. R. Aronson, J. G. Mork, C. W. Gay, S. M. Humphrey, and W. J. Rogers. 2004. The NLM Indexing Initiative's Medical Text Indexer. *Medinfo*, 11(Pt 1):268–72.

M. Van Assem, H. Rijgersberg, M. Wigham, and J. Top. 2010. Converting and annotating quantitative data tables. In *The Semantic Web–ISWC 2010*, pages 16–31. Springer.

S. Bamford, E. Dawson, S. Forbes, J. Clements, R. Pettett, A. Dogan, A. Flanagan, J. Teague, P. A. Futreal, M. R. Stratton, and R. Wooster. 2004. The COSMIC (Catalogue of Somatic Mutations in Cancer) database and website. *British Journal of Cancer*, 91(2):355–358.

I. Donaldson, J. Martin, B. de Bruijn, C. Wolting, V. Lay, B. Tuekam, S. Zhang, B. Baskin, G. D. Bader, K. Michalickova, T. Pawson, and C. WV. Hogue. 2003. PreBIND and Textomy – mining the biomedical literature for protein-protein interactions using a support vector machine. *BMC Bioinformatics*, 4(1):11.

V. Govindaraju, C. Zhang, and C. Ré. 2013. Understanding tables in context using standard NLP toolkits. In *Proceedings of the 51st Annual Meeting of the Association for Computational Linguistics*, volume 2, pages 658–664.

G. Hignette, P. Buche, J. Dibie-Barthélemy, and O. Haemmerlé. 2009. Fuzzy annotation of Web data tables driven by a domain ontology. In *The Semantic Web: Research and Applications*, pages 638–653. Springer.

N. Karamanis, R. Seal, I. Lewin, P. McQuilton, A. Vlachos, C. Gasperin, R. Drysdale, and T. Briscoe. 2008. Natural Language Processing in aid of FlyBase curators. *BMC Bioinformatics*, 9(1):193.

G. Limaye, S. Sarawagi, and S. Chakrabarti. 2010. Annotating and searching Web tables using entities, types and relationships. *Proceedings of the VLDB Endowment*, 3(1-2):1338–1347.

V. Mulwad, T. Finin, and A. Joshi. 2012. A domain independent framework for extracting linked semantic data from tables. In *Search Computing*, pages 16–33. Springer.

V. Mulwad, T. Finin, and A. Joshi. 2013. Semantic message passing for generating linked data from tables. In *The Semantic Web – ISWC 2013*, pages 363–378. Springer.

S. Oda, Y. Maehara, Y. Ikeda, E. Oki, A. Egashira, Y. Okamura, I. Takahashi, Y. Kakeji, Y. Sumiyoshi, K. Miyashita, Y. Yamada, Y. Zhao, H. Hattori, K. Taguchi, T. Ikeuchi, T. Tsuzuki, M. Sekiguchi, P. Karran, and M. A. Yoshida. 2005. Two modes of microsatellite instability in human cancer: differential connection of defective DNA mismatch repair to dinucleotide repeat instability. *Nucleic Acids Research*, 33(5):1628–1636.

J. P. Plazzer, R. H. Sijmons, M. O. Woods, P. Peltomäki, B. Thompson, J. T. Den Dunnen, and F. Macrae. 2013. The InSiGHT database: utilizing 100 years of insights into Lynch Syndrome. *Familial Cancer*, 12(2):175–180.

G. Quercini and C. Reynaud. 2013. Entity discovery and annotation in tables. In *Proceedings of the 16th International Conference on Extending Database Technology*, EDBT '13, pages 693–704, New York, NY, USA. ACM.

H. Shatkay and M. Craven. 2012. *Mining the biomedical literature*. MIT Press.

P. Venetis, A. Halevy, J. Madhavan, M. Paşca, W. Shen, F. Wu, G. Miao, and C. Wu. 2011. Recovering semantics of tables on the Web. *Proceedings of the VLDB Endowment*, 4(9):528–538.

W. Wong, D. Martinez, and L. Cavedon. 2009. Extraction of named entities from tables in gene mutation literature. In *Proceedings of the Workshop on Current Trends in Biomedical Natural Language Processing*, pages 46–54. Association for Computational Linguistics.

M. O. Woods, P. Williams, A. Careen, L. Edwards, S. Bartlett, J. R. McLaughlin, and H. B. Younghusband. 2007. A new variant database for mismatch repair genes associated with Lynch Syndrome. *Human Mutation*, 28(7):669–673.

A. Jimeno Yepes and K. Verspoor. 2013. Towards automatic large-scale curation of genomic variation: improving coverage based on supplementary material. In *BioLINK SIG 2013*, pages 39–43, Berlin, Germany, July.

M. A. Yosef, J. Hoffart, I. Bordino, M. Spaniol, and G. Weikum. 2011. Aida: An online tool for accurate disambiguation of named entities in text and tables. *Proceedings of the VLDB Endowment*, 4(12):1450–1453.

Deep Belief Networks and Biomedical Text Categorisation

Antonio Jimeno Yepes[♢♠], **Andrew MacKinlay**[♢♠], **Justin Bedo**[♢♠], **Rahil Garnavi**[♢], **Qiang Chen**[♢]
[♢] IBM Research – Australia, 380 La Trobe Street, Melbourne, VIC, Australia
[♠] Dept. of Computing and Information Systems, University of Melbourne, Australia
{antonio.jimeno,admackin,justin.bedo,rahilgar,qiangchen}@au1.ibm.com

Abstract

We evaluate the use of Deep Belief Networks as classifiers in a text categorisation task (assigning category labels to documents) in the biomedical domain. Our preliminary results indicate that compared to Support Vector Machines, Deep Belief Networks are superior when a large set of training examples is available, showing an F-score increase of up to 5%. In addition, the training times for DBNs can be prohibitive. DBNs show promise for certain types of biomedical text categorisation.

1 Introduction

Text categorisation is the task of automatically assigning pre-defined labels to text. In the biomedical domain, research in automatic text categorisation has mostly taken place in the context of indexing MEDLINE® citations with Medical Subject Headings (MeSH®).

MEDLINE is the largest collection of biomedical abstracts and contains over 23M citations with over 800k new citations every year, making it difficult to keep up-to-date with new discoveries. To help cataloging and searching biomedical documents, the US National Library of Medicine (NLM)® has produced the MeSH controlled vocabulary with over 26k headings. At NLM, each MEDLINE citation is manually assigned a number of relevant medical subject headings enumerating the topics of the paper. Machine learning for text categorisation in this context is appealing due to the large number of citations available to train machine learning algorithms.

In text categorisation, the most frequently used feature representation is *bag-of-words*, where text is converted into a feature vector in which each dimension corresponds to a word or phrase and stores either a binary value indicating its presence in the document or a numerical value indicating its frequency (Apte et al., 1994; Dumais et al., 1998; Sebastiani, 2002). This relatively simple approach has proven to be robust enough (Jimeno-Yepes et al., 2011) that it is difficult to improve on its performance with more sophisticated representations. In this work, we explore the use of Deep Belief Networks (DBN) to automatically generate a new representation in biomedical text categorisation. Since DBNs have a richer internal representation than SVMs, we wished to evaluate whether this would lead to improved classification performance compared to *bag-of-words*.

2 Related work

There are several approaches being used for text categorisation in the biomedical domain trying to reproduce the manual MeSH indexing. NLM has developed the Medical Text Indexer (MTI) (Aronson et al., 2004; Mork et al., 2013), which is used to suggest MeSH headings for new citations to indexers. MTI combines MetaMap (Aronson and Lang, 2010) annotation and recommendations from similar citations recovered using the PubMed Related Citations (Lin and Wilbur, 2007) tool that are post-processed to comply with NLM indexing rules. Results for the most frequent categories, as used in this work, indicate that machine learning methods can produce better results than MTI (Jimeno Yepes et al., 2013). Recently, there has been interest in comparing MeSH indexing approaches in the BioASQ challenge.[1] It has been found that bag-of-word representations without feature selection already provide competitive performance.

Recently, several studies have utilised different deep learning methods to build multiple layers of feature representation for documents, such as a Stacked De-noising Autoencoder (SDA) (Vincent et al., 2010; Glorot et al., 2011) and a DBN (Hinton

[1] http://www.bioasq.org/workshop/schedule

Antonio Jimeno Yepes, Andrew MacKinlay, Justin Bedo, Rahil Garvani and Qiang Chen. 2014. Deep Belief Networks and Biomedical Text Categorisation. In *Proceedings of Australasian Language Technology Association Workshop*, pages 123−127.

and Salakhutdinov, 2006) for tasks including spam filtering (Tzortzis and Likas, 2007). In this work, we apply DBN as our deep learning algorithm for biomedical text categorisation, trying to reproduce MeSH indexing for the 10 top most frequent MeSH headings.

3 Methods

3.1 Deep Belief Networks

Restricted Boltzmann Machines (RBM) A (restricted) Boltzmann Machine (RBM) (Salakhutdinov et al., 2007) is a parameterised generative model representing a joint probability distribution. Given some training data, learning an RBM means adjusting the RBM parameters to maximise the likelihood of the training data under the model. Restricted Boltzmann machines consist of two layers containing visible and hidden neurons.

The energy function $E(v,h)$ of an RBM is:

$$E(v,h) = -b'v - c'h - h'Wv; \quad (1)$$

where W represents the weights connecting hidden and visible units and b, c are the offsets of the visible and hidden layers respectively. The joint probability distribution is then given by the exponential family $P(v,h) = \frac{1}{Z}e^{E(v,h)}$, where Z is a normalisation factor. The likelihood of some data $X \subset \mathbb{R}^n$ is thus $\mathscr{L}(X) := \prod_{v \in X} \sum_h P(v,h)$ and b, c, and W are chosen to maximise this likelihood (or equivalently minimise the negative log likelihood):

$$\arg_{b,c,W} \min -\log \mathscr{L}(X) = -\sum_{v \in X} \log \sum_h P(v,h).$$

We used the Contrastive Divergence method (Hinton, 2002) to find an approximate solution.

Deep Belief Network A DBN normally is the stack of many layers of RBM model. Hinton and Salakhutdinov (2006) showed that RBMs can be stacked and trained in a greedy manner to form so-called Deep Belief Networks (DBN). DBNs are graphical models which learn to extract a deep hierarchical representation of the training data.

The hidden neurons extract relevant features from the observations, and these features can serve as input to another RBM. By stacking RBMs in this way, we can learn a higher level representation.

Practical training strategies In practice, the DBN training often consists of two steps: greedy layer-wise pretraining and fine tuning. Layer-wise pretraining involves training the model parameters layer by layer via unsupervised training. Fine tuning is achieved by supervised gradient descent of the negative log-likelihood cost function.

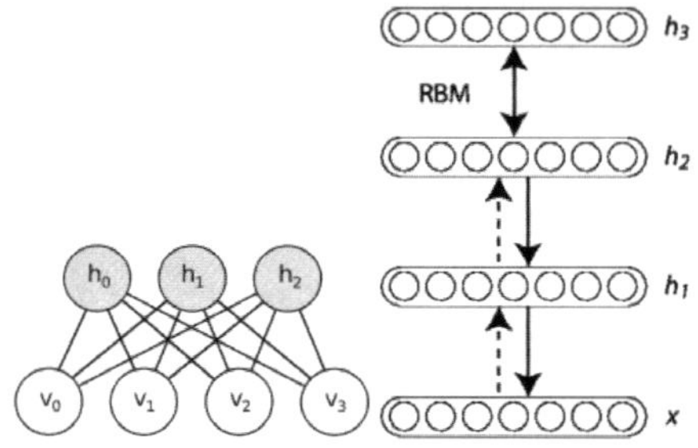

Figure 1: Deep Neural Network (left) and RBM (right)

The DBN implementation used in this work has been obtained from `http://www.deeplearning.net/tutorial` built on Theano[2]. Text data is very sparse with only a few dimensions having non-zero values. We modified the DBN code to deal with sparse matrices.

3.2 Support Vector Machine

We used a Support Vector Machine (SVM) with a linear kernel as our baseline method. SVM has shown good performance on text categorisation (Joachims, 1998) as well as in MeSH indexing (Jimeno Yepes et al., 2013) and within BioASQ. In this work, we have used the implementation from the MTI ML package[3] that follows the work of (Zhang, 2004) and uses Hinge loss with stochastic gradient descent.

3.3 Data set

Training and test sets have been obtained from the MTI ML site. There are 24,727 training citations and 12,363 test citations. From these data sets, we have selected the top 10 most frequent MeSH headings available from Table 1.

We have also used a larger set since we realised in the earlier stages of experimentation that more data was needed to train the DBN. This larger set has been obtained from the NLM Indexing Initiative[4] and is split into 94,942 training citations and 48,911 test citations. Results on both sets are reported for the same categories.

We processed the citations to extract the text from the title and the abstract. From the text, we

[2] `http://deeplearning.net/software/theano`

[3] http://ii.nlm.nih.gov/MTI_ML

[4] http://ii.nlm.nih.gov/DataSets/index.shtml#2013_MTI_ML

extracted tokens using a regular expression looking for white spaces and punctuation marks. Tokens were lowercased and filtered using a standard stopword list. Binary values for the features (present or absent) are considered. Only tokens that appear in at least two citations in the training set were considered, considerably reducing the number of features.

4 Results

The SVM and the DBN were trained and tested on the data sets. Binary classifiers predicting each individual category were trained for each one of the selected MeSH headings. For DBN, we used 2/3 of the training data for unsupervised pretraining and 1/3 for fine tuning the model due to DBN training cost, while for SVM we used all the training data.

Configuring the DBN requires specifying the number of hidden layers and the number of units per layer. We used one hidden layer to give three layers in total. We used two different configuration of training units, set empirically (and semi-arbitrarily) from data samples – *DBN 250* with 250 units in each of the three layers and *DBN 500*, with 500 units per layer.

Tables 1 and 2 show results for the small set with 16000 for DBN pretraining and 8727 for fine tuning and the large set with 63294 for DBN pretraining and 31647 for fine tuning.

As shown in Table 1, with the smaller datasets, SVM performance is superior to DBN, however DBN substantially outperforms SVM on the six most frequent categories. DBN results are much lower when the categories are less frequent and for *Adolescent*, DBN simply classified all citations as negative. *DBN 500* performs better than *DBN 250* in the top six most frequent categories.

Figure 2 shows learning curves obtained by training the three methods on increasingly large subsets of the small training set. SVM outperforms DBN when there is limited training data, but as the amount of training data is increased, for certain categories DBN, especially *DBN 500*, surpasses SVM (as expected from Table 1).

Results were obtained using the same subset and it could be interesting to see the behavior if different subsets of the training data are used. DBN results depend as well on the partition of the training data, using all the data for pretraining and fine tuning the perfomance of DBN on the small set improves (avg. F1: 0.7282).

Table 2 shows that when there is more training data available, the performance penalty for the DBN methods versus SVM over the sparser categories disappears. In addition, there is also less of a difference between results of 250 and 500 units per layer. Overall all three methods are more similar to one another over this larger data set, with better results for DBN on average. Absolute results between Tables 1 and 2 are not comparable since two different collections are used, e.g. some categories have significantly different performance.

5 Discussion

In our experiments, DBN overall performance is comparable to SVM with a linear kernel being better in some of the categories when a large set of training data is used. We also evaluated SVM with Radial Basis Function kernel (not reported) but the results were comparable to a linear kernel.

Compared to image processing, text categorisation has a larger dimensionality that varies with the size of the data set since there is the chance of finding new unique words, even though data is sparse and few of the citation features have a value. On the small set, with a batch size of 200 citations, the number of unique features is 2,531 and with a batch size of 8,000 it is 26,491, while in the larger set, 53,784 unique features were found.

6 Conclusions and Future Work

DBN shows competitive performance compared to SVM. We have tried a limited set of configurations with only one hidden layer. Deeper configurations with a more varied number of units can be explored but the pretraining phase is expensive. We would like to explore different pretraining and supervised tuning ratios to reduce training time. In addition, identifying the best DBN configuration can be expensive. (Rahimi and Recht, 2009) suggest approaches to avoid an explosion of possibilities which could be useful here.

Deep learning requires a significant amount of time to train, e.g. SVM was trained in several minutes while the DBN pretraining in the large set took five days. To alleviate this, we could consider methods to reduce dimensionality (Weinberger et al., 2009; Bingham and Mannila, 2001). Nonetheless, we believe that this work shows that DBNs show promise for text categorisation, as they are able to provide superior performance to SVM-based techniques traditionally for such tasks.

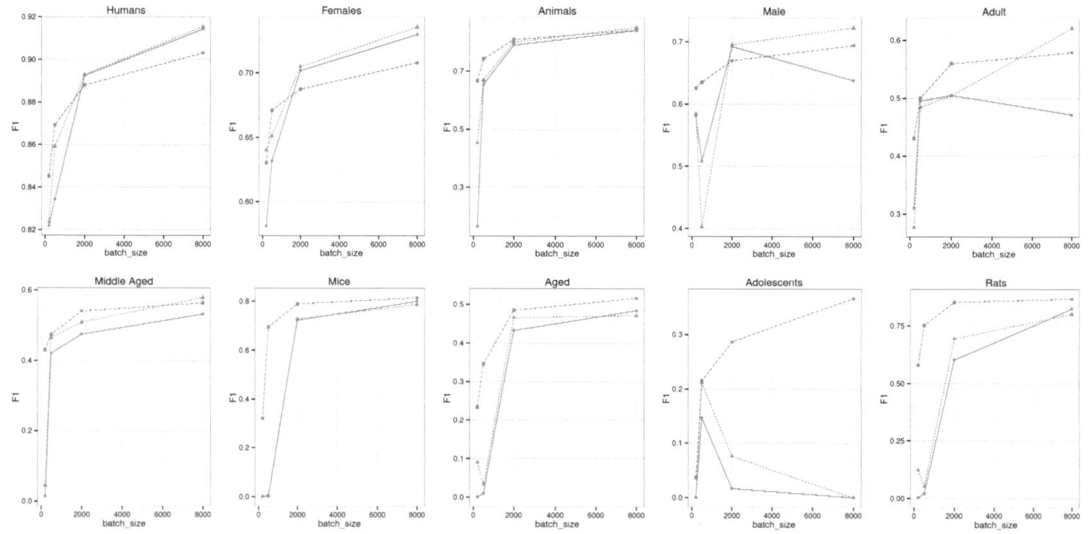

Figure 2: Training size vs F1 on the small set. There is one plot per category. Three methods are shown: SVM (slashed blue line, square shaped point), DBN with three layers with 250 units each (continuous red line, round shaped point) and DBN with three layers with 500 units each (dotted green line, triangle shaped point).

	Methods	SVM	(linear)		DBN	250		DBN	500	
Category	Positives	Pre	Rec	F1	Pre	Rec	F1	Pre	Rec	F1
Humans	7688	0.8983	0.9083	0.9032	0.9016	0.9273	0.9143	**0.9032**	**0.9282**	**0.9155**
Female	4616	**0.7215**	0.6950	0.7080	0.7001	0.7621	0.7298	0.6945	**0.7821**	**0.7357**
Male	4396	0.7034	0.6852	0.6942	0.4771	0.9627	0.6380	**0.7138**	**0.7318**	**0.7227**
Animals	4347	0.8585	0.8261	0.8420	**0.8797**	0.8042	0.8403	0.8476	**0.8548**	**0.8512**
Adult	2518	0.6092	0.5516	0.5790	**0.6397**	0.3737	0.4718	0.6098	**0.6330**	**0.6212**
Middle Aged	2108	0.5978	**0.5337**	0.5639	**0.7108**	0.4255	0.5323	0.7085	0.4900	**0.5794**
Aged	1467	0.5684	**0.4731**	**0.5164**	0.6806	0.3758	0.4842	**0.6813**	0.3599	0.4710
Mice	1304	0.8588	**0.7745**	**0.8145**	0.8102	0.7891	0.7995	**0.8890**	0.7063	0.7872
Adolescent	1066	**0.4059**	**0.3340**	**0.3664**	0.0000	0.0000	0.0000	0.0000	0.0000	0.0000
Rats	938	**0.9118**	**0.8262**	**0.8669**	0.8633	0.7878	0.8239	0.8702	0.7431	0.8016
Average	3045	**0.7134**	**0.6608**	**0.6861**	0.6663	0.6208	0.6428	0.6918	0.6229	0.6556

Table 1: Text categorisation results for the 10 selected categories with the small set and a batch size of 8000 citations. Results are reported in precision (Pre), recall (Rec) and F-measure (F1). Average results are shown at the bottom of the table. *DBN 250* means using three layers with 250 units each. *DBN 500* means using three layers with 500 units each.

	Methods	SVM	(linear)		DBN	250		DBN	500	
Category	Positives	Pre	Rec	F1	Pre	Rec	F1	Pre	Rec	F1
Humans	35967	0.9052	0.9354	0.9201	**0.9209**	0.9436	0.9321	0.9204	**0.9445**	**0.9323**
Female	16483	0.7464	**0.7176**	0.7317	**0.8305**	0.6964	0.7576	0.8216	0.7160	**0.7652**
Male	15530	0.7267	0.6889	0.7073	**0.7917**	0.7025	0.7444	0.7878	**0.7213**	**0.7531**
Animals	11259	0.8431	**0.7613**	**0.8001**	0.8895	0.6879	0.7758	**0.9407**	0.6337	0.7573
Adult	8792	0.5824	**0.5296**	**0.5547**	**0.6915**	0.4480	0.5438	0.6696	0.3592	0.4676
Middle Aged	8392	0.6323	0.5728	0.6011	0.7239	0.5654	0.6349	**0.7375**	**0.5853**	**0.6527**
Aged	6151	0.5616	**0.5079**	**0.5334**	**0.7147**	0.4076	0.5191	0.6937	0.4303	0.5312
Adolescent	3824	0.4641	**0.3690**	**0.4111**	0.5735	0.2529	0.3510	**0.6583**	0.2202	0.3300
Mice	3723	0.8386	0.7284	0.7796	0.8746	0.7268	0.7939	**0.8984**	**0.7295**	**0.8052**
Rats	1613	0.8461	**0.7601**	0.8008	**0.9150**	0.7204	0.8061	0.9123	0.7421	**0.8185**
Average	11173	0.7146	**0.6571**	0.6847	0.7926	0.6152	**0.6927**	**0.8040**	0.6082	0.6926

Table 2: Text categorisation results for the 10 selected categories with the large set and a batch size of 31647 citations. Results are reported in precision (Pre), recall (Rec) and F-measure (F1). Average results are shown at the bottom of the table. *DBN 250* means using three layers with 250 units each. *DBN 500* means using three layers with 500 units each.

References

Chidanand Apte, Fred Damerau, and Sholom M Weiss. 1994. Automated learning of decision rules for text categorization. *ACM Transactions on Information Systems*, 12:233–251.

Alan R Aronson and François-Michel Lang. 2010. An overview of MetaMap: historical perspective and recent advances. *Journal of the American Medical Informatics Association*, 17(3):229–236.

Alan R Aronson, James G Mork, Clifford W Gay, Susanne M Humphrey, and Willie J Rogers. 2004. The NLM indexing initiative's medical text indexer. *Medinfo*, 11(Pt 1):268–72.

Ella Bingham and Heikki Mannila. 2001. Random projection in dimensionality reduction: applications to image and text data. In *Proceedings of the seventh ACM SIGKDD international conference on Knowledge discovery and data mining*, pages 245–250. ACM.

Susan Dumais, John Platt, David Heckerman, and Mehran Sahami. 1998. Inductive learning algorithms and representations for text categorization. In *Proceedings of the seventh international conference on Information and knowledge management*, pages 148–155. ACM.

Xavier Glorot, Antoine Bordes, and Yoshua Bengio. 2011. Domain adaptation for large-scale sentiment classification: A deep learning approach. In *Proceedings of the 28th International Conference on Machine Learning (ICML-11)*, pages 513–520.

Geoffrey E Hinton and Ruslan R Salakhutdinov. 2006. Reducing the dimensionality of data with neural networks. *Science*, 313(5786):504–507.

GE Hinton. 2002. Training products of experts by minimizing contrastive divergence. *Neural computation*, 1800:1771–1800.

Antonio Jimeno-Yepes, Bartłomiej Wilkowski, James G Mork, Elizabeth Van Lenten, Dina Demner Fushman, and Alan R Aronson. 2011. A bottom-up approach to MEDLINE indexing recommendations. In *AMIA Annual Symposium Proceedings*, volume 2011, page 1583. American Medical Informatics Association.

Antonio Jose Jimeno Yepes, James G Mork, Dina Demner-Fushman, and Alan R Aronson. 2013. Comparison and combination of several MeSH indexing approaches. In *AMIA Annual Symposium Proceedings*, volume 2013, page 709. American Medical Informatics Association.

Thorsten Joachims. 1998. Text categorization with suport vector machines: Learning with many relevant features. In *Proceedings of the 10th European Conference on Machine Learning*, ECML '98, pages 137–142, London, UK, UK. Springer-Verlag.

Jimmy Lin and W John Wilbur. 2007. PubMed related articles: a probabilistic topic-based model for content similarity. *BMC bioinformatics*, 8(1):423.

James G Mork, Antonio Jimeno-Yepes, and Alan R Aronson. 2013. The NLM Medical Text Indexer system for indexing biomedical literature. In *BioASQ@ CLEF*.

Ali Rahimi and Benjamin Recht. 2009. Weighted sums of random kitchen sinks: Replacing minimization with randomization in learning. In *Advances in neural information processing systems*, pages 1313–1320.

Ruslan Salakhutdinov, Andriy Mnih, and Geoffrey Hinton. 2007. Restricted Boltzmann machines for collaborative filtering. In *Proceedings of the 24th international conference on Machine learning*, pages 791–798. ACM.

Fabrizio Sebastiani. 2002. Machine learning in automated text categorization. *ACM computing surveys (CSUR)*, 34(1):1–47.

Grigorios Tzortzis and Aristidis Likas. 2007. Deep belief networks for spam filtering. In *Tools with Artificial Intelligence, 2007. ICTAI 2007. 19th IEEE International Conference on*, volume 2, pages 306–309. IEEE.

Pascal Vincent, Hugo Larochelle, Isabelle Lajoie, Yoshua Bengio, and Pierre-Antoine Manzagol. 2010. Stacked denoising autoencoders: Learning useful representations in a deep network with a local denoising criterion. *The Journal of Machine Learning Research*, 11:3371–3408.

Kilian Weinberger, Anirban Dasgupta, John Langford, Alex Smola, and Josh Attenberg. 2009. Feature hashing for large scale multitask learning. In *Proceedings of the 26th Annual International Conference on Machine Learning*, pages 1113–1120. ACM.

Tong Zhang. 2004. Solving large scale linear prediction problems using stochastic gradient descent algorithms. In *Proceedings of the Twenty-first International Conference on Machine Learning*, ICML '04, pages 116–, New York, NY, USA. ACM.

Poster papers

Sinhala-Tamil Machine Translation: Towards better Translation Quality

Randil Pushpananda **Ruvan Weerasinghe**
Language Technology Research Laboratory
University of Colombo School of Computing
Sri Lanka
{rpn|arw}@ucsc.lk

Mahesan Niranjan
School of Electronics and
Computer Science
University of Southampton, UK
mn@ecs.soton.ac.uk

Abstract

Statistical Machine Translation (SMT) is a well-known and well established data-driven approach used for language translation. The focus of this work is to develop a statistical machine translation system for Sri Lankan languages, Sinhala and Tamil language pair. This paper presents a systematic investigation of how Sinhala-Tamil SMT performance varies with the amount of parallel training data used, in order to find out the minimum needed to develop a machine translation system with acceptable performance.

1 Introduction

Sri Lanka is a multi-ethnic, multi-lingual country. Sinhala and Tamil are the national languages of Sri Lanka. The majority of Sri Lankans do not have a good knowledge of languages other than their mother tongue. Therefore a language barrier between the Sinhala and Tamil communities exists. This language barrier and the problems that arose during the last 30 years in the country, encouraged us to a translation application using the SMT approach. This would reduce the language gap between these two communities and thereby help solve a burning issue in the country.

The choice of the Sinhala - Tamil language pair provides some opportunities as well as some challenges. The opportunity is that they share some affinity to each other, having evolved alongside each other in Sri Lanka. The challenges include the sparseness in the availability of data, and the limited research undertaken in them. Hence, developing a successful system with limited resources is our ultimate goal.

2 Background and Related Work

There is very limited research reported in the literature for Sinhala-Tamil machine translation. According to (Weerasinghe, 2003), the Sinhala-Tamil language pair gives better performance compared to the Sinhala-English pair in SMT since they are more closely related to each other owing to their evolution within Sri Lanka. Some important factors to consider when building SMT for the Sinhala-Tamil language pair have been identified in (Sakthithasan et al., 2010). The limited amount of data, and the restricted domain it represented, makes that word hard to generalize. Another study (Jeyakaran and Weerasinghe, 2011), explored the applicability of the Kernel Ridge Regression technique to Sinhala-Tamil translation. This research resulted in a hybrid of classical phrase based SMT and Kernel Ridge Regression with two novel solutions for the pre-image problem.

Owing to the limited amount of parallel data available, it has been not possible to analyze how the results vary with increasing numbers of parallel sentences in Sinhala and Tamil for general purpose MT.

2.1 Sinhala and Tamil Languages

Sinhala belongs to the Indo-Aryan language family and Tamil to the Dravidian family. Both Sinhala and Tamil languages are morphologically rich languages: Sinhala has up to 110 noun word forms and up to 282 verb word forms (Welgama et al., 2011) and Tamil has around 40 noun word forms and up to 240 verb word forms (Lushanthan, 2010). Also both these languages are syntactically similar. The typical word order of both these languages are Subject-Object-Verb. However both are flexible with the word order and variant word orders are possible with discourse - pragmatic effects (Liyanage et al., 2012; Wikipedia, 2014).

In addition there are some of the aspects of Tamil influence on the structure of the Sinhalese language. The most significant impact of Tamil on Sinhalese has been at the lexical level (Karunatilaka, 2011). අම්මා (/amma/: mother), අක්කා

Randil Pushpananda, Ruvan Weerasinghe and Mahesan Niranjan. 2014. Sinhala-Tamil Machine Translation: Towards better Translation Quality. In *Proceedings of Australasian Language Technology Association Workshop*, pages 129−133.

(/akka/: elder sister), අයියා (/ayya/: elder brother) are some loan words out of more than thousand words borrowed from Tamil to Sinhala (Coperahewa and Arunachalam, 2011).

3 Experiments and Results

3.1 Tools used

The open source statistical machine translation system: MOSES (Koehn et al., 2007) was used with GIZA++ (Och and Ney, 2004) using the standard alignment heuristic grow-diag-final for word alignments. Tri-gram language models were trained on the target side of the parallel data and the target language monolingual corpus by using the Stanford Research Institute language Modeling toolkit (Stolcke and others, 2002) with Kneser-Ney smoothing. The systems were tuned using a small extracted parallel dataset with Minimum Error Rate Training (MERT)(Och, 2003) and then tested with different test sets. Finally, the Bilingual Evaluation Understudy (BLEU) (Papineni et al., 2002) evaluation metric was used to evaluate the output produced by the translation system.

3.2 Data Collection and Data Preprocessing

To build a good baseline system, we need to have a sentence-aligned parallel corpus to train the translation model and a (possibly larger) monolingual corpus of the target language to train the language model.

Language	Characteristics		
	Total Words	Unique Words	Sentences
Sinhala	10,142,501	448,651	850,000
Tamil	4,288,349	400,293	407,578

Table 1: Characteristics of Sinhala and Tamil Monolingual Corpora

We used the *UCSC*[1] *10M words Sinhala Corpus* (Weerasinghe et al., 2007) and the *4M words Tamil Corpus* (Weerasinghe et al., 2013) to build the Sinhala and Tamil language models respectively. Both these are open domain corpora mainly with newspaper articles and Technical writing. The characteristics of the Sinhala and Tamil corpora is shown in Table 1.

Finding a good large Sinhala-Tamil parallel corpus was the main difficulty. For this purpose we collected a *Sinhala-Tamil Parallel Corpus* (Weerasinghe and Pushpananda, 2013) which consists of 25500 parallel sentences. This is also an open domain corpus which includes mainly newspaper texts and technical writing. The sentence length of sentences in this corpus was restricted to 8 - 12 words. Both Sinhala to Tamil and Tamil to Sinhala translation models were built using this corpus. The characteristics of the Sinhala-Tamil parallel dataset is shown in Table 2

Language	Total Words(TW)	Unique Words(UW)	UW/TW
Sinhala	252,101	37,128	15%
Tamil	219,017	53,024	24%

Table 2: Characteristics of parallel dataset

3.2.1 Baseline Systems

Using the above parallel corpus, we trained two baseline systems: Sinhala to Tamil and Tamil to Sinhala. First, 500 parallel sentences were extracted randomly as the tuning dataset. Then of the remaining 25000 parallel sentences, 5000 sentences were extracted randomly as the initial dataset. By applying *10-fold cross-validation* (Kohavi and others, 1995) (to get an unbiased result), we divided extracted 5000 sentences into 10 mutually exclusive partitions equally and then one of the partitions was used as the testing data and the other nine used as training data. Then we trained and evaluated the system iteratively for all combinations of the datasets and finally calculated the average performance of the results in order to obtain unbiased estimates of accuracy. We repeated the same procedure by adding 5000 more sentences to the initial dataset each time until the remaining dataset was empty.

Results Figure 1 shows the average BLEU score value variation against the number of parallel sentences in both Sinhala to Tamil and Tamil to Sinhala translation. However, it clearly indicates that much more data would be required to build an acceptable translation model for the Sinhala-Tamil language pair. The results of the Tamil to Sinhala translation system in figure 1 shows that the BLEU score approaches 12.9 when the dataset size reaches 25000. It also shows that results of the Sinhala to Tamil translation only approaches 10.1 for the full dataset of 25000 parallel sentences. The figure 1 shows that when the dataset size is increased from 5000 to 10,000 and 10,000 to 20,000, the increase in performance varies by

[1]University of Colombo School of Computing

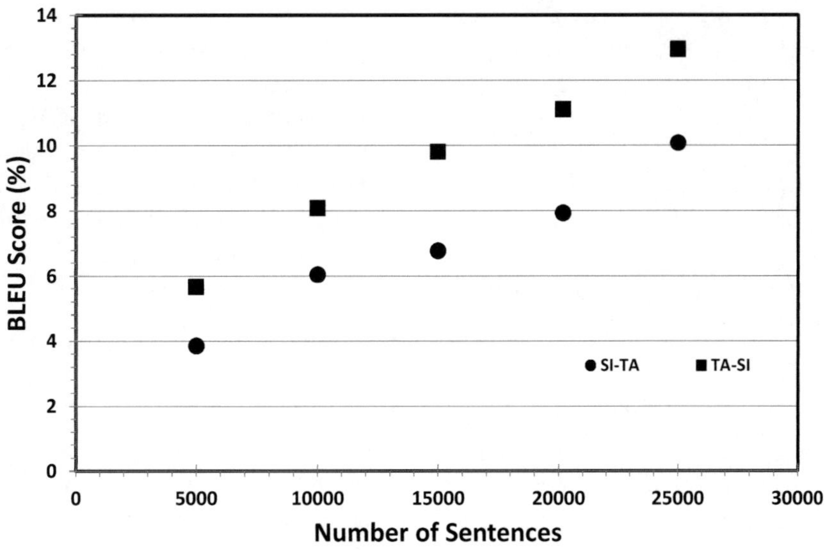

Figure 1: Average BLEU Score VS Number of Parallel Sentences

around 2 BLEU points for Sinhala to Tamil translation and around 2 to 3 BLEU points for Tamil to Sinhala translation. This is consistent with the results reported by Turchi et al. (2012).

Language	Sample Size (S)	Average Perplexity	Out of Vocabulary (OOV)	OOV/S
Sinhala	5000	1590.10	962	19%
	25000	997.33	2225	9%
Tamil	5000	6067.65	1295	26%
	25000	3819.94	3593	14%

Table 3: Average perplexity values and out-of-vocabulary values of the Sinhala-Tamil Parallel Corpus

Also, as shown in table 3, we can clearly see that as the number of sentences are increased, the average perplexity for both Sinhala and Tamil decreases. Sinhala and Tamil datasets were considered separately from the parallel corpus to calculate the perplexity values. These values are very high compared to those of the dominant European languages.

Here we did an error analysis to identify the problems of the methods we used and to find new methodologies to improve the results.

4 Error Analysis

The BLEU scores for test sets of 5000 and 25000 data samples were taken for the error analysis. The process for the error analysis stated as follows.

- Calculate the number of total words(TotW) and unique words(UniW) in each training (Tr) and test (Te) datasets.
- Calculate the number of out-of-vocabulary (OOV) words in the test dataset (as a percentage of test dataset).
- Calculate the number of untranslated words (UntransW)(as a percentage of test dataset).
- Calculate the number of translated words which are not in the reference dataset (TargetOOV)(as a percentage of test dataset).
- Calculate the number of translated words which are not in the target language model (Target LM OOV) (as a percentage of reference dataset).

Description	5000		25000	
	TotW	UniW	TotW	UniW
Training Dataset	44,806	13,723	224,959	34,858
Testing Dataset	4,985	2,884	24,678	8,890
OOV (%)	19.70	33.29	9.41	25.11
UntransW (%)	33.78	52.98	17.82	44.26
Reference Dataset	3,168	1,307	17,584	4,298
TargetOOV (%)	17.65	19.15	9.58	17.43
Target LM OOV (%)	0.29	0.33	1	1.55

Table 4: Results obtained from the error analysis of Sinhala to Tamil translation

The results obtained for the Sinhala to Tamil and Tamil to Sinhala translations are shown in

Description	5000		25000	
	TotW	UniW	TotW	UniW
Training Dataset	39,044	16,328	194,784	49,402
Testing Dataset	4,336	2,968	21,462	10,381
OOV (%)	30.32	43.67	16.84	33.85
UntransW (%)	40.68	57.14	25.08	48.58
Reference Dataset	3,168	1,307	17,584	4,298
TargetOOV (%)	10.88	14.94	5.01	11.45
Target LM OOV (%)	0.04	0.07	0.15	0.44

Table 5: Results obtained from the error analysis of Tamil to Sinhala translation

table 4 and 5 respectively. When considering the 5000 and 25000 datasets in table 4 and 5, we can see that the total number of words in the Tamil to Sinhala translation is lower than the Sinhala to Tamil translation in both training and testing datasets. However the unique number of words in the Tamil to Sinhala translation is much higher than the Sinhala to Tamil translation. This clearly shows the complexity of the Tamil language. However, as we expected OOV (unique word) rate is reduced by 8% - 10%, when the dataset size is increasing. That is one of the reasons for the increment of BLEU score value. We have identified mainly two problems. According to table 4, 20% of unique words in the test set are not translated even they were in the training set and 17% to 19% of words which are not in the target reference set is in the translated output. Those are occurred due to phrase alignment problems and also the decoding problems. For an example if we need to translate ගෙදර (*Home*) to Tamil, the phrase table consists only ගෙදර එන්න (*Come home*) and ගෙදර යන්න (*Go home*), then that word will not be translated even that word is in the training set. Since Sinhala and Tamil are low-resourced languages, we need to consider these issues to build a good translation system. We can clearly see that out-of-vocabulary rate and the untranslated word rate is much higher in Tamil to Sinhala Translation. Also when we consider the out-of-vocabulary words, we have found that those words consist of proper names, misspelled words, inflections, derivatives and honorifics. These are the main problems that we could identify from the error analysis. Since human evaluation is very costly, we used only the above technique to do the evaluation. According to the figure 1, we can see that even the OOV words are higher, BLEU score values of Tamil to Sinhala translation is higher. The main reason for this could be the size of the language model since words in the Sinhala monolingual corpus is more than twice as the words in the Tamil monolingual corpus. When consider the Target OOV and Target LM OOV in Tamil to Sinhala Translation is lower compared to the Sinhala to Tamil translation. That could be a another reason to get a higher BLEU score value for Tamil to Sinhala translation.

5 Conclusion and Future Work

The purpose of this research was to find out how the SMT systems perform for Sinhala to Tamil and Tamil to Sinhala translation. We can conclude that while Tamil to Sinhala and Sinhala to Tamil translation is unable to produce intelligible output with parallel corpus of just 25000 sentence pairs of relatively short length, we can expect performance to approach usable levels by collecting a large parallel corpora. Using this experience, we are currently collecting a more balanced parallel corpus.

However the error analysis shows that the sentence length limitations of the Sinhala-Tamil parallel corpus could not be the only reason for the comparatively lower BLEU scores, morphological richness may be the reason to get lower results since misspelled words and proper names are common to other languages too. Furthermore, a preliminary study shows that we can get better perplexity values for the same dataset we used for this research by stemming suffixes of the Sinhala and Tamil parallel sentences. In future, we are planning to investigate and find solutions to these problems and planning to implement a system capable of producing acceptable translations between Sinhala and Tamil for use by the wider community.

Acknowledgment

The authors would like to thank the anonymous reviewers for their helpful comments and suggestions. This work was supported by the National Research Council, ICT Agency and LK Domain Registry of Sri Lanka. The authors are grateful to past and current members of the Language Technology Research Laboratory of the UCSC, Sri Lanka for their significant contribution in developing the basic linguistic resources needed to carry out the research described above.

References

Sandagomi Coperahewa and Sarojini Arunachalam. 2011. *A Dictionary of Tamil Word in Sinhala*, volume 2. Godage International publishers, Sri Lanka.

Mahendran Jeyakaran and Ruvan Weerasinghe. 2011. A novel kernel regression based machine translation system for sinhala-tamil translation. In *Proceedings of the 4th Annual UCSC Research Symposium*.

WS Karunatilaka. 2011. *Link*. Godage International publishers, Sri Lanka.

Philipp Koehn, Hieu Hoang, Alexandra Birch, Chris Callison-Burch, Marcello Federico, Nicola Bertoldi, Brooke Cowan, Wade Shen, Christine Moran, Richard Zens, et al. 2007. Moses: Open source toolkit for statistical machine translation. In *Proceedings of the 45th Annual Meeting of the ACL on Interactive Poster and Demonstration Sessions*, pages 177–180. Association for Computational Linguistics.

Ron Kohavi et al. 1995. A study of cross-validation and bootstrap for accuracy estimation and model selection. In *IJCAI*, volume 14, pages 1137–1145.

Chamila Liyanage, Randil Pushpananda, Dulip Lakmal Herath, and Ruvan Weerasinghe. 2012. A computational grammar of sinhala. In *Computational Linguistics and Intelligent Text Processing*, pages 188–200. Springer.

Sivaneasharajah Lushanthan. 2010. Morphological analyzer and generator for tamil language. August.

Franz Josef Och and Hermann Ney. 2004. The alignment template approach to statistical machine translation. *Computational linguistics*, 30(4):417–449.

Franz Josef Och. 2003. Minimum error rate training in statistical machine translation. In *Proceedings of the 41st Annual Meeting on Association for Computational Linguistics-Volume 1*, pages 160–167. Association for Computational Linguistics.

Kishore Papineni, Salim Roukos, Todd Ward, and Wei-Jing Zhu. 2002. Bleu: a method for automatic evaluation of machine translation. In *Proceedings of the 40th annual meeting on association for computational linguistics*, pages 311–318. Association for Computational Linguistics.

Sripirakas Sakthithasan, ruvan Weerasinghe, and Dulip Lakmal Herath. 2010. Statistical machine translation of systems for sinhala-tamil. In *Advances in ICT for Emerging Regions (ICTer), 2010 International Conference on*, pages 62–68. IEEE.

Andreas Stolcke et al. 2002. Srilm-an extensible language modeling toolkit. In *INTERSPEECH*.

Marco Turchi, Cyril Goutte, and Nello Cristianini. 2012. Learning machine translation from in-domain and out-of-domain data. In *Proceedings of the 16th Annual Conference of the European Association for Machine Translation*, pages 305–312.

Ruvan Weerasinghe and Randil Pushpananda. 2013. Sinhala tamil parallel corpora subset with a total 1 million words. Technical report, University of Colombo School of Computing.

Ruvan Weerasinghe, Dulip Herath, Viraj Welgama, Nishantha Medagoda, Asanka Wasala, and Eranga Jayalatharachchi. 2007. Ucsc sinhala corpus - pan localization project-phase i.

Ruvan Weerasinghe, Randil Pushpananda, and Namal Udalamatta. 2013. Sri lankan tamil corpus. Technical report, University of Colombo School of Computing and funded by ICT Agency, Sri Lanka.

Ruvan Weerasinghe. 2003. A statistical machine translation approach to sinhala-tamil language translation. *Towards an ICT enabled Society*, page 136.

Viraj Welgama, Dulip Lakmal Herath, Chamila Liyanage, Namal Udalamatta, Ruvan Weerasinghe, and Tissa Jayawardana. 2011. Towards a sinhala wordnet. In *Proceedings of the Conference on Human Language Technology for Development*.

Wikipedia. 2014. Tamil language — wikipedia, the free encyclopedia. [Online; accessed 30-October-2014].

Analysis of Coreference Relations in the Biomedical Literature

Miji Choi[1,2] **Karin Verspoor**[1] **Justin Zobel**[1]
jooc1@student.unimelb.edu.au {karin.verspoor, jzobel}@unimelb.edu.au
[1]Department of Computing and Information Systems, The University of Melbourne
[2]National ICT Australia

Abstract

In this study, we perform an investigation of coreference resolution in the biomedical literature. We compare a state-of-the-art general system with a purpose-built system, demonstrating that the use of domain-specific knowledge results in dramatic improvement. However, performance of the system is still modest, with recall a particular problem (80% precision and 24% recall). Through analysis of features of coreference, organised by type of anaphors, we identify that differentiated strategies for each type could be applied to achieve further improvement.

1 Introduction

The peer-reviewed scientific literature is a vast repository of authoritative knowledge. However, with around 40,000 new journal papers every month, manual discovery or annotation is infeasible, and thus it is critical that document processing techniques be robust and accurate, to enable not only conventional search, but automated discovery and assessment of knowledge such as interacting relationships (events and facts) between biomolecules such as proteins, genes, chemical compounds and drugs. Biological molecular pathways, for example, integrated with knowledge of relevant protein-protein interactions, are used to understand complex biological processes.

Coreference resolution is an essential task in information extraction, because it can automatically provide links between entities, and as well can facilitate better indexing for medical information search with rich semantic information. A key obstacle is the low detection reliability of hidden or complex mentions of entities involving coreference expressions in natural language texts (Kim et al., 2011a; Miwa et al., 2010). Such anaphoric coreference expressions such as pronouns are mostly ignored by event extraction systems, and are not considered as term occurrences in information retrieval systems.

For example, the following passage includes an interacting relation; the *binding* event between the anaphoric mention *the protein* and a cell entity *CD40* is implied in the text. The mention, *the protein*, refers to the specific protein name, *TRAF2*, previously introduced in the same text.

(1) *...The phosphorylation appears to be related to the signalling events ... to be phosphorylated significantly less than the wild-type protein. Furthermore, the phosphorylation status of* ***TRAF2*** *had significant effects on the ability of* ***the protein*** *to bind to CD40, as evidenced by our ...* [PMID:10080948]

In this paper, we investigate the challenges of biomedical coreference resolution, and provide an evaluation of general domain coreference resolution system on biomedical texts. Prior work demonstrated the importance of domain-specific knowledge for coreference (Choi et al., 2014). We extend that work with a detailed analysis of features of coreference relations with respect to the type of the anaphor defined by a previously proposed framework (Nguyen and Kim, 2008), and propose an efficient strategy towards improved anaphoric coreference resolution in the biomedical literature building on that framework.

2 Background

Related Work

For general coreference resolution, several strategies and methodologies have been developed since 1990's. Centering theory was studied based on syntactic information for resolving pronominal expressions (Kehler, 1995), and a framework based

Miji Choi, Karin Verspoor and Justin Zobel. 2014. Analysis of Coreference Relations in the Biomedical Literature. In *Proceedings of Australasian Language Technology Association Workshop*, pages 134−138.

on the Centering theory was developed for the interpretation of pronouns by identifying patterns of coreference (Gordon and Hendrick, 1997).

An unsupervised system was developed to determine coreference links with a collection of rule-based models (Raghunathan et al., 2010), and the system has been extended by (Lee et al., 2011) with additional processes such as mention detection, discourse processing and semantic-similarity processing. The system was developed targeting to the newswire domain, but has been adopted for the clinical domain (Jindal and Roth, 2013; Jonnalagadda et al., 2012; Dai et al., 2012). The rule-based approach has been demonstrated to slightly outperform a machine learning approach for coreference resolution related to treatment, test and person (Jonnalagadda et al., 2012).

Recently, there was a community-wide shared task for coreference resolution in biomedical literature, the Protein Coreference task at BioNLP 2011 (Nguyen et al., 2011). Four out of six participants produced meaningful performance, but the overall performance of those systems was low with the best system (Kim et al., 2011b) achieving F-score=34% (73% precision and 22% recall).

A Framework in the Biomedical Domain

There have been attempts to define characteristics of coreference resolution in the biomedical domain (Gasperin et al., 2007; Gasperin, 2006; Lin et al., 2004; Castano et al., 2002). Pronominal mentions and definite noun phrases (NPs) are regarded as anaphoric references. A framework proposed by Nguyen and Kim (2008) organises anaphoric mentions into categories: Personal pronoun, Demonstrative pronoun, Possessive pronoun, Reflexive pronoun, and Indefinite pronoun. Additionally, antecedents are categorised into an NP or embedded within a larger NP, and by syntactic structure, including NP with a head noun (definite and indefinite), Conjoint NP (with more than one head), Coordinated NP, and NP with restrictive relative clause.

We will demonstrate that by analysing the performance of coreference systems according to these types, we can identify variation in system behaviour that depends on the type of an anaphor of a coreference relation. Our analysis taking advantage of this organisation points to the value of a differentiated treatment of coreference, where applicable rules depend on the specific characteristics of both anaphor and antecedent.

3 Experiment

We compare an existing coreference resolution system, TEES, that uses a domain-specific named entity recognition (NER) module with an existing general system, Stanford CoreNLP, that does not use a domain-specific NER. The aim is to explore how domain-specific information impacts on performance for coreference resolution involving protein and gene entities. The TEES system, which includes a biomedical domain-specific NER component for protein and gene mentions (Björne and Salakoski, 2011), and the Stanford CoreNLP system, which uses syntactic and discourse information but no NER outputs (Lee et al., 2011), are evaluated on a domain-specific annotated corpus.

3.1 Data Sets

We use the training dataset from the task Protein Coreference at BioNLP 2011 for evaluation of existing coreference resolution systems. The annotated corpus includes 2,313 coreference relations, which are pairs of anaphors and antecedents related to protein and gene entities, from 800 Pubmed journal abstracts. Table 1 presents descriptive statistics of the annotated corpus, in terms of the types identified by the coreference framework introduced previously.

Table 1: Statistics of annotations of the gold standard corpus

Anaphor	Relative pronoun	1,256 (54%)
	Pronoun	671 (29%)
	Definite Noun Phrase	346 (15%)
	Indefinite Noun Phrase	11 (0.5%)
	Non-classified	28 (1%)
Antecedent	Including protein	560
	Including conjunction	217
	Cross-sentence	389
	Identical relation	43
	Head-word match	254

3.2 Results

Performance for identification of coreference mentions and relations of each system evaluated on the annotated corpus is compared in Table 2. The Stanford system achieved low performance with F-score 12% and 2% for the detection of coreference mentions and relations respectively, and produced a greater number of detected mentions. The TEES system achieved better performance with F-score 69% and 37% for coreference mention and relation levels respectively, but detected a smaller number, reducing system recall.

Our investigation of low performance by each system at the coreference relation level appears in detail in Table 3. Several factors such as lack of domain-specific knowledge (*Including protein* columns), bias towards selection of closest candidate of antecedent (*Pronoun* row for Stanford), limiting analysis to within-sentence relations (*Cross-sentence* column for TEES), syntactic parsing error (*Relative pronoun* row for Stanford), and disregard of definite noun phrase (*Definite NP* row for TEES) have been observed. The main cause, lack of domain-specific knowledge, is explored below.

The annotated corpus contains 560 coreference relations, where anaphoric mentions refer to protein or gene entities previously mentioned in a text. For those coreference relations, the TEES system outperformed the Stanford system by identifying 155 true positives, far more than the 38 identified by the Stanford system, as shown in Table 4.

Table 4: Result of performance of existing systems for coreference relations involving protein names

		Stanford	TEES
Output	(TP)	38	155
	(FP)	1,732	46
Precision (%)		0.02	0.77
Recall (%)		0.07	0.28
F-score (%)		0.03	0.41

The Stanford system also produces a large number of false positives. The Stanford system also produces a large number of false positives. Many of these are coreference relations where an anaphor and an antecedent are identical, or have a common head word (the main noun of the phrase), for example, *IL-2 transcription* (anaphor) – *IL-2 transcription* (antecedent), or *1E8 cells* – *CD19 cross-linked 1E8 cells*. Such relations are not annotated in the gold standard, and hence are counted as false positives, while they may in fact be linguistically valid coreference relationships. The gold standard defines a different scope for the coreference resolution task than the Stanford system.

On the other hand, the TEES system achieved 77% precision, but still only 28% recall. The main reason for the low recall is that the system is limited to coreference relations where anaphors and antecedents corefer within a single sentence. Even though anaphors mostly link to their antecedents across sentences, the system still identified 155 correct coreference relations by taking advantage of domain-specific information provided through recognition of proteins.

Example 1 above demonstrates how the process of NER in the biomedical domain helps to determine correct coreference relations. The anaphor, ***the protein*** is correctly identified as referring to ***TRAF2*** by the TEES system, but the Stanford system links it to the incorrect antecedent *the wild-type protein* (underlined).

4 Discussion

4.1 Differentiated strategy by anaphor type

We have shown that domain-specific information helps to improve performance for coreference resolution, but the domain-specific system achieved lower recall, with 56% recall of coreference mentions and 24% recall of coreference relations. Features of coreference relations have been analysed following the framework focusing on types of anaphors, but the structure of antecedents have not been considered in this study. Differentiated approaches are considered for each type as shown in Table 5.

Table 5: Differentiated approaches based on anaphor types

Anaphor	**Approaches**
Relative pronoun	Syntactic information
Pronoun	Syntactic information Semantic information
Definite NP	Semantic information Head-word match

Relative Pronouns

As for the type of Relative pronouns, syntactic information results is critical for determining their antecedents. In our analysis, relative pronouns annotated in the gold standard corpus consist of *which*, *that*, and other *wh-* pronouns e.g., *whose*, and *where*. In particular, 100% of *which*, and 75% of *that* are tagged with the WDT Part-of-speech (POS) tag by the Stanford parser. A majority of antecedents for those relative pronouns are mentions placed directly before the relative pronouns,

Table 2: Results of evaluation of existing systems on the annotated corpus

	Stanford		TEES	
	Mentions	Relations	Mentions	Relations
Gold annotation	4,367	2,313	4,367	2,313
System detected	12,848	7,387	2,796	707
Exact match	1,006	112	2,466	564
Precision (%)	0.08	0.02	0.88	0.80
Recall (%)	0.23	0.05	0.56	0.24
F-score (%)	0.12	0.02	0.69	0.37

Table 3: Analysis of performance of existing systems comparing to the annotated corpus

		Stanford				TEES			
		Cross-sentence	Internal-sentence	Including protein	Including conjunction	Cross-sentence	Internal-sentence	Including protein	Including conjunction
Relative pronoun	TP	0	1	0	0	0	393	116	9
	FP	0	2	1	0	0	86	27	4
Pronoun	TP	7	62	28	10	0	162	37	9
	FP	675	302	197	132	0	47	15	2
Definite NP	TP	35	7	10	1	0	7	2	1
	FP	1,183	194	483	179	0	3	1	0
Nonclassified	TP	0	0	0	0	0	1	0	0
	FP	4,129	650	1,187	632	0	5	3	0

or close to the relative pronouns within a 10 character span in the same sentence. However, this approach has a defect that it would fail to find correct antecedents, if texts are incorrectly parsed by the syntactic parser. There are 63 *that* tokens tagged with the DT, that should be labelled with WDT.

Definite Noun Phrases

In the gold standard corpus, there are 127 out of 346 coreference relations where an anaphor that is a Definite NP has a biomedical named-entity as an antecedent, and 176 of the 346 anaphors share head-words e.g., *genes*, and *proteins* with the antecedent. For the relations neither involving proteins nor with shared head-words, other approaches are applied, such as Number Agreement to coreference relations e.g., *these genes* is plural and so must refer to multiple genes – *actin and fibronectin receptor mRNA* – and (domain-specific) Semantic Knowledge, such as the similarity between two terms. For example, "complex" and "region" in the coreference relation *the binding complexes – this region of the c-myb 5' flanking sequence* must be recognised as (near-) synonyms.

Pronouns

Pronouns are a more difficult type of anaphor to resolve than others, because they do not include helpful information to link their antecedents. In our data, the resolution scope of antecedents for Subject pronouns is defined within the previous sentence, while the Non-subject pronouns can refer anywhere in the text. For the Non-subject pronouns, semantic information based on its context is important. Among 238 coreference relations where an anaphor is a Pronoun, and their antecedents embed one or more specific protein names, 191 include protein-relevant words (defined by (Nguyen et al., 2012)), such as *binding, expression, interaction, regulation, phosphatase, gene, transactivation, transcription.*

5 Conclusion

In this study, we have explored how domain-specific knowledge can be helpful for resolving coreferring expressions in the biomedical domain. In addition, features of coreference relations have been analysed focusing on the framework of anaphors. By taking advantages of the framework, we expect that differentiated approaches for each type of anaphors will improve the task of coreference resolution, and further investigation according to antecedent types with syntactic characteristics is being left for future work.

Acknowledgments

This work was supported by the University of Melbourne, and by the Australian Federal and Victorian State governments and the Australian Research Council through the ICT Centre of Excellence program, National ICT Australia (NICTA).

References

Jari Björne and Tapio Salakoski. 2011. Generalizing biomedical event extraction. In *Proceedings of the BioNLP Shared Task 2011 Workshop*, pages 183–191. Association for Computational Linguistics.

José Castano, Jason Zhang, and James Pustejovsky. 2002. Anaphora resolution in biomedical literature.

Miji Choi, Karin Verspoor, and Justin Zobel. 2014. Evaluation of coreference resolution for biomedical text. *MedIR 2014*, page 2.

Hong-Jie Dai, Chun-Yu Chen, Chi-Yang Wu, Po-Ting Lai, Richard Tzong-Han Tsai, and Wen-Lian Hsu. 2012. Coreference resolution of medical concepts in discharge summaries by exploiting contextual information. *Journal of the American Medical Informatics Association*, 19(5):888–896.

Caroline Gasperin, Nikiforos Karamanis, and Ruth Seal. 2007. Annotation of anaphoric relations in biomedical full-text articles using a domain-relevant scheme. In *Proceedings of DAARC*, volume 2007. Citeseer.

Caroline Gasperin. 2006. Semi-supervised anaphora resolution in biomedical texts. In *Proceedings of the HLT-NAACL BioNLP workshop on linking natural language and biology*, pages 96–103. Association for Computational Linguistics.

Peter C Gordon and Randall Hendrick. 1997. Intuitive knowledge of linguistic co-reference. *Cognition*, 62(3):325–370.

Prateek Jindal and Dan Roth. 2013. Using domain knowledge and domain-inspired discourse model for coreference resolution for clinical narratives. *Journal of the American Medical Informatics Association*, 20(2):356–362.

Siddhartha Reddy Jonnalagadda, Dingcheng Li, Sunghwan Sohn, Stephen Tze-Inn Wu, Kavishwar Wagholikar, Manabu Torii, and Hongfang Liu. 2012. Coreference analysis in clinical notes: a multi-pass sieve with alternate anaphora resolution modules. *Journal of the American Medical Informatics Association*, pages amiajnl–2011.

Andrew Kehler. 1995. *Interpreting cohesive forms in the context of discourse inference*. Ph.D. thesis, Citeseer.

Jin-Dong Kim, Sampo Pyysalo, Tomoko Ohta, Robert Bossy, Ngan Nguyen, and Jun'ichi Tsujii. 2011a. Overview of bionlp shared task 2011. In *Proceedings of the BioNLP Shared Task 2011 Workshop*, pages 1–6. Association for Computational Linguistics.

Youngjun Kim, Ellen Riloff, and Nathan Gilbert. 2011b. The taming of reconcile as a biomedical coreference resolver. In *Proceedings of the BioNLP Shared Task 2011 Workshop*, pages 89–93. Association for Computational Linguistics.

Jin-Dong Kim, Yue Wang, and Yamamoto Yasunori. 2013. The genia event extraction shared task, 2013 edition-overview. *ACL 2013*, page 8.

Heeyoung Lee, Yves Peirsman, Angel Chang, Nathanael Chambers, Mihai Surdeanu, and Dan Jurafsky. 2011. Stanford's multi-pass sieve coreference resolution system at the conll-2011 shared task. In *Proceedings of the Fifteenth Conference on Computational Natural Language Learning: Shared Task*, pages 28–34. Association for Computational Linguistics.

Yu-Hsiang Lin, Tyne Liang, and T Hsinehu. 2004. Pronominal and sortal anaphora resolution for biomedical literature. In *ROCLING*.

Makoto Miwa, Rune Sætre, Jin-Dong Kim, and Jun'ichi Tsujii. 2010. Event extraction with complex event classification using rich features. *Journal of bioinformatics and computational biology*, 8(01):131–146.

Ngan LT Nguyen and Jin-Dong Kim. 2008. Exploring domain differences for the design of pronoun resolution systems for biomedical text. In *Proceedings of the 22nd International Conference on Computational Linguistics-Volume 1*, pages 625–632. Association for Computational Linguistics.

Ngan Nguyen, Jin-Dong Kim, and Jun'ichi Tsujii. 2011. Overview of the protein coreference task in bionlp shared task 2011. In *Proceedings of the BioNLP Shared Task 2011 Workshop*, pages 74–82. Association for Computational Linguistics.

Ngan Nguyen, Jin-Dong Kim, Makoto Miwa, Takuya Matsuzaki, and Junichi Tsujii. 2012. Improving protein coreference resolution by simple semantic classification. *BMC bioinformatics*, 13(1):304.

Karthik Raghunathan, Heeyoung Lee, Sudarshan Rangarajan, Nathanael Chambers, Mihai Surdeanu, Dan Jurafsky, and Christopher Manning. 2010. A multi-pass sieve for coreference resolution. In *Proceedings of the 2010 Conference on Empirical Methods in Natural Language Processing*, pages 492–501. Association for Computational Linguistics.

Finnish Native Language Identification

Shervin Malmasi
Centre for Language Technology
Macquarie University
Sydney, NSW, Australia
shervin.malmasi@mq.edu.au

Mark Dras
Centre for Language Technology
Macquarie University
Sydney, NSW, Australia
mark.dras@mq.edu.au

Abstract

We outline the first application of Native Language Identification (NLI) to Finnish learner data. NLI is the task of predicting an author's first language using writings in an acquired language. Using data from a new learner corpus of Finnish — a language typology quite different from others previously investigated, with its morphological richness potentially causing difficulties — we show that a combination of three feature types is useful for this task. Our system achieves an accuracy of 70% against a baseline of 20% for predicting an author's L1. Using the same features we can also distinguish non-native writings with an accuracy of 97%. This methodology can be useful for studying language transfer effects, developing teaching materials tailored to students' native language and also forensic linguistics.

1 Introduction

It has been noted in the linguistics literature since the 1950s that speakers of particular languages have characteristic production patterns when writing in a second language. This language transfer phenomenon has been investigated independently in a number of fields from different perspectives, including qualitative research in Second Language Acquisition (SLA) and more recently though predictive computational models in NLP (Jarvis and Crossley, 2012).

Such analyses have traditionally been conducted manually by researchers, and the issues that arise when they are attempted on large corpora are well known (Ellis, 2008). Recently, researchers have noted that NLP has the tools to use large amounts of data to automate this analysis, using complex feature types. This has motivated studies in Native Language Identification (NLI), a subtype of text classification where the goal is to determine the native language (L1) of an author using texts they have written in a second language or L2 (Tetreault et al., 2013).

Most work in SLA, NLI and NLP for that matter has dealt with English. This is largely due to the fact that since World War II, the world has witnessed the ascendancy of English as its *lingua franca*. While English is the native language of over 400 million people in the U.S., U.K. and the Commonwealth, there are also over a billion people who speak English as their second or foreign language (Guo and Beckett, 2007). This has created a global environment where learning multiple languages is not exceptional and this has fueled the growing research into language acquisition.

However, while English is one of the most prevalent languages in the world there are still a sizeable number of jobs and activities in parts of the world where the acquisition of a language other than English is a necessity.

One such example is Finland, where due to the predicted labour shortage, the government has adopted policies encouraging economic and work-related migration (Ministry of Labour, 2006), with an emphasis on the role of the education system. Aiding new immigrants to learn the Finnish language has been a key pillar of this policy particularly as learning the language of the host nation has been found to be an important factor for social integration and assimilation (Nieminen, 2009). This, in turn, has motivated research in studying the acquisition of Finnish to identify the most challenging aspects of the process.[1]

Finnish differs from English in many respects including verb tenses and forms (Karlsson, 2008). It is a highly inflectional agglutinative language with a flexible word order.[2]

[1] For example, the recent study by Siitonen (2014)

[2] More information about these differences can be found at http://esl.fis.edu/grammar/langdiff/

Shervin Malmasi and Mark Dras. 2014. Finnish Native Language Identification. In *Proceedings of Australasian Language Technology Association Workshop*, pages 139−144.

Given these differences, the main objective of the present study is to determine if NLI techniques previously applied to L2 English can be effective for detecting L1 transfer effects in L2 Finnish.

2 Background

NLI is a fairly recent, but rapidly growing area of research. While some early research was conducted in the early 2000s, most work has only appeared in the last few years. This surge of interest, coupled with the inaugural shared task in 2013 have resulted in NLI becoming a well-established NLP task. The NLI Shared Task in 2013 was attended by 29 teams from the NLP and SLA areas. An overview of the shared task results and a review of prior NLI work can be found in Tetreault et al. (2013).

While there exists a large body of literature produced in the last decade, almost all of this work has focused exclusively on L2 English. The most recent work in this field has successfully presented the first applications of NLI to a large non-English datasets (Malmasi and Dras, 2014b; Malmasi and Dras, 2014a), evidencing the usefulness of syntactic features in distinguishing L2 Chinese and L2 Arabic texts.

Finnish poses a particular challenge. In terms of morphological complexity, it is among the world's most extreme: its number of cases, for example, places it in the highest category in the comparative World Atlas of Language Structures (Iggesen, 2013). Comrie (1989) proposed two scales for characterising morphology, the index of synthesis (based on the number of categories expressed per morpheme) and the index of fusion (based on the number of categories expressed per morpheme). While an isolating language like Vietnamese would have an index of synthesis score close to 1, the lowest possible score, Finnish scores particularly high on this metric (Pirkola, 2001). Because of this morphological richness, and because it is typically associated with freeness of word order, Finnish potentially poses a problem for the quite strongly lexical features currently used in NLI.

3 Data

Although the majority of currently available learner corpora are based on English L2 (Granger, 2012), data collection from learners of other languages such as Finnish has also attracted attention in recent years.

finnish.htm

Native Language	Documents
Russian	40
Japanese	34
Lithuanian	28
Czech	27
German	21
Hungarian	21
Polish	12
Komi	11
English	10
Total	204

Table 1: The L1 classes included in this experiment and the number of texts within each class.

The present study is based on texts from the Corpus of Advanced Learner Finnish (LAS2) which is comprised of L2 Finnish writings (Ivaska, 2014). The texts are being collected as part of an ongoing project at the University of Turku[3] since 2007 with the goal of collection suitable data than allows for quantitative and qualitative analysis of Finnish interlanguage.

The current version of the corpus contains approximately 630k tokens of text in 640 texts collected from writers of 15 different L1 backgrounds. The included native language backgrounds are: Czech, English, Erzya, Estonian, German, Hungarian, Icelandic, Japanese, Komi, Lithuanian, Polish, Russian, Slovak, Swedish and Udmurt. The corpus texts are available in an XML format and have been annotated in terms of parts of speech, word lemmas, morphological forms and syntactic functions.

While there are 15 different L1s represented in the corpus, the majority of these have less than 10 texts and cannot reliably be used for NLI. Instead we use a subset of the corpus consisting of the top seven native languages by number of texts. The languages and document counts in each class are shown in Table 1.

4 Experimental Methodology

In this study we employ a supervised multi-class classification approach. The learner texts from

[3]http://www.utu.fi/fi/yksikot/hum/yksikot/suomi-sgr/tutkimus/tutkimushankkeet/las2/Sivut/home.aspx

the corpus are organized into classes according on the author's L1 and these documents are used for training and testing in our experiments.

4.1 Classifier

We use a linear Support Vector Machine to perform multi-class classification in our experiments. In particular, we use the LIBLINEAR[4] package (Fan et al., 2008) which has been shown to be efficient for text classification problems such as this. More specifically, it has been demonstrated to be the most effective classifier for this task in the 2013 NLI Shared Task (Tetreault et al., 2013).

4.2 Evaluation Methodology

Consistent with most previous NLI studies and the NLI 2013 shared task, we report results as classification accuracy under k-fold cross-validation, with $k = 10$. In recent years this has become a *de facto* standard for reporting NLI results.

5 Experiments

We experiment using three different feature types described in this section. Previous NLI research on English data has utilized a range of features types varying from surface features to more sophisticated syntactic ones (Malmasi et al., 2013). However, in most such studies the use of such deeper features is predicated on the availability of NLP tools and models for extracting those features. This, unfortunately, is not the case for Finnish and it was decided to make use of a simpler feature set in this preliminary study.

As our data is not balanced for topic, we do not consider the use of purely lexical features such as word n-grams in this study. Topic bias can occur as a result of the subject matters or topics of the texts to be classified not not evenly distributed across the classes. For example, if in our training data all the texts written by English L1 speakers are on topic A, while all the French L1 authors write about topic B, then we have implicitly trained our classifier on the topics as well. In this case the classifier learns to distinguish our target variable through another confounding variable. Others researchers like Brooke and Hirst (2012), however, argue that lexical features cannot be simply ignored. Given the small size of our data and the inability to reach definitive conclusions regarding this, we do not attempt to explore this issue here.

5.1 Finnish Function Words

The distributions of grammatical function words such as determiners and auxiliary verbs have proven to be useful in NLI. This is considered to be a useful syntactic feature as these words indicate the relations between content words and are topic independent. The frequency distributions of 700 Finnish function words[5] were extracted from the learner texts and used as features in this model.

5.2 Part-of-Speech tag n-grams

In this model POS n-grams of size 1–3 were extracted. These n-grams capture small and very local syntactic patterns of language production and were used as classification features. Previous work and our experiments showed that sequences of size 4 or greater achieve lower accuracy, possibly due to data sparsity, so we do not include them.

5.3 Character n-grams

This is a sub-lexical feature that uses the constituent characters that make up the whole text. From a linguistic point of view, the substrings captured by this feature, depending on the order, can implicitly capture various sub-lexical features including letters, phonemes, syllables, morphemes and suffixes. We do not consider n-grams of order 4 or higher as they may be capturing whole words.

5.4 Identifying Non-Native Writing

Our final experiment involves using the above-described features to classify Finnish texts as either Native or non-Native. To achieve this we use 100 control texts included in the LAS2 corpus that written by native Finnish speakers to represent the Native class. This is contrasted against the non-Native class which includes 100 texts sampled from each language[6] listed in Table 1.

6 Results

The results of the first three experiments are shown in Table 2. The majority baseline is calculated by using the largest class, in this case Russian,[7] as the

[4] `http://www.csie.ntu.edu.tw/~cjlin/liblinear/`

[5] These were sourced from pre-existing word lists from http://members.unine.ch/jacques.savoy/clef/index.html

[6] English only has 10 texts, so we include 2 extra Japanese texts to create a set of 100 documents.

[7] $40/204 = 19.6\%$

Feature	Accuracy (%)
Majority Baseline	19.6
Character unigrams	34.8
Character bigrams	42.6
Character trigrams	53.9
Function Words	54.6
Part-of-Speech unigrams	36.3
Part-of-Speech bigrams	55.2
Part-of-Speech trigrams	54.8
All features combined	**69.5**

Table 2: Finnish Native Language Identification accuracy for the three experiments in this study.

Feature	Accuracy (%)
Chance Baseline	50.0
Character unigrams	91.0
Character bigrams	94.0
Character trigrams	95.0
Function Words	94.0
Part-of-Speech unigrams	88.0
Part-of-Speech bigrams	89.5
Part-of-Speech trigrams	91.5
All features combined	**97.0**

Table 3: Accuracy for classifying texts as Native or non-Native (Experiment 4).

default classification label chosen for all texts. No other baselines are available here since this is the first NLI work using this data and L2 language.

The character n-gram models all perform well-above the baseline, with higher accuracies as n increases. Similarly, the distribution of function words is highly discriminative, yielding 54.6% accuracy. The purely syntactic POS n-gram models are also very useful for this task, with the best accuracy of 54.8% for POS trigrams.

Combining all of the models into a single feature vector provides the highest accuracy of 69.5%, around 15% better than the best single feature type. This demonstrates that the information captured by the various models is complementary and that the feature types are not redundant.

The results of our final experiment for distinguishing non-Native writing are listed in Table 3. They demonstrate that these feature types are highly useful for discriminating between Native and non-Native writings, achieving 97% accuracy by using all feature types. Character trigrams are the best single feature in this experiment.

7 Discussion

The most significant finding here is that the NLI methodology can be successfully applied to Finnish data with results that are largely comparable to state-of-the-art English NLI systems.

The main contributions of this work include the identification of a new dataset for NLI and employing it to demonstrate the cross-linguistic nature of NLI. This is one of the very first applications of NLI to a language other than English and an important step in the growing field of NLI, particularly with the current drive to investigate other languages.

NLI technology has practical applications in various fields. One potential application is in the field of forensic linguistics (Coulthard and Johnson, 2007), a juncture where the legal system and linguistic stylistics intersect (Gibbons and Prakasam, 2004). Here NLI can be used as a tool for Authorship Profiling (Grant, 2007) to provide evidence about a writer's linguistic background. There are a number of situations where a text, like an anonymous letter, is the key piece of evidence in an investigation. Clues about the native language of a writer can help investigators in identifying the source.[8] Accordingly, we can see that NLI can be a useful forensic tool for law enforcement agencies. In fact, recent NLI research such as that related to the work presented by (Perkins, 2014) has already attracted interest and funding from intelligence agencies (Perkins, 2014, p. 17).

In addition to applications in forensic linguistics, NLI can aid the development of research tools for SLA researchers investigating language transfer and cross-linguistic effects. Similar data-driven methods have been recently applied to generate potential language transfer hypotheses from the writings of English learners (Swanson and Charniak, 2014; Malmasi and Dras, 2014d). By using an error annotated corpus, which was not the case in this study, the annotations could be used in conjunction with similar linguistic features to study the syntactic contexts in which different error types occur (Malmasi and Dras, 2014c). Results from such approaches could be used to create teaching material that is customized for the

[8] e.g. for analysing extremist related activity on the web (Abbasi and Chen, 2005)

learner's L1. This has been previously shown to yield learning improvements (Laufer and Girsai, 2008).

There are a number of avenues for future work. A key limitation of this study, although beyond our control, is the limited amount of data used. We hope to evaluate our system on larger data as it becomes available. The application of more linguistically sophisticated features also merits further investigation, but this is limited by the availability of Finnish NLP tools and resources. Another possible improvement is the use of classifier ensembles to improve classification accuracy. This has previously been applied to English NLI with good results (Tetreault et al., 2012).

We would also like to point to the failure to distinguish between the L2 and any other acquired languages as a more general criticism of the NLI literature to date. The current body of NLI literature fails to distinguish whether the learner language is in fact the writer's second language, or whether it is possibly a third language (L3).

It has been noted in the SLA literature that when acquiring an L3, there may be instances of both L1- and L2-based transfer effects on L3 production (Ringbom, 2001). Studies of such second language transfer effects during third language acquisition have been a recent focus on cross-linguistic influence research (Murphy, 2005).

One potential reason for this shortcoming in NLI is that none of commonly used corpora distinguish between the L2 and L3; they only include the author's L1 and the language which they are learning. This language is generally assumed to be an L2, but this may not be case. At its core, this issue relates to corpus linguistics and the methodology used to create learner corpora. The thorough study of these effects is contingent upon the availability of more detailed language profiles of authors in learner corpora. The manifestation of these interlanguage transfer effects (the influence of one non-native language on another) are dependent on the status, recency and proficiency of the learner's acquired languages (Cenoz and Jessner, 2001). Accordingly, these variables need to be accounted for by the corpus creation methodology.

But it should also be noted that based on currently available evidence, identifying the specific source of cross-linguistic influence in speakers of an L3 or additional languages (L4, L5, etc.) is not an easy task. Recent studies point to the methodological problems in studying productions of multilinguals (De Angelis, 2005; Williams and Hammarberg, 1998; Dewaele, 1998).

From an NLP standpoint, if the author's acquired languages or their number is known, it may be possible to attempt to trace different transfer effects to their source using advanced segmentation techniques. We believe that this is an interesting task in itself and a potentially promising area of future research.

References

Ahmed Abbasi and Hsinchun Chen. 2005. Applying authorship analysis to extremist-group Web forum messages. *IEEE Intelligent Systems*, 20(5):67–75.

Julian Brooke and Graeme Hirst. 2012. Robust, Lexicalized Native Language Identification. In *Proceedings of COLING 2012*, pages 391–408, Mumbai, India, December. The COLING 2012 Organizing Committee.

Jasone Cenoz and Ulrike Jessner. 2001. *Cross-linguistic influence in third language acquisition: Psycholinguistic perspectives*, volume 31. Multilingual Matters.

Bernard Comrie. 1989. *Language Universals and Linguistic Typology*. University of Chicago Press, Chicago, IL, US, 2nd edition.

Malcolm Coulthard and Alison Johnson. 2007. *An introduction to Forensic Linguistics: Language in evidence*. Routledge.

Gessica De Angelis. 2005. Multilingualism and non-native lexical transfer: An identification problem. *International Journal of Multilingualism*, 2(1):1–25.

Jean-Marc Dewaele. 1998. Lexical inventions: French interlanguage as L2 versus L3. *Applied Linguistics*, 19(4):471–490.

Rod Ellis. 2008. *The Study of Second Language Acquisition, 2nd edition*. Oxford University Press, Oxford, UK.

Rong-En Fan, Kai-Wei Chang, Cho-Jui Hsieh, Xiang-Rui Wang, and Chih-Jen Lin. 2008. LIBLINEAR: A library for large linear classification. *Journal of Machine Learning Research*, 9:1871–1874.

John Gibbons and Venn Prakasam. 2004. *Language in the Law*. Orient Blackswan.

Sylviane Granger. 2012. Learner corpora. *The Encyclopedia of Applied Linguistics*.

Tim Grant. 2007. Quantifying evidence in forensic authorship analysis. *International Journal of Speech Language and the Law*, 14(1):1–25.

Yan Guo and Gulbahar H Beckett. 2007. The hegemony of english as a global language: Reclaiming local knowledge and culture in china. *Convergence*, 40:117–132.

Oliver A. Iggesen, 2013. *Number of Cases*. Max Planck Institute for Evolutionary Anthropology, Leipzig.

Ilmari Ivaska. 2014. The corpus of advanced learner Finnish (LAS2): database and toolkit to study academic learner Finnish. *Apples*, 8.

Scott Jarvis and Scott Crossley, editors. 2012. *Approaching Language Transfer Through Text Classification: Explorations in the Detection-based Approach*, volume 64. Multilingual Matters Limited, Bristol, UK.

Fred Karlsson. 2008. *Finnish: An essential grammar*. Routledge.

Batia Laufer and Nany Girsai. 2008. Form-focused instruction in second language vocabulary learning: A case for contrastive analysis and translation. *Applied Linguistics*, 29(4):694–716.

Shervin Malmasi and Mark Dras. 2014a. Arabic Native Language Identification. In *Proceedings of the Arabic Natural Language Processing Workshop (co-located with EMNLP 2014)*, pages 180–186, Doha, Qatar, October. Association for Computational Linguistics.

Shervin Malmasi and Mark Dras. 2014b. Chinese Native Language Identification. *Proceedings of the 14th Conference of the European Chapter of the Association for Computational Linguistics*, April.

Shervin Malmasi and Mark Dras. 2014c. From Visualisation to Hypothesis Construction for Second Language Acquisition. In *Graph-Based Methods for Natural Language Processing*, pages 56–64, Doha, Qatar, October. Association for Computational Linguistics.

Shervin Malmasi and Mark Dras. 2014d. Language Transfer Hypotheses with Linear SVM Weights. *Proceedings of the 2014 Conference on Empirical Methods in Natural Language Processing (EMNLP)*, pages 1385–1390.

Shervin Malmasi, Sze-Meng Jojo Wong, and Mark Dras. 2013. NLI Shared Task 2013: MQ Submission. In *Proceedings of the Eighth Workshop on Innovative Use of NLP for Building Educational Applications*, pages 124–133, Atlanta, Georgia, June. Association for Computational Linguistics.

Ministry of Labour. 2006. Hallituksen maahanmuuttopoliittinen ohjelma. *Tyhallinnon julkaisu 371*.

Shirin Murphy. 2005. Second language transfer during third language acquisition. *Teachers College, Columbia University Working Papers in TESOL & Applied Linguistics*, 3(1).

Tanja Nieminen. 2009. Becoming a new Finn through language: non-native English-speaking immigrants' views on integrating into Finnish society.

Ria Perkins. 2014. *Linguistic identifiers of L1 Persian speakers writing in English: NLID for authorship analysis*. Ph.D. thesis, Aston University.

Ari Pirkola. 2001. Morphological typology of languages for IR. *Journal of Documentation*, 57(3):330–348.

Hakan Ringbom. 2001. Lexical transfer in L3 production. (Cenoz and Jessner, 2001), pages 59–68.

Kirsti Siitonen. 2014. Learners' dilemma: an example of complexity in academic Finnish. The frequency and use of the E infinitive passive in L2 and L1 Finnish. *AFinLA-e: Soveltavan kielitieteen tutkimuksia*, (6):134–148.

Ben Swanson and Eugene Charniak. 2014. Data Driven Language Transfer Hypotheses. *EACL 2014*, page 169.

Joel Tetreault, Daniel Blanchard, Aoife Cahill, Beata Beigman-Klebanov, and Martin Chodorow. 2012. Native Tongues, Lost and Found: Resources and Empirical Evaluations in Native Language Identification. In *Proc. Internat. Conf. on Computat. Linguistics (COLING)*.

Joel Tetreault, Daniel Blanchard, and Aoife Cahill. 2013. A report on the first native language identification shared task. In *Proceedings of the Eighth Workshop on Innovative Use of NLP for Building Educational Applications*, pages 48–57, Atlanta, Georgia, June. Association for Computational Linguistics.

Sarah Williams and Bjorn Hammarberg. 1998. Language switches in L3 production: Implications for a polyglot speaking model. *Applied linguistics*, 19(3):295–333.

A Data-driven Approach to Studying Given Names and their Gender and Ethnicity Associations

Shervin Malmasi
Centre for Language Technology
Macquarie University
Sydney, NSW, Australia
shervin.malmasi@mq.edu.au

Mark Dras
Centre for Language Technology
Macquarie University
Sydney, NSW, Australia
mark.dras@mq.edu.au

Abstract

Studying the structure of given names and how they associate with gender and ethnicity is an interesting research topic that has recently found practical uses in various areas. Given the paucity of annotated name data, we develop and make available a new dataset containing 14k given names. Using this dataset, we take a data-driven approach to this task and achieve up to 90% accuracy for classifying the gender of unseen names. For ethnicity identification, our system achieves 83% accuracy. We also experiment with a feature analysis method for exploring the most informative features for this task.

1 Introduction

The study of the structure and phonology of given names and how they associate with gender and ethnicity is a topic that has been investigated over the last several decades (Cassidy et al., 1999). Such research generally aims to identify discriminative features that are predictive of gender and how they can be applied in other areas.

In addition to linguistic and psychological research, gender discrimination and inference has recently found practical uses in various areas. These include applications in NLP and text mining, as outlined in §2.

These applications generally rely on name databases which can be costly to construct. However, maintaining an exhaustive database is not always feasible for a number of reasons. Exact matching may not be possible due to spelling variations, portmanteaus and self-created nicknames. Names found on the Web can also be combined or shortened, particularly in usernames.

The main objective of this work is to evaluate a data-driven approach to inferring gender and ethnicity using machine learning and probabilistic models. Such methodology can help inform researchers about the structure of names and to build more robust name-gender inference systems for classifying unseen names.

In line with these goals, we also develop a publicly available dataset of names annotated with gender and ethnicity information.

2 Related Work

Linguistic research in name-gender relations has yielded some interesting results and demonstrated that phonology is quite informative about the gender of a name (Cassidy et al., 1999). It has also suggested that humans can often make gender attribution errors about other people due to the phonetic characteristics of their names.

In fact, through manual analysis, researchers have identified a slew of features strongly associated with gender (Barry Jr and Harper, 1995; Cutler et al., 1990), often from a linguistic viewpoint. One such example is that English female names are far more likely to end in a schwa vowel than male names (Slater and Feinman, 1985), most likely due to their Latin etymology. It is believed that humans implicitly learn these phonological cues and gender associations through exposure.

Names are also a useful demographic indicator to identify people that fit certain criteria or are members of particular groups. For example, manual analysis is often applied to phone directory or other data to identify potential candidates from a specific background for a biomedical study (Yavari et al., 2006).

Such applications have also expanded to language technology, given that names are found in social networks, news articles and many other document types. Inference of demographic details from social media and online content is useful for marketing, personalization, and forensic purposes and gender prediction has received much attention (Peersman et al., 2011; Argamon et al., 2007).

Shervin Malmasi. 2014. A Data-driven Approach to Studying Given Names and their Gender and Ethnicity Associations. In *Proceedings of Australasian Language Technology Association Workshop*, pages 145−149.

In a study on discriminating gender on Twitter, Burger et al. (2011) used names and screen names as features in their classification system, finding over 400k distinct values for each feature. They found the features to be highly discriminative and informative for this task. Similarly, Tang et al. (2011) take a name-centric approach to gender classification for Facebook, reporting that first names are highly informative for the task.

Name-gender info is also used in the NLP task of co-reference resolution and the state-of-the-art Stanford Deterministic Coreference Resolution System (Lee et al., 2011) uses a list of male and female names to resolve anaphora. However, more generic approaches that use probabilistic models of name features have also been recently applied for this task (Le Nagard and Koehn, 2010).

Name information has also been used in text mining (Patman and Thompson, 2003). One example is in the field of Onomastics where publicly available name information can be used to to infer diversity and gender statistics in various areas.

In computer vision, name information from associated text or captions has been used to aid image-based gender classifiers (Gallagher and Chen, 2008).

3 Data

Due to the paucity of publicly available, machine-readable name data that is annotated for gender we developed and make available our own dataset.

The MQ Names Corpus contains over 13k names from 5 cultural groups, as outlined in Table 1. These include names of Arabic, German, Iranian and Japanese origin. Romanized versions of all names are used. Additionally, a final set of the most common given names sourced from the 1990 US Census data[1] is also included. The data can be obtained by contacting the author.

4 Experimental Methodology

We take a supervised classification approach in this study. More specifically, a linear Support Vector Machine (SVM) classifier is employed.

For features we extract character n-grams of order $n = 1, 2, 3$. These n-grams can help capture orthography, syllables and phonemes. The start and end of names are marked with a special character "$". We do not consider n-grams of higher orders here since these could be capturing whole names instead of more generic patterns.

For evaluation, we report our results as classification accuracy under k-fold cross-validation, with $k = 10$. Results are compared with a majority baseline instead of a random baseline as the number of names in each class are unequal.

[1] http://www.census.gov/main/www/cen1990.html

Ethnicity/Culture	Male	Female	Total
Arabic	1090	1148	2238
German	497	576	1073
Iranian	1104	1529	2633
Japanese	1145	1005	2150
US	1219	4275	5494
Total	5055	8533	13588

Table 1: The ethnic groups included in our dataset and the number of names within each gender class.

Baseline (F)	CHAR1	CHAR2	CHAR3
62.8%	67.9%	78.6%	81.3%

Table 2: Gender classification results for the complete dataset using our character n-gram features.

5 Experiments and Results

In this section we outline our three experiments and present their results.

5.1 Gender Identification

Our first experiment assesses the classification accuracy of gender using our complete dataset.

The results for the baseline (Female) and the 3 feature types are shown in Table 2. All three feature types perform higher than the baseline and character trigrams provide the best performance with 81.3% accuracy. This result demonstrates the presence of gender-predictive features that may generalize across our chosen groups.

5.2 Ethnicity Identification

Our second experiment attempts to predict name ethnicity. 1000 names from each group were used and the ethnic/cultural groups are used as labels. Results are shown in Table 3.

	Baseline	CHAR1	CHAR2	CHAR3
All Cultures	20%	59.8%	72.8%	73.8%
US excluded	25%	70.7%	82.5%	83.5%

Table 3: Ethnicity identification results using 1k names from each group as the data.

While the accuracies across all data are quite high relative to the low baseline, our experiments showed that the US census data performed worse than the other groups. To investigate this we also experimented by excluding the US data. This yields a 10% improvement. In our experiments, all combination of cultures that included the US data performed worse than the combinations that excluded it, so we conclude that this is not just an effect of reducing the number of classes.

We hypothesise that this is because unlike the rest, the US data is sourced from a census, and given the diverse demographics of the US (Hirschman et al., 2000), it is likely to contain names from many ethnicities and cultural groups. For example, there are many names of German origin in the data and this is likely the case

5.3 Gender Classification within Ethnicity

We also experiment with gender prediction within each ethnicity, given that our previous experiment demonstrated that performance may be diminished when data from multiple groups are conflated.

Table 4 includes the results, which show that all languages had higher accuracies than when all the data was combined in experiment 1. Consistent with the results of experiment 2, we also see that the worst performance is on the US data, which is only some 6% above the already high baseline.

6 Feature Analysis

Beyond classification, another interesting task is to analyse the features that distinguish gender and cultural groups. Here, feature ranking could be performed with relevancy methods such as the F-score or Information Gain (Yang and Pedersen, 1997).

However, these methods are limited: they do not provide ranked lists for each gender or ethnicity, but rather an overall rankings. To achieve this, we propose the use of an alternative method using linear SVM weights, as described below.

Using the extracted features, we train linear SVM models for each class (either gender or culture). We use a one-vs-one approach to find features most relevant to each gender. For ethnicity classification, a one-vs-rest approach is used to identify culture-relevant features. L2-regularization is applied to remove noisy features and reduce the candidate feature set size.

Male Names	
Feature	**Examples**
r$	Gunther, Rainer, Heiner
f$	Kristof, Rudolf, Rolf
o$	Ingo, Botho, Waldo
an$	Maximilian, Bastian, Florian
us$	Klaus, Markus, Marius
Female Names	
Feature	**Examples**
a$	Ada, Gisela, Kristina
e$	Heide, Brigitte, Wilhelmine
ild	Hilde, Gerhild, Hildegard
ud$	Gertrud, Hiltrud, Irmtraud
lin	Alina, Karolina, Rosalinde

Table 5: Examples of the highly predictive features for classifying the gender of German names.

Ethnicity	**Features**
Arabic	al ah$ $Mu $Kh $Ab ali yya
German	ert $He ied lin ld$ sch rd$
Iranian	Far eh$ ee$ oo$ ehr okh Gol
Japanese	tsu $Ak ki$ aka suk u$ mi$

Table 6: Examples of features that are highly predictive of each cultural group.

In training the models for each feature, the SVM weight vector[2] is calculated according to (1):

$$\mathbf{w} = \sum_i \alpha_i y_i \mathbf{x}_i \tag{1}$$

After training, the positive and negative weights are split into two lists and ranked by weight. The positive weights represent highly predictive features, while features whose absence is indicative of a class will have large negative weights.

We applied this method to our data to extract the most predictive features for classifying the gender of German names. Some of these features, along with sample names containing them, are presented in Table 5. These features highlight that suffixes are an important cue in inferring the gender of German origin names.

We also applied this method to the ethnicity classification problem to extract lists of informative features for each group, shown in Table 6. Looking at the German features we see that they

[2]See Burges (1998) for a detailed explanation.

	Baseline	**CHAR1**	**CHAR2**	**CHAR3**
Arabic	51.3%	71.3% (+20.0)	80.1% (+28.8)	**81.4% (+30.1)**
German	53.7%	73.5% (+19.8)	88.1% (+34.4)	**89.3% (+35.6)**
Iranian	58.1%	68.2% (+10.1)	76.4% (+18.3)	**77.8% (+19.7)**
Japanese	53.3%	72.3% (+19.0)	88.8% (+35.5)	**89.9% (+36.6)**
US	77.8%	79.9% (+2.1)	**84.2% (+6.4)**	82.5% (+4.7)

Table 4: Gender classification results within each ethnic/cultural group of our data. Results include the accuracy and the relative improvement over the baseline. Best results for each group are in bold.

are mostly different than the ones useful for gender prediction.

Another advantage of this method is that it can also produce lists of features that are not associated with each gender or group, although this analysis has been omitted here for reasons of space.

7 Discussion

In this work we demonstrated the utility of a data-driven approach for name research and gender inference, where character trigrams provided the best results. An important finding here is that the gender cues in names are language and culture specific, and classification accuracy is higher when using a model that has been trained with data from the target culture or ethnicity. Since the ethnicity of an unseen name may not be known, this can be predicted first a name-ethnicity classifier, as we demonstrated in experiment 2. Once the most probable cultural group is known, a more specific gender predictor can be applied.

This method can be applied in various areas. It could be used in co-reference resolution systems in cases where unseen names are encountered and their gender must be determined. These methods could also enrich the output of Named-Entity Recognition systems with additional gender information. In text mining and NLP it could be applied to gender and demographic inference tasks for social media and other other big data.

Applications in name research, e.g. Whissell (2001), are also possible. The data-driven feature analysis methodology can help researchers investigating the structure and phonology of names. Additionally, since these gender cues are language-specific, the information extracted here could help non-natives wanting to familiarise themselves with the names of another culture.

The identified features can also be used in other areas. One example is to generate artificial names using features that are hypothesised to be informative about gender, and testing them on subjects to see if they generalize to new cases, e.g. Studies 1 and 2 by Cassidy et al. (1999). They can also be used for the research of product and brand names, which are often not explicitly gendered but strongly associated with customers of a specific gender. In fact, previous findings from applied psychology on phonological cues in product names show that consumers prefer gender congruent names (Cassidy et al., 1999, Studies 7 and 8).

One shortcoming here is the relatively small number of cultural groups included in the data. It would be interesting to assess the task performance with a large number of cultural groups. In the future we plan to expand our dataset with data from more cultural groups including Chinese, Korean, Kurdish, Turkish and Hispanic names. To assist with this, potential sources of publicly available name data need to be identified. Based on our results, data sources where language or ethnicity may not be clearly marked or possibly conflated under another variable, like the US census data, may not be suitable for this task. Wikipedia and public Facebook profiles can be a useful source for name data, although they would need to be annotated. Data sources which include names and gender annotations, such as IMDB, can also help.

Another issue is how to deal with gender neutral names. Unisex names, particularly those varying by culture, can pose problems for our system. One example is the name "Andrea", which is a feminine name in many cultures but considered a male name in Italy. Additional contextual information, if available, could aid in resolving the appropriate gender.

Another aspect that is how the names are categorized according to "origin": this could refer to ethnicity, country, language or a cultural group. It may be difficult to categorize all names according to one of these criteria due to confounding factors. One example is the influence of Islam and the Arabic language on Iranian names. Similarly, we also noted that immigration patterns can introduce Hispanic or German origin names into the US census name data. This is an issue that requires further investigation.

Several directions for future research exist. On a basic level, an error analysis could help identify the features causing misclassifications. Another promising avenue is to focus more on the phonetic features of the names by using phonetic encoding techniques such as Soundex or the more advanced Double Metaphone algorithm (Philips, 2000) to transform the representations of the names.

Another direction is to expand this research to surnames, which are also known to have their own unique structures and meanings (Reaney, 1991). Here, data-driven machine learning techniques could be applied to large-scale data to examine how patronymic, toponymic and locative aspects of last names from different cultures could be learnt algorithmically.

In sum, the results from this research, an intersection of linguistics, psychology and machine learning, can help inform name research and be applied in a variety of areas.

Acknowledgments

We would like to thank the reviewers for their insightful feedback and constructive comments.

References

Shlomo Argamon, Moshe Koppel, James W Pennebaker, and Jonathan Schler. 2007. Mining the Blogosphere: Age, gender and the varieties of self-expression. *First Monday*, 12(9).

Herbert Barry Jr and Aylene S Harper. 1995. Increased choice of female phonetic attributes in first names. *Sex Roles*, 32(11-12):809–819.

John D Burger, John Henderson, George Kim, and Guido Zarrella. 2011. Discriminating gender on twitter. In *Proceedings of the Conference on Empirical Methods in Natural Language Processing*, pages 1301–1309. Association for Computational Linguistics.

Christopher JC Burges. 1998. A tutorial on Support Vector Machines for Pattern Recognition. *Data mining and knowledge discovery*, 2(2):121–167.

Kimberly Wright Cassidy, Michael H Kelly, and Lee'at J Sharoni. 1999. Inferring gender from name phonology. *Journal of Experimental Psychology: General*, 128(3):362.

Anne Cutler, James McQueen, and Ken Robinson. 1990. Elizabeth and John: Sound patterns of men's and women's names. *Journal of linguistics*, 26(02):471–482.

Andrew C Gallagher and Tsuhan Chen. 2008. Estimating age, gender, and identity using first name priors. In *Computer Vision and Pattern Recognition, 2008. CVPR 2008. IEEE Conference on*, pages 1–8. IEEE.

Charles Hirschman, Richard Alba, and Reynolds Farley. 2000. The meaning and measurement of race in the US Census: Glimpses into the future. *Demography*, 37(3):381–393.

Ronan Le Nagard and Philipp Koehn. 2010. Aiding pronoun translation with co-reference resolution. In *Proceedings of the Joint Fifth Workshop on Statistical Machine Translation and Metrics*, pages 252–261. Association for Computational Linguistics.

Heeyoung Lee, Yves Peirsman, Angel Chang, Nathanael Chambers, Mihai Surdeanu, and Dan Jurafsky. 2011. Stanford's multi-pass sieve coreference resolution system at the conll-2011 shared task. In *Proceedings of the Fifteenth Conference on Computational Natural Language Learning: Shared Task*, pages 28–34. Association for Computational Linguistics.

Frankie Patman and Paul Thompson. 2003. Names: A new frontier in text mining. In *Intelligence and Security Informatics*, pages 27–38. Springer.

Claudia Peersman, Walter Daelemans, and Leona Van Vaerenbergh. 2011. Predicting age and gender in online social networks. In *Proceedings of the 3rd international workshop on Search and mining user-generated contents*, pages 37–44. ACM.

Lawrence Philips. 2000. The double metaphone search algorithm. *C/C++ users journal*, 18(6):38–43.

Percy Hide Reaney. 1991. *A dictionary of English surnames*. Psychology Press.

Anne Saxon Slater and Saul Feinman. 1985. Gender and the phonology of North American first names. *Sex Roles*, 13(7-8):429–440.

Cong Tang, Keith Ross, Nitesh Saxena, and Ruichuan Chen. 2011. What's in a name: A study of names, gender inference, and gender behavior in Facebook. In *Database Systems for Adanced Applications*, pages 344–356. Springer.

Cynthia Whissell. 2001. Sound and emotion in given names. *Names*, 49(2):97–120.

Yiming Yang and Jan O Pedersen. 1997. A comparative study on feature selection in text categorization. In *ICML*, volume 97, pages 412–420.

Parvin Yavari, T Gregory Hislop, Chris Bajdik, Alireza Sadjadi, Mehdi Nouraie, Masoud Babai, and Reza Malekzadeh. 2006. Comparison of cancer incidence in Iran and Iranian immigrants to British Columbia, Canada. *Asian Pacific Journal of Cancer Prevention*, 7(1):86.

ALTA Shared Task papers

Overview of the 2014 ALTA Shared Task: Identifying Expressions of Locations in Tweets

Diego Molla
Macquarie University, Sydney, Australia
diego.molla-aliod@mq.edu.au

Sarvnaz Karimi
CSIRO, Australia
sarvnaz.karimi@csiro.au

Abstract

This year was the fifth in the ALTA series of shared tasks. The topic of the 2014 ALTA shared task was to identify location information in tweets. As in past competitions, we used Kaggle in Class as the framework for submission, evaluation and communication with the participants. In this paper we describe the details of the shared task, evaluation method, and results of the participating systems.

1 Introduction

Locations are important pieces of information in social media. When people discuss an event, often they mention where that event is taking place or what they see where. In the case of emergencies, such locations could lead the right resources to the correct place or from the correct route. Also, recommender systems that locate suitable products and services for users require location information. This year, the fifth Australasian Language Technology Association (ALTA) shared task was set to identify expressions of locations identifiable on the map from Twitter messages. A total of 7 teams registered to the competition, with 4 teams submitting their results.

In this paper we describe the background of the shared task, evaluation methods, and results of participating systems. Section 2 describes the shared task. Section 3 gives a short survey of related research. Section 4 describes the data set that was used. Section 5 details the evaluation process. Section 6 shows the results. Section 7 discusses some of the key challenges and issues encountered during the organisation of the shared task. Finally, section 8 concludes the paper and points to the methods used by participating teams.

Tweet	Location
`France and Germany join the US and UK in advising their nationals in Libya to leave immediately http://bbc.in/1rVmrDJ`	`France, Germany, US, UK, Libya`
`Dutch investigators not going to MH17 crash site in eastern Ukraine due to security concerns, OSCE monitors say`	`MH17 crash site, eastern Ukraine`
`Seeing early signs of potential flash flooding with stationary storms near St. Marys, Tavistock, Cambridge #onstorm pic.twitter.com/BtogIxgQ5G`	`St. Marys, Tavistock, Cambridge`

Table 1: Example tweets and their location words.

2 The 2014 ALTA Shared Task

The goal of the 2014 shared task was to identify all mentions of locations in the text of tweets. *Location* was defined as any specific mention of a country, city, suburb, street, or POI (Point of Interest). Examples of POI include the name of a shopping centre, such as "Macquarie Centre" or the name of a hospital, e.g., "Ryde Hospital". This information extraction task is important for applications that attempt to find out where people are or whether they are talking about which location.

The shared task required the participants to only identify which word in the text of a tweet refers to a location, and did not expect the participants to find the location on the map. Table 1 shows example tweets and their locations.

Location expressions can be in the text itself, or in hashtags (e.g, #australia), URLs, or sometimes even in mentions (e.g., @australia). As location mentions can span over words, all these words had to be identified, however, partial identification of location names was rewarded. For example if the correct location mention is "eastern Ukraine" and

Diego Mollá and Sarvnaz Karimi. 2014. Overview of the 2014 ALTA Shared Task: Identifying Expressions of Locations in Tweets. In *Proceedings of Australasian Language Technology Association Workshop*, pages 151–156.

Figure 1: An example tweet with multiple location mentions.

a system only identifies "Ukraine", it was partially correct.

Participants were given a list of tweet IDs and a script to download the tweets from Twitter. Each system had to find the location mentions, and list them all in lowercase as blank separated words next to their tweet ID. For example, for the tweet shown in Figure 1, the expected output was `493450763931512832,france germany us uk libya`.

All punctuation in the word containing the location had to be removed, including the hash symbol (#). If a location was repeated in a tweet, it was expected that the systems to find all the occurrences. That is, each instance of a location is counted on its own, even if repeated.

Different instances of a location word were distinguished by appending a number. For example, if there were three mentions of Australia, the output would be
`australia australia2 australia3`.

Participants were also asked if a location had multiple words, to separate them with blank space so that, in effect, it does not matter whether it is one location expression with two words or two different location expressions. Table 2 shows an extract of the sample solution.

3 Related Work

Research community has been active in location extraction and inferencing locations based on the extracted location mentions from both formal text and social media. Below, we briefly cover two areas of named entity recognition and location extraction in social media, especially Twitter.

3.1 Named entity recognition in Twitter

Ritter et al. (2011) developed a set of tools designed specifically to perform tasks such as NER and part of speech tagging (POS) on tweets. They use distant supervision with topic modelling using an approach called LabelledLDA (Ramage et al., 2009). One of the entities in the NER tool provided by Ritter et al, was geo-location.

TwiNER (Li et al., 2012) is another NER system for Twitter. It follows an unsupervised approach which exploits the co-occurrence information of named entities in a tweet stream. A significant difference with Ritter et. al.. (Ritter et al., 2011) is that TwiNER does not rely on linguistic features asserting that they are unreliable in the tweet domain. Instead its algorithm relies on external sources such as Wikipedia. This system however only identifies named entities and it does not classify them into a type such as organisation or location.

3.2 Location extraction

A number of systems have been developed to extract location information from tweets. There are several studies that identify Twitter user's location based on their profile and their tweets. Some of these studies are briefly reviewed here.

Twitcident (Abel et al., 2012) is a system which uses NER to attach location information to tweets as part of a semantic enrichment stage. Other studies into NER in Twitter include Locke and Martin's (2009) work that investigated the performance of a classifier trained on a small Twitter corpus against an adapted classifier designed for a different text domain. They indicated that the tweet and newswire domains are very different.

Mahmud et al. (2012) proposed an algorithm to predict the home locations of Twitter users at different granularities at the state and city level. They used an ensemble of classifiers based on contents and temporal characteristics of tweets. Their system also leveraged external information sources such as gazetteers. Their dataset was limited to 100 cities in the United states.

Ikawa et al. (2012) studied the location of a tweet instead of the home location of the user who posted it. They learnt the associations between locations and relevant keywords from past messages to predict where a tweet is made. To evaluate their algorithm, they found tweets which have been geotagged with coordinates using Twitter's geotagging feature. Their dataset consisted of 12,463 tweets to train their algorithm and 20,535 tweets for evaluation.

TwitterStand (Sankaranarayanan et al., 2009) is a system that associates a cluster of tweets with a geographical focus by combining information extracted from analysing tweet content and user metadata. Hashtags were used to search Twitter for more tweets relating to specific topics. They used POS tagging and NER to identify location words and then use a gazetteer to resolve location words to specific places. They did not retrain their NER because at the time they stated that no annotated tweet corpus existed. They assigned a geographic focus to clusters of tweets which have been grouped by topic.

Finally, Lingad et al. (2013) compared the existing NER tools, such as out of the box Stanford NER and OpenNLP, re-trained Standford NER, TwitterNLP for their ability to identify locations. They also compared these tools with Yahoo! PlaceMaker, a geoparsing service that identifies place names in a given free-form text. Their main conclusion was that the existing NER tools should be re-trained before being applied to Twitter data.

The ALTA 2014 task was proposed on the level of identifying the location mentions from the tweets and did not cover finding where they refer to on the map.

4 Dataset

The dataset for the task was largely from the tweet collection created and annotated for a study of location extraction from disaster tweets (Lingad et al., 2013). Lingad's original collection was created using tweets from late 2010 till late 2012. It was later on augmented with a newer set of tweets (Yin et al., 2014). All these tweets were annotated in multiple stages, including whether or not they were related to disaster-related events, their location mentions, as well as their location focus (Karimi and Yin, 2012; Yin et al., 2014). Only location mention annotations were used in the ALTA shared task.

The size of the final set was 3,220 tweets, though, as mentioned in Section 7.1, a smaller set of 3,003 tweets had to be used for the shared task. Of this data set, 2,000 tweets were made available for training and development, and the rest was used for a public and a private evaluation as described in Section 5. The split between training and test partitions was based on the date of the tweet postings, so that the training test use older tweets, and the test set used newer tweets. By splitting according to time there is a lesser risk of contaminating the test set, since it has been observed that tweets may focus on special topics and locations at particular points in time. In practice, since Twitter generates tweet IDs sorted by time, we used the IDs to implement the partitioning. The partitioning of the test set into the public and the private sets was random, using the framework provided by Kaggle in Class.

Annotations for the dataset was crowdsourced using the CrowdFlower service.[1] Annotators were required to be from English speaking countries. Each tweet was annotated by three different annotators and only those with majority agreement made it to the final set.

To comply with Twitter policy, we only provided tweet identifiers and their corresponding annotations. Participants were required to download the tweets that were still publicly available directly from Twitter.

5 Evaluation Measures

To evaluate the results we used the setup provided by Kaggle in Class.[2] With this setup, a random partition of the test set (501 tweets) was allocated for a public evaluation, and a disjoint partition (502 tweets) was allocated for a private evaluation. The participating teams returned the output of their systems on the combined public and private partitions, but they did not know what part of the data belonged to what partition. When a team submitted a result, the team received instant feedback on the results of the public partition. In addition, a public leaderboard was maintained by Kaggle in Class, listing the results of the public partition for all teams. The final ranking of the systems was made based on the private partition.

The rationale of keeping these two partitions is that participating systems can receive instant feedback on their progress but the risk of overfitting their systems to the test results was minimised. To limit overfitting to the public test set, each team was allowed to submit at most two runs every day. The public leaderboard was based on the best run of the public partition for each team, and the parallel leaderboard that would be used for the final ranking was based on the best run of the private partition for each team.

[1]http://www.crowdflower.com/

[2]http://inclass.kaggle.com/

Team	Category	Public	Private
MQ	Student	0.781	**0.792**
AUT NLP	Open	0.748	0.747
Yarra	Student	0.768	0.732
JK Rowling	Open	0.751	0.726

Table 3: Results of the best runs.

To evaluate the results we used the F1 evaluation metric implemented in Kaggle in Class.[3] Table 2 shows some of the rows of the test set.

The first two columns indicate the tweet ID and the expected output as explained above. The last column indicates whether the row belongs to the public test set or to the private test set. Participating teams had access to the first column only.

For each row of the test data, the F1 score was computed, and the average F1 was used for scoring the run. The formula for F1 is:

$$F1 = 2\frac{pr}{p+r},$$

where p is the precision, measuring the ratio of correct location mentions returned by the participating system among all mentions returned by the participating system, and r is the recall, measuring the ratio of location mentions returned by the system among all location mentions.

Thus, if, for example a system returns `senegal christchurch brighton` for the third tweet in Table 2 with tweet id 255773531281960961, then

$$\begin{aligned} p &= 1/3 \\ r &= 1/2 \\ F1 &= 0.4 \end{aligned}$$

6 Results

Table 3 shows the results of the participating systems for both the private and the public partitions, sorted by private partition in descending order.

As in past years, participant teams belonged to two categories:

Student: All participants are undergraduate or post-graduate students. No members of the team can be full-time employed or can have a PhD.

Open: There are no restrictions.

[3]https://www.kaggle.com/wiki/MeanFScore

The final prize is awarded to the top student team.

The top team, MQ, is from the student category and it achieved the best results both in the public and private partitions of the data. They are therefore the winning team. Team Yarra was also a student team, and there were three other student teams registered in the competition but they did not submit any runs. Teams AUT NLP and JK Rowling belonged to the Open category.

The results produced by the systems are lower than those reported by Lingad et al. (2013), who reported a top F-measure of 0.902. But note that the amount of training data available to the teams was more limited. Also, note that the partitions used in the shared task were split in time, and as mentioned in Section 4, probably this will produce lower results compared with random partition and represent the results of a more realistic scenario.

7 Discussion

The organisation of this task presented a number of challenges, both in the collection of the data and the evaluation process.

7.1 Collection of the data

Due to policy restrictions from Twitter we were not authorised to distribute the text of the tweets. We therefore made available the tweet IDs, and a script that could be used to download the tweets directly from Twitter. Unfortunately, the number of tweets that could be downloaded could be different on different days, due to changes in the network, and on changes by the owners of the tweets, who can at any time decide to change their availability. When the shared task was announced in August 2014, out of the original 3,220 tweets available in the original dataset (Lingad et al., 2013), only 3,047 were available. Some of them were duplicates, so that the final number of distinct tweets available was 3,003. The tweet IDs of these available tweets formed the training and test sets for this shared task. However, there were comments in the discussion forum hosted at Kaggle in Class that still 87 of the tweets were not available. Thus, some participants who joined later, or perhaps who did not have luck at the time they downloaded the tweets, were disadvantaged against other teams.

TweetID	LocationMentions	Usage
255647812950306817	NONE	Private
255736037089873920	brighton salem kansasville	Public
255773531281960961	senegal senegal2	Private
255804975408635905	christchurch	Private
255805039300460544	chch eqnz	Public
255867997271502849	gambia gambia	Public

Table 2: Sample lines of the test set.

Team	Category	Public	Private
MQ	Student	0.759	**0.778**
AUT NLP	Open	0.736	0.742
Yarra	Student	0.758	0.720
JK Rowling	Open	0.738	0.712

Table 4: Results of the best runs using the original test set that had some annotation errors.

7.2 Evaluation process

Location mentions could be based on multiple words, and there could be repeated locations. However, Kaggle in Class had some constraints on the data format and the choice of evaluation metrics.[4] We therefore converted the annotations from multiple-word expressions to single words, and numbered repeated instances of a word as described in Section 2. However, the conversion process incorporated a bug which resulted in some duplicated words not having the correct numbering. A new evaluation using corrected data revealed that the results returned by the systems were slightly higher than posted in the public leaderboard (about 0.01–0.02 higher for each run), and the rankings were not changed. Possibly, the small impact of this error was due to the fact that the training data had the same annotation inconsistencies, and the number of data affected was small. Table 4 shows the results using the original test set.

8 Conclusions

The 2014 ALTA shared task focused on identifying location mentions in Twitter data. The organisation was facilitated by the framework provided by Kaggle in Class. As in previous runs of the ALTA shared task, this framework facilitated the maintenance of registration, evaluation of the runs, and communication with the teams. On the other hand, the limited choice of submission formats and evaluation metrics added some challenge to the organisation of the task.

The number of participants in this year's shared task was reduced in comparison with past years. This was due to the fact that the task was not incorporated in the assessment component of existing academic subjects, in contrast with, for example, the shared task of 2013. Still, some of the participants were very active, and for example, the total number of runs submitted among the 4 teams was 168.

The details of some of the systems participating in this year's competition have been included in the proceedings of the 2014 Australasian Language Technology Workshop (ALTA 2014). The systems used a range of techniques, including the use of sequence labellers, feature engineering, and combination of classifiers following ensemble and staking processes. Parma Nand et al. (2014) report on AUT NLP's team. They used the Stanford named entity recogniser without training it with the tweed data due to the reduced amount of training data available, in conjunction with various rule-based modules and knowledge infusion. Fei Liu (2014) report on Yarra's team. They use a variety of lexical, structural and geospatial features together with CRF++'s Conditional Random Field (CRF) sequence labeller. They also experimented with classifier stacking and methods for self-training. Finally, Bo Han et al. (2014) report on JKRowling's team. They used a CRF sequence labeller and experimented with topic labelling and semi-supervised learning.

Acknowledgments

The data and the task original idea is from John Lingad's Honours project (The University of Sydney) co-supervised with Jie Yin (CSIRO).

The shared task prize was sponsored by IBM

[4]The constraints are partly due to the fact that Kaggle in Class is free, and as a consequence it has limited support. The paid version of Kaggle does not necessarily have these constraints.

Research.

References

Fabian Abel, Claudia Hauff, Geert-Jan Houben, Richard Stronkman, and Ke Tao. 2012. Semantics + filtering + search = Twitcident. exploring information in social web streams. In *Proceedings of the 23rd ACM conference on Hypertext and social media*, pages 285–294, Milwaukee, Wisconsin.

Bo Han, Antonio Jimeno Yepes, Andrew MacKinlay, and Qiang Chen. 2014. Identifying twitter location mentions. In Gabriela Ferraro and Stephen Wan, editors, *Proceedings of the 2014 Australasian Language Technology Workshop (ALTA 2014)*, Melbourne, Australia.

Yohei Ikawa, Miki Enoki, and Michiaki Tatsubori. 2012. Location inference using microblog messages. In *the 21st international conference companion on World Wide Web*, pages 687–690, Lyon, France.

Sarvnaz Karimi and Jie Yin. 2012. Microtext annotation. Technical Report EP13703, CSIRO.

Chenliang Li, Jianshu Weng, Qi He, Yuxia Yao, Anwitaman Datta, Aixin Sun, and Bu-Sung Lee. 2012. Twiner: named entity recognition in targeted twitter stream. In *the 35th international ACM SIGIR conference on Research and development in information retrieval*, pages 721–730, Portland, Oregon.

John Lingad, Sarvnaz Karimi, and Jie Yin. 2013. Location extraction from disaster-related microblogs. In *The 22Nd International Conference on World Wide Web Companion*, pages 1017–1020, Rio de Janeiro, Brazil.

Fei Liu, Afshin Rahimi, Bahar Salehi, Miji Choi, Ping Tan, and Long Duong. 2014. Automatic identification of expressions of locations in tweet messages using conditional random fields. In Gabriela Ferraro and Stephen Wan, editors, *Proceedings of the 2014 Australasian Language Technology Workshop (ALTA 2014)*, Melbourne, Australia.

Brian Locke and James Martin. 2009. Named entity recognition: Adapting to microblogging. Senior thesis, University of Colorado.

Jalal Mahmud, Jeffrey Nichols, and Clemens Drews. 2012. Where is this tweet from? inferring home locations of Twitter users. In *The International AAAI Conference on Weblogs and Social Media*, pages 511–514, Dublin, Ireland.

Parma Nand, Rivindu Perera, Anju Sreekumar, and He Lingmin. 2014. A multi-strategy approach for location mining in tweets: AUT NLP group entry for ALTA-2014 Shared Task. In Gabriela Ferraro and Stephen Wan, editors, *Proceedings of the 2014 Australasian Language Technology Workshop (ALTA 2014)*, Melbourne, Australia.

Daniel Ramage, David Hall, Ramesh Nallapati, and Christopher D. Manning. 2009. Labeled lda: a supervised topic model for credit attribution in multi-labeled corpora. In *Conference on Empirical Methods in Natural Language Processing*, pages 248–256, Singapore.

Alan Ritter, Sam Clark, Mausam, and Oren Etzioni. 2011. Named entity recognition in tweets: an experimental study. In *Proceedings of the Conference on Empirical Methods in Natural Language Processing*, pages 1524–1534, Edinburgh, UK.

Jagan Sankaranarayanan, Hanan Samet, Benjamin E. Teitler, Michael D. Lieberman, and Jon Sperling. 2009. Twitterstand: news in tweets. In *Proceedings of the 17th ACM SIGSPATIAL International Conference on Advances in Geographic Information Systems*, pages 42–51, Seattle, Washington.

Jie Yin, Sarvnaz Karimi, and John Lingad. 2014. Pinpointing locational focus in microblogs. In *The 19th Australasian Document Computing Symposium*, Melbourne, Australia.

Identifying Twitter Location Mentions

Bo Han, Antonio Jimeno Yepes, Andrew MacKinlay, Qiang Chen
IBM Research
Melbourne, VIC, Australia
bohan.ibm@au1.ibm.com, antonio.jimeno@au1.ibm.com,
admackin@au1.ibm.com, qiangchen@au1.ibm.com

Abstract

This paper describes our system in the ALTA shared task 2014. The task is to identify location mentions in Twitter messages, such as place names and point-of-interests (POIs). We formulated the task as a sequential labelling problem, and explored various features on top of a conditional random field (CRF) classifier. The system achieved 0.726 mean-F measure on the held-out evaluation data. We discuss our results and suggest ideas for future work on location mention recognition in social media.

1 Introduction

The ALTA shared task 2014 aims to identify location mentions in Twitter data. The input is plain text messages, and the expected output is location entities such as country names, city names and POIs for each message. For instance, *Auckland* and *#eqnz* are identified as location mentions in *@USER are you considering an Auckland visit after #eqnz today?*.[1] This shared task is very similar to a well-established NLP task — named entity recognition (NER) but with a focus on location entities in social media. Each token in a text message is categorised as either a location mention or not. The nearby tokens (i.e., context) may influence a token's labelling, hence we incorporate context information in our system. Following the literature on NER (Lingad et al., 2013), we formulate it as a sequential labelling task and use a conditional random field (CRF) as the classifier.

The main contributions of the paper are: (1) A sequential labeller for identifying location mentions in social media; (2) Feature analysis and comparison in NER between social media and other genres. (3) Discussion on errors and extensions to current sequential labeller.

[1] *#eqnz* is a short form for earthquake in New Zealand.

2 Challenges

Although CRF models for NER are widely used and are reported to achieve state-of-the-art results in literature (Finkel et al., 2005; Liu et al., 2011; Ritter et al., 2011), NER in social media still raises several non-trivial challenges.

First, Twitter text is noisy, with more non-standard words than polished text (Baldwin et al., 2013) including typos (e.g., *challanges* "challenges"), abbreviations (e.g., *ppl* "people") and phonetic substitutions (e.g., *4eva* "forever"). These non-standard words often cause generalisation issues (Han and Baldwin, 2011). For instance, lexical variants (e.g., *Melb*, *Mel*, *melbn*) will not be recognised in the test data when only standard forms (e.g., "Melbourne") are observed in the training data.

In addition to non-standard words, informal writing style further reduces NER accuracy. One example is that conventional features relying on capitalisation are less reliable. For instance, *LOL* is capitalised but it is not a location entity, while *brisbane* may be a valid location mention even though it is in lowercase.

Similarly, Twitter specific entities sometimes are sentence constituents, e.g., *#Melbourne* in *#Melbourne is my fav city.* However, they may be a topic tag that does not form part of the syntactic structure of the sentence, such as the hashtags in *I like travel to beautiful places, #travel #melbourne*, in which case syntactic features would be less effective.

For this reason, widely-used NER features may need to be re-engineered for use over social media text.

Bo Han, Antonio Jimeno Yepes, Andrew MacKinlay and Qiang Chen. 2014. Identifying Twitter Location Mentions. In *Proceedings of Australasian Language Technology Association Workshop*, pages 157−162.

3 Feature Engineering

3.1 Related work for NER

The starting point for our features comes from some other representative systems that are summarised in Table 1.

STANFORD NER (Finkel et al., 2005) combined Gibbs sampling and a widely used CRF model. The Gibbs sampling offers non-local constraints to the conventional CRF model that utilises a range of local features. The features in the CRF model are based on words, POS tags, character n-grams , word shapes and the presence of words in a predefined window. The word and POS tag features also include the surrounding tokens and tags to capture the local context information.

Liu et al. (2011) proposed a two-stage CRF-based tagger MSRA for Twitter NER. First, a k-NN classifier pre-categorises words, and then feeds results to a downstream CRF modeller. The features they adopted in k-NN are two word text windows including the target word (i.e., five words in total). The gazetted resources (from Wikipedia) are also utilised and shown to be effective in their experiments. As for the features for building the second stage CRF model, they followed Ratinov and Roth (2009) and made use of tokens, word types (e.g., whether the word is alphanumeric or capitalised), word morphological features (e.g., suffix and prefix of words), previous tagging labels, word context windows, and conjunction features that combine both tags and word context windows.

Recently, another WASHINGTON NER tool (Ritter et al., 2011) was developed by rebuilding a Twitter-specific NLP pipeline (from tokenisation and POS tagging to chunking and NER). They adopted rich information generated in the pipeline, such as POS tags, chunking and predicted capitalisation information, as well as clustering of lexical variants (Brown et al., 1992) and gazetted features from Freebase.

3.2 Proposed Features

Based on the previous representative NER work, we considered the following features:

- `Word`. Lowercased word types are included as a default feature as suggested by existing systems. Previous and next two words are also included to capture local context information. Larger context window size is not considered as Twitter data is fairly terse and ungrammatical (Baldwin et al., 2013), so incorporating long distance context may bring little context information and introduce more noise.
- `POS`. Based on the fact that location named entities are primarily nouns. A reliable POS tagger generates valuable clues for locations. Instead of re-building a NLP pipeline, we adopt an off-the-shelf Twitter POS tagger CMU that generates coursed-grained POS tags with high accuracy ($\geq 90\%$) (Owoputi et al., 2013). Similar to `word`, the previous and next two `POS` tags are also included. We also consider `POS` bigrams.
- `Capitalisation`. Instead of predicting token case in Twitter (e.g., (Ritter et al., 2011)), four types of capitalisation information are retrieved based on the original surface form. Namely, they are all character uppercased (AU), all character lowercased (AL), first character uppercased and the rest are lowercased (UL) and mixed capitalisation (MC). We also consider `capitalisation` bigrams.
- `Domain`. Twitter specific entities such as user mentions, hashtags and URLs are considered as normal words. This is because many location mentions are embedded in these entities. For instance, *@Iran*, *#brisbane* and `http:www.abc.net.au/melbourne/`. Furthermore, we distinguish whether a word is in a stop word or not. Moreover, some location clues such as *street* are also categorised as task-specific features in this feature group.
- `Gazetteer`. Literature has shown that external gazetted resources are helpful in identifying named entities. Therefore, we incorporate features based on external place names, e.g., whether a current word is in a refined list of locations. Details are in Section 3.3.
- `Gazetteer Morphology`. As an extension of previous `gazetteer` features, we also observed that gazetted names may form part of a token and this is particularly common for Twitter specific entities, e.g., *#IranEQ* and *@zdnetaustralia*. As a result, we also perform partial string matching in Section 3.4.

Features	STANFORD	MSRA	WASHINGTON
`Word`	✓	✓	✓
`Word Context`	✓	✓	✓
`Word Morphology`	Character *n*-gram	Affix	Brown Cluster
`POS`	✓	✗	in-domain POS tagger
`Chunking`	✗	✗	in-domain chunker
`Capitalisation`	✗	✓	in-domain capitalisation restoration
`Gazetteers`	✗	Wikipedia	Freebase

Table 1: Features comparison of representative NER Systems

3.3 Gazetteers

We adopted `GeoNames` as our primary source of gazetted features. It is a geographical database with information about all countries with over eight million places, such as cities and points of interest.[2] However, as noted by Liu et al. (2011), some place names are also commonly used to denote something other than a location. Examples of these terms include people's names, natural disasters (e.g., *storm*), and names that usually do not denote a location (e.g., *Friday* or *Friend*). To alleviate the negative impact of these unreliable place names, we collected stopwords starting with a standard one and then added 5K most frequent English terms,[3] natural disaster names from Wikipedia and a list of popular personal names.[4]

After extracting and cleaning the terms from `GeoNames`, the list had over 9.8 million terms.[5] The dictionary was used to annotate the tweets using ConceptMapper (Tanenblatt et al., 2010) and the `GeoNames` annotation was used as a CRF feature.

On top of refined gazetteers, we also collected country names, state abbreviations, airport IATA codes and place abbreviations (e.g., *st* for street) in some English speaking countries from Wikipedia and Google.[6] The list is also filtered by stopword removal so that it represents a high quality place names and we can separately use them as gazetted features from `GeoNames`.

[2]`http://www.geonames.org`

[3]`http://www.wordfrequency.info`

[4]`https://online.justice.vic.gov.au/bdm/popular-names`

[5]Locations might have more than one name to include variants.

[6]The data is available at `https://github.com/tq010or/alta-shared-task-2014-ibm`

3.4 Gazetteer Morphology

The unique genre in Twitter generates many composite and non-standard location mentions. For instance, *chch* represents Christchurch in New Zealand in *Thoughts with everyone in chch #eqnz - not again!*; A standard place name may be concatenated with other tokens, e.g., *#pakistanflood*. A naive string match will miss these gazetted terms, therefore, we also match the prefix and suffix of all refined gazetted terms in Section 3.3 for each token in the tweet. The side effect of this approach is it also produces some false positives, e.g., *sa* (as South Australia or South Africa) also matches *samsung*. To avoid matching false positives, we further restrict the other part (e.g., *msung* in the *samsung* example) must be a valid word from a 81K English lexicon.[7].

Additionally, we also stripped spaces for higher order *n*-gram for this gazetteer morphology matching so that *newzealand* and *losangeles* would be recognised as well.

4 Experiments and Discussion

The training/dev/test data is offered by ALTA-shared task organisers. The collected and filtered tweets correspond to short time period when several disastrous events happened. 2K tweets are used to training and 1K tweets are randomly selected and equally split for dev and test purpose. The data set, however, is skewed to a number disastrous events such as New Zealand earthquake and Queensland floods.

The evaluation metric is mean-F score which averages the F1 number for each tweet. In addition to this official evaluation metric, we also present precision, recall and F1 numbers.

We adopted a state-of-the-art CRF implemen-

[7]2of12inf.txt in `http://goo.gl/4c49gv`

tation named CRF-SUITE (Okazaki, 2007) with default parameters. We used built-in tokenisation and POS tags in CMU and all our string matching is in lowercase. Furthermore, the features are represented in BIO notation, in which B and I represent the beginning and continuity of a location entity, respectively. O denotes non-entity words. Using lowercased features and BIO (instead of BIOLU (Ratinov and Roth, 2009)) notations are to avoid potential data sparsity issues in generalisation, as we only have 2K training tweets and many labels such as *#eqnz* are repeated fairly frequently.

To correct CRF tagging errors and misses, we further imposed some post-processing rules. Words satisfying the following rules are also added as location mentions:

1. A word is in the refined `GeoNames` dictionary or a Twitter-specific entity is a gazetted term combined with an English word;
2. A word is in a closed set of direction names (e.g., *north*, *nth* or *north-east*) or location clues (e.g., *street*, *st*);
3. An URL contains an entry in the refined `GeoNames` dictionary;
4. If the tokens preceding and following *of* are labelled as locations, then the middle *of* is counted as part of a location mention, e.g., *north **of** Brunswick Heads*;
5. *CFA* and *CFS* with the following two words are labelled as location mentions, e.g., *CFA district 123*.

The evaluation numbers of our system for overall and feature ablations are presented in Table 2. Kaggle's site shows the results on the test set of our system compared to other systems.[8] Our system seems to perform below other participating systems, which is cannot be discussed since we are not aware of the implementation of the other systems. Overall, our best tagger achieved 0.758 and 0.726 mean-F1 on dev and test data, respectively. The noticeable disagreements between the results on the dev and test data indicates that there is a large difference between the two sets and that larger training sets are required to avoid overfitting or that additional sets of features might be considered.

[8]Challenge results on the dev set: `https://inclass.kaggle.com/c/alta-2014-challenge/leaderboard`, and public and private split of the test set: `https://inclass.kaggle.com/c/alta-2014-challenge/forums/t/10702/and-the-winner-is/57341#post57341`

Among all features, we saw that `word` and `post-processing` are the most important features to NER. By contrast, `domain`, `gazetteer` and `gazetteer morphology` contribute little to the overall performance. It makes sense that `word` are effective features, because many specific tokens (e.g., *eqnz*) are strong signals showing the token is a location mention. However, it is counter-intuitive that `gazetteer` and `gazetteer Morphology` failed to boost the performance (Ratinov and Roth, 2009; Liu et al., 2011). We hypothesise this may be because our CRF model down-weighted `gazetteer` features, when some location mentions (such as non-gazetted POIs) are not in the refined `GeoNames` and there might be common words that share the same surface forms with entries in `GeoNames`. Nonetheless, this doesn't indicate the gazetted data is not useful, but rather it should be integrated appropriately. Because when we added gazetted data in the `post-processing`, a considerable boost in performance is observed.

Notably, `capitalisation` and `POS` are useful in identifying location mentions. This suggests developing reliable capitalisation restoration and NLP pipeline will be beneficial to downstream NER.

5 Error Analysis

Our system incorrectly identified some tokens as locations. Most of the false positives were due to CRF mistakes. Examples of these mistakes are annotation of tokens like *bushfires*, Probably a larger data set would allow the CRF model to avoid these mistakes. On the other hand, many false positives produced by our system look as genuine locations. For instance, *bakery* was not annotated in *Chinatown bakery* but was annotated in *Manchester Wong Wong's bakery* a few tweets below. Some locations such as *Kumbarilla State Forest* seem to be false positives as well. Possibly the noise in the data set is also responsible for errors produced by our CRF tagger.

Even with our best efforts to remove location names that would not typically denote a location, there are some `GeoNames` locations in our dictionary that typically do not denote a location, e.g., *The End of the World*.

Our system missed some Twitter user names or hashtags with location information, e.g., *@FireRescueNSW*, *@abcsouthqld*. Although these lo-

Data	Dev				Test			
Evaluation metrics	mean-F1	F1	P	R	mean-F1	F1	P	R
`Overall`	0.758	0.774	0.784	0.764	0.726	0.756	0.770	0.742
`-Word`	0.716	0.738	0.717	0.760	0.683	0.715	0.702	0.729
`-POS`	0.744	0.767	0.780	0.755	0.713	0.742	0.772	0.715
`-Capitalisation`	0.748	0.761	0.769	0.752	0.723	0.753	0.769	0.737
`-Domain`	0.758	0.772	0.781	0.763	0.715	0.749	0.768	0.732
`-Gazetteer`	0.751	0.770	0.776	0.763	0.725	0.749	0.758	0.741
`-Gazetteer Morph.`	0.754	0.772	0.780	0.763	0.727	0.756	0.770	0.742
`-Post-processing`	0.714	0.743	0.814	0.684	0.700	0.736	0.814	0.672

Table 2: Overall experiment results and feature ablations

cations contain an acronym or abbreviation denoting a location as prefix or suffix, the rest part is not a valid single word in our English lexicon. For some locations, their variants were not in our location dictionary, e.g., *Melb* for *Melbourne*.

Some location names were not in our `GeoNames` dictionary and nor were identified by the CRF. Examples of these location names include *Coal Quay* or *Massabielle grotto*. Some two letter US state abbreviations were not recognised by our system, e.g., *OR* or *ID*; this could possibly be alleviated by less aggressively filtering the stopwords such as *OR* from the gazetteer but this would in many cases result in many false positives.

In a few cases, our system missed part of the location name when it was a generic location token attached to a specific named location. For instance, *markets* was not annotated in *Kelvin Grove markets* and *grounds* was not annotated in *UTS grounds*.

6 Discussion

In addition to standard CRF experiments and feature ablation analysis, we also tried to improve the accuracy through two extensions. First, we leveraged embedded topics to represent features, i.e., a feature is represented by the distribution of a limited number of related topics. The feature to topic distribution map is generated on a larger number of English tweets using WORD2VEC.[9] The results, compared with the CRF experiments, turn to be negative or minor positive in various settings. We infer this may be due to the sub-domain difference in the representation. We used general English tweets from Twitter Streaming API to obtain the embedded topics, which is different from disaster-related tweets with location mentions. Alternatively, this may be due to the high noise/signal ratio, i.e., expanding original feature to embedded topics brings more noise than the useful information.

Additionally, we also tried semi-supervised learning by first training a CRF model to annotate locations in a large amount of unseen new tweets, then feeding all locations and tweets into a CRF learner to train a new model for future tagging. This approach didn't show improvement either. We hypothesise that this is due to the data set being skewed towards disaster-related location mentions, adding more training data from general tweets does not improve the results.

7 Conclusion and Future Work

In this paper, we described our system in participating ALTA-shared task — identifying location mentions in Twitter. We formulated the problem as a location entity recognition task to scope our efforts in NER literature. Having examined and compared NER feature of existing systems, we proposed our own feature set with justifications. We further built a CRF-based location mention tagger and analysed the feature contributions. Overall, our tagger achieved 0.726 mean-F1 in the shared task. Although our extension experiments both show negative results, there is certainly room for further improvements. Our discussion and error analysis shed light on the future work in this research topic.

[9] `https://code.google.com/p/word2vec/`

References

Timothy Baldwin, Paul Cook, Marco Lui, Andrew MacKinlay, and Li Wang. 2013. How noisy social media text, how diffrnt social media sources? In *Proceedings of the Sixth International Joint Conference on Natural Language Processing*, pages 356–364, Nagoya, Japan, October. Asian Federation of Natural Language Processing.

Peter F. Brown, Peter V. deSouza, Robert L. Mercer, Vincent J. Della Pietra, and Jenifer C. Lai. 1992. Class-based n-gram models of natural language. *Computational Linguistics*, 18(4):467–479.

Jenny Rose Finkel, Trond Grenager, and Christopher Manning. 2005. Incorporating non-local information into information extraction systems by gibbs sampling. In *Proceedings of the 43rd Annual Meeting of the Association for Computational Linguistics (ACL 2005)*, pages 363–370, Ann Arbor, USA.

Bo Han and Timothy Baldwin. 2011. Lexical normalisation of short text messages: Makn sens a #twitter. In *Proceedings of the 49th Annual Meeting of the Association for Computational Linguistics: Human Language Technologies (ACL HLT 2011)*, pages 368–378, Portland, USA.

John Lingad, Sarvnaz Karimi, and Jie Yin. 2013. Location extraction from disaster-related microblogs. In *WWW 2013 Companion*, pages 1017–1020, Rio de Janeiro, Brazil.

Xiaohua Liu, Shaodian Zhang, Furu Wei, and Ming Zhou. 2011. Recognizing named entities in tweets. In *Proceedings of the 49th Annual Meeting of the Association for Computational Linguistics: Human Language Technologies (ACL HLT 2011)*, pages 359–367, Portland, USA.

Naoaki Okazaki. 2007. CRFsuite: a fast implementation of conditional random fields (CRFs).

Olutobi Owoputi, Brendan O'Connor, Chris Dyer, Kevin Gimpel, Nathan Schneider, and Noah A. Smith. 2013. Improved part-of-speech tagging for online conversational text with word clusters. In *Proceedings of the 2013 Conference of the North American Chapter of the Association for Computational Linguistics: Human Language Technologies (NAACL HLT 2013)*, pages 380–390, Atlanta, Georgia.

Lev Ratinov and Dan Roth. 2009. Design challenges and misconceptions in named entity recognition. In *Proceedings of the 13th Conference on Natural Language Learning (CoNLL-2009)*, pages 147–155, Boulder, USA.

Alan Ritter, Sam Clark, Mausam, and Oren Etzioni. 2011. Named entity recognition in tweets: An experimental study. In *Proceedings of the 2011 Conference on Empirical Methods in Natural Language Processing (EMNLP 2011)*, pages 1524–1534, Edinburgh, UK.

Michael A Tanenblatt, Anni Coden, and Igor L Sominsky. 2010. The conceptmapper approach to named entity recognition. In *Proceedings of the 7th International Conference on Language Resources and Evaluation (LREC 2010)*, Malta.

A Multi-Strategy Approach for Location Mining in Tweets: AUT NLP Group Entry for ALTA-2014 Shared Task

Parma Nand, Rivindu Perera, Anju Sreekumar
Natural Language Processing Group
Auckland University of Technology
Auckland 1010, New Zealand
{pnand,rperera,anjus}@aut.ac.nz

He Lingmin
Department of Computer Science
China Jiliang University
Hangzhou, China
helm@cjlu.edu.cn

Abstract

This paper describes the strategy and the results of a location mining system used for the ALTA-2014 shared task competition. The task required the participants to identify the location mentions in 1003 Twitter test messages given a separate annotated training set of 2000 messages. We present an architecture that uses a basic named entity recognizer in conjunction with various rule-based modules and knowledge infusion to achieve an average F score of 0.747 which won the second place in the competition. We used the pre-trained Stanford NER which gives us an F score of 0.532 and used an ensemble of other techniques to reach the 0.747 value. The other major source of location resolver was the DBpedia location list which was used to identify a large percentage of locations with an individual F-score of 0.935.

1 Introduction

The objective of the ALTA competition was to identify a wide range of location mentions in Twitter messages. Among the various types of information that can be mined from Twitter messages, location mining has attracted a lot attention because of its application in identifying the geographical location of a topic in the Tweet, whether it be an accident, a natural disaster, a concert or an open invitation party gone out of hand. Location mining is a special case of a generic NLP task called Named Entity Recognition (NER), which involves identifying and classifying entities into person, organization and location type entities. This particular competition focussed on only identifying location type entities, however had a wider scope compared to a typical NER task. The objective of the task was to identify the string which specifies the most specific possible locations in the message. A typical NER tool such as the Stanford[1] and OpenNLP[2] only identifies word based locations which has to be then composed into noun phrases consisting of multiple words identifying the full location. In addition to the locations identified by noun phrases, the task required the identification of the specific locations defined by propositional attachments such as "40km south of tenterfield2" and "100 mi from nations capital".

Our approach to solving the location mining task at hand was to use a NER system to attain a benchmark performance and then to use various techniques to fine tune the system to account for the noise in Twitter messages. The architecture forms part of a bigger project called the *Twitter Miner*[3]. This project is a higher level research project currently underway at Auckland University of Technology which is meant to extract information for various purposes from microblogging type texts such as Twitter.

For the NER, we used the Conditional Random Field (CRF) based, Stanfod NER system as this has been tested to give the highest accuracy on Twitter messages (Lingad et al., 2013). In this paper Lingad et al. (2013) reported the re-trained Stanford NER to achieve an F-value of 0.902 compared to 0.576 for the pre-trained NER. We however found that, re-training the Stanford NER with bare training data provided by the organizers gave us F scores around the 0.4 mark at token level compared to approximately 0.57 for the pre-trained model. Analysis of the errors for both the models showed that due to loose capitalization in twitter messages, a lot of the locations could not be identified simply because they did not exist in the training data. Since the pre-trained model was trained with much larger training set

[1] http://nlp.stanford.edu/software/CRF-NER.shtml
[2] http://opennlp.apache.org
[3] http://staff.elena.aut.ac.nz/Parma-Nand/projects.html

Parma Nand, Rivindu Perera, Anju Sreekumar and He Lingmin. 2014. A Multi-Strategy Approach for Location Mining in Tweets: AUT NLP Group Entry for ALTA-2014 Shared Task. In *Proceedings of Australasian Language Technology Association Workshop*, pages 163−170.

it could detect a larger number of locations giving us a higher precision value. We tried incremental training of the Stanford NER, however ran into technical difficulties with memory and computational time required. Hence, we adopted the approach of ensemble system consisting of a pre-trained Stanford NER, knowledge infusion, regular expression identifier and use of rules. Instead of a pipeline architecture with no re-processing we adopted a parallel architecture to cater for the copious amount of noise in Tweets. The parallel architecture enabled us to revisit previous decisions and correct them.

The rest of the paper organized as follows. Section 2 gives an overview of related works for location mining in Twitter messages as well as some generic NER works. Section 3 describes the task description followed by our methodology. The results are detailed in Section 5 followed by conclusion.

2 Related Works

Location Mining is a subtask of the more generic information extraction task of named entity recognition. There are numerous works on NER in the formal domains, however this section gives an overview of the recent work specifically in the informal domain of microblogging, mostly for "Twittersphere".

Ritter et. al. (2011) presented an NER system named *T-NER*, which uses Freebase as an information source to enhance supervision for the Stanford NER to classify entities into 10 classes, one of which was Geo-location. Their system achieved an overall F score of 0.66 and a Geo-location F score of 0.77. Li et al. (2012) present a random walk model which exploits the gregarious properties associated with Tweets in addition to the textual content to determine the named entities. The gregarious property is based on named entities mentioned together in media other than Twitter. The authors used Microsoft N-Gram and Wikipedia as the corpus to compute the gregarious property value. This system attained an F score of 0.419 on their data compared to 0.466 for the previously mentioned system and 0.423 for the Stanford NER on the same data.

The task of location mining specifically from Twitter messages has attracted a lot of attention because Twitter is current up to the minute hence can be used for information about uptodate events around the globe. One of its immediate use is for almost real time disaster detection so that services can be deployed as soon as possible. There are multiple other uses for Twitter location mining such as location based advertising and geography based sentiment mining. Lingad et al. (2013) present test results for using 4 off-the-shelf NER's to determine locations with varying degrees of granularity from Country, State, City, Area, Suburb to Point of Interest. The results from this paper showed that the retrained Stanford NER was the the best performer at 0.872 and the standard Stanford NER 4-class classifier attained a value of 0.691. We used the results of this paper to choose the NER used to be used for our location miner.

Twitter messages may also have meta data indicating the location from which a Tweet was sent. This is only present in Tweets sent from mobile devices equipped with GPS hardware, however note that this feature can also be turned off for privacy reasons by the user. Ikawa et al. (2012) present a model which exploits the GPS location as well as the textual content of the Tweet. This model uses associations between locations and relevant keywords from past messages during training, which is then used to estimate where the new message was issued from. The identified location is then allocated a geographical square and the errors were calculated based on the distance within 10 kilometres. The study reports a precision value of 0.45 with a dataset of 20,535 messages out of which 16,380 were used for training. A large part of the error in this was that the location mentions in the text of the Tweet might not necessary correlate with the location of the user.

Mahmud et al. (2012) also present a system for predicting the home locations of Twitter users. Unlike the previous system, this paper uses an ensemble of statistical and heuristic classifiers to predict Google's geo-coding bounding box for Twitter corresponding to the Twitter users. The paper reports accuracies at various granularities which range from 0.54 to 0.78 recall values.

Sankaranarayanan et al. (2009) present a system which also does location mining for a different purpose. The object of this work is to cluster Twitter messages according to the news content based on geographical locations. This work again uses ensemble learning, similar to out approach. It uses references to geographic locations in the text, called toponyms, to determine the coordinates which then used to resolve using various techniques such as NER, POS tagging and a look up database containing countries, city, river etc. In addition to this the textual content of the Tweet is extended using its metadata about the location of the Tweeter. The metadata information is added as textual content of the Tweet which is then treated similarly as the rest to the message. The paper does not report any location specific accuracy, however illustrates another use for location mining and the enforces the use of ensemble architecture for the purpose the purpose.

Apart these there are several other papers (e.g., Kinsella et al., 2011; Li et al., 2011) who have done work on location mining focussed on either the location from where the Tweet was sent or the geographical location of the Tweeter. Something that is common in these works is that they all use some kind of ensemble of techniques rather than any one particular technique. This paper reports the results of a system with a similar architecture which uses an ensemble of techniques, however the task being tackled there is slightly different. It is more akin to location extraction from the text rather than anything to do with the location of the Tweeter or the location from which the Tweet was sent. They may be the same for some Tweets, however the tasks are quite distinct in that a Tweeter can tweet about a location quite different from his or her registered location or current location.

3 Shared Task Specification

The organizers provided a set of 2000 Twitter Id's with identified locations for training and another set of 1003 Twitter Id's for testing. The locations in the test set were not released, hence the participants had to make their own test sets based on the training data. The participants were allowed two uploads per day to test the accuracy, which was calculated with a confidential subset of the testing data giving the participants an approximation of the level of accuracy achieved. The output was submitted as a comma separated (csv) file with tweet Id's and the locations separated by a space on each line. The order of the locations on a line was immaterial so "New Zealand" and "Zealand New" are both correct.

The overall goal of the task was to identify all mentions of locations in the text of a twitter message. This includes all single and contiguous word mentions such as "guatemala" and "new zealand" and similar mentions as abbreviations such as "nz" for New Zealand. The following examples give an overview of the wider scope of the task.

- "#eqnz" - location is "eqnz"
  In this case we need to check for location within strings, however extract the whole token if one is found.

- "http:www.abc.net.au/melbourne/" - location is "http:www.abc.net.au/melbourne/"

- "cork city...#Cork" - locations - "cork city cork2"
  In this case locations such as city had to be identified and words in locations appearing more than once had to be tagged with the count.

- "Morrison's Island - S Terrace" - location is"morrisons island s terrace"
  Punctuations need to be removed leaving the strings as they appear in the text.

- "U.S. EPA on Twitter" - location is "NONE"
  In this case "U.S." is not a location, but a user.

- "Our house" - location is "our house"
  Common nouns with possessive pronouns need to be identified since they are specific locations.

- "Southwest towns of San Marcos" - location is "Southwest towns of San Marcos"
  In this case we need to retain the preposition "of".

- "60 miles east starting from Stamford CT" - location is "60 miles east Stamford CT"
  This involves removing the verb and the preposition from the location.

4 Methodology

The schematic representation of the method is shown in Fig. 1. We utilized the parallel processing strategy with multiple modules to identify locations.

The proposed location mining architecture adheres to the parallel processing of five major modules. These modules take the cleaned twitter text generated by text cleaning utility. The Named Entity Recognition (NER) module attempts to identify location entities using pre-trained model file.

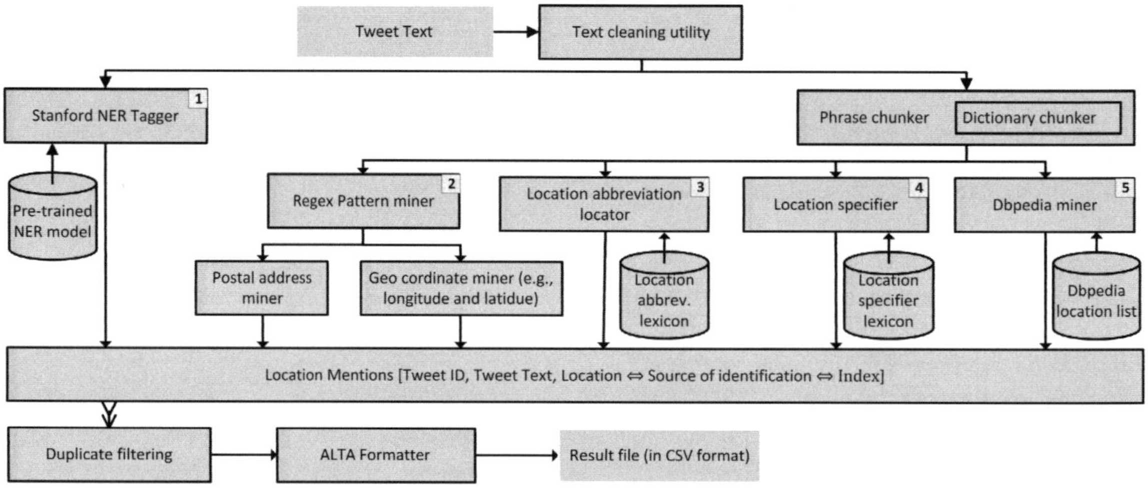

Figure 1: Schematic representation of the Twitter location mining framework

The Regular Expression (Regex) pattern miner is composed of two subcomponents; postal address miner and geo-coordinate miner. Locations can also be specified using abbreviations. This is more common in microblogging type texts. To address this need, the framework utilizes a module that can identify the location abbreviations (e.g., chch, au, nz) using a location abbreviation lexicon. The location specifier module contains the logic to identify locations based on list of location specifiers such as beach, coast and street. We have also utilized the exponentially growing Linked Data cloud in location mining through DBpedia miner.

All these modules are configured to write the results to a single data structure called "*Location Mention*" consisted of tweet id, tweet text, location phrases. Each location phrase has another three attributes; location text, source of identification and the index. The source of identification attribute is used to identify from which module the phrase is identified as a location and index specifies the index of the location phrase in the tweet text. The framework is also equipped with two other modules to merge locations and to format the final result according to the ALTA formatting guidelines. The following sections explore aforementioned modules in detail.

4.1 Cleaning Twitter text

Compared to normal text, microblogging type text contains different features. The most common features that can be seen in Twitter are hashtags and mentions. Existence of such features can disturb the location identification process. To overcome such noise we employed a text cleaning utility that can identify these features and convert them back to the normal textual form. The library is based on one of our previous work (Nand et al., 2014) in Twitter text mining that uses Hidden Markov Model (HMM) based tagging.

4.2 Location mining using NER

Named Entity Recognition (NER) is a widely used technique to extract elements in text into predefined categories such as organizations, cities, person names. The proposed framework utilizes NER to identify cities and countries from the tweet text. We have integrated the Stanford NER toolkit (Finkel and Manning, 2009) with MUC-3 class pre-trained model to locate cities and countries. Fig. 2 shows an example scenario for NER based location mining. This Tweet example and the rest of the following examples are taken from ALTA test set unless specified otherwise.

Tweet ID: 255741958625062912
Cleaned Text: Aus Weather Warnings on Twitter: Queensland : Fire Weather Warning: http://t.co/knVkydSB
Locations: Queensland
Source: [NER]

Figure 2: Example scenario for Named Entity Recognition based location mining

4.3 Phrase and dictionary chunking

Except for the NER module which takes the raw Tweet text, all other modules are designed to process chunked text. In essence, the framework first chunks text based on a predefined rule set. This rule set is implemented with the use of LingPipe library [4] which makes it a scalable module. Table 1 shows the list of rules used for this task. The chunked text is analysed again to check whether there is a possibility to chunk it further. The framework utilizes a dictionary based chunking technique for further chunking if needed. Each token appearing in the phrase is checked whether it can be chunked into multiple words using a lexicon list. The lexicon list is a combination of words extracted from dictionary and a location abbreviation lexicon (see Section 4.5).

Rule	Description
(NN)(NNP)(NNS)	Adjacent noun, singular proper noun or plural noun phrases
(JJ)(NN/NNP/NNS)	Adjective with a noun phrase
(JJR)(NN/NNP/NNS)	Comparative adjective with a noun phrase
(JJS)(NN/NNP/NNS)	Superlative adjective with a noun phrase

Table 1: Phrase chunking rules

4.4 Regex Pattern miner

Locations can also be represented in postal addresses and geo coordinates such as longitude and latitude. Therefore, the framework is equipped with a regular expression pattern miner which takes a predefined template and identifies whether a given text phrase is a location or not. An example scenario of Regex pattern miner is depicted in Fig. 3.

4.5 Location abbreviation miner

Abbreviations are more abundant in microblogging type texts due to space limitations. Essentially, when mining locations it is important to consider abbreviations that can specify a locations (e.g., chch ⇒ Christchurch, nz ⇒ New Zealand). These abbreviations can appear in the text as a single word or in a combination with another word. The latter case makes it difficult to identify because the combination can form different textual

[4]http://alias-i.com/lingpipe/index.html

`Tweet ID:` 255729069977636864
`Cleaned Text:` Weather Underground on Twitter: Watching area near 9.3N 48.3W for tropical development Invest 98L: winds 30 mph moving W at 24 mph http://t.co/ml1PrSJW hurricane
`Locations:` 9.3N 48.3W
`Source:` [R-GEO]

`Tweet ID:` 264171210596831232
`Cleaned Text:` SEQ incidents on Twitter: Reports of Fire Services Incident ? near 333 Manly Road Manly West http://t.co/c2c0GAcm
`Locations:` 333 Manly Road Manly West
`Source:` [R-POSTAL]

Figure 3: Example scenario of Regular Expression based pattern mining

`Tweet ID:` 269641336326615041
`Cleaned Text:` QLD Times on Twitter: Deebing Heights house badly damaged by a fire this morning: http://t.co/U7X06IOh. QldFire
`Locations:` QLD Qldfire
`Source:` [ABBREV]

Figure 4: Example scenario of location abbreviation based mining

representations. This is addressed in our framework by performing the abbreviation mining in two steps. First, phrase chunker attempts to identify phrases from the given text as discussed in Section 4.3. Then single words appearing in these phrases are chunked again using a location abbreviation lexicon list and a set of English words. If it is found that the phrase contains an abbreviation of a location (e.g., nzquake ⇒ nz, quake), the complete phrase is tagged as a location. Fig. 4 shows an example case taken from the test dataset.

4.6 Location specifier based identification

Tokens like beach, street and coast are generally used to specify locations. As a preprocessing task we used the ALTA training data to create a location specifier list. This list is further enriched with another set of location specifiers extracted using a thesaurus. We iteratively searched *Thesaurus.com*[5] with seed words selected from the ALTA training set based location specifier list. From this we were able to list 183 location speci-

[5]http://www.thesaurus.com/

- X? [km,mi,ft,miles] [south][north][east[west] [of,from] Y?
- X? [km,mi,ft,miles] (away) from Y?
- X? near Y?
- X? [km,mi,ft,miles] [outside] [of,from] Y?

Figure 5: Sample set of templates created to identify locations which are prepositional attachments

`Tweet ID:` 260164937983340546
`Cleaned Text:` Daily Examiner on Twitter: Clarence Valley bushfire update. http://t.co/TxnorR7X
`Locations:` Clarence Valley
`Source:` [SPEC]

Figure 6: Example scenario of location specifier based identification

fiers. This list is used with a template based matching to identify whether an extracted phrase is a location. An example scenario is shown in Fig. 6 which shows how the specifier "*Valley*" is used to identify a location.

In addition to these predetermined location specifiers, this module also selects locations which use prepositional attachments. This identification is accomplished using a set of templates that we created based on the ALTA training data and twelve Wikipedia pages related to locations. Sample set of templates are shown in Fig. 5. The complete template set is composed of 28 unique templates.

4.7 DBpedia based location mining

DBpedia[6] based location mining module uses the most extensive knowledge about locations compared to the other four processes described previously. DBpedia is a Linked Data resource which is built based on the Wikipedia[7] text. In general a Linked Data resource is made up of triples which represent vast domain knowledge and categorized into predetermined classes.

In DBpedia, the ontology class "*Place*" is used to categorize all location specific entities. Under this main entity class "*Place*", there are 149 sub classes that denote places such as theatres, lakes, pyramids, etc. Since DBpedia does not offer a database from which we can easily filter out these locations, we have created a database with all the

[6]http://dbpedia.org/About

[7]http://en.wikipedia.org/wiki/Main_Page

`Tweet ID:` 264099474564075520
`Cleaned Text:` 702 ABC Sydney on Twitter: The bushfire at Lake Macquarie near Teralba is now under control. Homes are no longer under threat
`Locations:` Lake Macquarie
`Source:` [DBPEDIA]

Figure 7: Example scenario for DBpedia based location mining

information required to filter only locations from the DBpeda data files. Table 2 shows few records from this database. The phrases which match with the entity literal value (shown in Table 2) were tagged as locations. Fig. 7 shows an example scenario of DBpedia based location mining where the phrase "*Lake Macquarie*" is identified as a location.

4.8 Merging module

Since the framework follows the parallel processing architecture utilizing five individual modules, there was a need for a merging module which can generate accurate representations of multiple location identifications which ultimately point to one location in Tweet text. The ultimate goal of this merging module is to present the most informative location as the final result. This was accomplished using a text merging utility that takes the index of each location mention and merges them according to the same order of tokens appearing in the tweet text. An example scenario is shown in Fig. 8 which depicts the process of merging two location identifications; one identified by DBpedia miner and other identified by location specifier list based identification module. In this example scenario, compared to the location identified by the DBpedia miner, the location specifier based module has identified a more informative location. In this case we analyse the index of the tokens from both process and since the DBpedia based identification is a subset of the specifier list based identification, we merge two and output the result as "*40km south of Tenterfield*".

4.9 ALTA formatter

ALTA shared task requires special formatting of the result as a comma separated file which was accomplished by this module. In essence, the formatter was based on the following four rules:

- remove all punctuations from the phrase

Ontology class	Entity literal value	Link	Data file
Theatre	Stephen Joseph Theatre	http://dbpedia.org/page/Stephen_Joseph_Theatre	Stephen_Joseph_Theatre.rdf
Lake	Lake Macquarie	http://dbpedia.org/resource/ Lake_Macquarie_(New_South_Wales)	Lake_Macquarie.rdf
Museum	BritishMuseum	http://dbpedia.org/resource/British_Museum	British_Museum.rdf
Airport	Glasgow Airport	http://dbpedia.org/resource/Glasgow_Airport	Glasgow_Airport.rdf
Mountain	Mount Vesuvius	http://dbpedia.org/resource/Mount_Vesuvius	Mount_Vesuvius.rdf

Table 2: Sample set of records from DBpedia entity database

`Tweet ID:` 255914885928583168
`Cleaned Text:` Live Traffic NSW on Twitter: TENTERFIELD: NewEnglandHwy closed in both directions 40km south of Tenterfield due to a bushfire.

`Locations:` Tenterfield
`Source:` [DBPEDIA]

`Locations:` 40km south of Tenterfield
`Source:` [SPEC]

`Output`: 40km south of Tenterfield

Figure 8: Example scenario for merging two locations

- if locations are repeated in a tweet, number them from the second occurrence
- if there is no location for the tweet, then mark it as *NONE*
- lowercase all extracted location phrases

The resulting phrases were converted to a Comma separated file with two fields; tweet id and the location phrases.

5 Results

Our location miner achieved an average F-value of 0.747 which was in the second place compared to the winner which had an F score of 0.77807. The F-value was calculated based on the "bag of words criteria" for each tweet as described in the Section 3. If a tweet did not contain any locations, the participants were required to label them with "NONE". The overall results for the test dataset is shown in Table 3.

The precision and recall values were computed for individual Tweets, which were then averaged to compute the overall F-value. Hence the precision and recall values for a Tweet with no location mentions was taken as 1.0 for "NONE" to indicate no location. Any other strings instead of "NONE" were counted as false positives. Table 3 shows that there were 115 Tweets (11.5%) with no locations. It should be noted that this strategy for accuracy approximation will tend to boost the F-value if a large number of Tweets have no location mentions.

Test Data Property	Value
No. of Tweets	1003
No. of Location tokens	3179
No. NONE Tweets	115
Av. Recall	0.7279
Av. Precision	0.7905

Table 3: Dataset details and Results

Module	Number	F Score
Stanford NER	1003	0.532
Postal Address Miner	6	0.167
Geo coordinate	8	0.242
Location Abbreviation Miner	607	0.710
Location Specifier	202	0.884
DBpedia Miner	1867	0.935
Total	3680	–

Table 4: The number of locations resolved by individual modules with respective F score.

Table 4 gives the number of the locations specified by the individual modules of the ensemble system used for the task. The total is much higher than the total number of locations because of the false negatives and some of the locations were identified by more than one module. The majority of false negatives were identified by the *Location Specifier* module which was primarily based around rules based on the use of the prepositions of place such as, “at”, “on” and “in”. The *DBpedia miner* module was able to identify a total of 1867 locations which is even higher than then the *Stanford NER* module. Furthermore, DBpedia miner has achieved the highest F score of 0.935 compared to other four modules. The results illustrate that as comprehensive information sources become available, their use in conjunction with machine learning algorithms can be effectively used for improved accuracy.

6 Conclusions and Future Work

This paper showed the use of an ensemble approach to solve the problem of location mention identification. We presented an ensemble architecture that uses a basic general purpose NER, with a combination of various rule based modules in conjunction with DBpedia knowledge base to achieve an F score of 0.747. A critical aspect of any ensemble architecture is how to combine the results at the end. This was also illustrated by the Merger module which takes outputs from the various ensemble modules and combines them into a noun phrase location phrase as was required by the shared task specification. The design of the architecture enables us to exclude a class of location mentions and also to include any new ones that a task at hand might dictate. The final results can also be easily modified to output single token locations or full noun phrase locations. In future we intend to further improve the accuracy and to classify the locations into types such as country, site and address for specific applications.

References

[Finkel and Manning2009] Jenny Rose Finkel and Christopher D Manning. 2009. Joint Parsing and Named Entity Recognition. In *Proceedings of the North American Association of Computational Linguistics (NAACL 2009).*

[Ikawa et al.2012] Yohei Ikawa, Miki Enoki, and Michiaki Tatsubori. 2012. Location inference using microblog messages. In *Proceedings of the 21st international conference companion on World Wide Web - WWW '12 Companion*, page 687, New York, New York, USA, April. ACM Press.

[Kinsella et al.2011] Sheila Kinsella, Vanessa Murdock, and Neil O'Hare. 2011. "I'm eating a sandwich in Glasgow". In *Proceedings of the 3rd international workshop on Search and mining user-generated contents - SMUC '11*, page 61, New York, New York, USA, October. ACM Press.

[Li et al.2011] Wen Li, Pavel Serdyukov, Arjen P. de Vries, Carsten Eickhoff, and Martha Larson. 2011. The where in the tweet. In *Proceedings of the 20th ACM international conference on Information and knowledge management - CIKM '11*, page 2473, New York, New York, USA, October. ACM Press.

[Li et al.2012] Chenliang Li, Jianshu Weng, Qi He, Yuxia Yao, Anwitaman Datta, Aixin Sun, and Bu-Sung Lee. 2012. TwiNER. In *Proceedings of the 35th international ACM SIGIR conference on Research and development in information retrieval - SIGIR '12*, page 721, New York, New York, USA, August. ACM Press.

[Lingad et al.2013] John Lingad, Sarvnaz Karimi, and Jie Yin. 2013. Location extraction from disaster-related microblogs. *Proceedings of the 22Nd International Conference on World Wide Web Companion*, pages 1017–1020, May.

[Mahmud et al.2012] Jalal Mahmud, Jeffrey Nichols, and Clemens Drews. 2012. Where Is This Tweet From? Inferring Home Locations of Twitter Users. In *ICWSM*.

[Nand et al.2014] Parma Nand, Ramesh Lal, and Rivindu Perera. 2014. A HMM POS Tagger for Micro-Blogging Type Texts. In *Proceedings of the 13th Pacific Rim International Conference on Artificial Intelligence (PRICAI 2014).*

[Ritter et al.2011] Alan Ritter, Sam Clark, Mausam, and Oren Etzioni. 2011. Named entity recognition in tweets: an experimental study. pages 1524–1534, July.

[Sankaranarayanan et al.2009] Jagan Sankaranarayanan, Hanan Samet, Benjamin E. Teitler, Michael D. Lieberman, and Jon Sperling. 2009. TwitterStand. In *Proceedings of the 17th ACM SIGSPATIAL International Conference on Advances in Geographic Information Systems - GIS '09*, page 42, New York, New York, USA, November. ACM Press.

Automatic Identification of Expressions of Locations in Tweet Messages using Conditional Random Fields

Fei Liu, Afshin Rahimi, Bahar Salehi, Miji Choi, Ping Tan, Long Duong
Department of Computing and Information Systems
The University of Melbourne
{fliu3,bsalehi,joocl,pingt,lduong}@student.unimelb.edu.au
afshinrahimi@gmail.com

Abstract

In this paper, we propose an automatic identification model, capable of extracting expressions of locations (EoLs) within Twitter messages. Moreover, we participated in the competition of ALTA Shared Task 2014 and our best-performing system is ranked among the top 3 systems (2nd in the public leaderboard). In our model, we explored the validity of the use of a wide variety of lexical, structural and geospatial features as well as a machine learning model Conditional Random Fields (CRF). Further, we investigated the effectiveness of stacking and self-training.

1 Introduction

With the rise of social media, people have developed a fondness for posting not only their thoughts and opinions, but also content regarding their whereabouts (Liu et al., 2014). While the spatial information carried by tweets is crucial to a wide variety of location-based applications ranging from real-time disaster detection (Sakaki et al., 2010; Núñez-Redó et al., 2011; Yin et al., 2012) to targeted advertising (Tuten, 2008; Evans, 2012), only 26% of Twitter users specify their locations as granular as a city name (e.g. *Melbourne, Australia*) in their profile according to Cheng et al. (2010). Further, as little as 0.42% of all the tweets investigated by Cheng et al. (2010) are associated with the per-tweet geo-tagging feature (i.e. a latitude and longitude). To add to the complexity, on such highly-interactive yet informal social media platforms, people make heavy use of informal language, such as acronyms (e.g. *NYC*) and word shortenings (e.g. *St.*) due to the 140-character limit (Agarwal et al., 2011; Eisenstein, 2013; Han et al., 2013), making the identification task even more difficult. Despite the difficulties, identifying geospatial information in social media text has drawn much attention (Lingad et al., 2013).

Our focus in this paper is the automatic identification of EoLs in the text of tweets consisting of any specific reference to a geospatial location. A location, as defined by Lingad et al. (2013), consists of both *geographic location(s)*, such as country, city, river, or suburb, and *point(s)-of-interest* (POI (s)) which refer to hotels, shopping centres, and restaurants.

The task is closely related to Named Entity Recognition (NER). In this regard, Liu et al. (2011) and Ritter et al. (2011) report F-score of 77-78% at identifying spatial named entities in tweets. Matching place references in a gazetteer (Hill, 2000) is another widely-used approach. Paradesi (2011) investigated the approach of combining NER and external gazetteers. Further, Gelernter and Balaji (2013) built a geoparser incorporating the results of four parsers.

In our attempt to build an automatic EoL identification system, we employed a conditional random field (CRF) (Lafferty et al., 2001), which can be found and has proved to be successful in various Natural Language Processing (NLP) tasks (Sha and Pereira, 2003; Gimpel et al., 2011; Finkel et al., 2005; Ritter et al., 2011). In this paper, we present our approach to building such a system as well as a variety of features, such as lexical, structural and geospatial features and show major improvements on the task of EoL identification over earlier attempts. Our best-performing system is ranked among the top 3 systems (2nd in the public leaderboard).

The paper is organised as follows: the dataset and external resources used in our system is described in Section 2 and Section 3. We introduce the tools involved in this paper in Section 4. In Section 5 and Section 6, we provide the description of our system and analyse its performance with different feature sets respectively. We present

Fei Liu, Afshin Rahimi, Bahar Salehi, Miji Choi, Ping Tan and Long Duong. 2014. Automatic Identification of Expressions of Locations in Tweet Messages using Conditional Random Fields. In *Proceedings of Australasian Language Technology Association Workshop*, pages 171−176.

the conclusions in Section 7.

2 Dataset

We used the dataset introduced by (Lingad et al., 2013) to evaluate our proposed system. This dataset was also used in ALTA shared task 2014 and contains 1,942 tweets in the training set and 1,003 tweets were selected for the test set. According to (Lingad et al., 2013), around 89% of the tweets contain at least one location. The location mentions can be either in the text, in hashtags (e.g. #Australia), URLs or in mentions (e.g. @australia).

The dataset contains the list of tweet IDs and the locations mentioned in the respective tweets. At the time of extracting the tweets from twitter, 58 tweets in training set were not accessible.

3 External Resources

Apart from the training and test datasets, we introduce the additional datasets and resources involved in this project in this section.

3.1 User Meta Data

We extracted location meta information of the authors of the messages in the training data and created a list of such location mentions.

3.2 Text Retrieved from URLs

Additionally, for the purposes of self-training, we also downloaded the text of the articles whose URLs are contained in the tweets (37% contain URLs in the training set). Due to the unavailability of some URLs, we were only able to retrieve some of the articles.

3.3 GeoNames

As an external gazetteer, we adopted *GeoNames*[1] whose data can be downloaded to increase the coverage of our model since only a limited number of tweets were provided for training.

4 Tools

In this section, we introduce the tools we utilised in our system.

CRF++

`CRF++` is an open source, general-purpose implementation of CRF by Kudo (2005) and can be applied to a wide variety of NLP tasks. Since it only takes CoNLL format training and test data, we converted the training and test data.

Retrained StanfordNER

The Stanford named entity recogniser (Finkel et al., 2005) has proved to be effective when retrained over data containing EoLs (Lingad et al., 2013) even though evidence found by Liu et al. (2014) indicates otherwise. We retrained it over the training data and will refer to it as `Re-StanfordNER`.

GeoLocator

`GeoLocator` is a geoparser created by Gelernter and Balaji (2013) to geoparse informal messages in social media. The training data for this model was extracted from Twitter following the Februray 2011 earthquake in Christchurch New Zealand. It incorporates the output of four parsers: a lexico-semantic named location parser, a rule-based street name parser, a rule-based building name parser and a trained NER.

5 System Description

In this section, we describe our approach to creating an automatic EoL identification system.

5.1 Pre-processing

We pre-processed both the training and test dataset with lexical normalisation (using the dictionary created by Han et al. (2012)), POS tagging and full-text chunk parsing. Recognising the incompetent performance of traditional NLP tools when applied to social media text (Java, 2007; Becker et al., 2009; Yin et al., 2012; Preotiuc-Pietro et al., 2012; Baldwin et al., 2013; Gelernter and Balaji, 2013), we adopted `ARK Tweet NLP POS Tagger v0.3` (Owoputi et al., 2013) with the Penn Treebank tagset model for the task of word tokenisation and POS tagging. For chunk parsing, we used `OpenNLP`[2].

5.2 Features

We trained our model (based on `CRF++`) with various features, which can be categorised into three categories: lexical features, structural features and geospatial features. Note that we used a context window of 2 for each feature.

- Lexical features include lemmatised words (using NLTK (Bird et al., 2009), POS,

[1] `http://www.geonames.org/`

[2] `http://opennlp.apache.org/`

brief word class introduced by Settles (2004) where capitial and lowercase letters are replaced with 'A' and 'a', digits with '0' and all other characters with '_' and consecutive identical characters are collapsed into one (e.g. *#Adelaide* $\rightarrow$ *_Aa*), capitalisation and locative indicator (Liu, 2013).

- Structural features include position of the word in the chunk and POS of the first word in the chunk.

- Geospatial features include *GeoNames* geospatial feature class described by Liu (2013).

As pointed out by Wolpert (1992), stacking is able to generate better results than any single one of the trained model. We therefore also applyed stacking by combining the output of our `CRF++`-based model, `Re-StanfordNER` and `GeoLocator` and using them as three distinct features.

5.3 Self-training

Self-training, a semi-supervised learning algorithm, has proved to be successful, as reported by Plank et al. (2014), in Twitter POS tagging and NER tasks with an error reduction of 8–10% over the state-of-the-art system. We employed self-training using text retrieved from the URLs in the training and test dataset as the new test data. First, we train `CRF++` over the original gold-standard training data. Next, we predict on the new test data and expand the training data by including new instances from the new test data with prediction confidence higher than or equal to a threshold value. This process is repeated until there is no instance from the new test data to be added. Furthermore, we experiment with various threshold values.

5.4 Post-processing

In order to improve the recall of our model, we further include two post-processing methods: gazetteer matching and aggregation.

Gazetteer Matching

In addition to the machine learning approach, we also explored the use of external gazetteers and a matching algorithm. The algorithm, based on dynamic programming, searches the gazetteer case-sensitively for the maximum number of matched words in a sentence.

To further enable our model to detect directional words (e.g. *north*, *northern*) and common elements of toponyms (e.g. *street*, *road*), we also compiled a list of generic terms which are frequently used as part of an EoL by splitting entries in *GeoNames* into single tokens and including the top 500 most frequent words. Also, we created an algorithm capable of finding case-insensitive partial as well as whole-word matches.

Aggregation

Similar to the union operation of sets, we aggregated the prediction results of `CRF++` and `Re-StanfordNER` in the attempt to achieve higher recall, classifying a word as part of an EoL as long as it is identified in the output of at least one of two machine learning tools.

6 Evaluation

In this section, we present the performance of our system as well as analyses of the results. All the evaluation is based on the test data and the gold-standard annotations provided by the organiser. In addition to the mean F-score generated by the evaluation script provided by *Kaggle in Class*, we also include macro-averaged precision, recall and F-score to better understand the performance of our system with various feature setups.

The performance of our system is presented in Table 1. The performance attained using only word ($\mathcal{W}$) and POS ($\mathcal{P}$) with `CRF++` is better than `Re-StanfordNER` in precision but inferior in recall, resulting in a slightly lower macro-averaged F-score ($\mathcal{F}$) than that of `Re-StanfordNER`. Aggregating the two achieves a substantial gain in performance, boosting the macro-averaged F-score from 67.39 to 72.07. As we improved the performance of `CRF++` by adding more sophisticated features incrementally, the benefits of aggregation became less substantial, which is not that surprising considering the output of the `Re-StanfordNER` is already included and used as a feature in stacking. In most cases, the results with aggregation are better than those without aggregation. However, applying aggregation has negative impacts on the recall of `CRF++` with stacking, even though it enables the model to achieve a modest gain in F-score. The reasons for this remain unclear.

We also observed that stacking improved the performance on the whole test data substantially (a 3.85 increase in mean F-score without aggregation). Upon closer investigation of the impact of stacking on the performance on the test data, we discovered that stacking was less effective on the private test set (a 3.01 increase in mean F-score) than on the public one (a 4.7 increase in mean F-score), which might have been caused by the fact that GeoLocator, Re-StanfordNER and CRF++ (with lexical, structural and geospatial features) overfit the public test data. Based on this, we suspect that the public test data is more similar to the training data than the private test data. Further, we created a Venn diagram of the output of the three systems and discovered that there is room for further improvement with stacking and that a 13.35 F1 point increase can be achieved if we had an oracle stacking algorithm.

		$\mathcal{GL}$	$\mathcal{RS}$	**CRF++**		
				$+\mathcal{W},\mathcal{P}$	$+\mathcal{L},\mathcal{S},\mathcal{G}$	$+\mathcal{ST}$
$-\mathcal{A}$	$\mathcal{P}$	61.76	62.96	65.53	68.81	72.22
	$\mathcal{R}$	65.31	72.34	69.35	72.95	**76.87**
	$\mathcal{F}$	63.48	67.32	67.39	70.82	74.47
	$\mathcal{MF}$	60.84	64.94	64.57	68.56	72.41
$+\mathcal{A}$	$\mathcal{P}$	–	–	72.33	74.14	**74.60**
	$\mathcal{R}$	–	–	71.81	74.07	76.49
	$\mathcal{F}$	–	–	72.07	74.10	**75.54**
	$\mathcal{MF}$	–	–	69.48	71.93	**73.57**

Table 1: Macro-averaged precision ($\mathcal{P}$), recall ($\mathcal{R}$), F-score ($\mathcal{F}$) and mean F-score ($\mathcal{MF}$) attained by using GeoLocator ($\mathcal{GL}$) and Re-StanfordNER ($\mathcal{RS}$) out of the box and adding each feature incrementally to CRF++. Features include word ($\mathcal{W}$), POS ($\mathcal{P}$), lexical features ($\mathcal{L}$), structural features ($\mathcal{S}$), geospatial features ($\mathcal{G}$) and stacking ($\mathcal{ST}$). $\mathcal{A}$ stands for aggregation. Evaluation based on the test data (the best $\mathcal{P}$, $\mathcal{R}$, $\mathcal{F}$and $\mathcal{MF}$ are in bold).

Also, we investigated the impact of the use of external gazetteers. The results are summarised in Table 2. Note that the two gazetteer matching algorithms were applied upon our best performing system so far, which is able to achieve a macro-averaged F-score of 75.54. Further, we discovered that including GeoNames was not beneficial to the overall performance as it introduces a number of false positives.

Additionally, we also applied self-training with 4 different confidence threshold values ranging from .70 to .95 and the results are shown in Table 3. Note that self-training was applied to

Method	$\mathcal{P}$	$\mathcal{R}$	$\mathcal{F}$	$\mathcal{MF}$
$+\mathcal{U},\mathcal{DT}$	**76.88**	**77.00**	**76.94**	**74.98**
$+\mathcal{U},\mathcal{G},\mathcal{DT}$	76.75	76.42	76.58	74.64

Table 2: Macro-averaged precision ($\mathcal{P}$), recall ($\mathcal{R}$), F-score ($\mathcal{F}$) and mean F-score ($\mathcal{MF}$) attained by using user meta data ($\mathcal{U}$), Geonames ($\mathcal{G}$) and the list of directional words and toponyms ($\mathcal{DT}$) (the best $\mathcal{P}$, $\mathcal{R}$, $\mathcal{F}$and $\mathcal{MF}$ are in bold).

CRF++ with lexical, structural and geospatial features, which results in a macro-averaged F-score of 70.82. While precision and recall fluctuate, no significant improvement can be observed in F-score despite the claim of 8–10% error reduction by Plank et al. (2014). Rather, the overall performance declined to around 68–69 in F-score.

Threshold	$\mathcal{P}$	$\mathcal{R}$	$\mathcal{F}$	$\mathcal{MF}$
.70	66.21	72.61	69.26	67.12
.80	65.59	**72.65**	68.94	66.76
.90	65.94	72.12	68.89	66.72
.90	**67.16**	72.23	**69.60**	**67.39**

Table 3: Macro-averaged precision ($\mathcal{P}$), recall ($\mathcal{R}$), F-score ($\mathcal{F}$) and mean F-score ($\mathcal{MF}$) attained by self-training with various threshold values (the best $\mathcal{P}$, $\mathcal{R}$, $\mathcal{F}$and $\mathcal{MF}$ are in bold).

7 Conclusions

We proposed an automatic EoL identification model which is able to work on Twitter messages. In this paper, we described our approach to building such a system based on a CRF. Moreover, we presented the performance of our system with various feature setups and discovered a variety of features which are helpful to the task, such as lexical, structural and geospatial features as well as stacking. Further, evidence indicates that the inclusion of external gazetteers and matching algorithms works well and contributes to the boost of the overall performance with the exception of *GeoNames*. Lastly, we found that self-training did not improve the performance. As future work, possible enhancement can be done on the stacking algorithm and the gazetteer matching approach.

References

Apoorv Agarwal, Boyi Xie, Ilia Vovsha, Owen Rambow, and Rebecca Passonneau. 2011. Sentiment analysis of Twitter data. In *Proceedings of the Workshop on Languages in Social Media (LSM 2011)*, pages 30–38, Portland, USA.

Timothy Baldwin, Paul Cook, Marco Lui, Andrew MacKinlay, and Li Wang. 2013. How noisy social media text, how diffrnt social media sources. In *Proceedings of the 6th International Joint Conference on Natural Language Processing (IJCNLP 2013)*, pages 356–364, Nagoya, Japan.

Hila Becker, Mor Naaman, and Luis Gravano. 2009. Event identification in social media. In *Proceedings of the 12th International Workshop on the Web and Databases (WebDB 2009)*, Providence, USA.

Steven Bird, Ewan Klein, and Edward Loper. 2009. *Natural Language Processing with Python*. O'Reilly Media.

Zhiyuan Cheng, James Caverlee, and Kyumin Lee. 2010. You are where you tweet: A content-based approach to geo-locating twitter users. In *Proceedings of the 19th ACM International Conference on Information and Knowledge Management (CIKM 2010)*, pages 759–768, Toronto, ON, Canada.

Jacob Eisenstein. 2013. What to do about bad language on the internet. In *Proceedings of the 2013 Conference of the North American Chapter of the Association for Computational Linguistics: Human Language Technologies (NAACL HLT 2013)*, pages 359–369, Atlanta, USA.

Dave Evans. 2012. *Social media marketing: An hour a day*. John Wiley & Sons.

Jenny Rose Finkel, Trond Grenager, and Christopher Manning. 2005. Incorporating non-local information into information extraction systems by Gibbs sampling. In *Proceedings of the 43rd Annual Meeting of the Association for Computational Linguistics (ACL 2005)*, pages 363–370, Ann Arbor, USA.

Judith Gelernter and Shilpa Balaji. 2013. An algorithm for local geoparsing of microtext. *Geoinformatica*, 17(4):635–667.

Kevin Gimpel, Nathan Schneider, Brendan O'Connor, Dipanjan Das, Daniel Mills, Jacob Eisenstein, Michael Heilman, Dani Yogatama, Jeffrey Flanigan, and Noah A. Smith. 2011. Part-of-speech tagging for twitter: Annotation, features, and experiments. In *Proceedings of the 49th Annual Meeting of the Association for Computational Linguistics: Human Language Technologies: Short Papers - Volume 2 (ACL 2011)*, pages 42–47, Portland, USA.

Bo Han, Paul Cook, and Timothy Baldwin. 2012. Automatically constructing a normalisation dictionary for microblogs. In *Proceedings of the 2012 Joint Conference on Empirical Methods in Natural Language Processing and Computational Natural Language Learning (EMNLP-CoNLL 2012)*, pages 421–432, Jeju Island, Korea.

Bo Han, Paul Cook, and Timothy Baldwin. 2013. Lexical normalisation of short text messages. *ACM Transactions on Intelligent Systems and Technology*, 4(1):5:1–5:27.

Linda L. Hill. 2000. Core elements of digital gazetteers: Placenames, categories, and footprints. In *Proceedings of the 4th European Conference on Research and Advanced Technology for Digital Libraries (ECDL 2000)*, pages 280–290, Lisbon, Portugal. Springer-Verlag.

Akshay Java. 2007. A framework for modeling influence, opinions and structure in social media. In *Proceedings of the 22nd Annual Conference on Artificial Intelligence (AAAI 2007)*, pages 1933–1934, Vancouver, Canada.

Taku Kudo. 2005. Crf++: Yet another crf toolkit. *Software available at* `http://crfpp.sourceforge.net`.

John D. Lafferty, Andrew McCallum, and Fernando C. N. Pereira. 2001. Conditional random fields: Probabilistic models for segmenting and labeling sequence data. In *Proceedings of the Eighteenth International Conference on Machine Learning (ICML 2001)*, pages 282–289, San Francisco, USA.

John Lingad, Sarvnaz Karimi, and Jie Yin. 2013. Location extraction from disaster-related microblogs. In *Proceedings of the 22Nd International Conference on World Wide Web Companion (WWW 2013)*, pages 1017–1020, Rio de Janeiro, Brazil.

Xiaohua Liu, Shaodian Zhang, Furu Wei, and Ming Zhou. 2011. Recognizing named entities in tweets. In *Proceedings of the 49th Annual Meeting of the Association for Computational Linguistics: Human Language Technologies - Volume 1 (ACL 2011)*, pages 359–367, Portland, USA.

Fei Liu, Maria Vasardani, and Timothy Baldwin. 2014. Automatic identification of locative expressions from social media text: A comparative analysis. In *Proceedings of the 4th International Workshop on Location and the Web (LocWeb 2014)*, pages 9–16, Shanghai, China.

Fei Liu. 2013. Automatic identification of locative expressions from informal text. Master's thesis, The University of Melbourne, Melbourne, Australia.

Manuela Núñez-Redó, Laura Díaz, José Gil, David González, and Joaquín Huerta. 2011. Discovery and integration of web 2.0 content into geospatial information infrastructures: a use case in wild fire monitoring. In *Proceedings of the 6th International Conference on Availability, Reliability and Security (ARES 2011)*, pages 50–68, Vienna, Austria.

Olutobi Owoputi, Brendan O'Connor, Chris Dyer, Kevin Gimpel, Nathan Schneider, and Noah A. Smith. 2013. Improved part-of-speech tagging for online conversational text with word clusters. pages 380–390, Atlanta, USA.

Sharon Myrtle Paradesi. 2011. Geotagging tweets using their content. In *Proceedings of the 24th International Florida Artificial Intelligence Research Society Conference (FLAIRS 2011)*, pages 355–356, Palm Beach, USA.

Barbara Plank, Dirk Hovy, Ryan McDonald, and Anders Søgaard. 2014. Adapting taggers to twitter with (less) distant supervision. In *Proceedings of the 25th International Conference on Computational Linguistics (COLING 2014)*, pages 1783–1792, Dublin, Ireland.

Daniel Preotiuc-Pietro, Sina Samangooei, Trevor Cohn, Nicholas Gibbins, and Mahesan Niranjan. 2012. Trendminer: An architecture for real time analysis of social media text. In *Proceedings of 1st International Workshop on Real-Time Analysis and Mining of Social Streams (RAMSS 2012)*, Dublin, Ireland.

Alan Ritter, Sam Clark, Mausam, and Oren Etzioni. 2011. Named entity recognition in tweets: An experimental study. In *Proceedings of the Conference on Empirical Methods in Natural Language Processing (EMNLP 2011)*, pages 1524–1534, Edinburgh, UK.

Takeshi Sakaki, Makoto Okazaki, and Yutaka Matsuo. 2010. Earthquake shakes twitter users: Real-time event detection by social sensors. In *Proceedings of the 19th International Conference on World Wide Web (WWW 2010)*, pages 851–860, Raleigh, USA.

Burr Settles. 2004. Biomedical named entity recognition using conditional random fields and rich feature sets. In *Proceedings of the International Joint Workshop on Natural Language Processing in Biomedicine and Its Applications (JNLPBA 2004)*, pages 104–107, Geneva, Switzerland.

Fei Sha and Fernando Pereira. 2003. Shallow parsing with conditional random fields. In *Proceedings of the 2003 Conference of the North American Chapter of the Association for Computational Linguistics on Human Language Technology - Volume 1 (HLT-NAACL 2003)*, pages 134–141, Edmonton, Canada.

Tracy L Tuten. 2008. *Advertising 2.0: social media marketing in a web 2.0 world.* Greenwood Publishing Group.

David H Wolpert. 1992. Stacked generalization. *Neural networks*, 5(2):241–259.

Jie Yin, Andrew Lampert, Mark Cameron, Bella Robinson, and Robert Power. 2012. Using social media to enhance emergency situation awareness. *Intelligent Systems*, 27(6):52–59.